THE NEWSPAPERMAN

AND

THE LAW

THE NEWSPAPERMAN

AND

THE LAW

By

WALTER A. STEIGLEMAN

Associate Professor of Journalism,
State University of Iowa

*Formerly on Staff of Press Services and Newspapers
in Harrisburg, Pa., Philadelphia, Pittsburgh,
New York, and Washington.*

GREENWOOD PRESS, PUBLISHERS
WESTPORT, CONNECTICUT

TABLE OF CONTENTS

Preface

There are many good books on newspaper law. They have come from teachers of journalism and of law, practicing lawyers, newspapermen, and from authors fortunate enough to possess training and experience in two or more of these fields.

Why, then, should there be another book on the same subject? The reasons must lie in the author's own appraisal of the situation.

My experiences on newspapers and in classrooms have led me to the conclusion that *what is needed is both a new thesis and a new presentation.*

It seems to be that too often law of the press is studied as an isolated phenomenon affecting only the newspaper and the legal system. More practical value, I feel, comes when law of the press is recognized as merely one phase of an organized system of social control.

Too much emphasis also has been placed on the negative side of law. Often the study of newspaper law is merely a recital of the prohibitions and restraints which it exercises against complete freedom of publication. Law also has a positive side. But even more important than a negative or positive approach to law is an examination of the reasons for both.

The whole problem of law as it affects all aspects of journalism has been accentuated by the coming of mass communications. New problems have arisen which must be recognized, examined, and interpreted, both in the interests of the press and of society as a whole. This new interpretation must stress responsibilities as much as rights and privileges. For the social implications of the law are just as important today as the strict legal implications.

Law of the press must be rid of its mystery and specialized language and re-examined in the light of the functions for which society created it. The newspaperman, beginner or veteran, must be asked to accept law as not merely a series of "do's" and "don'ts," but as a long-planned method of social control. He should be asked also to cease to regard law as his "enemy" and accept it as his partner in order that both together may do their part in maintaining order, stability, and regularity in society.

This partnership, however, must not be one of "conspiracy" against society or the individual, nor should it be one of mutual acquiescence in the mistakes or short-sightedness of each partner. At times, the press has chafed at the law's seemingly greater concern for form and ritual than for the best interests of a dynamic society. The law, in turn, has shown impatience at persistence of journalism in believing it is more in touch with the needs and wishes of the people than the venerable legal institutions. Modern society needs both stability and malleability.

The thesis of this book, then, is that the law, like journalism, is a social agency. Both were created by society to serve its needs, and both are entitled to those prerogatives only which will accrue to the advantage of the group as a whole. Resolution of conflicts between the law and the press must not be regarded as victories or defeats for either, but only as gains for society. The new keyword for law of the press is neither rights nor privileges, but—responsibilities.

In presentation, what seems to be needed is, first, an explanation of the origin and development of the whole legal system. For what purposes was it designed? Why did society feel it had a need for such a system?

No one can understand a specific phase of the legal system —such as newspaper law—until he knows the general nature of the whole institution of law. For that reason, the early chapters are devoted to such a discussion.

Freedom of the press, too, has only a partial meaning to those unfamiliar with the underlying principles. Why did society grant to the press immunities given to no other institution?

The second need seems to be for a presentation that will relate the functions of the law to its direct application to specific circumstances. And, finally, the presentation should be legal but not "legalistic."

For these reasons, the stress in this book is upon continuity of related phases. For example, the coverage of courts involves contempt, privacy, libel, fair comment, and other aspects which custom seems to have placed in isolated and "water-tight" compartments. Rather than scatter such particular phases of the same problem throughout the book, I have placed them together so that the rights and privileges and responsibilities in covering courts begin with the commission of the crime and continue right through the final disposition of the case.

Other problems have been organized in a similar manner. As far as possible, the presentation aims to develop the problems as reporters would find them on their day-to-day beats, ranging from covering Congress down to reporting the meeting of a service club in a small community.

One annoyance common to practicing newspapermen and students alike is to find that definitive answers are not given in all cases. There are a number of reasons for this apparent defect. All law cases are not carried to final conclusion. Newspapers, knowing libel suits are expensive to win as well as to lose, often are reluctant to let the issue go to the courts if the other party is at all reasonable. A sense of fair play brings from many newspapers prompt contrition and the complainant is satisfied.

Another annoyance to newspapermen or students is for them to discover that cases which seem similar produce varying opinions from the courts. One reason is that each state has its own legal system and, in addition, there is a federal jurisdiction. Principles of law are rather uniform, but interpretations of particular applications may vary.

A further reason is that no two cases really are exactly alike.

For example, the same case may involve both libel and the invasion of privacy. One court may elect to let the issue stand on libel; another court might have decided that privacy was the better cause for action.

Then, too, cases differ because of evidence permitted to be introduced. And they differ also in the manner in which the attorneys present them and the varying weight which juries give to what looks to be identical evidence. Judges, attorneys, and

x THE NEWSPAPERMAN AND THE LAW

jurors also are not detached from the world, and changing social conditions often are reflected in the courtroom.

Although the emphasis in this work is upon newspapers, much of the material applies also to radio. The problems peculiar to radio only are dealt with in a comprehensive chapter.

* * *

In the preparation of this book, I had the advice and encouragement of a number of men at the State University of Iowa. Professors Norman C. Meier and Harold W. Saunders were helpful in making me see the social aspects of law, Professors Leslie G. Moeller and Arthur M. Barnes in the general subject matter and arrangement, and Professor James Jordan in the legal interpretations.

Over a period of years, Professor Frank Thayer of the University of Wisconsin has encouraged me in a serious study of the subject, and Wray E. Fleming, general counsel for the Hoosier State Press Association, from time to time has been most helpful in his interpretations of various aspects of the whole field of law of the press.

None of these men, naturally, bears any responsibility for the views, expressions, or interpretations in this book. That responsibility is mine alone.

—WAS

Iowa City, Iowa
June, 1950

SECTION I

"The Origin and Growth of Press Laws"

How to Find a Law or Court Decision

One doesn't have to be a lawyer to look up specific laws for himself or to determine what a court actually ruled in a given case.

The constitutions of the United States and of the several states are generally available in newspaper morgues and public libraries.

Each state (and the federal government) has a compilation of its laws called a code. Some codes bear the name of the state and others still go by the name of an early compiler or publisher, such as *Burns Code Annotated*. Any lawyer has a copy of the state code. The indexing generally is poor and laws affecting the press may be listed under newspapers, publication, printing, press, etc.

Since judges draw upon precedents, past court decisions are important. Each state and the United States has its major decisions filed in so-called Reporter Series. In addition, there are regional reporter series such as Atlantic, Northeast, etc. County law libraries will have these series.

The citation (or reference) is important in looking up a decision. Cases are cited this way: 23 Fla. 341. That means Volume 23 of the Florida reports, page 341. Or 23 N.E. 645 which means Volume 23 Northeast Reports, page 645.

Each decision is preceded with explanatory material setting out sharply the points of law involved and how the court ruled on each. In addition, the decision generally reviews the circumstances over which the case arose. The language at times is stilted and "legalistic," but surprisingly enough, the courts usually get right down to earth in their discussions.

CHAPTER I

"Introduction"

A newspaperman once said that a good reporter knows 95 per cent of everything and knows where to find the other 5 per cent in a hurry.

In the 5 per cent unknown sector no subject bulks larger than law. Many reporters and copyreaders try to blaze their way through this unknown area by the insertion of a generous number of "alleged's" and "it was reported's," and then are amazed when the story explodes in their faces.

The law of the press has two fundamental aspects. In its narrow sense, law tells the newspaperman what he can do and what he cannot do. Even in this narrow area, newspapermen trudge along many times without realizing that beneath what appears to be solid ground is a layer of quicksand.

In its broader view, law, either directly or by implication, has wide social aspects that point up the responsibilities which society is becoming more insistent that the newspaper meet now that the press has become communicator to the masses. The Supreme Court's decision in the government's anti-trust suit against the Associated Press, for example, is not nearly so important for the specific issues which it decided as for the social implications. For the first time, a high court called attention to the fact that the press must recognize duties to the group at large as well to the individual.

Justice Frankfurter, who concurred with the majority, went even further and insisted that the press recognize a public service function. Society, too, is becoming more insistent that the First Amendment is not a fortification erected to permit an entrenched press to go its independent way, but rather that the Amendment is a common bulwark behind which both society and the press can protect the liberties of all.

Only a few critics thus far have expressed openly the conviction that the change must come from the group itself speaking through mandatory laws rather than leaving the method to the conscience of the newspapers themselves. But if from a lack of understanding of its social responsibilities or if from inertia or editorial contumacy, the press should forfeit its chance, these critics may sweep on to full advantage. In that event, it is not unlikely that these critics by so cheerfully accepting government aid may awaken to find a yoke around their necks far more burdensome than the faults of which they now complain. Too late they may discover they have destroyed one of America's greatest contributions to the world — a truly free press.

Law is an instrument for social control. Laws affecting the press, then, cannot be studied as phenomena so detached from every day life that a hoop can be passed through them without touching any of society's other activities. What a specific law is, often is not so important as the circumstances which prompted its enactment or the situation which it is intended to promote or restrict. Throughout this book, it must be borne in mind that a law is not a commandment from Mt. Sinai, but merely a formalized expression of the people's needs, wishes, or desires.

What society gives, it also can take away from those who persist in using it for purposes other than those for which it was designed. And society always retains the right to modify or alter a law to meet changing situations.

While this broader aspect of law is the more important one, the narrow phase should not be neglected. This narrow phase is the study of specific principles of law as applied to the press, either to permit it to serve its function better or to restrict it in the interests of the superior right of the individual or the group. A newspaperman who doesn't know these general rules and their practical application hasn't learned his profession.

But the newspaperman who thinks he can be his own lawyer by merely reading a book is as foolish as the man who buys half a dozen bottles of assorted pills and undertakes to cure himself of any ailment.

The sick or injured man, however, can give himself some "first aid" until the doctor arrives. And by a general knowledge of the body and its functions, he can eliminate some visits to a doctor's office. He knows which of nature's laws he can violate with a certain degree of immunity as well as those to which he must adhere rigidly. He can grasp such fundamental principles as the fact that if he uses his teeth to crack nuts, tear string, or test coins for genuineness, he sooner or later will be calling upon his dentist without waiting for that twice a year checkup.

If he persists in going out in his shirt sleeves to have a snowball battle with the children or habitually eats pumpkin pie or chocolate cake for breakfast dessert, or at 50 believes he has all the vitality and stamina he had at 18, he should be well informed about the doctor's visiting hours.

By the same token, a newspaperman who persists in printing anything that comes to his knowledge or attention, sooner or later will require the services of a good lawyer. The Bible, conscience, and a sense of ethics may be good guides to human conduct but they are not necessarily sufficient for the operation of a newspaper.

A book on newspaper law is not intended as "ten easy lessons" on how to become a lawyer. Its use is that merely of a formal guidepost to make the dealer in the printed word aware of his rights, responsibilities, and privileges. And to see all of them in their proper social setting.

As far as procedural law (adjective law) goes, Daniel Webster probably would be just as much at home in today's courtroom as he was when he was making legal history with his arguments before the Supreme Court. But Webster would be considerably confused by some of the present social manifestations of legal science. For law which we are prone to think of as static, is really as dynamic as the conflicting views and philosophies of those who interpret it. Law, on the other hand, is neither magical nor mysterious. It operates in well-defined ways with principles that remain relatively steadfast.

It is the aim of this book to develop those principles and to explain them in their proper setting. If it does nothing more than make a newspaperman aware that he has a problem involving both privilege and responsibilities, it will have served its purpose. A newspaperman never loses if he delays publishing a story until he has time to reflect upon all its implications and possible consequences to the community, or if a specific point of law is involved, until he has had a chance to consult with his attorney, just as a man never loses if he talks promptly with his physician about a sudden ache or sickness. As the makers of one brand of aspirin say: "If you need quick relief, take two tablets. If your headache persists, see a doctor."

If your knowledge of the general principles of law tell you danger still lurks in that story — see a lawyer. A newspaperman's job is to report court news, not to sit in court as a defendant.

CHAPTER II

The Nature of Law

In the limbo of American wisecracks is one: "There ought to be a law." Unknowingly, the man in the street in his jest has hit upon the way laws come into being. For, as pointed out in the preface, there is nothing magical in the way a law appears on the statute books.

Someone (or a number of individuals) feels a situation needs to be corrected, limited, or formally defined. Those feelings become articulate and surge upward until in some assembly hall such a bill is dumped into the hopper and begins its way through the legislative process. The chief problem in making a law is not its passage through a legislative body but in first determining just what form the remedy should take.

Long before General Marshall made his modest statement at Harvard, many people in the United States believed this country should do something to aid Europe to regain its feet. Congress then set about to translate into legislative action this general policy of the man in the street.

Unfortunately, the American legal system is made up more of revising and amending than initiating and discarding. Initiating means heading off into a different direction which takes time and considerable experimentation. Amending requires only addition to or deletion from basic rules already in existence. The federal income tax laws are examples of this amending process which have pyramided until the average citizen needs legal advice simply to fulfill one obligation to his government.

Laws affecting the press are in just about as much confusion. Amendments have been made, courts have interpreted and sometimes reversed themselves until both bench and bar and the press realize a general overhauling is a long-delayed need.

Radio, in particular, made courts thumb through statute books and precedents and the makeshift answers they arrived at satisfy no one. Now television has added another complication.

Precise definitions of law should be left to the legal fraternity. The journalist will find more understanding in seeking his definitions from the social scientists who give to their terms the broader concept the newspaperman of today needs.

J. O. Hertzler says: "By law we mean the rules of the game of organized society." (1) Those rules, however, must be enforceable rules as Kimball Young suggests in saying: "Law is but a form of social control through the systematic application of the power of a political agency in society." (2)

Harry Elmer Barnes emphasizes the changing nature of laws, a factor of which the newspaperman must be cognizant. To him, laws are "the publicly enforceable rules of human conduct and social behavior which prevail in any country at any given time." (3)

One principal school of jurisprudence, however, bases its definition of law on practically the same concept as the social scientists.

Frank R. Kennedy, professor of law at the State University of Iowa says this school — the historical school —

"insists that it is the social pressure behind legal rules that makes law obligatory; that the efficacy of the legal order rests on the sanction of public opinion, which is the source of the social standard of justice." (4)

Speaking for the legal fraternity, Kennedy defines law this way:

"If men are to exist together, so that each can develop his individuality as fully as possible without hindering the efforts of others, limits of the activities of each individual must be recognized. These limits are established by law." (5)

Justice Frankfurter of the Supreme Court, in commenting that the American mind too often is preoccupied with the constitutionality of legislation rather than its wisdom, emphasized also the social nature of laws.

---

(1) This footnote and all further footnotes in this book may be found by chapter title in the footnote section at the rear of the book.

"Reliance for the most precious interests of civilization, therefore must be found outside of their vindication by courts of law. Only a persistent positive translation of the faith of a free society into the conviction and habits and action of a community is the ultimate reliance against unabated temptations to fetter the human spirit." (6)

Both bar and laymen are in agreement, then, that the crux of law is that it is a rule that can and will be enforced. Residents and businessmen of a city may customarily decorate their houses and stores with bunting to welcome a convention. If one refuses to go along on the decoration plan, the courts will not compel him. Neither will the courts interfere if a merchant refuses to abide by the agreement of a businessmen's association to close all stores at the same time daily. The courts, too, will not interfere if a church congregation finds itself divided on the method by which a particular ritual should be performed.

Thus the elements of law which concern a newspaperman, are: laws are social rules, they are enforceable, they change, they may be repealed, and their only purpose is to permit the life of the group to have coherence, stability, and regularity.

Laws that no longer command the sanction of public opinion or are outmoded by changing conditions either are repealed or remain on the statute books as legal relics. Prohibition was repealed when Americans showed they didn't want it enforced. Every state code is cluttered with legal relics or silly laws such as the attempt of one midwestern state to cope with the automobile when it first appeared. That law, still buried in the books, reads: "When two automobiles approach a railroad crossing, both must stop, and neither must proceed until the other has passed."

Massachusetts still has a law that permits a husband to whip his wife when she needs it provided he uses a stick no thicker than the width of his thumb. Presumably the husband is the sole judge of when his wife needs to be punished. A husband, however, who insisted upon exercising his legal right today would find himself before a jury on a charge of assault and battery. It's not because knighthood again is in flower but because the status of women has changed. Most rights of husbands are like those of pedestrians. The law says the husband is the head of the house and that the pedestrian has the right of way. Both are fairly safe until they try to exercise those rights.

Laws are both attributive and distributive. If they restrict one individual they at the same time confer a right upon another. The laws of libel, for example, restrict a newspaper from printing any bit of gossip or rumor that comes to its attention. Many a newspaperman has come across what in his language is a "hot story" but he knows he can't touch it.

But the laws of libel which restrict the newspaper at the same time confer some rights on the individual. They give the individual the privilege of living the "good, clean life" in anonymity, no matter how dull. He forfeits that right when he bangs his automobile into another car, goes into court to adjudicate a dispute with a rival, runs off with his neighbor's wife, gets hit by a taxicab, is married or divorced, eats more oysters than anybody in the county, expresses himself too loudly in a taproom and is shushed with a right to the jaw, throws his hat into the political ring, makes a speech, writes a book, or otherwise brings himself to the attention of the public. Society then feels it must be informed about him or at least give recognition to him, no matter if his participation in the public view is voluntary or has been forced upon him.

The Oregon woman school teacher, who was known principally to her landlady and her pupils, soon found newspapers exercised their right to comment and print pictures when she got up at a Parent-Teachers' meeting and performed a hula hula dance. She discovered the public suddenly had developed an esthetic sense and she had no legal ground for complaint against the press when the rhythmic movement of her hips swung her right out of her job.

If the journalist will keep in mind this dual function of the law — to restrict and at the same time to confer — he will not only understand but also will not be so bitter at the laws of libel which at times prevent his publishing an item that he knows would obtain high readership interest. Then he will regard law as a kind of Jimminy Cricket to prevent his printing a story which his news judgment tells him is "terrific" but which his ethical sense tells him he should not use.

The journalist must keep in mind one thing more. Too many publishers cling to the theory that a newspaper is an institution with special rights and privileges that are inviolable. To them, a newspaper is not established but ordained.

The newspaper must first of all be a good citizen. As a business, it must subject itself to all the laws, rules, and regulations that apply to other commercial organizations. The newspaper is distinct only by virtue of having its principal commodity —news — enjoy a peculiar status in society. No other enterprise can turn out its products with such protection. The law, for example, will not tell an automobile manufacturer what designs, colors, etc. he may use, but it does insist that his product meet certain safety requirements. A cereal maker cannot stuff his boxes half with sawdust although the public might find the new product has more tang and believe it's twice as nourishing.

The newspaper, however, must not use its special privilege to become the community bully. The Supreme Court in deciding labor board cases, made short shrift of publishers' contentions that a newspaper in the general conduct of its business enjoys rights and immunities not accorded to other commercial organizations. (7)

Although the general public is prone to regard law as magical and beyond its power of comprehension, most newspapermen view it as mysterious and confusing. In the United States, much of that confusion arises because there are so many different legal jurisdictions. A state is limited only by the federal constitution, and the courts are most liberal in permitting states to use their police powers to regulate the lives, health, comfort, and convenience of their citizens.

A roving newspaperman when he adds up his expense account in New York, whether from timidity or honesty, knows that two and two are four. If his next assignment takes him to San Francisco, the two plus two on his "swindle sheet" again add to four if mathematics is still his sole guide.

Law is not that exact. A decision of a New York court may be the reverse of the opinion of a California court in cases which seem identical. That there is room for even the most learned judges to disagree in their interpretations is seen frequently in the five to four decisions of the United States Supreme Court. And sometimes such as in the Associated Press anti-trust case, the justices produced five different opinions. (8)

The same act may be defined differently by the several states. In an eastern state a press photographer went to the home of a girl who suddenly figured in the news. No one was at home but the back door was ajar. He pushed his way in and found a framed picture of the girl on a dining room shelf. The enraged family demanded action. The district attorney, thumbing through the statutes, decided the most serious case that could be brought against the photographer was a charge of trespassing, a misdemeanor. The prosecutor, however, may have wanted the paper for a friend more than the family, and he may have searched the books without his spectacles.

In another state, a press photographer under almost the same circumstances, was arrested on a charge of breaking and entering although the "breaking" consisted of just standing by while an obliging neighbor woman used the key which the family had entrusted to her. Fortunately, the mere issuance of the warrant pacified the family, and the prosecutor, of the same political faith as the paper, was happy to dismiss the charge on grounds of "insufficient evidence."

A New Yorker got a quick lesson on changing laws. In 1932 he walked down the street with a bottle in his hand and a $10 gold piece in his pocket. A judge commended him for his American virtue of thrift but gave him 30 days for violating the prohibition law.

A few years later the same gentleman repeated his performance. This time the judge dismissed the bottle as a mere sign that the man was a gentleman of good spirits but was forced to jail him for failure to turn in his gold money as the government required.

Laws, or perhaps more properly decisions, affecting the press may change as rapidly. In 1945, Russia was our ally and her victories on the eastern front were helping to bring the war to a successful close. Less than three years later, a New York court ruled that to call an American a Communist, if he actually were not a member of the Communist party, was libelous. Several papers paid dearly for so labeling three college professors.

Yet for almost two years after this decision, an avowed Communist occupied a seat on the New York City council and the party appeared legally on the official ballot of several states.

During the war, it was libelous to call an American a Nazi or a Fascist, but today that man probably would have to prove special damages in order to collect. This may be just one more bit of evidence that judges also read newspapers.

Furthermore, the interpretations may be only sectional. To call a man a rat in most communities might lead to fisticuffs or a damage suit. But to shout "Rat" at a youth swinging along the streets of Lexington, Va., might bring only a friendly greeting if he is a student at Virginia Military Institute. An Arizona court ruled that the word "racket" is not necessarily damaging. (9) Even newspapermen fondly refer to their profession as a "racket."

More confusion comes with the "mumbo jumbo" language of the law. If a writ is served on the ordinary layman he doesn't know if he is being cited for meritorious service or being charged with a crime until a lawyer tells him. Lawyers themselves are recognizing that they have lost touch with the people, and a committee of the American Bar Association is at work to make their language understandable. The committee already had recommended cutting down on the "to wits," "aforesaids," and the "did and" caused to be "dones."

A lawyer in a Boston court trying a $100,000 damage suit asked a doctor a question that took the attorney 20 minutes to state. When he finished, the doctor answered "yes." (10)

Sometimes this seeming "mumbo jumbo" is necessary. A public official once was "empowered, authorized, and directed" to do something. Each word was important. Empowering him made him the official responsible for the act, authorizing him gave him the sanction to do it, and directing was a command that he do it. Libel suits have hung on such words as these. A Texas paper lost because it printed a defendant's confession. The state Supreme Court ruled that the law "authorizing" prosecutors to take a confession was simply a notice to them that they could do so if they wished but were not compelled to do it. Therefore, the court ruled, the confession had no standing in law since it was purely a discretionary proceeding.

While the late William Howard Taft, President of the United States and later Chief Justice of the United States, was professor of law at Yale, a student disputed sharply the instructor's interpretation of a particular case.

The usually genial Taft, becoming provoked at the student's persistence, blurted:

"That's the law. If you don't like it, I suggest you get on the Supreme Court and change it."

In 1949, that student had the last laugh because he became Justice Sherman Minton of the United States Supreme Court.

Taft was not speaking too idly because another Chief Justice, Charles Evans Hughes, is credited with the remark: "The law is anything the Supreme Court says it is."

To those steeped in the school book tradition that the Congress (and the several legislatures) makes the laws, the Chief Justice's reputed assertion may sound like usurpation of powers by one branch of our check and balance government. Hughes, however, certainly didn't mean laws are the product of judicial whimsy or even indigestion. He may have been illustrating the fact that it's the interpretation of a law that gives it direction and force. And those interpretations are influenced by the changing sentiments of the times.

Congress discovered that when it attempted to regulate child labor. First, it tackled the problem through one of its most important powers — the regulation of interstate commerce. The Supreme Court declared the law was unconstitutional.

Next Congress tried its second important power — its taxing authority. Again, the Supreme Court said "no." Then Congress decided a constitutional amendment was the remedy, but its proposal was not ratified by a sufficient number of states.

Finally, Congress returned to its original idea of getting at the problem through its regulation of interstate commerce. This time the law won approval of the court. Although all these actions came within a relatively few years, there had been drastic changes meanwhile in the makeup of the court, in economic conditions, and in the sentiments of the people regarding child labor.

Hughes, if he made that statement, may have had something else in mind. He might have meant that there is no certainty what a law really does mean until the courts have interpreted it. Judges never go out looking for business but act only when a case comes before them. Once they decide there is no guarantee that at some later date they won't reverse themselves.

The federal income tax law is another example of not knowing what the law is until the courts speak. For years, it was assumed that federal salaries were not subject to the income tax law. The same cynic who probably asks "Why?" when told "the show must go on," decided to find out about the tax law. As a result, today even the President of the United States finds his pay check bears tax wounds.

Businessmen, always quick to assert their rights, sometimes are caught asleep. A large eastern state back in 1904 placed a $500 a year tax on all store keepers handling oleomargarine. For 43 years, merchants, big and little, paid the tax promptly. In 1947, a small store keeper decided he needed the $500 more than the state did, and he refused to pay.

When the case got to the state Supreme Court, the learned justices ruled the tax violated the state constitution. Of course, under the theory of supreme sovereignty of the state, the merchants got no refunds for back taxes paid, but they could look forward to a future of the "more abundant life."

By this time you probably have decided that law is so muddled and confused that a study of it is unprofitable. A girl who was a graduate of a school of journalism where law of the press is not a required subject, held that view. She went from school to a position of responsibility on a daily paper and within a month had her employers involved in three libel suits. They found it profitable to dispense with her otherwise brilliant service.

A number of factors prevent law from being as fixed and certain as mathematics. For one thing, there are those 48 states and the federal jurisdiction which were mentioned. Another factor is that one great base of our legal system — the common law — is a product of development and adaptation rather than of specific creation. An English justice 100 years ago remarked he wished it were possible to start over again and make all laws from rational enactment.

A further reason is that cases which seem similar may vary greatly because each one involves not only a set of facts but also the manner in which those facts are presented to the jurors and accepted by them. Some great lawyers of the past (and probably of the present, too) were skilled more in forensics than in law. They made a set of bare facts come to life for the jury.

If legal situations at times seem confused, take courage. The late Justice Rutledge, in commenting that reporters often report legal news badly simply because they do not understand it, sympathized with them by saying:

"With too rare exceptions their capacity for misunderstanding the significance of legal events and procedures, not to speak of opinions, is great. But this is neither remarkable nor peculiar to newsmen. For the law, as lawyers best know, is full of perplexities." (11)

Law may not be an exact science but it certainly is not made up of mere whimsies and vagaries. There are well-established guiding principles that hold relatively firm. As the Washington bureaucrat said during the war: "It's true that there is confusion here. But it's organized."

For Further Reading

The story of the "evolution" of law from folkways to formalized legal systems is told in many general books on sociology, especially those dealing with social institutions.

The two listed below were not selected because they are necessarily outstanding in their field but because they present two of the conflicting views of social science.

Barnes, Harry Elmer, *Social Institutions*, New York: Prentice-Hall, Inc., 1942.

Professor Barnes believes the legal system is the most important factor in today's society. He takes a rather dismal view of the control law exercises today.

Young, Kimball, *Sociology*, New York: The American Book Company, 1942.

Professor Young discusses law as one of the means of social control but not necessarily the most important nor the most effective.

Some of the points of conflict between law and journalism are discussed in:

Siebert, Fred S., "The Law and Journalism," 32 *Virginia Law Review*, June, 1946.

CHAPTER III

Types of Laws Affecting the Press

Law, as the advertisements of a well-known business firm say, also comes in "a dozen assorted colors and sizes."

Two men marooned on a South Sea island have little use for a set of law books or codes, for a few simple rules serve their needs. Enforcement depends upon the "sportsmanship" of the pair or the superior physical strength of one.

Primitive groups had no lawyers and judges as separate functionaries, because the men in council and the chief handed down, made, altered, and enforced the rules. As society grew complex, the legal system had to keep up with new conditions although the law seldom moves as rapidly as social changes.

Today law and lawyers are necessary. One social scientist even takes an extreme view by calling them the most important directive element in modern civilization.

"We hear much talk about 'our scientific age,' 'our industrial society,' 'our mechanical civilization,' and 'our empire of machines.' Nevertheless, ours is still a lawyer-made civilization, and one made by jurisprudence which reached its present character in 1825, before most of our great scientific and mechanical advances had taken place." (1)

Some idea of how the law shifted to meet new conditions or as society itself assumed more group responsibility is seen in today's laws on bodily assault and murder. Once such acts were "private affairs." Money payments to the injured or to the survivors were the only punishments. Further action was taken only if the accused refused to pay. In that event, group action was similar to today's contempt of court. Medieval laws compiled a "price list" for such wrongs, and since the physically handicapped in those days were virtually thrown on humanity's scrap heap, it cost more to injure a man permanently than to kill him.

The most brilliant lawyer today is not the one who can recite from memory the statutes and decisions. Just as self-service markets discourage any attempt on the part of checkers to memorize prices which may change overnight, legal training emphasizes not rote recall but the ability to look up the law and apply it.

Here, too, the lawyer is limited, and those who command the highest fees are specialists in particular fields just as doctors specialize. The corporation attorney who commands a $100,000 fee may not serve you as well on a traffic violation charge as the lawyer struggling to make office rent.

Few lawyers, for example, have made themselves specialists on libel, invasion of privacy, and the other laws that restrict editorial content. For one thing, there are not the same demands or rewards for their services in these fields as in other practices. Another reason, no matter how society regards it, newspapers, being staffed by human beings, generally relegate to future editorial oblivion the lawyer who wins a case against them.

An editor, with human emotions, feels no more kindly toward such lawyer than any individual does toward the person who injures him, no matter where the fault lies. For it is expensive even for a paper to win a libel suit.

In this respect, the newspaperman is no better and no worse than men in other professions and business, few of whom follow the Biblical injunction to turn the other cheek to their enemy.

Laws are like the Biblical sands of the sea, and every session of Congress and state legislatures deposits more residue on the legal shores. The First Congress beginning in 1789 considered 268 bills and resolutions and enacted 118 of them into law. The 78th Congress, starting in 1943, considered 7,845 bills and resolutions and approved 1,157 of them. (2)

From the first Congress until the close of the 78th Congress, representatives and senators dumped into the legislative hoppers 762,702 bills and resolutions. (3)

That staggering total does not include the rulings of commissions and independent agencies which to particular industries and businesses have all the effect of law. Sometimes regulations gush forth from administrative agencies in book form, 100,000 words or more at a time.

The newspaperman should at least have a general awareness of the fields of law that affect him if he does not care to strike up a more usable acquaintanceship.

In the classification of fields of law, there are just about as many ideas as there are in journalism on what makes a good headline. The following list is meant to be neither definitive nor precise, but is intended only to serve as workable information.

The principal basic types or fields of law the newspaper as a unit encounters include:

COMMON LAW

Colonists, exercising their rights as Englishmen, borrowed as much of the common law as they wished. After the Revolution, it was necessary to retain some legal base for no people can start all over again. American common law continued to follow that of England, but the American concept of a free press is different as the next chapter shows.

Common law has been defined variously as unwritten law, the residue of customs and sanctions which served society from the day when men first lived together, and judge-made law. Each element has some truth and also some falsity.

Common law is a blend of abstractions, expediency, and articulated customs. It is unwritten in the sense that a good part of it has never been put into statute form. It is the result of custom because its antecedents go back into early rules of the group. It's judge-made law because it was given substance and direction by the early English royal courts, and today judicial precedents loom large in the determination of many cases. To win their suits, lawyers look up records of cases in the past in which the issues involved were similar to those of the present dispute. Some of the cases they cite may go back hundreds of years. They hope the same line of legal reasoning will prevail again. Following precedents gives a measure of stability to the law, but judges do not follow them blindly.

A few years ago in an eastern state, a farmer closed off a road which ran through his property. Neighbors went to court. The county surveyor testified that the road actually was on the property of the farmer. The judge, however, dipped back into common law as far as the common pasturage customs of medieval England, and decided since the farmer for years had not objected to use of the road, it now became a public highway.

Newspapermen frequently cover cases involving a popular conception of the "unwritten law." Husbands (or wives) who shoot the rival who broke up their marriage go back to the common law to plead justification on the ground they were defending the sanctity of the home. Despite the statutes governing murder, juries often accept such pleas.

Common law played a major role in the growth of freedom of the press in England, and as we shall see in a later chapter, some authorities persist in the view that Americans borrowed that concept.

In written communication, American writers are protected under a common law copyright. The courts recognize an unpublished manuscript as the property of the creator unless he forfeits his rights by giving it to the world without protecting himself under statutory copyright.

Americans, however, have enacted most of the legal rights of the press into more concrete law.

MORAL LAW

Moral law, growing out of religious concepts, finds no distinct place in our modern legal system. It is important however to the press because it exerts a negative control to a degree not often suspected.

The newspaperman pays respect to the "moral law" when he withholds a story because his own code of ethics tells him it violates "good taste." Rightly, or wrongly, he feels his readers will be disturbed at a particular story or more often at the phrasing of an individual sentence or two. Only in recent years, for example, have such words as "rape," "syphilis," "hell" and even the milder "liar" shown up in newspapers. For years, no one ever died of cancer in a newspaper, and many went back to that old custom of refusing for a long time to tell the reader the disease which was sapping the strength of Babe Ruth. Doctors often went to jail for "unethical practices" but only recently for performing abortions.

Once it was almost standard practice for newspapers to print no pictures of bodies, especially those mangled in accidents. Many newspapers have abandoned this self-imposed rule on the ground that horror is part of life, and in the case of automobile accidents, may even have a salutary effect.

The New York *Daily News* in 1928 regarded as a "scoop" its photograph of Ruth Snyder as she sat in Sing Sing's death chair, but many other papers criticized its publication. An electrocution picture published in 1949 by a Chicago paper drew about the same reaction. (4) But neither New York nor Illinois has a specific law against such pictures.

A city editor on an eastern paper insists that his reporters write suicides as merely "sudden deaths" on the theory that the family wants to file that obituary clipping in its Bible or memory book. In the handling of other news, this city editor likes to regard himself as a "hard-boiled newspaper man of the old school."

Many papers formerly invoked this "good taste" principle on certain labor news on the ground "agitators" should not be encouraged with publicity. When former Senator Burton K. Wheeler campaigned for vice president on the Progressive ticket in 1924, a Pennsylvania newspaper gave him a three-column "spread" when he talked in that city. Just before the United States entered World War II, Senator Wheeler returned to that city. This time the paper ignored his speech by reasoning it violated "good taste" to print views contrary to those held by the "best people" in the community.

Moral law is not a law in the legal meaning because it is not enforceable by the state. But its restraining force in shaping the appearance of the printed word in the newspaper and in deciding what is "fit to print," cannot be underestimated or dismissed without comment. American readers, for example, were aware of the Wally Simpson story before the rank and file of Englishmen knew a crisis was approaching because most English papers, by tacit agreement, refuse to put their sovereigns in a "gold fish bowl."

American journalism faced just as delicate a situation in reporting the activities of President Franklin D. Roosevelt. Even during the heat of political campaigns no attention was called to his infirmity nor any pictures printed that revealed the heavy apparatus that permitted him to walk nor the special ramps built for his convenience.

Paul W. White, former news editor of the Columbia Broadcasting System, discloses that a radio announcer who in 1936 watched Mr. Roosevelt fall in the mud of Franklin Field, Philadelphia, as the president entered to deliver his address, kept up a running talk of description of the crowd and the weather but made no mention of the mishap. (5) All of radio's "good taste" cannot be attributed to fear of the wrath of the Federal Communications Commission when license renewal time comes around.

If an editor decides that "good taste" forbids his publication of a story or picture, or compels him to alter a story to spare his readers, who can deny his decision is just as effective for the community as if there were legal censorship?

CONSTITUTIONAL LAW

A constitution is a statement of the basic principles, organization, and powers which a people have granted to their government. All rights not granted by the constitution are retained by the people to insure themselves of being ruled by a government of law and not of men. And the people reserve the right to alter that constitution as they deem necessary.

The constitution is the newspaperman's fountainhead of freedom. The people of the United States were distrustful that a government could be relied upon to permit them to continue the enjoyment of freedom of speech, press, and worship. They sought to make certain by expressly stating in the constitution that there must be no tampering with these basic rights. Today, many critics of the press find fuel in the theory that this freedom is not an absolute right. Future battles over the press no doubt will be fought out along this line, and newspapers should be aware of the implications in it.

Each state, too, adopted a constitution, and it took a war to determine finally that the federal constitution was supreme.

Americans put their constitution in writing; some other countries have not set down in print their basic tenets of government. To an Englishman, however, his largely unwritten constitution is just as real as the American document that can be read, seen, and touched.

The constitution has made the American government one of delegated and implied powers. The founding fathers might be compared roughly with directors of a modern corporation. They set up the general policies and leave to the officers the day-to-day rules necessary to carry on the business.

STATUTORY LAW

As Charles A. Beard suggests, the delegates to the Philadelphia convention knew that the general language of the constitution they were framing could become concrete only with statutes. (6)

Washington expressed the same thought in saying: "Establishment of certain general doctrines of law does not make a government." (7)

The Constitution itself provided for those "day-to-day" operations by declaring:

> "This constitution and all laws of the United States made in pursuance thereof, and all treaties made and which shall be made under the authority of the United States, shall constitute the supreme law of the land." (8)

Statutory law simply means laws enacted by a law-making body such as Congress or state legislatures. For practical newspaper purposes, enactments or ordinances by minor political divisions such as cities may be considered in the same category.

A number of cities at the moment are taking advantage of their taxing power to levy a tax for permission to conduct business. Courts have interfered only when this special tax applied just to newspapers or attempted to classify newspapers by a yardstick of circulation. (9)

Distribution of printed matter, other than general newspapers, has also encountered municipal regulation and some of those ordinances have been annulled by the courts. (10)

Since statutes (or ordinances) are creations of law-making bodies as they attempt to discharge their duties, no statute can be superior to the constitution. If a law conflicts with the limitations imposed upon Congress (or the legislatures or city councils) by the constitution, the courts declare the law void. Such decisions, unfortunately, may leave the injured party without redress for injury, and without means to retrieve an unlawful tax paid. Newspapers generally have shown reluctance to force a test case on such laws, and act only when they believe the law has become "oppressive."

Statutes deal with every phase of modern life. A popular conception is that statutes deal only with offenses called crimes, but hundreds of them, collectively called private law, regulate commerce, industry and all enterprises or activities upon which people embark.

CRIMINAL LAW

A crime is an offense against society. The law assumes a particular act is injurious to the best interests of the group as a whole. The state then steps in and prosecutes the offender.

Unlike some private law (also called civil law) criminal law has well-defined punishments. The paper which libels a person doesn't know until the jury speaks if the wrong will cost it six cents or $100,000. The offender against criminal statutes knows in advance the limits of his punishment. The murderer is aware that if convicted the minimum sentence will be the penalty fixed for voluntary manslaughter and the maximum will be death.

On the editorial side, the newspaper is concerned with several types of criminal law. If the story it prints incites, or tends to incite, people to commit a breach of the peace, the state may prosecute for criminal libel.

A brutal murder once prompted a midwestern newspaper, after the suspect was caught, to comment editorially:

"There is talk among some red-blooded men that the county may be spared the expense of a trial."

A mob bent on lynching gathered around the jail, but finally was dispersed. The district attorney went through the formalities of drawing up a charge of criminal libel but abandoned the attempt.

Contempt also is dealt with by the courts as an offense with the penalty a fine or imprisonment or both. Publication of lottery news, obscene and blasphemous stories also can be handled under the penal code.

On the business side, the printing of advertisements known to be fraudulent may be dealt with by penal statutes as well as civil actions. Several executives of a magazine once went to jail for padding their circulation figures in an attempt to defraud advertisers.

Any criminal statute affecting other businesses also applies to the newspapers. A newspaper publisher once was fined $10 and costs for permitting the editorial room to be cluttered with discarded back copies and waste paper which the city contended created a fire hazard. Had the publisher read his paper that morning he may have noticed that according to the news column the city was conducting a "vigorous campaign" against fire law violations.

CIVIL LAW

Some authorities prefer the term "private law" to "civil law." They have a good point because it covers suits between individuals. The state takes no part except to set up the rules and provide the court machinery.

The editorial side is concerned chiefly with civil law in libel, invasion of privacy, and unfair competition. All three in law are torts. A tort for practical purposes may be defined as a personal injury suffered through a wrongful act. "Personal" does not refer to physical injury but, as in the case of libel, to loss of reputation or good name or "mental anguish." Only a person himself can destroy his good name with impunity.

The peril to a newspaper in libel, we have seen, is the unfixed limits of the damages which may be assessed against it. Courts do not interfere with a jury's award unless convinced the sum is all out of proportion to any injury, real or apparent. The governor of a southern state in 1948 won a libel suit of $375,000 against a magazine, but the court cut the sum in half on the ground it was excessive. A typographical error cost a Texas paper only $100, but a Pennsylvania paper paid $15,000 for a printer's mistake.

A newspaper or a press association which finds a rival (or radio) stealing its news has an action in civil court. The editorial side also encounters civil law if it wants to sue for infringement of a copyrighted article or to protect its trademark from being appropriated by another paper.

Invasion of privacy is a relatively uncharted field. Courts disagree not only in its interpretation and application but also in whether there is such a wrong. Pictures and advertisements have provided most of the few cases. The crux is: What use can be made of the photograph of a person not directly in the news if the paper for some reason wishes to publish the picture? In advertising, some states have statutes and in other states courts have applied the rule that a person's picture, testimonial, etc. cannot be used in an advertisement without his permission.

On the business side, the newspaper encounters civil law when it signs a contract to sell or buy goods or services, insures its building or employees, or performs any of the acts a corporation must do to carry on its affairs.

Civil and criminal law sometimes are confused because the same set of circumstances may give rise to both kinds of cases. After an automobile accident, one or both motorists may be charged with drunken driving. That's a crime. The state takes over and prosecutes so that the man may be punished. Both cars may be badly damaged, but society will not concern itself because that is a matter between the two motorists. If the driver at fault refuses to pay for the damage to the other car, that motorist brings a civil action. The state takes no part in that case except to provide the courts and the procedure for hearing it.

EQUITY

It may be just a reflection of today's mores, but ordinarily, time or money, or both, are thought to heal everything. In the lush 1920's, many chorus girls, broken-hearted on Page 1 with pictures, because some "sugar daddy" reneged on a proposal usually made after he had looked upon the wine while it was red, found the wounds healed miraculously when the foreman of the jury, almost like a radio quiz master, boomed: "Give the little lady $50,000."

It would have been repugnant to society if the courts through their equity powers had compelled "daddy" to make good on his promise, and besides the little lady then probably would have had a real heart attack.

The courts, however, recognize that in less tender affairs, money cannot always be the answer. Early England recognized the inadequacy of the law in certain situations by permitting some pleas to go directly to the king. The busy sovereign simply delegated a chancellor as the "royal conscience."

Sometimes the complainer does not want damages, but instead wants the defendant to do a particular thing or to refrain from doing an act. He prays to the court for relief either in the form of specific performance or an injunction. The branch of law which decides his plea is equity. Popularly, the best-known equity cases are divorce suits. One (or both parties) wants release from a "contract."

Perhaps no group in modern American life felt this power of the courts more than labor unions. On the plea that his property or business was in danger of irreparable damage, an employer went into court to ask that a striking union be compelled to desist from barring entrances to his plants, wholesale picketing, interfering with men who remained at work, or to oust workers on a "sit down." If the court accepted the plea, it granted an injunction, violation of which was punishable as contempt of court.

A baseball player who jumps his contract also may be enjoined from playing with any other team. The courts, wise in the ways of the world, would not tell the player he had to pick up his glove and resume work, because he might just stand like a statue at his position. They simply tell him that until he fulfills his contract he can't play with any other team.

An active partner in a publishing firm who refuses to give his colleagues an accounting of his stewardship may be compelled by an equity court to provide those records.

Editorially, the newspaper is not so much concerned with equity because the injunctive powers of the courts cannot be used to prevent publication of an article. Relief to an injured person comes after publication only.

A Washington judge in 1949 did enjoin a newspaper from printing a series of stories criticizing the Federal Housing Authority, but the injuction was dissolved before it could be tested. (11)

Judges also have acted to ban the circulation of comic books, but again, there have been no rulings by appellate courts.

Minnesota once enacted a law that had the effect of prior censorship. The law forbade the publication of papers (or periodicals) of "undesirable character." One paper, devoted principally to attacks upon public officials, was enjoined from further publication until the owner gave promises of "good behavior." He appealed, and the United States Supreme Court in 1931 held the Minnesota statute was unconstitutional. (12)

When the government proceeded against the Associated Press, it sought a remedy through equity. The government wanted to prevent the press association from enforcing certain of its by-laws which the justice department said "restrained trade." (13)

An equity court once refused to enjoin a Texas newspaper from using the same name as a paper in St. Louis. The court, in effect, ruled the St. Louis paper had not proved any actual injury. (14)

At times, newspapers, press associations, and magazines have resorted to equity in disputes over the rights to features, to protect news dispatches from being used without permission or payment, and to prevent interference by administrative agencies.

ADMINISTRATIVE LAW

A phenomenon of modern American government is the growth of administrative law. The Interstate Commerce Commission, created by Congress in 1887, is considered to be the parent of commissions and independent agencies that are still growing.

Congress (and the legislatures) can delegate some of its powers to commissions for regulating particular industries or activities.

Constitutionally, a commission, as an agent of Congress, can have no power that Congress does not enjoy. A commission exercises legislative, judicial, and executive functions. The regulations it makes have all the effect of law. Its interpretation of the way an industry meets those requirements usually is not reviewed by the courts unless there is a clear question of arbitrary use. It can call upon the full powers of the government to enforce its edicts if necessary.

The commission best known to journalism is the Federal Communications Commission which has jurisdiction over leased wires and radio message transmission as well as radio broadcasting.

The newspaper itself is more concerned with the Postoffice Department since a loss of its second-class mailing privileges may be a financial death sentence. The Supreme Court in 1945 effectively limited the Post Office Department's right to pass on contents of a periodical. (15)

At present, the postoffice and newspapers are disputing over the Department's fluctuating interpretation of what violates the lottery laws, and this issue, too, some day may head into the courts.

The business side of the newspaper is concerned with administrative law through regulation of advertising by the Federal Trade Commission and the Securities and Exchange Commission as well as the agencies or commissions handling the common industrial problems of social security, workmen's compensation, unemployment insurance, and others.

The continued growth of administrative law promises future conflicts. In the opinion of many authorities, administrative agencies and commissions are developing into a fourth branch of American government.

For Further Reading

The story of the development of customs and rules into a system of constitutional government is a fascinating one.

For the story of the English constitution see:

Hallam, Henry, *Constitutional History of the English Constitution*, New York; E. P. Dutton & Co., 1912.

May, Sir Thomas Erskine, *Constitutional History of England*, London; Armstrong & Co., 1895.

For the American constitution:

Curtis, G. T., *History of the United States Constitution*, New York; Harper & Bros., 1897.

Hamilton, Alexander; Madison, James; and Jay, John, *The Federalist*, New York; Henry Holt & Co., 1898.

Warren, Charles, *The Making of the Constitution*, Boston; Little Brown & Co., 1928.

For a blending of both American and English stories with special reference to freedom of the press, see:

Patterson, Giles, J., *Free Speech and a Free Press, Boston;* Little Brown & Co., 1939.

Chafee, Zechariah, *Freedom of the Press*, Chicago; University of Chicago Press, 1947.

For general information on the American legal system see:

Bush, Chilton R., *Newspaper Reporting of Public Affairs*, New York; Appleton-Century Co., 1940.

MacDougall, Curtis D., *Covering the Courts*, New York; Prentice-Hall, Inc., 1946.

CHAPTER IV

"What Is Freedom of the Press?"

When the historian of a far distant age sets down the record of our times, he undoubtedly will list as two of America's major contributions to the world – objective reporting and a distinctive concept of freedom of the press.

The story of objective reporting belongs properly to the journalism historian. The story of America's unique concept of a free press belongs here, but a subject that volumes have not exhausted hardly can be made definitive in one chapter. (1) The purpose here, however, is to see just what freedom of the press means to the newspaper of today. Only by a knowledge of historical perspective can present-day laws of the press be understood.

Some of the questions to be explored are:

1. Is it really a distinctive concept, or is it, as some authorities say, a mere borrowing from England?

2. If it is a distinctive concept, how did it originate?

3. Is freedom of the press an absolute right?

4. What are the signs that indicate the trend toward the future?

The newspaperman by the very nature of his work cannot live apart from the world. Quick to note man's progress in other fields, he often fails to observe the currents that swirl about his own feet. As freedom of the press is the backbone of his profession, the newspaperman is foolish to dismiss these currents with blissful assurance that his liberty always will remain as firm as that foundation of solid rock upon which Biblical man was directed to erect his house.

To assume, as some do, that America merely borrowed its concept from England is to ignore, as one Supreme Court justice has said, all the lessons of history. (2) Those lessons may serve well as guideposts in resolving the growing criticism in some quarters that there must be changes in the modern press, by law, if necessary.

There is no denying that early America borrowed on the principles of freedom of the press (and speech) that still were evolving in England after several centuries of struggle. When the barons forced the *Magna Charta* from King John at Runnymede, the liberties they won were pretty dubious. The sovereign promised that: "To no one will we deny right or justice."

The royal idea of right and justice, however, did not extend to the individual the privilege to speak his opinion freely. It took centuries more for those rights to be won.

There is evidence that the colonists used England more as a negative example to demonstrate what they did not want. Realizing full well the restrictions their brothers in England still were fighting, the colonists were determined to settle the issue almost at one blow.

More convincing evidence is the fact that half a century after freedom of the press was written into the American Constitution, England still struggled with newspaper taxes that were ill-disguised attempts to shackle criticism of public officials.

In April, 1949, the editor of the *London Daily Mirror* went to jail for three months and his paper was fined $40,000 for a journalism escapade that America probably would have dismissed as being in about the same category as the "invasion from Mars."

The *Mirror* in a page 2 feature, claimed a vampire man had killed a number of persons, presumably to drink the blood. The feature clearly was based on the murder of an elderly woman which had brought sensational stories in other London papers, even the most conservative press. (3) Several had alluded to rumors of a vampire angle. London papers, just alloted more news print, had been engaging in a circulation war.

The *Mirror*, in its feature story, reported a vampire man had been arrested in connection with the murder. The *Mirror* and its editor were penalized on the ground the story made it difficult for the defendant to receive a fair trial. Buried in the legal phrasing of the judgment, however, was the impression that the court also was prompted by the desire to teach the newspaper "good manners."

For the justice said: "In the opinion of the court, this (the publication of the article) has been done, not as an error in judgment, but as a matter of policy, pandering to sensationalism for the purpose of increasing the circulation of the paper." (4)

The court, in branding the article a "disgrace to journalism," went back to 1742 for its major precedent. American judges, in dealing with constructive contempt, seem more prone to consider cases in the light of modern developments in mass communications.

No American newspaper, not even those most blatant in "trying cases in print" ever has felt such judicial wrath. In the United States, the most usual result is to grant a change of venue for the defendant. This evidence is cited, not as justification for a free rein of pre-trial comment, but simply as another indication of the difference between the English and American judicial mind in one phase of newspaper activity.

Although there is always danger in attempting to draw parallels in law, American newspapers have gone further and editorially have tried to "quicken the conscience of the court" while the judges were making up their minds on sentences or motions for new trials. In some of the most striking examples of this type of editorial "command" to the judiciary, the Supreme Court has upheld "freedom of the press" with an admonition to judges not to be so sensitive to "the winds of public opinion." (5)

In civil libel, the *London Daily Mirror* on Nov. 20, 1949, reported a case which does offer some contrast with the American view of what constitutes damages. A former British heavyweight boxer in attempting a "come back," was matched in what promoters described as his "first full-out test" since he lost the title. One newspaper, *The People,* described the match as the "craziest, quaintest, promotion of the year," and added: "The suckers, of course, rolled up to see it. The promoters cleaned up."

The promoter was awarded $10,000 in a libel action. (6)   A few years ago, an eastern metropolitan newspaper, in commenting upon a sports event arranged as a charity benefit, not only criticized the spectacle sharply but also inferred none too subtly that the promoters had been so liberal in listing expenses that charity would continue to "suffereth long and endureth much." The promoters failed to collect in a libel action.

In contempt cases, it doesn't seem logical that American courts have refrained from taking drastic action either from lack of zeal toward protecting defendants or from failure to realize their inherent powers.   In civil libel, the courts also know of the rules on fair comment.

A more logical explanation seems to be that American courts are aware that we have a different concept of press freedom than that of England.   This will be borne out by a more detailed study, in a later chapter, of constructive contempt—those acts committed outside the immediate jurisdiction of the court. In 1918, with Supreme Court blessing, judges began to stray far from direct contempt — acts committed within the court's immediate jurisdiction — but in the past few years, the highest court has brought them back to the more narrow interpretation.   In cases from Texas and two from California, the Supreme Court within the past few years, has insisted that judges be "men of fortitude, able to thrive in a hardy climate." (7)

One of the tightest fetters on the English press down through the years was the crime of seditious libel which most times took the form of penalizing criticism.   Yet not until 1843 by the Lord Campbell's Act was the English journalist permitted to plead a defense of truth.

Today English papers may print only the fact that divorces have been granted.   American judges often impound divorce evidence but the public by that time usually knows the charges, the property settlement, the child custody arrangements, and are busy speculating on a new spouse for each party.

In November, 1949, a British cabinet minister thought it necessary again to remind the House of Commons that members will not be permitted to ask questions about stories in the press or to call for a committee of inquiry into a newspaper report. His reason was that no minister had official responsibility for the press. If the American concept of the press coincides with that of Britain, why must a British minister remind the Commons about a subject which no American Speaker ever finds necessary to mention?

More evidence that America views the press in a different light than does England, or most of the continent, is seen in the operation of press associations. More than a hundred years ago, Paul Julius Reuter became, in effect, a British minister without portfolio by setting up a news service.

The effective tie-in between Reuters and the British government grew in importance as England became master of most of the world-wide cables. From Downing Street, the official interpretation of the British government regarding questions that affected the empire went out to the world in Reuters' dispatches. News from outlying empire possessions or other world points, came back by the same process. To some authorities, this was cooperation between a news service and a government; to others it was a form of prior restraint or "censorship." The practical mind doesn't need to be told that no Reuters' reporter was going to stray far from "official interpretation."

For a long time, one American press association received most of its world news through an exchange arrangement with Reuters. Later, France, Italy, Germany, and Japan had their "official news agencies," and today Russia still permits only "official versions" to go out. It was not until the 1940's that Reuters went under "private ownership" of British newspapers. For one thing, radio transmission was dooming any attempt to control news through ownership of cables.

In all American history, the government has had no such connection with a press service. The world always has received its news of the United States from private American sources or news services or from correspondents maintained here by papers of other countries.

The close connection in the latter part of the 18th century and early 19th century between one or more American papers and the administration produced "official interpretations" in those few papers, but the remainder of the press and news services went their independent ways. The whole history of American journalism is a story of practices which belie any tie-in between government and press on either domestic or foreign news. The American concept has never conceived of any affinity between the two.

The American State Department, especially in the immediate years before World War II, frequently was called upon by foreign legations to explain a press story. The American secretary each time patiently had to tell the inquirer that the government exercises no control over the press and has no way of making it conform even to the Department's own policy.

In 1927, the State Department tried to exert some influence by asking the press to print a report that the Department was concerned over a growing foreign hegemony in Mexico. The Department was eager for the story to reach the American reader without its source being traced to officialdom. The press responded by roundly denouncing the subterfuge.

Historically, the events leading to the adoption of the First Amendment guaranteeing freedom of press, speech, religion and the right of petitioning and peaceable assembly, are replete with evidence that the founding fathers deliberately set about to correct what they regarded as the evils of the English system. Colonists were neither unaware nor disdainful of the part Englishmen had played and were playing in the battle for free expression. At times, there was cooperation between groups abroad and in the colonies.

Colonists themselves had been waging such a struggle. America's first newspaper was suppressed. Massachusetts' governor and council were outraged not only by some of the contents of Benjamin Harris' *"Publick Occurrences Both Foreign and Domestic"* but also because he printed without a royal license. Royal governors, in their credentials from the crown, were warned that liberty of printing might give rise to "great inconvenience" and that nothing should be printed "without your especial leave and license first obtained." (8)

When Andrew Hamilton by his forceful argument that the jury should pass on the fact as well as the law, won a verdict of "not guilty" for John Peter Zenger, publisher of the *New York*

Weekly Journal, against a charge of seditious libel, the verdict was applauded in England.

One correspondent of the *Pennsylvania Gazette,* writing from England, observed:

"The greatest Men at the Bar have openly declared that the Subject of Libels was never so well treated in Westminster Hall as at New York."

He quoted a "Goliath in learning and politics," as saying of Hamilton's argument: "If it is not law it is better than law, it ought to be law, and will always be law wherever justice prevails." (9)

The colonists set out to make into law not only Hamilton's contention that juries should pass upon both fact and law but also that truth should be admitted as a defense. Under the English law of the time, neither of Hamilton's contentions was valid, but the trial was a landmark because it gave evidence that the colonists were going to develop an institution that soon would beat off the challenges of government.

The progress of that development can be measured to some extent by the action of the First Continental Congress in 1774. Freedom of press was one of the five inviolable rights the Congress inserted in its Declaration of Rights. (10) Soon afterward, the colonies began drawing up written constitutions which contained freedom of press provisions.

One argument of those who maintain the American concept of freedom of the press was borrowed from England is that the completed draft of the Constitution made no mention of it. Since the delegates again followed the custom of meeting secretly and only later published their journal, the best record of the discussions is in the notes of James Madison. Freedom of the press, it is true, did not receive much attention but a clue as to the reason is given in the comment of Delegate Richard Sherman of Connecticut.

Quoting Sherman's reason why a proposal to appoint a committee to draft a bill of rights was voted down, Bancroft has him saying:

"The State declaration of rights are not repealed by this Constitution and, being in force, are sufficient." (11)

After the Constitution was completed, the fight began for a specific Bill of Rights. The First Congress directed that such a bill should be drawn up and left the work to a committee headed by James Madison. The struggle sometimes is referred to historically as being between the schools of Hamilton and Jefferson although Jefferson was in France at the time. Such designation doesn't mean that Hamilton and Jefferson alone bore the brunt but is a simple way of designating two principal ideas.

As a result, Hamilton often is regarded as opposed to a free press but a reading of his defense of Harry Croswell in 1804 shows his opposition was to the method and not to the goal. (12) A generalized statement of opinion is that he believed freedom of the press, and similar ideas, depended in the final analysis on the sentiment of the people and not on written guarantees. A rough parallel might be the case of money which has no value in itself but receives value from confidence in the government and the economic system as a whole. A statement of principle, then, has only the effect which public opinion or sanction gives it.

The Jefferson school, on the other hand, wanted an expressed declaration of restrictive clauses. Jefferson had such faith in free institutions that he once wrote:

"... the basis of our government being the opinions of the people, the very first object should be to keep that right; and were it left to me to decide whether we should have a government without newspapers or newspapers without a government, I should not hesitate a moment to prefer the latter." (13)

Writing about nine years later to criticize the Sedition Act passed by Congress in 1798, Madison was emphatic in claiming a distinction between the American and British government. He wrote that the First Amendment must be considered in the light of that difference. (14)

Concretely, the evidence that Americans were fully aware they were blazing a new trail toward individual freedom, may be summed up under these general classifications:

1. America, despite some debunkers, was settled primarily by people fleeing from what they regarded as shackles on their liberty. It is incongruous to believe that such people would

impose upon themselves the same shackles that drove them from England.

2. As Americans applied common law, seditious libel, long a press control in England, was unknown. The political party that attempted to impose it — the Federalists — not only was swept from power at the next election but the party disappeared. The Federalists' motive was punishment and revenge for criticism, the use to which England put seditious libel.

3. The American Bill of Rights is a creation of the people themselves and expressed in a constitution. It is not, as in England, the creation of a governing body. The English Bill of Rights was directed at the crown and was not intended to apply to Parliament which gave it.

4. The American Bill of Rights recognized the difference between America and England by also forbidding a state religion. There was an established church in England.

5. The American government was a novel political creation. The people were not wresting power from the crown but were setting up a government based only on powers they granted to it. It was to be government by consent of the governed. It was unlikely in such circumstances the people were going to sign away rights to a creature of their own making which at some future time might be turned against them.

6. After the constitution was completed, there came insistent demands from state after state that guarantees of individual liberties be expressly set forth and that implied guarantees were not sufficient. It is inconceivable that such demands would have arisen had the people deliberately set out to copy English institutions or if they elected to put their trust in English common law.

7. When the American Bill of Rights was adopted, the press situation in England was roughly this:

The press was free from license and censorship. But seditious libel was still a matter for the courts to determine because not until the Fox Libel Law of 1792 did juries pass on the fact and the law. Even that law did not stop such prosecutions, and not until 1843 was truth a defense.

There was a tax on the English press which exercised strong control.

8. The use of the word "abridge" in the First Amendment indicates the Constitution meant no prohibitions. It could have used "censor," "regulate" or some other word capable of being interpreted as conferring only a qualified right.

9. Years later, the American people reinforced that Bill of Rights in the Fourteenth Amendment which prevents states from infringing upon the rights or immunities of any citizen. True, it was not aimed specifically at the rights in the First Amendment but judicial interpretation has given it that effect.

> The Supreme Court has said: ". . . by the First Amendment it was meant to preclude the national government, and by the Fourteenth Amendment to preclude the states from adopting any form of previous restraint upon printed publications." (15)

The weight of evidence, then, is that the American Bill of Rights is a recognition of the differences in the ideologies of the English and the American people. Those differences, as they affect the press, have become more pronounced over the years both by custom and by judicial interpretation.

But let's submit the case to a panel of experts:

James Madison, who sat in on the constitutional convention, often stressed this difference. In his argument for the Bill of Rights, he wrote that the First Amendment should be considered in the light of the essential difference between the British government and the American Constitution. And he added:

> "Freedom of the press and the rights of conscience, those choicest privileges of the people, are unguarded in the British constitution." (16)

> Again, he wrote: ". . . the freedom exercised by the press and protected by public opinion far exceeds the limits prescribed by the ordinary rules of law." (17)

By "ordinary rules of law," Madison clearly had in mind common law.

T. M. Cooley, the great authority on constitutional law, wrote:

> "The English common law which made libels on the Constitution or the government indictable, as it was administered

by the courts, seems to us unsuited to the condition and circumstances of the people of the United States, and therefore never to have been adopted in the several states." (18)

Further on he says: "The common-law offense of libelling a government is ignored in constitutional systems, as inconsistent with the genius of free institutions." (19)

Schofield goes even further in saying: "One of the objects of the Revolution was to get rid of the English common law on Liberty of speech and press." (20)

The courts have spoken frequently on the subject. In Grosjean v. American Press Co., the majority opinion declared: ". . . the restricted rules of English common law in respect to freedom of the press in force when the constitution was adopted were never accepted by the American colonies." (21)

Another decision was even more emphatic:

"No purpose in ratifying the Bill of Rights was clearer than that of securing for the people of the United States much greater freedom of religion, expression, assembly, and petition than the people of Great Britain ever enjoyed. Ratified as it was while the memory of many oppressive English restrictions on the enumerated liberties were still fresh, the First Amendment cannot reasonably be taken as approving prevalent English practices. On the contrary, the only conclusion supported by history is that the unqualified prohibitions laid down by the framers were intended to give to liberty of the press, as to other liberties, the broadest scope that could be countenanced in an orderly society." (22)

In rejecting the argument of the government in the Abrams case, brought under the Amendment to the Espionage Act of 1917, Justice Holmes said:

"I wholly disagree with the argument of the government that the First Amendment left the common law as to seditious libel in force. History seems to me against the notion." (23)

Again, Justice Holmes has said:

"But when men have realized that time has upset many fighting faiths, they may come to believe even more than they believe the very foundations of their own conduct that the ultimate good desired is better reached by free trade in ideas

— that the best test of truth is the power of the thought to get itself accepted in the competition of the market, and that truth is the only ground upon which their wishes safely can be carried out. That, at any rate, is the theory of our constitution." (24)

Is the Freedom of the Press an Absolute Right?

Are the rights and privileges which the American people have given to the press unqualified and absolute? Do those rights and privileges set the newspaper apart from all other commercial and industrial institutions?

Publishers who adhered to the theory they were living in a cloister untouched by law or public opinion, received probably their greatest shock during the depression days of the 1930's. First, the publishers were embroiled with the National Recovery Act which encouraged industries to set up self-regulating codes and to fly the "Blue Eagle." The second shock came in the dealings of the press with the National Labor Relations Act.

Colonel Robert R. McCormick, publisher of the *Chicago Tribune*, possibly represented the extreme view in his embracing theory that the First Amendment would be violated by any law that had the effect of unreasonably raising the cost of production "or unreasonably decreasing by indirect means the return from publishing, as these would destroy its freedom as effectively as would excess taxation." (25)

He included in these factors all regulations affecting labor conditions, and preservation of business competition, and regulations superintending "accuracy in advertising." (26)

The Supreme Court spoke in a number of cases but nowhere made its message more clear than in a suit growing out of the discharge of Morris Watson of the Associated Press for Guild activities.

The court said:

"The publisher of a newspaper has no special immunity from the application of general laws. He has no special privilege to invade the rights and liberties of others. He must answer for libel. He may be punished for contempt of court. He is subject to antitrust laws. Like others he must pay equitable and non-discriminatory taxes on his business." (27)

The newspaper, then, is a business institution and so regarded by the law.

On the editorial side the story is different. Publishing a newspaper is a business but the content of the paper cannot be regulated by ordinary business laws or rules.

As Justice Sutherland said:

"A free press stands as one of the great interpreters between the government and the people. To allow it to be fettered is to fetter ourselves." (28)

But as the Supreme Court has indicated, an orderly society must have some limit on the free play of opinions. (29)

The newspaperman must never forget that liberty of the press is not his exclusive right but that it belongs to all people just as the other freedoms of the First Amendment. That an orderly society must impose some limits, actual or implied, on all liberties is obvious if any liberty is to be worthwhile. Absolute and total liberty results only in irresponsibility. Justice Holmes made that clear when he said that freedom of speech certainly gives no man the right to cry "fire" in a crowded theater. (30)

The First Amendment guards freedom of religion but Congress interfered with that liberty by outlawing the polygamous practices of one religious group. (31) The Supreme Court upheld the government's contention that polygamy is a crime against the orderliness of society.

On the other hand, if any restriction is to be imposed because of some doubtful and remote danger, the effect is to destroy all liberty. In some Latin American countries, the president is empowered to suspend all constitutional guarantees whenever a crisis arises or is threatened. Liberty there, then, fluctuates at the will of an executive or legislature.

Down through American history from the birth of the Constitution, there have been a number of times when the First Amendment was threatened. The Alien and Sedition Acts, which have been mentioned, were aimed directly at critics of the government. The Federalists were following an historic pattern, for the pages of the past are filled with examples of how men or governments in control used that power to perpetuate themselves.

Authorities are pretty well in agreement that the acts were unconstitutional. What would have happened had any test cases reached the Supreme Court is conjecturable, because the court in those days had not established the doctrine of judicial nullification of an act of the legislature. Instead the people spoke by repudiating at the polls the party which placed the acts on the statute books, and the laws themselves expired.

Even Jefferson, probably the most ardent champion of a free press, later believed it necessary to restrict some of that freedom. He thought, however, that it was a matter for the states and not for federal action.

Stung by the vituperative attacks on his administration in Federalist organs, Jefferson in 1803 wrote to Governor McKean of Pennsylvania:

> "The Federalists, having failed in destroying the freedom of the press by their gag-laws (Alien and Sedition Acts), seem to have attacked it in the opposite form, that is, by pushing its licentiousness and its lying to such a degree of prostitution as to deprive it of all credit . . . The press ought to be restored to its creditability if possible. The restraints provided by the laws of the states are sufficient for this if applied. I have therefore long thought that a few prosecutions of the most prominent offenders would have a wholesome effect in restoring the integrity of the presses. Not a general prosecution, for that would look like persecution, but a selected one." (32)

The pre-Civil War agitation in the several states for a time threatened to strain the First Amendment, and the courts may have had that situation in mind when later they interpreted the Fourteenth Amendment as forbidding states to interfere with the liberties granted by the federal constitution.

During the Civil War years, the government acted principally through the military. Papers were suppressed or suspended, but the crisis passed without the First Amendment being placed on trial. World War I and the immediate post-war years led to restrictions from two sources.

By the Espionage Act of 1917 and the amendment to it in 1918, certain newspapers, mostly organs of minorities or special groups, were punished for interfering with the war effort.

Free speech of individuals also was restricted. In a series of cases growing out of those acts, the Supreme Court brought forth what has since been referred to as the "clear and present danger" construction.

The principle is that a society cannot permit itself to be destroyed from within while it is fighting for its life against external forces. At the same time, the freedom for which that society is fighting is worthless if the people in waging that struggle lose the liberties they already enjoyed.

As Justice Holmes said:

> "When a nation is at war many things that might be said in time of peace are such a hindrance to its effort that their utterance will not be endured so long as men fight." (33)

Writing more than a century before, Alexander Hamilton expressed the broader idea in saying:

> "The circumstances that endanger the safety of a nation are indefinite; and for that reason no constitutional shackles can wisely be imposed upon that power." (34)

The rule of reason on limitations was expressed by the Supreme Court this way:

> "Any attempt to restrict those liberties (First Amendment) must be justified by clear public interest, threatened not doubtfully nor remotely, but by clear and present danger. Only the gravest abuses endangering paramount interests, give occasion for permissible limitations." (35)

The court, however, came to the aid of the states when they had to deal with a wave of syndicalism. The states were permitted by the Supreme Court to avert the danger through their police powers although there was some restriction on the First Amendment's freedom. The court, in effect, held it not only to be the state's right but its duty to protect its citizens.

That right, however, does not include the power to suppress a newspaper because its contents are objectionable nor to penalize the press through taxes. We have seen that Minnesota was not permitted to enjoin the publication of a paper which state officials held to be scandalous nor was Louisiana able to use its taxing authority as a penal power. (36)

And more recently the courts have decided that a press association cannot refuse to render service to a newspaper if the refusal tends towards monopolistic practices. (37)

On the other hand, a newspaper cannot take refuge in the First Amendment to avoid its liability for injuries it causes.

The American Concept and the Foreign Press

That the American concept of freedom of the press is distinctive is reinforced by a brief look at other countries. Before World War I, a free press could be considered to have existed in England, Switzerland, Holland, the Scandinavian countries, and possibly France. But "freedom" was patterned more on the English concept than on the American because libel and sedition took its pattern from the British press laws rather than from the American. And no country now shows signs of swinging more to the American ideas.

Many French reporters "worked" for an organ of fact and a journal of opinion at the same time and often used their press connections for obtaining other sources of revenue. Americans rely on press agents to put over special views but special, and even foreign, interests in France bought their own organs of opinion.

Russia has a freedom of the press clause in the constitution adopted by the Soviet Republics. Back in 1920 Lenin, however, gave his views on such freedom in a speech in Moscow. He asked:

> "Why should freedom of the press and freedom of speech be allowed? Why should a government which is doing what it believes to be right allow itself to be criticized? It would not allow the opposition lethal weapons. Ideas are much more fatal things than guns. Why should a man be allowed to buy a printing press and disseminate pernicious opinions calculated to embarrass the government?" (38)

During World War II, field men of a United States government information service were shocked at the reaction of some Latin American papers to the news articles proffered them, telling the story of how the United States was meeting the war challenge of the Axis. Some of these field men report the first question asked them was:

"How much will we be paid for printing these stories?"

In 1949 alone, three newspapers in Argentina were forced to suspend for criticizing Dictator Peron, and two of the largest papers found themselves defendants in government suits for suggesting Peron had not suffered financially by becoming head of the state.

By direct control or by subtle suggestion, newspapers in many parts of the world are feeling the power of the state. And in the areas where freedom does seem to exist, the different concept of the rights and privileges of the press are reflected in varying restrictions upon content.

Resumé and Analysis:

If the winds of the future portend anything, it is likely that the whole subject of freedom of the press in the United States will come in for more and more discussion.

In 1942, through a grant of $200,000 by Henry R. Luce of Time, Inc. and $15,000 from the Encyclopedia Britannica, Inc., a commission undertook an inquiry into "the present state and future prospects of the freedom of the press." (39) Later the work was broadened to include other major agencies of mass communications: Radio, motion pictures, magazines, and books.

The Commission, reporting its work in several volumes, found freedom of the press in danger for three reasons:

1. "The importance of the press to the people has greatly increased with the development of the press as an instrument of mass communication. At the same time the development of the press as an instrument of mass communication has greatly decreased the proportion of people who can express their opinions and ideas through the press.

2. "The few who are able to use the machinery of the press as an instrument of mass communication have not provided a service adequate to the needs of society.

3. "Those who direct the machinery of the press have engaged from time to time in practices which the society condemns and which, if continued, it will inevitably undertake to regulate or control." (40)

But the commission found no agreement on the methods that control or regulation should take. As J. Edward Gerald suggests:

"The dilemma which chills the ardor of those who think the press should be required to change in some way is whether the job should be left to the individual editorial virtue or to the social conscience of the group expressed in mandatory law. In either case, the means appears inadequate for the task. Individual control, ideal under the theory of democratic government effected through Benham's formula of instruction, excitation, and correspondence, tends to bog down in complacency, thus converting a great social instrument into a mere personal property.

"Government control, which has prevailed for practically all of recorded history, tends to make the press either an inert, colorless government circular or an instrument of propaganda by which the group in power seeks to maintain political control." (41)

If critics ever come to as much agreement upon the method as they do upon the goal, some editorial complacency may be badly jarred. For this reason, the newspaperman should be alert as to the true meaning of freedom of the press.

For practical, working purposes, he may regard it as meaning simply no prior restraints either by licensing or censorship. On the other hand, he must not regard it as an absolute and inviolable right, nor worst of all, as his own personal property to do with as he will. It must be a balance between rights and privileges on the one hand, and responsibilities on the other.

With that perspective as his guide to bolster America's unique conception of a free press, the newspaperman of today can repeat in earnest the declaration by Thomas Jefferson of more than 150 years ago:

"As long as the press remains free, this nation shall remain free."

For Further Reading

The literature on freedom of the press is endless. Chafee and Patterson referred to at the end of Chapter 3 well repay the reading. The following additional reading is suggested:

Mott, Frank, *American Journalism*, New York; Macmillan Co., 1941.

Lee, Alfred McClung, *The Daily Newspaper in the United States*, New York; Macmillan Co., 1937.

A smaller but good readable account is:

Bleyer, Willard G., *Main Currents in the History of American Journalism*, New York; Houghton Mifflin Co., 1927.

COURT CASES

A good historical account as seen through the eyes of the courts is in:

Grosjean v. American Press Co. 297 U.S. 233.

The series of cases growing out of the Espionage Act of 1917 and the amendment to it in 1918, shows the thinking of the court. The most important of those cases are:

Schenck v. United States 249 U.S. 47.

Frowerk v. United States 249 U.S. 204.

Debs v. United States 249 U.S. 211.

Abrams v. United States 250 U.S. 616 (first case under the amendment).

Schafer v. United States 251 U.S. 466.

Pierce v. United States 252 U.S. 239.

An interpretation of cases after 1931 is found in:

Gerald, J. Edward, *The Press and the Constitution, 1931-47.*

CHAPTER V

"Problems of News and Newsgathering"

The newspaperman going about his daily work soon realizes he is in probably the most unusual business in the world.

It is unusual in a number of ways. A manufacturer, either from memory or from records, if his is a large corporation, can describe his products exactly. A newspaperman cannot because no one ever has hit upon a completely satisfactory definition of news.

This lack of a concrete definition of news is of more than academic or philosophical interest. Some of the conflicts between the press on the one hand, and society, either group opinion or law, on the other, have arisen because these two have found no agreement in determining just what is, or is not, news. Some of the most vigorous critics of the press base their principal attack on what they call the failure of newspapers to print "significant" news. So far, these critics have failed to agree among themselves as to what is either "significant" or "news."

Some other critics are still dismayed by the press accounts of the death in 1942 of Movie Actress Carole Lombard and 11 aviators, killed in a plane crash as Miss Lombard was being flown to Hollywood after a war bond appearance in Indiana.

Practically every newspaper featured Miss Lombard in the headlines. These critics believed 11 aviators were more "important" to a country at war. They could not understand that the press made no attempt to evaluate the "importance" of any one on that plane. To millions of Americans, Miss Lombard was not just a detached movie star but a "living personality" as close to them as a neighbor or personal acquaintance although many had never seen her. Certainly, the country appreciated those 11 aviators, but none of them had the warmth and personal appeal that Miss Lombard had exerted on the average American. Americans regret the passing of many public figures but seldom do they genuinely mourn as they did on the death of Franklin D. Roosevelt.

Courts and administrative agencies, in particular, try to define news by limiting access to or refusing outright to divulge certain information which to the press is "news." The State Department from time to time has been reluctant to "fill in" a story or report on the ground the "information" is not news but "diplomatic secrets."

When the angels dropped down on the hills around Bethlehem, they hastened to reassure the frightened shepherds that their mission was only to bring "glad tidings." Had there been newspapers in those days, the "tidings" probably would have been buried in the birth announcement columns because often an event is not news until it is interpreted and its significance evaluated days, weeks, or years later.

A Paris cobbler who relieved the monotony of his drab existence by keeping a diary, noted in it one July that "the day is quiet." Little more than a block down the street, the Bastile had been stormed to give us the symbol for a new era of the rights and dignity of man. The Wright brothers discovered their first sustained flight brought only a notice in their home town paper that "two popular bicycle merchants are expected home for Christmas."

Medieval kings greeted visitors with: "What tidings?" which is the equivalent to today's salutations: "What's new?" His Majesty, however, wanted more than a casual reply, for the visitor often told the king whether he could continue to relax in the banquet hall, or should buckle on his armor and head out to battle. The courier who raced a frothing horse to report that "William had landed" would have been just as amazed as any chronicler of his day to know that his "news" was so "significant" it was to change the destinies of most of the world.

Many writers in journalistic history or methods who must attempt to pin down with thumb tacks specific definitions of news realize they are engaging in mental jujitsu with semantics without adding much to working knowledge. Chilton R.

Bush says: "News is not always mere information; it is more frequently information that is interesting, that is to say, information that the ordinary human being derives satisfaction or stimulation from reading." (1)

Charles C. Clayton, a practicing newspaperman besides being a writer on journalism, concludes that "whatever interests people is news." (2)   He admits that interest is a word that is indefinable.   The Kansas Editorial Association believes news is: ". . . an impartial report of the activities of men, mind, and matter, which does not offend the sensibilities of the more enlightened people." (3)   The words "impartial" and "enlightened" can start more arguments than they settle.   Curtis D. MacDougall believes news is: ". . . an account of an event which a newspaper prints in the belief that by so doing it will profit." (4)   The word "profit" hardly will go unchallenged in either newspaper or academic circles.   *Webster's Collegiate Dictionary*, trying its hand, comes up with: ". . . news is a report of a recent event, information about a thing unknown, recent intelligence."   *The New American College Dictionary*, of Harper and Bros., also likes the word "recent" because it defines news as "a report of any recent event, situation, etc."

When King Tut's tomb was uncovered, the excavation was a "recent" event, but the life and times of Tut, including his burial service, was a vital part of the story although it happened 5,000 years or more ago.   Stressing the "unknown" doesn't help too much because one of the top stories every day is about a "situation" which the reader already has observed for himself when he stepped out onto the porch to get his morning paper — the weather.

Wilbur Schramm brings a different concept into the discussion by declaring that "news exists in the minds of men.   It is not an event; it is something perceived after the event." (5)

Social scientists, following along this same theory, produce a result not too much unlike the old argument as to whether there is a sound if no one is around when a tree falls in the forest.   This theory finds a rough parallel in criminal libel in which the words themselves are regarded only from the standpoint of the actions, potential or actual, they arouse in the reader.

Newspapermen themselves are of little help in arriving at a definition of news. Many of them like to quote an early leader in American journalism that "when a man bites a dog, it's news." This definition, however, is more facetious than accurate because if enough men go around biting dogs, the report of such happenings will soon work its way from Page One, back to the classified advertising section, and finally out of the paper entirely. Unless a man eating fish chokes, he is unlikely to receive public recognition, but the boys at Harvard hit the front pages simply by eating fish in a peculiar way — they swallowed goldfish.

If newspapermen by chance should find themselves in agreement on what is news, they may be chagrined to discover the reader has another idea. Reader interest surveys have shown that subscribers frequently reject editorial judgment as to what was the top news of the day. Definitions, nebulous at best, change from year to year as shown by the fact that today press associations and larger papers have full-time reporters, and smaller papers part-time reporters, for education, business, finance, real estate, religion, aviation, movies, health, and other activities for a long time ignored by most of the general press. The president of the United States once was not "news" and as late as the 1920's, a vice-president discovered many people in his home city knew only that he had "some sort of government job in Washington."

There is some justification for newspapermen believing that "advertising is anything a person wants in the paper; news is anything that person wants kept out." A Washington woman, feuding with her neighbor, turned her pet goat loose to eat the dessert the neighbor had set out to cool on her back doorstep. The unusual "revenge" attracted press attention when the woman goat owner was arrested, but she "threatened" newspapers if they dared to print it. A week before, she cancelled her subscription to one of those papers because it had printed only two paragraphs of the inconsequential talk she had made before a small neighborhood club.

The newspaper business is unusual also because its indefinable raw material — news — is free to everyone. The manufacturer owns exclusively the raw material he takes into his plant and only health and safety regulations prevents his fashioning any products he wishes. The newspaper, however, can claim no monopoly or title to news. Anyone who sees, hears, or becomes aware of a happening may publish freely his version and opinions about it.

Since the press can claim no exclusive ownership in news, the ordinary rules of property rights cannot apply to the newspaper's raw material. This, too, at times raises problems. (6)

The newspaper business is still more unusual because unlike most industries, it cannot produce for stock. At the end of each day, it throws out its used and unused raw material and starts fresh again the next morning. This puts a premium on speed in gathering the raw material which, in turn, leads to conflicts with society as well as to frequent errors in judgment on the part of the newspaper staff.

The product it finally fashions is probably the most perishable goods in the world. Basically, the wag had a point when he said: "There is never any new news. It's just the same old thing happening to different people." Today's issue upon which the staff labored so hard becomes history tomorrow. The public each day greets its news heroes with a shower of confetti made from newspapers that told the story of yesterday's idol.

In the coverage of courts, especially, newspapers at times may transgress in their zeal to print "news" instead of "reviews" and "history." In other areas, rumors and reports are substituted for actual facts which may not be available for another day or two. Sometimes the printing of the rumor makes the disclosure of the actual happening anticlimactic. Both press and reader are impatient. Most of the so-called "trial by newspaper" can be blamed on this inability to wait until the story unfolds from the witness stand.

Finally, the newspaper business is unusual because society has conferred upon it privileges accorded to no other industry. Most of these privileges come about because society itself recognizes that the democratic form of government cannot operate unless the citizenry is informed on all matters on which it eventually must make decisions, or about all events to which it thinks it should give recognition. By law, custom, and judicial interpretation, the newspaper is recognized as having a special and peculiar function.

As the newspaperman goes about his routine, doors swing open, records are put at his disposal, public officials and private citizens talk freely and often about matters they would not discuss with their neighbors, and most of society's activities are put on parade so that the reporter may observe and record. The social theory that an individual has the privilege of anonymity loses out continually to the principle that society should be informed or at least be made aware of actions and conditions.

By law, custom, and judicial interpretation also, society insists that a business so unusual as the newspaper must in turn assume responsibilities for the privileges granted to it. Society never can give any of its institutions a blanket power to roam and pry at will without any regard for the individual or the group as a whole. The attempt to strike a balance between these privileges and responsibilities produces most of the conflicts with which this book deals. It is the purpose of this chapter to look into the general nature of those privileges and responsibilities and then in later chapters to discuss them more fully.

For a society to order that the press shall be free, as the American constitution and the people command, and then deny it access to the news would be inconsistent. It would be just as inconsistent for a government based on the worth and dignity of man to say that every person must live in a "goldfish bowl" for the edification of his fellow citizens. Society by custom and through its coercive power, as expressed in law, must attempt to define these areas so that neither the principle nor the operation of democratic government suffers.

Since in the following pages there will be much discussion of rights and privileges, it is well to fix those terms more precisely. To this point, those terms have been used practically synonymously. In statutory law, however, there is a sharp distinction between a right and a privilege. Often that distinction is the key to a press law.

Political scientists who specialize in the operation of governmental systems, give us more understanding than lawyers on the practical use of the words. Courts, however, make a sharp distinction between legal and political language. The constitution contains both legal and political terms. When a statute comes before a court for interpretation, the judges go over it and try to give to each word a legal meaning. If a particular word does not lend itself to a legal meaning, the courts regard it as political. Only legal words are enforceable.

Political scientists define rights and privileges in terms of statutory interpretation. It is helpful, however, if we use their definitions as a kind of "guide" and keep in mind that the purpose is to make a workable distinction rather than to be legally precise. (7)

For purposes of statutory interpretation, a political scientist would define a right as a benefit conferred upon the public generally.

A privilege is a benefit conferred upon certain persons or classes less than the whole public.

A power is a privilege to be used for the benefit of others. The "power of the press" is a popular term without standing in law. It simply means the newspaper, directly or indirectly, has brought pressure to bear upon a particular situation or problem. If the pressure is exerted by persons or groups outside the "newspaper family," the newspaper still feels it invoked the power of the press by calling attention to the conditions that needed remedying.

Subjects of the law are the sum total of people affected favorably or unfavorably, including those charged with enforcing the law. An official charged with the duty of enforcing a press law is just as much a subject of it as the newspaper against which it is enforced.

Although these definitions are not legally precise for the purposes to which we will use them, they do provide a basis for determining workable distinctions that must be kept in mind. Rights of the press are a misnomer, for the whole public shares them, too. Freedom of the press therefore becomes, under this distinction, a right, not a privilege, because it is conferred upon everybody. Anyone with a hand press and a few sticks of type can publish a "paper" if he so chooses, and his right to do so is just as valid as that of the *New York Times*. Unless he runs afoul of criminal statutes and civil liability (which apply also to the metropolitan press) the man with the hand machine is given just as substantial protection under the First Amendment as the publisher down the street with his multiple unit presses.

Early English and colonial struggles for free expression were waged over the "printing press" and not over newspapers, for newspapers did not appear until more than a century after printing was introduced into the western world. Early state constitutions reflected this trend by inserting provisions for "freedom of the printing press."

The invention of printing from moveable type meant that ideas could spread rapidly, and the church, and later the state, took immediate steps to control it. The church feared the spread of heresy which was defined as any idea or opinion contrary to church canons. The state feared its authority would be undermined by criticism, and ideas and opinions were "quarantined" and permitted to circulate only after they had been "disinfected" by the censor.

Although the press likes to speak of its privileges, actually it has few of them. What the press regards as privilege often is only "courtesy."

Members of Congress during debates and proceedings have absolute privilege. They are accountable to no court or other agency for any statement made in the pursuance of their official duties. A member of Congress cannot be sued for libel for any statement he makes during debate, no matter how false or how damaging it may be to an individual or group.

Each house, however, can discipline its own members if it chooses. During the Hoover administration, a ranking member of the Republican party was stripped of his committee positions and patronage for declaring that the president had "sold out" to Europe by agreeing to a moratorium on debts owed to the United States by its World War I allies. This punishment was purely a party matter, and the congressman did not have to answer to anyone else for his charges.

A congressman, however, on a campaign swing has no privilege but only the right of free speech. He can be sued for libel just as any private citizen.

Lawyers and judges also have this absolute privilege in order that all the evidence may be produced and weighed. It would handicap the operation of the whole legal proceedings if judges and lawyers were held accountable for their courtroom remarks as long as those statements are germane to the case. A witness, however, has no such privilege because if it can be proved he lied, he may be charged with perjury.

Newspapers are permitted to defend libelous statements if they can show the stories were a fair and true report of legislative or judicial proceedings. If a congressman makes a libelous charge during debate, the press can print it without danger provided it does not go beyond the statement and add matter or comment of its own. Since this privilege does not originate with the newspaper but is dependent upon another party — the legislator or the judge — it is called conditional privilege, or more popularity, qualified privilege.

Members of state legislatures also have absolute privilege. Whether city councilmen, county commissioners, and minor legislative bodies enjoy absolute privilege has not been established definitely in all cases, but a reasonable assumption is that a county commissioner or city councilman is permitted wide latitude if his statement bears directly upon the business at hand and is made without hate or spite.

Newspapers have courtesies of many kinds that set them apart from individuals or other businesses, but which are "privileges" only in a popular sense rather than in legal standing. Theoretically, the Congress should be meeting in closed sessions, as early Congresses did, but reporters not only are admitted, but special galleries are provided for their comfort and convenience. The press has direct wires into the house and senate press galleries and convenient telephones. Individuals sitting in the regular spectator galleries are not permitted to make notes, but a reporter from his seat looking down on the presiding officer can write as much and as long as he wishes.

In most courtrooms, special tables are set aside for the convenience of the press. Ordinarily, any person may drop into a courtroom and scramble for a seat, but only reporters accredited by the judge can sit at the press table. The press table is usually opposite the jury box and right beneath the bench so that reporters can see and hear advantageously. If a judge decides the testimony by its nature should not be heard by the general public, especially youths, he may clear the room. Sometimes he may "invite" the press to leave also, but if he does it consistently society may take a hand to make certain the defendant is receiving justice and not persecution.

The respect and close understanding between many judges and the press was illustrated in the perjury trial of Alger Hiss, onetime State Department official whom the government charged permitted secret documents to fall into the hands of Communist agents. After the jury had returned a verdict of guilty, Federal Judge Henry W. Goddard warned the 12 men and women jurors not to discuss their deliberations after they returned home.

And his warning, he said, applied to any discussion with those "very likeable newspapermen who will approach you as you leave." (8) The jurors scampered down the courthouse steps and scattered, while the correspondents watched ruefully some "good stories" vanish around the corner.

Sometimes a right and privilege blend. Records kept by many officials are public records and anyone may examine them. But if people trooped into some offices just to scan records out of idle curiosity, or merely to kill time while waiting for a rain to cease, public business would be inconvenienced. In some instances, therefore, examination is restricted but in those cases the courts usually hold that a newspaper has a peculiar interest in the records because its function is to inform the public about them. Such interest permits reporters to scan the records while individuals may be denied access to them. A public official who refuses to permit a reporter to see a public record usually can be compelled by court order to open his books.

In attempting to make a definitive list of the rights, privileges, and restrictions of the press, difficulties are encountered.

Some rights and privileges shade into each other and are still further confused because "courtesies" also play a part. Again, some restrictions apply generally and others only under specific conditions.

The following list is intended to be neither precise nor definitive, but is simply a classification of convenience in order that they may be studied more fully in later chapters.

RIGHTS

Freedom: To print without prior licensing or censorship.

To determine for itself what it will print and what it will not.

To gather the news.

To examine public records.

To scan the police blotters in some states.

To make fair comment and criticism of movies, plays, books, or other public performances.

To cover public meetings, often with special courtesies to permit it to operate better than the ordinary spectator there.

To take pictures of persons or events in the news if it does not have to break a law to snap those photographs.

To comment on and to criticize public officials and their official actions.

To protect its work and skill by a quasi-property right in the news after it is gathered.

To refuse any advertisement it does not wish to publish.

PRIVILEGES

To defend certain libelous statements with the defense of qualified privilege.

To receive a special mailing rate from the Post Office Department.

Protection in some states against being given false information.

To keep secret in 12 states the sources of any information.

RESTRICTIONS

The press is accountable under libel laws for everything it prints.

May not in some states print the names of juveniles involved in crimes.

Cannot print obscene words or statements.

Can use copyrighted material only under certain circumstances.

Must respect the privacy of the individual who is not in the news.

Cannot comment too freely upon a court case or criticize the conduct of it while it is still underway.

Cannot print anything that tends to incite, or actually does incite, a breach of the peace.

Cannot print anything, in time of war, that interferes with the war effort such as calling upon men to ignore the draft or printing information that may give "aid and comfort to the enemy." How far the Alien Registration Act of 1940 may affect news of this type in peace time is not yet determined.

Cannot print pictures of money, stamps, government bonds, etc. if such reproductions could be passed off as genuine or if such reproduction would aid in counterfeiting.

Cannot print advertisements which it may have reason to believe are fraudulent.

Cannot print advertisements as news stories without danger of losing its second-class mailing privileges.

Cannot print lottery news.

Of all rights, none is so important to the press as the guarantees of the First Amendment. And of restrictions, none is so severe as libel. For that reason, libel is always a substantial section of any book on law of the press.

For Further Reading

Ernst, Morris, *The First Freedom,* New York; The Macmillan Co., 1946.

Chafee, Zechariah, Jr., *Government and Mass Communications,* Vol. 1, Chicago; University of Chicago Press, 1947.

Chafee, Zechariah, Jr., *Free Speech in the United States,* Cambridge; The Harvard University Press, 1942.

Field, Marshall, *Freedom Is More Than a Word,* Chicago; University of Chicago Press, 1945.

Villard, Oswald Garrison, *The Disappearing Daily,* New York; Alfred Knopf Co., 1944.

Siebert, Fred S., *The Rights and Privileges of the Press,* New York; Appleton-Century, 1934.

SECTION II

"Rights and Privileges of the Press"

CHAPTER VI

"Reporting the Federal Government"

The most frequent and probably the most important dateline in today's newspaper is Washington.

Founders of the nation generally believed the federal government would operate principally in the field of external affairs, leaving states to handle most of the domestic matters except interstate commerce, defense, currency, and other problems calling for uniform and united action. Many of them believed the state legislatures should take the place of parliament in regulating most of the activities of citizens. (1)

The swing toward Washington as a news center, in evidence for years, was hastened by World War I, accelerated greatly by the depression of the 1930's and gained new momentum from the crisis that led to World War II. Despite those who decry centralization, Washington will continue to be the most important news source for Americans, and for the world, down into the unforseeable future.

A natural outcome of the tremendous growth of the federal government is that the executive branch and the independent agencies have eclipsed Congress in the year-round headlines. With 42 billion dollar budgets, Congress no longer can make appropriations in detail as it once did, right down to the amount of ink a department might use. The President draws up the budget, and the executive branch also has cut into another congressional function by initiating more than half of the legislation.

Congress has not abdicated its powers but simply has come to recognize the inevitable. It now legislates, appropriates, and supervises in terms of general policies, and leaves to the executive department the carrying out of the broad program. The government is too big for Congress to continue to argue for three weeks over such things as a two-cent tariff margin on a specific commodity.

But Congress, in and out of session, continues to be a prime news source. It dictates all revenue and expenditures, controls all executive structure but the elective offices of president and vice-president, has an almost absolute power over personnel, can create or abolish departments, commissions, agencies and offices, and has general supervisory authority over the operation of the government. And when these vast powers are exercised by 531 members of Congress, bound by no authority except rather nebulous party responsibility, there will always be much material for correspondents to fashion into news stories.

Today's coverage of Congress by press associations and individual papers and even magazines and radio stations, has produced situations that show some new interpretations of the rights and privileges of the press. More than 600 men and women are accredited to the Capitol press and radio corps to report the activities of Congress.

The First Congress under the constitution met behind closed doors as was the custom in those days of all such legislative bodies. When the first reporter wandered into a Congressional sitting, he remained there by tacit permission. And that is the situation today, although Congress has been liberal in providing quarters and other aids for correspondents in their daily work. (2)

Reporters now pick up copies of bills and calendars as fast as they come from the government printing office for use of members of Congress, call members from the floor for interviews or to answer queries, ride in elevators marked "for members and press only," attend all but a few committee hearings, and, in general, act as if they had a legal right to be there.

The theory of deliberative bodies is that they have an inherent privilege of meeting secretly and of publishing only their official actions. When the government moved from Philadelphia to Washington, four newspapers — two Republican and two Federalist — quickly began publishing in the new capital.

When Congress convened in Washington for the first time, Samuel Harrison Smith, who with the help of Thomas Jefferson had published the *National Intelligencer,* memorialized the House for permission to sit within the bar and take shorthand notes. The House, evenly divided between Federalists and Republicans, stalemated the petition with a tie vote, and Speaker Thomas Sedgwick settled the issue by deciding against Smith.

Smith, denied a place inside the railing, took notes from the gallery but within a month was expelled. Speaker Sedgwick claimed Smith's stories contained many false statements. Smith retaliated by charging the Speaker was angry at Smith's "fair statements of the Speaker's blunders."

When the Republicans took control of the House at the next session, the Speaker was directed to provide places on the floor for reporters and stenographers. Smith obtained a seat beside the Speaker.

Along in the second Congress the Senate also permitted reporters, and the press began its systematic coverage of Congress. From time to time, however, both houses have served notice that they retain their inherent privileges by expelling reporters who angered them. A few were expelled for becoming too active in legislation.

In modern times, no reporter has been expelled by formal Congressional action, but in 1935 the House threatened to discipline the press corps for reporting the results of a teller vote.

A teller vote is one of the devices the House uses to avoid having each member placed on record on a particularly "hot" issue. Sometimes, however, it is used merely to expedite passage of minor measures.

In 1935, the House was considering a bill to forbid holding companies which controlled many public utility companies. Aware that the decision would come by teller vote rather than by a roll call, the *Washington Daily News* in an editorial on June 30, 1935, served notice it would attempt to record the vote. (3) Fourteen Scripps-Howard reporters came early to get front seats in the press gallery. As House members filed past two tellers, Scripps-Howard reporters kept tally.

The next day the *Daily News* reported the bill had lost, 152 for, and 224 opposed. (4) Actual figures later were disclosed as 146 for, and 216 opposed. The *News* invited any Congressman who wished, to call up and have his vote changed if the paper were wrong. Only two availed themselves of this opportunity.

Some House members demanded the press be disciplined, but none apparently wanted to take the initiative. The Speaker rebuked the press and subtly reminded it that reporters had no legal right to be there, and the flurry ended.

Long usage, however, sometimes gives "unofficial privilege," and today no one can conceive of a time when reporters will not be permitted to go about the job of covering Congress. A member once expressed his views on the importance of reporters by reminding a colleague who was droning on and on that he might as well cease talking because "the gentlemen in the press gallery have stopped taking notes." The member, glancing at the press gallery, confirmed his colleague's observation, and promptly sat down. (5)

The British House of Commons maintains the same fiction as the American Congress. Reporters are simply "strangers in our midst," and since no official attention is called to their presence, no action is taken. But more than a quarter of a century after American reporters had comfortable places to write up Congress, British correspondents in the House of Commons were still sitting on the steps or any vantage points they could seize. The Commons long since has provided press galleries. In 1949, the Commons did recognize the reporters "unofficially" by granting them permission to work without their coats. (6)

Proceedings of Congress, in the chambers and in the committee rooms, carry absolute privilege for members who may express themselves freely without being held legally accountable for their remarks. What members say officially, the press can report without fear of libel suits. A "fair and accurate report of a legislative proceeding" absolves a newspaper from libel under the principle of qualified privilege, no matter who may be damaged by the story.

When a congressional committee moves to any part of the country for a hearing or investigation, privilege goes with the members. The press can report those proceedings with the same immunity as actions within the halls of Congress itself.

Legally, a member away from Washington on congressional business has no privilege for statements made on his own initiative or for remarks not a part of the official proceedings. Courts, however, have been liberal in interpreting what is "official congressional business." A committee touring the country on an investigating mission often releases statements or comments before returning to Washington. In theory, the committee should make no statement until it transmits its report to Congress, but there have been no successful libel suits growing out of these away-from-Washington comments.

A reporter, however, should exercise care in printing such material, particularly if the statement is merely the expression of one or more members and not of the committee as a whole. Congressmen while on such trips often are wined and dined, but the speeches they make at banquets can hardly be classified as "official business."

A member of Congress on a campaign swing, however, is a private citizen. He then is accountable for what he says, and the press is responsible for its reports of such statements. Reputations cannot be traduced with impunity under such circumstances.

The Senate, which must ratify treaties, may bar reporters and go into executive session to consider such documents transmitted to it by the president.

Treaty-making was once an important part of American diplomatic procedure. President Washington was incensed, and foreign ambassadors to the United States were thunder-struck, by the temerity of newspapers in printing the text of the Jay Treaty with England before the Senate had ratified it.

The United States now uses executive agreements in its foreign relations more than formal treaties. Secret hearings of the Senate have been few in recent years and ineffective. If the Senate is to consider a treaty, every senator, by the time the document reaches the Senate, has publicly declared his stand so that a secret session would be anticlimatic.

Executive sessions for ratifying treaties or for other matters have been mere formalities in modern times. Each reporter simply "waylaid" his "favorite" senator, and few were reluctant to talk. Sometimes the presiding officer, for the record, reminded senators the next day that executive sessions were secret, and thus having done his duty, the matter ended.

In 1848, a *New York Herald* reporter was jailed for contempt for printing a treaty then being considered by the Senate in executive session, but today such action probably would find little support. (7)

No libel suits have grown out of any secret session but presumably qualified privilege does not attend upon matters which technically the press has no right to publish.

The few secret committee meetings also receive about the same treatment, for in some mysterious manner the committee rooms develop "leaks" despite the solid masonry of the Capitol. Many times, a member disgruntled by committee action, leaves early so that his side of the debate can "leak out" first, and thus get the "news play." In 1937, two correspondents made a wager as to how many members they could persuade to disclose what had happened at a secret conference. Within a short time, they had information from 13 of the 17 senators who had participated. (8)

The House can go into secret session whenever "confidential communications" are received from the President, but in modern times apparently no such "secret information" has come from the White House. Committees from time to time do receive "confidential documents" from the President. Most of them deal with defense matters which the press respects; the contents of the others appear soon in print because reporters seem to have remarkable acumen in "guessing" at what they contain.

Aside from the flurry over the House teller vote, the chief disputes between Congress and the press in recent years have been over release dates and the refusal of reporters to divulge the sources of their information.

In 1930, a House committee was angered because several papers broke a release date in printing tax refunds. The committee made the information available December 8 with a December 29 release date in order that stories could be mailed to member's papers by press associations or moved during slack times on their regular news circuits. Chairman William Williamson threatened to revoke such courtesies in the future if the newspapers persisted in violating release dates. (9)

Several times individual newspapers or reporters have aroused congressional wrath by premature releases, but in most instances Congress accepted the explanations that these violations were unintentional, and no formal action was taken. Of course, Congress could refuse to give out any information in advance, but it shows no inclination to penalize the whole press corps for spasmodic actions of a few members. Press associations often penalize member papers who refuse to abide by release dates on stories sent in advance. The problem is simply a "gentleman's agreement," without standing in law. If a newspaper violated a release date and later Congress revised its report, an interesting legal question would arise as to whether the premature story carried qualified privilege, or whether it, in effect, was like court testimony that a judge ordered stricken from the record.

In the same classification of "gentleman's agreement" is "off-the-record" news. The only recourse of the official whose anonymity is not respected is to deny the statements and to bar offending reporters from future press conferences. For a time, "off-the-record" conferences threatened to become a major press problem as many petty officials began taking refuge in that method to avoid responsibility for information they wished printed. By tacit agreement among themselves, press representatives began to "smoke out" these anonymous sources. The "off-the-record" technique is used now principally for background material to round out a story.

Twice in the last few years, congressional committees have tried officially to force reporters to disclose the source of their information. Both times members of Congress admitted that "newspaper ethics" were stronger than any of their pleas or threats.

During the war, an Ohio paper charged that merchant seamen had refused to unload a vital war cargo on Sunday at

Guadalcanal. The city editor declined to tell a subcommittee of the House Naval Affairs Committee the names of the marines who provided his information.

The committee did not press him for the names but commented:

> "It would have been helpful had the paper seen fit to submit to us these names, which we assured the publisher would be kept in confidence so as to minimize the possibility of military recrimination. We are aware, however, of the customary practice of newspapers in not revealing the sources of such stories." (10)

In 1945, Albert Deutsch, a reporter for the *New York PM*, wrote a series of articles criticizing the medical program of the Veterans Administration. All he would tell the House Veterans Affairs Committee was that most of his material came from "five officials" of the administration. The committee voted 13 to 5 to cite him for contempt. (11) Four days later, however, Rep. Edith M. Rogers, Massachusetts, a member of the committee, said the "Deutsch case is dead." (12) The committee never sent the contempt citation to the Department of Justice for prosecution.

The committee's action loosened a storm in Congress. One member of the committee denounced it on the ground that the committee "is supposed to be investigating veterans' facilities and not newspapermen." (13)

Later, Representative Rogers declared the contempt citation should be rescinded because "it isn't fair to the press here on the Hill." (14)

The Republican leader in the House, Joseph W. Martin, Jr., himself a newspaper publisher in Massachusetts, told the House:

> "As a newspaper publisher I know that a good reporter never discloses the sources of his stories if he is requested to keep them confidential." (15)

Rep. M. J. Monroney, a former political writer for the Scripps-Howard's *Oklahoma City News*, went even further:

> "The committee's action strikes at one of the most fundamental rights of a free press. If any government body can muzzle the press by forcing a reporter to disclose news sources

that are confidential, then all newspapers will eventually face disintegration and deterioration to mere bulletin board existence." (16)

Through editorials and resolutions, most of the nation's press joined in condemning the action of the committee. (17)

Legally, Congress could have compelled both the Ohio city editor and Deutsch to disclose their sources or go to jail for contempt. In 12 states, (as will be noted later) reporters by statute need not disclose their news sources, but there is no such provision in federal law.

Except for these infrequent clashes with congressional committees, reporters roam pretty freely about the Capitol and the Senate and House office buildings. Newspapermen covering committee hearings often pass up questions which members later put to witnesses and also provide information that committee investigators may not have uncovered. It is not unknown either for a senator or representative to issue a "ringing statement" that was born in the typewriter of some correspondent. (18)

Although reporters are not permitted on the floor of either house, few representatives or senators ignore the word that a newspaperman is waiting to see them in the cloakroom. In 1931, there was a move to restore to newspapermen an old privilege of access to the Senate floor, but the resolution did not pass. Newspapermen, as a group, felt there was no need for this privilege since contact with members can be made so easily. (19)

When committees meet to draft a final report on bills, many times after public hearings, the press is excluded. News of committee action however quickly bobs up in the press. In 1950, the powerful House Rules Committee by a tie vote, refused to speed to the floor a Fair Employment Practices bill. By the time committee members had returned to their offices, newspapers were printing the exact vote in that "secret session," and the House took no notice of the "leak." (20)

Some of this camaraderie between press and Congress is explained by noting that 34 members of the 81st Congress were newspaper publishers or editors. (21) Most of it, however, is due to the fact that a member of Congress needs the basking

light of publicity for political health as much as he requires the
ultra-violet rays of the sun for physical well-being.

The Press and the Administration:

In "downtown" Washington the situation is a little different.
It's physically impossible for even hundreds of correspondents
to cover administrative Washington without the help of department press agents.   For most routine news, the press agent's
"handout" is adequate, but good correspondents use their own
initiative to ferret out stories.   Even the staid old State Depart-
men has discovered frequently that news just can't be "bottled
up."

Most policy-making officials, from the President on down,
hold regular press conferences.   A Washington official can evaluate his "importance" objectively by simply noting how many
and what reporters show up at his press conference.

One of Franklin D. Roosevelt's secretaries of state saw attendance at his conferences steadily dwindle although normally
the Department is a fertile news source.   The secretary, inept
at handling such meetings, frequently was outmaneuvered by
the correspondents and finally took refuge in innocuous statements.   Reporters do not troop into conferences merely to get
polite comments about the weather nor for learned discussions
on the proper spelling of Chinese cities.

On the other hand, the Department of Agriculture, which
might be expected to yield mostly routine news, periodically
has one of the most spirited conferences.   These lively conferences come on the day the Department releases crop estimates.
A Department official holds the printed copies of the report
and watches the clock.   When release time arrives, the official
dumps the copies on a desk and steps back as gingerly as a
hockey referee putting the puck in play.   Reporters grab and
streak for a telephone.

Handling of administrative news differs from coverage of
Congress primarily because the courts are not in agreement on
what privileges attach to departmental information.   It is well-
established that administrative officers, in the performance of
their duties, have absolute privilege, the same as the legislative
and judicial branches of government.   The lack of uniformity

comes in the courts' interpretation of how far official action carries qualified privilege for newspapers.

Some officials, such as the attorney general, have a quasi-judicial function. An official action by the attorney general then in all likelihood would carry qualified privilege for the press.

One complication comes because officials play several distinct roles. The President, for example, is chief executive, titular leader of his party, and a citizen. The governor of a state plays the same multiple roles.

No one, however, is going to sue the President on the ground that his utterance overstepped the absolute privilege of his office. It is hardly likely either that any one will sue a newspaper for libel for printing a story based on presidential remarks unless the paper should stray far afield in its comment on those utterances.

The President is quoted only with his permission. Some presidents have been reluctant to give that permission, and newspapers then have been forced to set up the subterfuge of a "White House spokesman." During the Coolidge administration, a New York paper, irked because the president refused to be quoted, described the "White House spokesman." It was no coincidence that the description fitted Mr. Coolidge perfectly.

At times, the "White House spokesman" may be the President, and at other times it may be one of his official aides. Only the correspondents know. Most direct news from the President comes from his regular press conferences. Deskmen even on the smallest papers know when these conferences are held because over the wire comes a flood of bulletins all starting: "The President is reported today to be considering this or that."

Moving down from the President, the situation becomes more muddled. If the Secretary of the Interior, for example, announces that a contract with a company drilling oil on a government reserve is being canceled because the firm is guilty of fraud, a newspaper could print the news with reasonable safety. But if the Secretary merely says he *believes* the company *may* be guilty of fraud, the press should tread warily. Of course, it is inconceivable that a cabinet officer would be that reckless with charges.

The increase in the number of Washington columnists has added a further problem. Many columnists write of rumors that most newspapers would not touch if the gossip originated in their home cities. Somehow, many newspapers must feel there is magic in a columnist's name or in the fact that his story came over the wire or by special delivery mail. There have been a number of libel suits arising from statements in Washington columns. Gossip and rumor seldom carry privilege unless the story can be defended on ground of fair comment and criticism about the acts of a public official.

The courts have held that a War Department report does not carry qualified privilege. A New York paper paid because it printed a "slacker list" that came to it in an official War Department release. (22)

During World War II, the commanding general of an army reception center provided a newspaper in his area with regular lists of men who had been inducted by draft boards but who failed to arrive at his camp. The newspaper wisely refrained from printing the names and explained to the puzzled general that he should turn over his information to proper federal authorities and if charges of draft dodging were brought formally, the newspaper would be glad to publish the news. An inductee, with the best of patriotic intentions, might fall from a train enroute to the reception center, miss connections, get hit by a taxi, become ill suddenly, or suffer amnesia.

The general finally saw the point when one absentee wired from a hospital that he had left a train to undergo an emergency operation for appendicitis but expected to report within two weeks. Had the paper hinted that this draftee was a "slacker" it would have been liable.

Washington is filled with administrative commissions and independent agencies. Those which conduct hearings, frequently permit the press to attend, especially if one or more parties to the dispute request it. Mere permission for the press to attend, does not in itself carry qualified privilege although there is a trend in that direction. However, there would be no privilege for any remarks the trial examiner makes to reporters out in the hall.

The right of newspapermen to attend hearings of federal administrative bodies and independent agencies has never reached the courts for interpretation. In theory, many such meetings can be closed to the press, but Washington today is operating on a more practical basis. A congressman once attacked from the floor a decision of the Internal Revenue Department to bar newspapermen from a hearing on a tax on oleomargarine. He complained because he said representatives of farm and dairy interests and lobbyists were admitted.

"In this case," he told the House, "the Press would have served a particularly helpful function in bringing this important question before the people." (23)

Three Houston, Texas, reporters who showed up to cover an immigration hearing were barred but they got a stepladder and looked in the transom. A harassed examiner called upon a United States attorney for advice. The attorney said the newsmen could not be routed from their perch. The examiner then covered the transom with cardboard, and the hearing resumed. (24) Fortunately, the matter of privilege for what they printed never came up.

There are more grounds for claiming qualified privilege in official decisions of commissions and agencies than there are at the actual hearings. Newspapers, for example, for years have printed decisions of the Federal Trade Commission that have reflected unfavorably on companies and corporations.

Other important sources of Washington information are public records. Definitions of what a public record is are about as plentiful as definitions of news. If the law requires a public officer or a public agency to keep a written document of official acts that document is a public record. (25) Under the democratic theory of government, citizens should have access to all public records, or at least those citizens who have a legitimate interest in them. Information taken from a public record carries qualified privilege provided the newspaper does not augment the data or interpolate comment of its own.

The mere fact that a public officer keeps a record does not make it a public document. Reporters certainly could not peer into diplomatic pouches or insist upon seeing information the

Federal Bureau of Investigation has compiled in its checkup of suspected criminals. The Attorney General has ruled that the President and heads of departments may publish "any information, or as much" as they "may deem important and material." (26)

Sometimes if there is a dispute between a department head and the press over how much information should be released, Congress may resolve it by calling for the data.

Once the information is in the hands of Congress, the inevitable "leaks" develop or a committee may make it part of its proceedings. A wag has suggested that the surest way to get publicity in Washington is to give the item in confidence to a columnist or whisper it to a congressman.

In 1924, Congress authorized the publication of all income tax returns. Some people had a field day going into their district offices of the Internal Revenue Department to satisfy their curiosity about neighbors' salaries. Congressmen also received complaints from men whose wives discovered for the first time the actual salaries of their husbands. Two years later, Congress repealed the publicity law and now only salaries above $100,000 are made public. (27)

An Indiana minister bent on reform once tried to obtain a list of slot machines in operation in the state. State authorities refused any access to their information, but the federal Internal Revenue Department permitted him to examine the list of those persons paying the annual federal tax on such machines.

On the other hand, no federal department or agency could operate efficiently if all its internal routine, including correspondence, were open to inspection. Citizens would be reluctant to file complaints against officials or to provide certain information if they knew their letters could be published. One of the fights in Congress over the 1950 census centered around the question of asking people their incomes. Some congressional critics were not allayed by assurances from the Census Bureau that all census information is secret, and that the replies on income, in particular, would not be sent to the Internal Revenue Department.

A good general rule, then, is that ultimate actions and decisions of governmental bodies, including court rulings, are open for inspection to those who have a legitimate purpose for examining the records. Such open records, it can be assumed in the absence of specific decisions to the contrary, carry qualified privilege which permits them to be published.

In one area, however, Washington news sources have "tightened up." The "cold war" between Russia and the Western Powers, which started soon after the shooting ended in World War II, produced for the first time in America's peace years, a serious problem about "security information."

The war brought into the American vocabulary a new expression — top secret — which the armed forces borrowed from England. (28) Obviously, the top military command and the press will not always agree on what is "top secret" and more especially on the other types of restricted information. For example, if material can be restricted because it might cause "unwarranted injury to an individual" there is always the danger that blunders, honest mistakes, and accidental errors might be kept from the public.

In August, 1948, a military plane crashed in the Maine mountains, and an army sergeant threatened to shoot two news photographers who beat their way through the woods to take pictures of the wreckage. An air force captain from the home base of the plane later permitted photographers to take pictures but then confiscated the plates and destroyed them. The Commandant of Grenier Field — the plane's home base — afterwards said the sergeant and the captain had acted "contrary to Air Force policy." (29)

The dispute among the several branches of the armed forces over a unification program produced more attempts to suppress information and criticism on "security" grounds. A navy captain found it necessary to sneak into a hotel corridor and meet reporters by pre-arrangement to give them the views of one naval faction as the unification dispute grew intense.

The development of the atomic bomb during the war and the post-war plans for a triton (hydrogen) bomb also presented a grave security question and Americans for the first time heard reports that unidentified planes might be shot down for flying over certain military installations. This was the type of news Americans heretofore had read only under foreign datelines.

In 1940, as the United States headed into the crisis that finally led to war, Congress passed the Alien Registration Act to strengthen the Espionage Act of World War I. The 1940 act was made operative in peace times.

The Supreme Court in 1944 interpreted the Alien Registration Act in much less severe terms than some early cases under the Espionage Act but this decision came before the hydrogen bomb placed increased emphasis on security. (30)

Washington early in 1949 was stirred because a capital tap-room posted on the wall an aerial map of the city. When the attention of some top officers was called to the fact that a similar photograph also had been displayed publicly, they admitted that the picture itself did not concern them but they wanted suppressed the fact that the photograph had been made from a record altitude. Apparently, the development of a camera to photograph at such heights was a "secret".

In February 1950, correspondents queried President Truman about the effect of a new executive order prohibiting the publication of "uncensored photographs, maps, or drawings" of military installations and equipment.

The President referred the reporters to the Department of Justice where it was said the Solicitor General was "studying" the order. A Department of Defense press secretary explained the new order was only a change in language to include the air force as well as the army and navy, and also to add the classification of "top secret". (31)

Later correspondents came across the case of an air force colonel who sent to Washington an envelope marked "secret". When it was opened in the Pentagon Building, the envelope contained nothing but magazine and newspaper clippings.

Questioned by his superiors as to why he had marked it "secret," the colonel said that was the only way he could get his communications read by the proper officers. (32)

The nice balance between what is really "security information" and what is withheld capriciously or to cover up mistakes, promises to put part of the Washington news scene in an atmosphere of tension until more explicit rules are worked out by the press and the armed services.

Elsewhere in Washington, the trend in recent years is for more and more governmental activities to be made public. The emphasis now is not on whether the people have a right to know but on whether an official has a right to keep the information secret.

There is also a growing tendency for persons damaged by statements of congressmen or Washington officials to fight it out in the public forums rather than resort to the courts. Newspapers are always ready to print both sides of any dispute. A person who is sincere in his demand for vindication is probably more content with an opportunity to present his side publicly than he is to collect damages. The only exception may be the man who is villified deliberately and not as an incident to the normal gathering and printing of news.

The new trend is illustrated by the case of Alger Hiss, former State Department official. When Whittaker Chambers told a House committee that Hiss had given him confidential documents for transmission to Russia, Hiss challenged Chambers to repeat the accusations in a place where he would have no immunity. Chambers took the challenge and repeated his charges on a radio program. Hiss sued for libel but at a pretrial conference information developed that Department of Justice agents followed up. Hiss was indicted and convicted. (33)

Although the tendency in government affairs today is to permit a free interplay of facts, opinions and criticisms, it doesn't mean there should not be any limits to what is legitimate news and what is unfounded gossip or rumor. The press should always pay for irresponsibility.

For Further Reading

Chafee, Zechariah, Jr., *Government and Mass Communications*, Vol. 1, Chicago; University of Chicago Press, 1947.

Cushing, Luther S., *Elements of the Law and Practice of Legislative Assemblies in the United States*, 9th ed., Boston; Little, Brown and Company, 1908.

Dawson, S. A., *Freedom of the Press*, New York, Columbia University Press, 1924.

Hinds, A. C., *Precedents of the House of Representatives*, Washington; Government Printing Office, 1907.

Siebert, Fred S., "Newspapers' Rights to Public Records," *Editor and Publisher*, March 8, 1930.

Steigleman, Walter, "Press Rights and Congress," *Newspaperman*, April, 1944.

A new popular account of the Washington news scene is:

Cabell, Phillips (ed.), *Dateline: Washington*, New York; Doubleday & Company, 1949.

COURT DECISIONS

Most of the court decisions dealing with records refer only to state documents. For some decisions affecting federal records see:

United States v. Baltimore *Post*, 268 U.S. 388.

Hubbard v. Mellon, 5 Fed. (2d.), 746.

CHAPTER VII

"Reporting State Governments"

The Press and Legislature

Unlike the reporter who sits in Congress as a "legal stranger," the newspaperman covering a legislature may be there not only with the expressed permission of the assembly but also of the state constitution.

The constitution of the State of Texas, for example, says "the doors of each house shall be kept open". Presumably, Texas legislators may hold no secret meetings for any purpose although there has been no judicial interpretation of the right of committees to go into executive sessions. Since Texas is practically a one-political-party state, legislative leaders conceivably could meet "informally" in private and agree upon a course of action which might become merely routine when officially brought before the assembly. Only a vigilant press can prevent such evasions of the constitution.

A number of other states provide constitutionally for open meetings of their legislatures except when circumstances dictate that a session should be secret. By practical necessity, the constitutions leave to the assemblies the determination of the circumstances requiring secrecy.

In this group of states are: Alabama, Arkansas, California, Connecticut, Delaware, Florida, Illinois, Indiana, Iowa, Maryland, Michigan, Mississippi, Missouri, New Hampshire, New York, Ohio, Pennsylvania, Tennessee, Vermont, and Wisconsin.

The constitutions of all other states make no mention of the right to attend legislative sessions, but one of them, Maine, permits by statute, a reporter to have access to the floor of both houses, provided the newspaperman has no interest in the passage of any measure before the assembly. (1)

In most states, the legislatures have provided galleries for the press and in some, such as Pennsylvania, the correspondents have permanent quarters from which to cover news of the capital between sessions. Pennsylvania correspondents are governed by their own association which passes on qualifications for membership and sets up working rules. The state retains only nominal authority by providing a paid superintendent of the news room whose principal duty is that of liaison between the various capital correspondents and the press room to see that routine news is made available promptly. The governor and principal state officers hold regular press conferences, and reporters roam as freely as do their colleagues in Washington.

In general, the informal ties between legislature and the press are stronger than those between Congress and the Washington correspondents. For one thing, the smaller geographical area of the state often means that the reporter long has been acquainted with the legislator and may even be from his home district. Then, too, legislatures usually meet only every two years and, to the member, it is just a part-time job which lasts but a few months of each biennium. Members, especially those of the House, often are inexperienced in legislative matters and welcome help and suggestions from their friends in the press corps. The reporter may even have handled the member's election publicity or his campaign.

For these reasons, reporters often sit in on committee sessions when bills are drafted into final form, attend party caucuses and, at times, act as unofficial "secretaries" for committees or commissions. Closed meetings of legislative committees or other groups develop "leaks" even more readily than similar congressional sessions because of the more personal relationship between the assembly members and the press.

In the twenty states whose constitutions require open meetings, except under special circumstances, no case involving secret sessions has gone to the courts. In all likelihood, the courts would be most liberal in their interpretation of "special circumstances" because such a question is apt to be more political than legal. Both houses of legislature, like those of Congress, have power to regulate their proceedings and to pass on the qualifications of members.

Moreover, if a court did receive such a case, its decision would be in the nature of a "post-mortem" because the legislature probably would have adjourned before the question was adjudicated. It would be a hollow victory for a newspaper to discover months later that a certain session should have been open to it. (2)

Most disputes between legislatures and newspapers involve individual members of the assembly and one or more reporters. In 1949, however, a committee of the Colorado legislature attempted to hold secret hearings to investigate the state's Fish and Game Department.

The *Denver Post* insisted that its reporter was going to remain in the room unless the attorney general ruled he could not stay. Committee members then recessed the hearing. Palmer Hoyt, editor and publisher of the *Post*, said his reporter was instructed to remain until ejected because "that sort of sets it down for the record that we don't like that kind of dealing with the public matters." (3)

A reporter for the *Miami Herald* was punched in the face by the chairman of the Senate Rules Committee and barred from further 1949 senate sessions. The reporter had commented to another senator that the action of the Rules Committee in making a horse race bill a special order of business "looked like a smooth play." (4) The incident brought a wave of newspaper protests, and copies of papers with editorials denouncing the action, were placed on desks of every member of the senate and house. (5) Ten reporters accredited to the senate protested by refusing to use the special press facilities during the remaining four days of the session. (6)

Correspondents covering the North Carolina legislature walked out when the Joint Appropriations Committee ruled the newsmen, although present, must not report discussions of the "executive session." The committee objected particularly to publication of the names of members who made various motions.

The reporters argued that state law required the joint committee to meet in open session. The chairman countered with the statement that since 1929 reporters had abided by the "custom" of not printing executive session discussions. (7)

The newsmen staged their walkout to bring the situation to the attention of the public.

Like a member of Congress, a legislator enjoys absolute privilege for the remarks he makes during legislative proceedings. This privilege extends to his work in committees and to all activities directly authorized by the legislature. Sometimes a legislature may set up an investigating committee that is to report after the session adjourns. The report may be made to the governor or to a permanent officer of the assembly. Such a report also carries privilege.

In all cases in which the legislator has absolute privilege, the press obtains qualified privilege. An editorial based on a legislative activity would not, in itself, carry qualified privilege but, unless the editorial writer went far afield in his comments, it might be defended successfully on the ground of fair comment on a public proceeding.

One of the danger areas involving news coverage of legislatures is the predilection of some members to issue statements from their own offices between sessions, especially if the legislator is a party officer or leader. There is a large difference between a statement issued by a legislator as part of legislative proceedings and a statement he makes merely concerning state or legislative matters.

As a party officer or leader, the legislator has no more privilege than the ordinary citizen. If he says that at the next session he intends to introduce a bill to stop some fraudulent practices and, directly or by implication, names the people he believes are engaging in those practices, his statement carries no privilege and a newspaper prints it at its own risk. Unless the statement of a member is issued as part of the business specifically authorized by the legislature, the press must regard it simply as the views of a private citizen.

Several papers have experienced trouble because they printed statements a legislator made in advance of a session. A Pennsylvania paper was sued for publishing the remarks made by a man soon after he was elected to legislature in November on a "reform ticket." The courts ruled that the man actually was not a member of the legislature until he was sworn into office when the general assembly convened and organized in January. Many elective offices carry a provision that the incumbent serves for a specified term or until his successor is qualified and sworn in. Several months may elapse between the election and the swearing-in of an official. During those months, he remains a private citizen.

The Press and the State Administration

A governor, like the President of the United States, usually is the titular leader of his party. His multiple roles—as chief executive, party leader, and private citizen—are not so interwoven legally as those of the President.

A governor, especially of a smaller state, may spend only a portion of his time at the state capital. Many times he retains at least a nominal control of the business in which he was engaged before his election. The governor of one state who operated a large farm got into a dispute with a neighbor and, in the argument, harsh words were exchanged. The governor accused his neighbor of having sold cattle on the "black market" during the war.

Later, the governor retracted his hasty accusations and apologized to his neighbor. Papers which printed the charges, however, had no valid defense of qualified privilege because the chief executive had spoken only as a private citizen.

In the discharge of his official duties, the governor has absolute privilege. It would be contrary to the principles of democratic government to say that a legislator in assembly or a judge in his courtroom has absolute privilege but that the chief executive of the state enjoys no such power. In some states, by judicial decision, and by inference in most other states, a governor cannot be mandamused—that is, be required to do a particular thing or be restrained from doing it unless there is specific constitutional provision on the subject. If the governor, however, by inaction, in effect annuls laws of legislature he may be impeached.

The press may report the official acts of the governor and the reasons he assigns for taking that particular action. The borderline cases usually grow out of the multiple roles of the chief executive. While on an official inspection tour of state institutions, he may be tendered a banquet by party or civic leaders of a community. In his speech to the diners, he may discuss state issues and reflect adversely on some persons. A paper which printed the speech probably would fare better by trying to maintain a defense of fair comment on public affairs rather than to rely on qualified privilege.

Among state officers, other than the governor, the courts are not in agreement about privilege. The growing tendency seems to be to accord absolute privilege to the principal administrative officers. The paradox, however, is that courts have been very slow to recognize qualified privilege in the actions of these lesser officials. Only in four states—Arizona, Michigan, Ohio, and Texas—is such qualified privilege definitely established by statute.

The attorney general, however, occupies a slightly different status in his legal relationship to the press. Most courts agree that an official opinion of the attorney general is in the nature of a quasi-judicial proceeding and therefore carries qualified privilege. Extradition hearings and sessions of the Board of Pardons usually are regarded in the same classification. (8)

In many states, this legal question is averted to some extent by the practice of subordinate state officers in issuing many of their decisions or actions through the governor's office. The head of a department, for example, who uncovers a fraud or questionable practice, may draw up a report only for the governor. The chief executive then makes it public along with the action he is taking on the matter.

If subordinate officers are elected by the voters rather than appointed by the governor, publication of their actions presents a more obscure legal status for the press. The elective state superintendent of schools, for example, may say he is removing (if he has that power) a high school principal on the ground the principal has stolen school funds. Here is some information to which the public, especially residents in the affected community, is entitled. But if the "theft" turns out to be nothing more than careless bookkeeping, the paper which printed the superintendent's charge may be in for trouble.

A wise editor would make no mention of theft unless a warrant were sworn out and served upon the principal. The first announcement could be printed, however, if changed to read that the superintendent said he was removing the principal because a shortage was found in school accounts. Such a statement makes no charges against the principal.

Minor state employees should never be quoted or used as a source for any defamatory statements unless their charges are sustained by documentary proof that would stand up in court. A clerk in the state treasurer's office has no more business talking about shortages or thefts than a washroom janitor has of accusing the corporation president of manipulating the company's finances.

Since it has been established that qualified privilege attaches to the proceedings of semi-judicial federal agencies such as the Federal Trade Commission, it may be assumed that proceedings of similar state agencies also carry the same right. (9) A state Public Utility Commission is likely to have such a privilege attached to its proceedings.

Municipal and County Offices

Since the days of the old New England town meetings, the local governmental units have been regarded as the heart of American democracy. Here is where citizens not only are more concerned about issues but also where they are better informed about them. The citizen who has only a sketchy notion about corporation taxes or regulations or tariffs, or reciprocal trade agreements, has rather definite ideas on how his city should regulate traffic, make the tax assessments, or provide recreational facilities.

In smaller towns, the citizens can go to council chambers and present their views. In metropolitan centers, the residents have less interest, are not so well informed about local matters and, either by limitations of experience or time, have no inclination to attend meetings. Most courts recognize that the press has an important function of laying the issues before the public and enabling all sides to be heard. (10)

Open meetings of city councils are provided for in some states by statutes and in other states by provisions in the city charters.

In the other states there is neither a statute nor a charter provision, but general practice is for council to meet in open session. In some states, the term "open session" has been judicially construed as applying also to meetings of the committee of the whole. (11) If the city charter sets up boards or agencies, the meetings of these bodies also are open. But subcommittees of council may meet in secret. Their final actions, however, must be approved by council in open session.

Reporters who make a fair and accurate report of a council meeting can defend such stories under qualified privilege. The courts of one state held that defamatory statements made by a city water board also carried qualified privilege. (12) Under the theory that open discussion of issues is healthy for the community, the press may be considered as having such leeway in its daily coverage of official municipal actions. There is no privilege, however, for matters not germane to the business at hand.

If, during the discussion in city council of a proposal to raise water rates, a member arises and accuses a businessman of fraudulent dealings, his statement can hardly be construed as having a bearing on the matter at hand. The press must regard that statement as the extraneous utterance of a private citizen.

Likewise, there is no privilege in matters over which a city council has no jurisdiction. (13) Council can tell a manufacturing company where it may locate its factory, regulate traffic around it, and set local taxes on the plant. But aside from health, fire, and safety regulations, it has no jurisdiction over working conditions in the factory nor over the internal management of the company. A councilman during a discussion of the plant's tax rate could not claim privilege for statements charging the company operated a "sweat shop" or that it produced shoddy products. The press has no defense if it should print such statements.

The mayor of Lake Wales, Florida once "instructed" the local paper, the *Daily Highlander,* to print everything he said at council meetings or else publish nothing. He suggested the council purchase a wire recorder to take down his remarks.

The paper declined the mayor's "request." (14) To claim a defense of qualified privilege for such meetings, a paper need only print a "fair and accurate" report. Courts do not expect the press to publish a verbatim account of any proceedings unless a paper so wishes. Nor can the courts compel verbatim publication.

In Carleton County, Minnesota, a paper which did wish to print a verbatim account of the meeting of county commissioners was refused permission to use a wire recorder or a stenotype machine. The commissioners, however, had no objection if a stenographer took down the proceedings. (15)

In communities governed by boards of supervisors or other political devices, the same general rules hold as those for city councils. They hold good also for school districts.

Counties are governed in various ways in the several states. In some states a board of commissioners of three to five or seven members is the legislative unit. Some states have boards of sixty or more members who meet at stated intervals. Other states call their county legislative body a board of supervisors. Most of the boards and commissions exercise both executive and legislative functions.

Most of the meetings of these boards and commissions are open but, except at tax assessment time, few persons other than reporters attend the sessions. For one thing, it would mean a trip to the county seat at a time inconvenient for many citizens. The public usually relies on the press to be the link between it and the commissioners. Reports of these meetings generally carry qualified privilege for newspapers.

In practically all jurisdictions, committees of these boards or commissions may hold executive sessions. As a matter of custom, reporters are admitted to many committee meetings.

In Rockford, Illinois, reporters were barred from meetings of committees of the county board of supervisors and the right of the board to exclude them was upheld by the Attorney General. He cited precedents of English common law in his opinion. Whereupon, the *Rockford Morning Star* wrote to an attorney in England for clarification. The English lawyer advised the American paper that admissions to meetings of local governing bodies in England was not based on common law, but regulated by the Admissions of the Press to Meetings Act of 1908, which leaves the question to local authorities for determination. (16)

Public Meetings

The reporter's daily work takes him to meetings of many clubs, organizations, and associations that have no official standing.   Or, the meeting may be a general one, such as a taxpayers' group, a citizens' committee to obtain better traffic regulation, or even an unorganized group called together suddenly by mutual interest in a certain problem.

If the meeting is that of a formal organization, the assumption is that it is for members and invited guests.   A reporter covers a meeting of a service club, a stamp club, a hobby club, or similar association only through the courtesy of the organization.   Nothing that is said at such meetings can be defended on the grounds of qualified privilege.   The speaker who at a service club luncheon accuses the mayor of the city of accepting graft can be sued, as well as the paper that prints his speech.

Any organization or club can hold a "public meeting" if it so wishes by extending a general invitation for all to attend. Clubs do that sometimes if their speakers are of national prominence or intend to discuss issues in which the city is vitally interested.   Again, there is no privilege for the remarks of the speakers.

Club members may discuss among themselves any matter pertinent to their organization.   A church, for example, may call its congregation together to discuss charges against the Sunday School superintendent.   Or a medical society may meet to debate charges of unethical practices against one of its members.   Unless the statements made by members in the course of the discussion show a reckless disregard of rights or truth, courts generally regard such disputes as "family matters."   But a newspaper cannot print them without risking a suit for libel.

School and college classrooms are strictly private meetings. Truth cannot be arrived at if a teacher can offer no facts or evidence except those which can be legally proved. For that reason, the press has no right to print any classroom discussion. Or, if the subject is not defamatory but of general interest, a student cannot sell an article based on the lecture without the permission of the instructor, for he owns the material he gives to the class.

Associations which expel members often couch the reason in general terms. A medical society which expelled a doctor said he was dropped for "non-payment of dues." Every reporter in town knew the real reason was that the society had adjudged the member guilty of performing an abortion, but no paper dared print that fact.

The meetings which bring the most serious problems are those called to discuss an important issue. A school board once invited all parents to an open meeting to discuss charges that male teachers in the high school had been "too familiar" with girl pupils. The one newspaper in the town had to handle the story in vague terms because most of the charges were too serious. Later, when four male members of the faculty resigned, the paper merely said the resignations had come after a public discussion of charges of misconduct on the part of some high school teachers. This judicious handling of the story was vindicated later when it was proved that one of the teachers quit in protest against the manner in which the board handled the affair and that he in no way had been involved in any of the charges.

Courts are not in agreement as to just what constitutes a public meeting. If twenty non-members wander into a club meeting by mistake and are not challenged, their presence does not mean it is a public meeting. An association, too, can have invited guests without making its session public.

Only in three states does the law afford the reporter any help or protection. Texas permits qualified privilege for "fair, true, and impartial reports of public meetings, dealing with public purposes." (17) But when the matter ceases to be of public interest or concern, the qualified privilege is lost if the same report is republished. California and Utah have a similar law but without this latter provision. (18)

The reporter in Texas, California, and Utah, then, has some statutes to guide him. The newspaperman in other states does well to adopt the policy of regarding all statements made at meetings as the views of private individuals which have no standing in law.

For Further Reading

Cushing, Luther S., *Elements of the Law and Practice of Legislative Assemblies in the United States*, (9th ed.) Boston; Little, Brown and Company, 1907.

COURT DECISIONS

For court decisions other than those cited in the notes bearing upon the right of the press to report various meetings, see:

Stanley v. Prince, 118 Maine 360.

Cafferty v. Southern Tier Publishing Co., 173 NYS 774.

Iddings v. Houser, 237 Ill. App. 236.

Tiles v. Pulitzer Publishing Co., 241 Mo. 609.

Evans v. American Publishing Co., 8 S.W. (2s) 809.

For discussions of these rights, see:

23 *Michigan Law Review* 420.

22 *Columbia Law Review* 374.

CHAPTER VIII

"Public Records as News Sources"

Basically, a newspaper obtains its news from people, events, or records. The discussion in an earlier chapter showed how federal records affected the press generally, but the immediate problem about them concerns primarily news associations and a specialized group of reporters.

A small Midwestern daily may condemn editorially any attempt of a Washington official to withhold records and may sign a protest petition originated by a publishers' association or a press service. The problem, however, is no longer remote when city, county, or even state officials start suppressing records or denying that a reporter has a right to see them.

The concern of the press over public records is twofold. First, they are a source of what newspapers regard as "legitimate news" about which the public should be informed. Second, if the record is a public document, a newspaper may set up a valid defense of qualified privilege for any information it takes from them. A non-public record must be regarded by the press as simply a memorandum that carries no more privilege than the statement of an individual.

In recent years, there has been a growing tendency on the part of many local officials to conceal records, and in 1949 the problem became serious for many local publishers. Some of these officials have acted upon what they have thought was the correct interpretation of their duties, but others seem to have decided arbitrarily to work in secrecy. Any explanation of this new tendency on the part of many officials to withhold records must be largely conjecture, but some clues to their behavior may be found in a discussion of the areas in which this practice has grown.

The definition of a state or local record follows that given for federal documents. In a number of cases, state courts have been specific in definitions of what constitutes a public record. State courts, too, have been emphatic that a newspaper has a sufficient interest in the records to permit it to examine them if the documents are intended to be public.

State Records

There is little quarrel between the press and legislature over records. As indicated in the previous chapter, the press finds little difficulty in covering legislature.

But in the day-to-day operation of the state government, information and records are accumulated which have definite news value. Some of them, the press recognizes, must be regarded simply as "thoughts in writing" between a department head and his staff or between heads of departments.

In some states where heads of departments constitute virtually a governor's "cabinet," the chief executive holds regular meetings with them much as the President does with his cabinet. Neither in the federal government nor in a state does a cabinet have legal sanction but is merely a group of advisers. The state situation is complicated because many department heads may be elected by the voters instead of being appointed by the governor.

When a governor meets with his "cabinet," a secretary may take down notes which later are transcribed and given to each participant as a memorandum of the actions agreed upon. Such memoranda are not public records although the governor or a department head may provide the press with a copy for "background information."

The governor's office itself accumulates few public records because many of the chief executive's actions are based on information prepared by one or more departments. If the governor has the power to grant pardons or commute sentences, his actions become public records although sometimes they are withheld until the prisoner has been released, especially if the convict has figured prominently in the news. Some states adopt this policy to prevent a prisoner from being pounced upon by reporters as he leaves the penal institution. They feel he can begin his rehabilitation better if not subjected to such interviews.

In other states, it is recognized that if the prisoner is of sufficient news interest, reporters will ferret him out and it is better to have the interview early and then let the man go his way. Many times the interview is in the office of the penitentiary warden.

If a governor in his other activities keeps records and refuses to permit them to be seen, the press has no legal remedy. As a practical step, it might ask the legislature to try to obtain the records or attempt to bring "public opinion" to bear on the situation. A minor official can be mandamused and compelled to show records which are public, but such legal action does not hold against the chief executive. (1)

As chief law officer of the state, the attorney general compiles records on crime and law violations. Information upon which the attorney general intends to ask for indictments is not public, and should he disclose any of it "off the record," a paper prints it at its own risk. However, once an attorney general orders a warrant drawn up and served, a report of the arrest can be printed.

An official opinion of the attorney general, as indicated previously, does carry qualified privilege because it is regarded as quasi-judicial.

The information gathered by state police officers also is not public although again a paper may print news of an actual arrest. State police keep a docket similar to the police blotter of a city or town police force, but only in one state—Connecticut—is this "blotter" a public record. In other states, if a reporter is permitted to see the docket, he must realize his only defense, if he uses any material from it, is truth.

Sub-stations of the state police usually are connected with each other and with central headquarters by teletype. Local reporters who are on good terms with sub-station officers, frequently watch the teletypes grind out criminal information, but there is no privilege in this "news." Even in Connecticut it is doubtful whether such information can be printed because it is not actually on the "blotter."

Reporters, however, can resort to the bromide: "State police are seeking John Jones for questioning in connection with the death of ————." They might go on to tell who Jones is and to describe the circumstances surrounding the death. But any suggestion, direct or implied, that Jones might be guilty of the crime can lead to action against the paper.

Reports of the state fire marshal's office in its investigation of a fire have brought conflicting decisions. A Massachusetts court has ruled such a report is privileged, but a Wisconsin court has taken the opposite view. (2) The Massachusetts case was decided in 1903; the Wisconsin case in 1929. The reporter, confused by this conflict, should wait for the fire marshal to bring criminal action against those he blames for the fire.

Since a citizen has a right to know how his tax money is spent, most records of the offices of state treasurer and auditor general are public. In some states, both officers must publish their receipts and disbursements in designated newspapers as paid advertisements. The payments made by individual tax-payers, however, usually are confidential. Virtually every state has a statute providing heavy penalties for circulation of false reports about the financial condition of banks. It is not surprising, therefore, that bank examiners' records are secret.

If the secretary or commissioner of banking is forced to close a bank or have the state take it over for liquidation, his decision can be printed along with the reasons he gives for his action. But a newspaper could not conjecture that the bank's trouble grew out of speculation by its officers if the commissioner simply said it was due to "unwise investments." They may have been the result of errors in judgment only.

If a state wants to exercise its right of eminent domain and condemn land or buildings, the report of its appraisers is not a public record. The state, however, may permit publication of the report to justify the price it has set on the property.

Records of the state bureau of motor vehicles generally are public records and facilities usually are provided to enable any person to obtain readily the ownership of a license. The owner of a new car often finds his mail box flooded with literature from gasoline and accessory companies whose representatives obtained his name from the motor vehicle bureau.

The bureau not only may keep a record of drivers whose licenses have been suspended but also may issue a report on them at frequent intrevals. A Pennsylvania paper prints in bold-face type the names of drivers who lose their licenses for intoxication. Other revocations are printed in light face type. A motorist sued on the ground the heavy type showed the paper printed the information "with malice," but the suit was dismissed.

If purchases are made or state jobs let through competitive bidding, the records of the bidding are public. The usual custom is for the bids to be opened in public although few but contractors or dealers attend such sessions.

Records of other departments — health, insurance, schools, agriculture, labor, etc. — are generally open. The Indiana legislature, however, in 1945 passed a law prohibiting state employees from disclosing data in the Office of Vital Statistics. Three years later, the attorney general gave the law a rather novel interpretation by declaring "there is involved in the statute no censorship of the press, nor is there involved the rights of anyone to utter or publish any information. All information which anyone can properly obtain may be discussed and published. . . . The sources which would be available if there were no vital statistics law are still available." (3)

Presumably, a paper which obtains the information from other sources can print it but may not get the data from the state office after it is assembled there.

The Hoosier State Press Association was concerned not only by this interpretation but also by two later opinions, one by the attorney general holding that the legislature has power to forbid or to limit access to public records "and this policy (of the legislature) may not be abrogated by the courts unless the act . . . in question contravenes some constitutional provision." (4)

The attorney for the Office of Vital Statistics elaborated further in an opinion which held:

"I doubt if any authority can be found to sustain a proposition that the freedom of the press to print information which newspapers have, also guarantees to them the source or availability of the information." (5)

If carried to its logical conclusion this reasoning of the attorney general means, in effect, that the legislature has sole power over information about most of the state's activities. The reasoning of the attorney for the agency, if pursued, has the effect of thwarting the constitutional provision of freedom of the press by establishing negative censorship. Denial of access to the news is just as effective a censorship as positive prohibition against publication. (6)

Iowa editors got into a flurry with the State Tax Commission over an order prohibiting employees or department heads from giving out any news, either factual or relating to policies of the commission, unless the item were approved first in written form by the three-man commission.

The commission, however, said it "realizes that the public and the press are entitled to full information as to its activities so that the public may be correctly informed." (7)

The commission maintained the order was not intended as censorship but to assure that adequate and correct information be given out on all matters. (8)

The flurry was started over the status of protests against tax evaluations. Commission personnel divided on the question as to whether the protests were public records.

Newspapermen pointed out that there have been no instances of commission employees giving out personal tax information which is secret. Finally, the commission offered to work out a compromise with the editors. (9)

Since the depression of the 1930's, there have been disputes between state officials and newspapers over records of persons receiving financial or job aid. In a number of cities, as for example Philadelphia, newspapers have uncovered stories of people receiving state aid long after they had gone back to their regular employment or had obtained new jobs. A number of persons, by shuttling across the Delaware River, have collected relief in two states.

Newspapers contend that such frauds are uncovered more readily at the local level than by state inspectors from the capital. No newspaper wants to identify in print a family on relief when such a story might embarrass the family and particularly their children in school. At the same time, the newspaper feels the community has a right to know how public relief funds are being spent. Relief agencies, however, have been reluctant to entrust newspapers with any information except lump statistics. By law, especially when all or part of the money is paid from federal funds, these records are secret.

Local Records

Local records are a primary news source for all newspapers. It is on the local level that most of the conflicts arise between officials and the press.

Whether records, on the local level, are public records is determined primarily by three methods. The state, by statute, defines many local public records. City ordinances or charters also may designate which records are open. Courts furnish the third means by which the status of records is determined. Court records themselves will be discussed in a later chapter.

County Records

Most county records are open and may be examined by the press and published under qualified privilege. The principal exception to this rule (other than some court records discussed in the next chapter) is criminal information filed either with the district attorney or with the sheriff as the chief enforcement officer of the county. The findings of a coroner's autopsy or inquest may be withheld temporarily until an accused person is arrested.

The county usually is the authority for handling all elections, municipal, state, and national. The public may check to see what nominating petitions are taken out and later filed, petitions for local referenda and check the official tally sheets of the voting. Ballot boxes, however, may be opened only by court order and under official supervision.

The public has a right to know what real estate is bought, sold or mortgaged, who is married or divorced, details of county revenues and expenditures, the opening of new roads or streets, judgments secured and filed against persons or property, wills admitted to probate, guardianships approved, jurors drawn for service, tax assessments and appeals, health regulations and enforcement, eviction notices filed and executed, commitments to the county jail, almshouse, or mental institutions (but not necessarily the full record of these cases), contracts let or intended to be let for purchases or construction, bond issues floated by school or municipal districts (if the law permits certain loans without a popular vote on them), hunting, fishing and dog licenses issued, payments made to farmers for cattle killed by dogs, school bus contracts, the personnel of the county (usually including salaries paid to each employee) and practically every detail about the operation of the county.

Reporters, as they go about their daily routine of gathering news, generally find that county offices are cooperative. Even on the last of the month, when county officers are jammed with accumulated bookkeeping, most of them will pause long enough for a reporter to look over the records and fill him in on last-minute items not yet entered on the books.

If a reporter is denied access to a record, he first should ask the official to cite the specific law or court decision which says the document is not open. This procedure most times brings the desired result.

If the official persists in withholding it the reporter should consult the newspaper's lawyer, the district attorney, or the county judge, or, if he knows how, the newspaperman should check state statutes. In a certain county, the woman clerk of the marriage license bureau persisted in using her own judgment as to which applications she would keep secret. Since licenses are numbered, reporters had no difficulty in telling when the record was incomplete. A number of times after she withheld a license, a box of candy or a bouquet of flowers appeared mysteriously on her desk.

A newspaper, after missing several newsworthy wedding stories, consulted its lawyer and discovered the remedy was simple. The next time the record of a license was missing, the paper through its attorney, obtained a writ of mandamus from the county judge.

The clerk fainted when the sheriff appeared with the writ. The sheriff just waited until she was revived and then did his duty. The clerk thereupon resigned with a swan-song statement that the public just didn't appreciate her "long and faithful service." Similar writs have opened up other records after officials consistently kept them from inspection.

Some officials write on the margin of certain records such notations as: "this is not for publication," or "the parties request this not be published."

A newspaper should consider such notations as simply requests and make its own decision about publication. If the record has been designated as a public document, no elective or appointive official can deny access to it nor instruct the paper which portions may be printed and which may not be published. As pointed out previously, the request for examination of the record must be reasonable, must be made during normal office hours, and usually must be by a person having an interest in the information. A newspaper can always show sufficient interest in public records.

Smaller papers at times have made arrangements with officials to send over copies of these records. If under these circumstances, the officials omit part of the records, the newspaper cannot compel delivery of a full report since the arrangement is purely a matter of courtesy. The paper's remedy is to send its own reporter over to make a copy.

Municipal Records

With the exception of two classes — police and hospital — municipal records follow the same pattern as county records. Again, state statutes, city charters, or court decisions designate which records are open. The remedy against an official who refuses access to a municipal public record is an appeal to the county court for a writ of mandamus.

The Rhode Island Superior Court ordered tax abatement lists made available to reporters of the *Providence Journal* and *Evening Bulletin*. (10) The city council and mayor of Titusville, Pa., adopted an ordinance that city hall news could be released only by the mayor or the head of a department. The next day, when a storm of protests broke, one councilman commented: "We were fools. I didn't realize what we had done until I read the paper the next day." (11)   Editor E. S. Stevenson of the *Titusville Herald* said his front page editorial of protest brought him so many handshakes at church the following Sunday ;you would have thought I was the minister." (12)

In Phoenix, Arizona, reporters had difficulty gathering City Hall news but when a new acting city manager took over, he issued these instructions:

"We are fully cognizant of the great importance of keeping the public informed as to the activities and plans of the city government. It is important that all department heads give the fullest cooperation at all times to reporters." (13)

Hospital News

Hospitals present a legal problem to the reporter for several reasons. Many hospitals are private institutions although some of their financial support may come from tax funds or from public subscription.

A person entering a hospital for medical treatment or surgery is not presumed to be giving up his privacy. The broken arm I suffer in a traffic accident may be a matter of public information, but when my appendix misbehaves it's a matter between myself and my doctor. If I fail to survive the operation, my death is a public record, but successful convalescence is mine alone to enjoy.

In most accident cases, the reporter has a dual or multiple check because the police department may require a record of it. Should the accident result in a fatality, the coroner also must be notified. The doctor who in the privacy of his office treats a bullet wound is required to make a report despite the wishes of his patient.

If the hospital is supported entirely from public funds, the assumption still is that medical patients are private cases. The reporter's best procedure is to establish rapport with the hospital which is not too difficult in many instances because the institution's administrative staff is cognizant that it needs public support and goodwill. This has become true especially now since most hospitals have come to the realization that the direct-

ing heads should be men trained in administration of institutions rather than men trained in medicine only.

Only a few medical patients have news value. In such
cases, there is a wide-spread custom for the hospital to release
the bare fact that the person is a patient and leave additional
information to the discretion of the attending physician. If the
patient is very prominent, usually the family cooperates with
the newspaper to inform the public of his progress.

Iowa editors and the Iowa State Medical Association and
Iowa Hospital Association drew up a "code" in 1949 to govern
news about patients.

Provisions of the "code" include:

"The presence of certain persons in a hospital is news.
Their presence should generally be acknowledged by the hospital unless expressly forbidden by the patient or attending
physician.

"The death of any patient is presumed to be public property. A statement that the patient died should be made by
the hospital. . . ." (14)

On accident and fire cases where records must be kept by
municipal departments anyway, the "code" recommends to hospitals that they should give to newspapers immediately:

"Name, age, address, occupation, and sex. Extent of injuries although it is recognized that pending complete prognosis (sic), these statements may of necessity have to be hedged
with 'possible fractures,' condition, 'apparently' good, fair or
serious." (15)

If the patient is newsworthy, there is little likelihood that
he can remain in a hospital very long before the press becomes
aware of it. A man or woman of prominence doesn't disappear
without friends or relatives knowing about it and discussing it.

If the hospital or attending physician refuses such information,
there is little the newspaper can do except to attempt to "reason"
with them on the basis that the community is concerned. The
public has been educated pretty well to the role of reporters
and to the knowledge that newspapermen on a "death watch"
are not "ghouls" but simply men bent on the task of keeping
people informed about an event in which there is much interest.

Hospital records are not privileged and thus a paper's only defense against publication of them is truth. To say that a patient is hospitalized for treatment of a kidney condition when the disease actually is diabetes is not libelous since neither ailment is a "derogatory affliction." But the paper heads for trouble if it reports a patient entered a hospital for treatment of one of the so-called social diseases or for mental disorders when the ailment was appendicitis. Cancer was long America's "hidden disease" but now people talk freely about it and realize that it may be contracted by the best of people with the best of health and social habits. Leprosy, however, is still regarded as a loathsome disease which may bring virtual social ostracism to the patient. Erroneously attributing leprosy to a hospital patient would no doubt sustain an action in libel. (16)

Since an erroneous report of a death is not libelous in itself, there is no libel in a mistake in the report of a patient's condition. If a paper says a patient is in a critical condition when actually he has passed the crisis and is recovering, the only damage is to the paper's reputation for veracity.

Hospital methods and administration may be criticized the same as any other activities affected with public interest provided there is no direct or implied inference of incompetence, especially on the part of the medical staff. The law neither presumes that any one is infallible nor that there is only one correct way of doing everything. But the law does presume that a person trained in special skills and licensed to perform those skills, is competent. Physicians may make mistakes in diagnosis and prognosis, but in print those errors must be due to other factors than lack of ability or the paper may find itself in serious trouble.

Municipal Police Records

Local police in the various communities keep a record popularly known as the "police blotter." This document is practically a diary of police activities, for, besides arrests, it also lists fire calls (since police answer alarms to direct traffic and prevent spectators from interfering with firemen), and complaints from citizens regarding matters ranging from prowlers, to broken street lights or stray dogs.

When a policeman brings an arrested person to headquarters the officer in charge determines if he will be held or released on bond (called forfeit by police) or freed on simply his promise to be in police court at an appointed time.

The blotter lists the arrested person's name, address, age, sex, offense, disposition of case, and name of arresting officer. By custom, in most communities, the police reporter heads first for the blotter to see what has happened since he made his last check. One or more checks may be made by telephone and an obliging desk sergeant, if he is on good terms with the reporter, often reads off the blotter listings.

By state law, Kansas and Utah have designated the police blotter as a public record. Laws in Georgia and Idaho indicate, but do not conclusively designate, the same status. (17)

In the following states an unofficial opinion or belief of the attorney general, holds the police blotter is a public record: Alabama, Florida, Iowa, Kentucky, Minnesota, North Carolina, Oklahoma and Washington.

In Massachusetts and New York the courts have definitely held the blotter is not a public record.

These states leave the matter to municipalities to determine: Arizona, Pennsylvania, Tennessee, Texas, Washington, and West Virginia.

In three states, statutes indicate the blotter is not a public record: Connecticut (except state police), Louisiana, and South Dakota.

In six states, an unofficial belief or opinion of the attorney general is that the blotter is not a public record: Michigan, Montana, Ohio, Rhode Island, South Dakota, and Wisconsin.

In all other states, there are no laws, ordinances, legal opinions, or court decisions to guide the reporter. As a practical matter, a newspaper in defending a libel suit in any of these states probably would contend that the blotter is a public record and hope the court accepted that interpretation. But the press in these states should realize that there are no indications of judicial sentiment on the question.

Reporters in states in which the blotter is a public record are protected only for the information they actually take from it and their stories must be accurate. Failure to copy from the blotter the middle name or initial of an arrested man may result in a libel suit if it leads to confusion with an innocent person. (18) Typographical errors in street addresses have plagued so many papers that a common custom now is to say: Harry Jones of the 400 block of Third street, instead of giving the exact house number.

If the reporter goes beyond the information on the blotter and obtains additional facts from the arresting officer or from the chief of police, those extra facts are generally printed at the paper's risk. The danger is even greater if the additional facts imply that the defendant is guilty.

The newspaper's desire to avoid libel suits and also to be fair has produced rather trite writing in police stories. Readers may be irked by the constant repetition of: ". . . was arrested for questioning in connection with the theft of $500 etc." but the newspaper staff can breathe more easily with that version than if it says ". . . was arrested *for* the theft of, etc.", or ". . . was arrested *in* the theft of, etc."

Reporting that a man was arrested for questioning about a crime is libelous if the man actually were not arrested. Many times a person is asked or "invited" to come to the police station for questioning or he may show up without any notice because he was at or near the scene of a crime and knows that sooner or later the police may want a few words with him.

Although the United States Supreme Court has ruled that a defendant must be arraigned within a reasonable time, in many jurisdictions either by law or custom which has never been contested, people often are held on "open charges" or on a nominal charge such as vagrancy for 24 to 48 hours while police continue their investigation. At the end of that period, either a formal charge is brought or the man is released. A paper may say (if it is true) that a man is being held on an open charge while police continue their investigation of a certain crime. But there must be no inference that the man is guilty or even involved in that crime.

A paper paid damages because its account of a routine arrest said the suspect had attempted to escape from the officer. The arresting policeman had done a little embellishing of his report to gain some personal glory. The defendant, cleared the next day in police court, later convinced a jury in a libel suit that he had gone willingly to the police station and that the report of his attempted escape had branded him as guilty.

A trite but safe practice is to make no specific identification of an arrested man unless that identification is positive. A prisoner may tell the desk sergeant that his name is John Jones and give a street address. He may have a wallet full of cards bearing that name and address. But wallet and cards may have been stolen.

If there is any doubt about identification, the paper should say "a man whom police listed as John Jones," or "a man identified by police as John Jones." If the man is a local resident, the paper usually can check other sources.

Many times persons arrested on minor charges, especially traffic violations, fail to appear for a hearing and the money they posted as bond is forfeited and the cases dropped. The story should say that "John Jones today forfeited $10 bond on a charge of, etc." There should be no inference or assumption that the man was guilty. He may have believed it more convenient to lose $10 than take the time off to attend the hearing or he may have slipped up on the date, or he may have been compelled to go out of town suddenly.

In cities where the blotter is not a public record, there is no defense except truth for any police story. Any information obtained from the blotter or from policemen is printed strictly at the paper's own risk. In those jurisdictions, the blotter must be regarded simply as a record kept by the police department for its own convenience. Although by custom reporters may be permitted access to it, the legal status is about the same as if the police chief showed a reporter one of his private letters.

Serving of a warrant is an act of arrest. (19) Reports of investigations by law enforcement officers carry no privileges except in unusual circumstances. (20)

An Indiana paper made a settlement out of court for enlarging upon a story from a chief of police who had assigned a man to investigate the disappearance of a woman. The mother of the missing woman was quoted by the police chief as saying she was certain her son-in-law had "done away" with her daughter. Printing that police were looking for a woman reported missing could be defended on ground of truth but there is no defense for calling a man a murderer.

A Pennsylvania paper paid because a careless police officer linked the disappearance of a girl and a married man. The paper's story began: "Police today said they are looking for a 15-year-old girl and a married man who disappeared from their homes a week ago." The implication was the two had gone away together, which was untrue.

Minor errors in a police story usually do not destroy any qualified privilege the item otherwise might possess. To say a man was arrested on a charge of stealing $200 when actually the sum was only $150 would not destroy privilege. Neither would a minor mistake in the amount of bond required destroy privilege but a typographical error making a $10 forfeit read $1,000 or more might be ground for contention that the bail figure placed the defendant in a more serious light in the community. (21)

One paper discovered, however, that the courts do find a difference between saying a man was arrested for being drunk and disorderly and that he was arrested for "annoying young girls." His drunken banter among a group of young girls actually prompted his arrest but he was charged formally with only drunkenness and disorderly conduct. Since the community had been concerned with a growing number of sex offenses, the man convinced a libel jury that the words "annoying young girls" imputed to him a morals offense.

Confessions

A perennial source of danger to the press in police news, no matter what the status of the blotter may be in a particular jurisdiction, is the printing of confessions.

Many decisions have established that a confession has no legal standing until it is introduced into evidence and accepted by the court during a trial. (22) In all jurisdictions the taking of a confession is regarded as being merely a discretionary act of law enforcement officers. The procedure is authorized neither by law nor by the courts, but a police officer may obtain a confession if he is able and so chooses. (23)

Veteran court reporters know that some of the most bitter legal fights in criminal trials have come about through the efforts of the defense to prevent the introduction into the evidence of a confession the defendant made to police. If defense counsel can show the confession was made under duress or coercion or even under the threat of duress or coercion, the courts usually will bar its use by the state. The courts also will not permit a confession to be used as evidence if counsel can show the defendant was not aware of his constitutional rights. The constitution does not compel a man to testify against himself either in a confession or from the witness stand.

The courts also generally will bar the confession if defense can show the prisoner made it on the promise, direct or implied, that he would profit from it by having the charge reduced or by having the district attorney recommend leniency.

To aid the state in having a confession introduced into evidence at the trial, police officers insist that the suspect agree to a "preamble" declaring the statement is being made without "threat, duress, coercion, or promise" and that the prisoner is aware of his constitutional rights.

If a paper prints a confession and later the defendant is acquitted by a jury, he probably has a good case of libel. His case is strengthened if at the trial the court refused to admit the confession into evidence. An acquittal means legally that the defendant did not commit the crime with which he was charged, no matter what people in the community may think or believe. Therefore, to have printed that he did commit the crime, even by his own admission, is dangerous. If the confession were barred from the trial, it means the court found it was obtained illegally which is further damaging evidence against a paper in a libel suit.

A confession, always dangerous to print, becomes an even greater risk if the statement implicates other persons. The prisoner who confesses may be naming others just for "spite." One man, arrested in the holdup of a gasoline station in which an attendant was wounded seriously, implicated two friends as being with him. Later it was proved that, although the two friends had been with him that night, they left him several hours before the holdup and had no knowledge that he was planning a robbery.

A paper which printed the confession naming the two friends was fortunate to escape liability by publishing a correction and an apology. The two men were satisfied that the apology restored their standing in the community and did not press for damages.

It is not fantastic to say that the confession even of a murderer may flare back on the paper which prints it. An Indiana man was convicted of murder and the execution date set. But his lawyers, after a two-year fight, won a reversal from the United States Supreme Court which ordered a new trial. By that time, the state's principal witness had died. The district attorney felt he could not hope for another conviction and he reluctantly was forced to ask for a dismissal of the charge. He and others in the community had no private doubts as to the guilt of the man but the case went back into the files among the "unsolved murders."

Confessions are "news," and few papers refuse to print them. If the defendant later is convicted and denied an appeal, the paper is fairly safe. But an acquittal gives it cause to be concerned. As long as prisoners confess, papers probably will publish the statements, but the press should be aware that this is one story that legally may be "highly inflammable". About the only defense for the paper in event of a libel suit is to prove that the confession actually was made and signed and then hope that the jury will regard it as a report of an event and not as the paper's inference that the defendant was guilty of the crime charged against him. It is not a good legal defense but it may mitigate damages which is about all the paper can expect under such circumstances.

Resumé and Analysis:

In only a few states is the police blotter established as a public record either by statute, city ordinance, or court decision. In jurisdictions where the blotter is a public document, qualified privilege is possessed only by the information taken accurately from the blotter. There is no privilege for any additional facts obtained from police or from private citizens.

Where the police blotter either is not a public record or its status has not been determined, the press is liable for all the information it prints about crime. Since even in protected jurisdictions, the general practice is to add to the bare facts on the police blotter, the paper's "first line of defense," as the Judicial Council of Massachusetts suggests, is truth. "Privilege is a second line of defense." (24)

Since the police beat is a fertile source of news, there have been endless disputes between press and the police. Philadelphia reporters discovered that in a neighboring township three bankers were involved in a country club brawl in which a policeman was beaten. Township police merely noted the arrests on the blotter and beside them wrote: "not for newspapers." The papers dug around and unearthed the facts but later the charges were dropped without a formal hearing. Their stories then had no legal sanction but none of the bankers brought an action against the papers. (25) Truth would have been the only defense left to them.

A Detroit chief of police became embroiled with police reporters and photographers because he insisted that each one take a "loyalty oath" to show he had no affiliation or sympathy with the Communist party. His ruling was fought bitterly in Detroit as an unwarranted interference with the press and as infringement on personal liberty. A survey by *Editor and Publisher* showed publishers and newspapermen over the country were divided on the question. Later, the order was modified to exclude reporters for Detroit dailies.

When the police chief finally issued press badges, after withholding them for months during the argument over the loyalty oath, the press found they were exact duplicates of police sergeant badges with the exception of the word "reporter" in small type. The similarity led to many mixups.

Some newspapermen found people talked more freely at the sight of their badges and presumably the newsmen did not call attention to the word "reporter" on them. One reporter, on the way downtown by bus, decided this transportation was too slow. He alighted and hailed a taxi. The driver noticed the badge and sped him to headquarters.

He waved aside the proffered fare with the assurance:

"Always glad to do the department a favor, officer."

The furore over the loyalty oath ended when the incoming mayor appointed a new police chief. (26)

The mayor of Phoenix City, Alabama, in 1949 rescinded, in effect, a three-year-old order forbidding the police blotter to be inspected by anyone. The new order said there would be no objection to anyone looking at the blotter "as long as he did not defame the city." The prohibition had gone into effect after newspaper criticism of the handling of gambling cases. (27)

In 1950, the press and radio in Baltimore won an 11-year-old fight over the publication of crime news. After a bizarre murder in 1939, the Supreme Court of Baltimore promulgated a press "code," Rule 904 of which prohibited the publication of confessions and certain other "pre-trial statements."

The battle drew to a climax in 1948 when an 18-year-old girl was found strangled in an automobile. Beside her body was her fiance in a serious condition from what police said were self-inflicted bullet wounds.

Before lapsing into a coma, the youth made statements to police. Baltimore papers, in printing the story, alluded to the statements but carried an editorial note informing readers that Rule 904 prohibited them from disclosing what the youth had said. Washington papers printed the statements and sent copies into Baltimore. Later five Baltimore radio stations and a news commentator carried the statements and were adjudged in contempt and fined.

Maryland papers outside Baltimore began showing concern when the other courts indicated the "code" might be adopted state-wide. The Maryland Court of Appeals, with one justice dissenting, reversed the convictions on June 8, 1949, and held invalid the section of Rule 904 under which the men were found guilty. In January, 1950, the United States Supreme Court refused to grant an appeal to the state of Maryland. (28)

In New York City, police have established more friendly relations with the press. The New York police department, in drawing up a new "Public Relations Manual," inserted a section directing officers to cooperate with the press by releasing promptly "such information as is permissible." The section concluded that:

". . . a cooperative attitude (with the press) and a courageous explanation when necessary (to show why certain information cannot be divulged) will usually result in a more desirable presentation of the facts from the police viewpoint." (29)

From time to time, newspapers in states where the police blotter is not a public record, have threatened court action to obtain access to the docket, but finally had to admit that there was no legal remedy in the absence of statutes, charter provisions, or court decisions. (30)

Some newspapers like to break in new reporters by putting them on the police beat on the theory it quickly teaches them accuracy and attention to details. Papers with more prudent editors assign only experienced men to the police run. Teaching a man the lessons of accuracy may prove expensive for a newspaper. For the police beat which is one of the best sources of news is also the area of the newspaper's biggest legal headache.

For Further Reading

For a detailed study of the status of the police blotter in the several states see:
Steigleman, Walter, "The Legal Problem of the Police Blotter," *Journalism Quarterly*, March, 1943.
For a fuller discussion of the dangers in the printing of confessions see:
Steigleman, Walter, "I Confess — But It May Be Libel," *Quill*, Nov. 1944.

COURT DECISIONS

Courts have been concerned with the status of police news for at least 100 years. One of the earliest cases which determined that there was no privilege in police news was: Cincinnati Gazette Co. v. Timberlake, 10 Ohio,

548, decided in 1860. Statutes, ordinances, and decisions have since modified that interpretation in a number of jurisdictions. The recitation of a pertinent point or two from a decision may be misleading or too assuring. The cases should be read in their entirety. Some leading cases other than those already cited dealing with police news are:

McAllister v. Detroit Free Press Co., 43 N.W. 431.

Hubert v. New Nonpareil Co., 82 N.W. 928.

Norfolk Post Co. v. Wright, 125 S.E. 656.

Burrows v. Pulitzer Publishing Co., 255 S.W. 925.

Switzer v. Anthony and Denver Express Publishing Co., 71 Colo. 291.

Behrendt v. Times-Mirror Co., 96 Calif. App. 3.

Republican Publishing Co. v. Conroy, 38 P. 423.

Dement v. Houston Printing Co., 37 S.W. 985.

McClure v. Review Publishing Co., 80 P. 303.

Houston Chronicle Publishing Co. v. Bowmen, 182 S.W. 61.

CHAPTER IX

"Reporting Crime and Courts"

The Press and the Minor Judiciary

The underlying theory of the American legal system is based on two assumptions: (a) a person accused of a criminal offense is presumed to be innocent until he is proved beyond a reasonable doubt to be guilty, (b) the accused person is entitled to a fair hearing or trial. (1)

If every minor offense such as spitting on the sidewalk, walking over a newly-planted lawn, driving with one headlight burned out, etc., were permitted to go into county court for a trial before a jury, the courts either would become so congested there would be long delays or else the number of judges necessary would be so large as to cause an undue hardship on taxpayers.

For those reasons, every state has set up what is popularly known as the minor judiciary. Members of the minor judiciary are known by such various names as justices of the peace (squires), aldermen, police magistrates, et al. Most of these minor justices are elected by the voters and their powers are prescribed rigidly by law.

In minor cases, they have final authority known as summary conviction. Unless the law specifically permits a jail term, a man accused of spitting on the sidewalk may be fined a few dollars and costs and committed to prison only if he fails to pay. Minor traffic offenses provide only fines in the absence of contrary statutes.

From such minor charges, there is no appeal unless the accused can show a violation of his constitutional rights or that the justice was influenced by factors other than facts. Many such cases involve nothing more than the accused's word against that of the arresting officer.

The magistrate usually lends more weight to the evidence of the arresting officer than he does to the defense. For one thing, the arresting officer is supposed to be "neutral" and have no other motive than performance of his duties.

The "sour note" in the system comes in the fact that most minor justices are paid only in fees. If the case is dismissed for lack of evidence or other reasons, the justice receives no money. The traffic officer who feels a justice seems to side with the motorist, is apt to find ways to take his "business" before some other squire, and the justice discovers his receipts suffer. Appealing such a case is expensive, and a motorist who conscientiously believes he is in the right, may decide it is cheaper to pay the fine. Such appeals also are difficult to win because the county court will not reverse the justice unless it can be shown definitely that he was in the wrong or exceeded his authority.

In more serious offenses, the justice sits only as a committing magistrate. He decides whether or not there is enough evidence to bind the defendant over to the county or district court and the amount of bail that should be required.

If the bail seems excessive, the defendant can ask the county court for a reduction. If the justice decides the evidence does not warrant holding the accused, the district attorney may overrule the decision and the defendant finds himself re-arrested.

A murder suspect, for example, is entitled to a preliminary hearing before the minor judiciary, but the justice except in unusual circumstances has authority only to go through the formality of binding him over for action by the county grand jury.

But no matter whether the offense is a major or minor one, when the justice mounts his bench (which may be just a chair in his ordinary business office), he assumes most of the prerogatives of the county court. He can hold the defendant, a witness, or a spectator in contempt for disturbing the proceedings or for any other cause that would bring similar action in the county court.

For his official actions, the justice is accorded the same absolute privilege as the judge on the county bench, provided he does not abuse his office. The justice, for example, could not say he was not fining a traffic violator because if he did "some one at City Hall would just steal the money anyhow." Nor can he use his office for unwarranted attacks upon persons not a party to the proceedings.

The county coroner, at a formal hearing or inquest, is a minor justice. He, too, just as the other justices, can issue subpoenas for witnesses, compel a party to the case to produce certain records, and in general proceed as though the case were being heard by the regular county court.

The justice also may sit in equity in minor matters. Through an injunction by a justice, I can restrain the man who continually walks over my flower bed or who permits his dog to run over my garden or property.

When the justice holds a hearing or takes official action, the newspaper may print "a fair and accurate" report of the proceedings under qualified privilege. It may not embellish its report just to "liven it up" or to turn it into a sparkling human interest story. Most justice hearings are more informal than those before the county court and at times there may be considerable "by-play" on the part of the participants. The reporter who seizes upon this "by-play" as the best part of the story may find he printed it at his own risk. Many times, too, a participant, mistaking the general informality for license to "wise crack" may call out a remark that "brings down the house." As far as the reporter is concerned, he must realize such remarks are those of private citizens. If they are defamatory, he may find himself in trouble for printing them. (2)

Once the justice has rendered his decision, the newspaper may criticize the case just as it comments on actions of the county court. The paper, however, may not hold the justice up to ridicule nor can it infer that his decision was based on any factors but his findings of fact and conclusions of law.

An Iowa justice received considerable newspaper attention because he held court in the rear of his taproom. A newspaper was free to express the opinion that justice should not be dispensed in a tavern but it could not imply that either the justice

or participants in a case tarried too long in the front of the shop
before court opened.

Records of the minor judiciary are open for inspection. The
public has the right to all information necessary to evaluate the
operation of its legal system, from the lowest to the highest
court. (3) The remedy for a paper denied access to such records
is a writ of mandamus from the county court.

The Grand Jury

The defendant bound over to county court by a justice finds
the next stop in his case is the grand jury. The number of grand
jurors varies from six to 23 in the several states. (4)

Only the state's case is presented to the grand jury. The
defendant cannot appear nor be represented there by counsel.
The jurors examine the evidence and determine if it is sufficient
to warrant the case going to trial. The proceedings of the
grand jury are secret and may not be published, even if known,
until a formal report is made. The grand jury either returns a
"true bill" which sends the case to trial, or returns a "no bill,"
popularly known as a refusal to indict. A "no bill" ends the
case. A "true bill" means the defendant has been indicted.

The grand jury also has wide investigating powers. It may
look into any matter in the county which it believes needs investigation. The investigation may come on the jury's own
initiative or by direction of the court. While investigating, it
has power to subpoena witnesses or records and may hold in
contempt witnesses who refuse to appear or who balk at testifying. The grand jury also examines county institutions, such
as the jail or almshouse, and makes such recommendations it
believes necessary or desirable.

Since the grand jury proceedings are secret, there is no privilege attached to publication of them before the jury makes a
formal report to the court. Should a newspaper have a "pipe
line" into the jury room, it can be cited for contempt for printing the day-by-day proceedings.

A reporter, however, can take a position as near to the
room as permitted and print the names of witnesses he sees
entering. In many jurisdictions a list of witnesses called is

made public by the grand jury usually through the district attorney. Their testimony, however, is kept secret.

In some states, a witness before he enters the grand jury room may give a reporter the gist of what he expects to testify. Once he is before the jury and is sworn, he usually is bound by secrecy and may be cited for contempt for disclosing his testimony, along with the paper that prints it. The inexperienced reporter covering his first grand jury often will save himself and his paper grief by consulting the district attorney and the judge.

A Pennsylvania grand jury, investigating charges against high state officials, attracted reporters from a number of cities. The judge assigned to preside met with reporters daily to "brief" them. Reporters talked freely with witnesses on the way in and often as they emerged. On the basis of such information, one newspaper predicted what indictments would be returned and against whom. The story was so accurate that after the trials, a convicted state official cited it in his appeal as evidence that the grand jury proceedings were not secret as required by law. The supreme court rejected the appeal. In another jurisdiction, such procedure by the reporters might have involved them in a contempt citation, especially if they had not worked so closely with the presiding judge.

When the grand jury makes a formal report to the court, its statement becomes part of a judicial proceeding and carries qualified privilege. (5) Many times a grand jury may indict as a result of its investigation and the person named may not yet be under arrest. The customary procedure is for this indictment to remain secret until the judge issues a bench warrant and the sheriff serves it. Otherwise, premature publication might warn the defendant in time for him to leave the jurisdiction.

Since a grand jury's report is often brief and stated in legal phraseology, the district attorney may fill in reporters. In some jurisdictions, the statement of the district attorney is regarded as part of the grand jury proceedings; in other jurisdictions the courts hold it is "mere conversation." "Conversation" can be defended only by truth or, in some circumstances, by a plea of fair comment.

The Press and the Courts

When the actual trial begins, the reporter is on probably the safest ground since the crime was committed. A fair and accurate report of a judicial proceeding carries qualified privilege.

The reporter not only sits in court but, as pointed out in an earlier chapter, he generally finds certain conveniences provided for him. The position of the press table usually enables him to see and hear clearly every part of the proceedings, even to "eavesdropping" on conferences between judge and counsel as the lawyers huddle around the bench. How much of such overheard material he may use depends upon the subject being discussed and the ruling of the judge. The results of most such conferences show up in a formal ruling from the bench and then may be printed.

A fair and accurate report does not mean that equal space must be given daily to both prosecution and defense. Since the state presents its evidence first, early days of a trial look mighty dark for the defendant. The district attorney presents witness after witness whom he expects will add to the web of evidence he is trying to weave. The press may report all such testimony, no matter how damaging it may be for the defendant. After each state witness completes his testimony, he is subject to cross-examination by defense counsel. This cross-examination may bring out facts favorable to the defendant which the reporter notes, not only because he wants to be fair, but because it is news. The reporter's job is to tell the reader what is happening and not to take sides.

When the state rests, the defendant gets his day in court. Then, witness after witness will take the stand to refute the testimony offered by the state. The reporter doesn't have to worry about giving the exact space to the defense as it did to the prosecution.

The prosecution may have presented its side on a day when other news was light and much space could be devoted to the trial. On the day the defense opens, community or world-shaking events may trim the space that can be devoted to the case. Or the defense testimony may be nothing but straight denials of that presented by the state. If the state received a front-page streamer for each of its days of testimony, however, and the defense story is relegated to the classified advertising page, the paper's fairness is open to question. Court coverage, however, is not based on the mere number of inches given to each side but on fairness and accuracy. The court is concerned with seeing that the defendant receives a fair trial; the newspaper must be concerned with seeing that he is given a fair presentation of his story.

If the reporter observes court rules and is accurate, there are only two chief problems that need worry him. One is to refrain from interposing his own comments in the story. He is not there to sit in judgment and must not express his opinions as to the guilt or innocence of the defendant. He also must not imagine he has a sport spectator's prerogative of criticizing the officials—judge, counsel, or jurors.

His own sense of ethics must be his guide as to whether he writes: "The witness trembled at the question," or "the defendant clutched his hands nervously." A witness who hesitates before answering a question is not necessarily panicky or clever. He may be only trying to arrange his thoughts before speaking. To infer, then, that the question had the witness "on the ropes" or that the witness "sparred for time," may not only be inaccurate but also unfair. The reporter who writes that "the district attorney scored heavily," may be chagrined an hour later when defense counsel neatly parries away the effect.

Ordinarily, the court takes no notice of such comments. But if the reporter strays too far from facts the judge may snap him back or even bar him from further session. Too drastic comments may lead to a contempt citation, especially if the jury is permitted to go home at night. Although such jurors are instructed not to read about the case, courts recognize the weakness of human flesh to seize upon printed accounts of an event in which they are playing a part.

The second area of danger comes in testimony or remarks ordered stricken from the record. A court trial cannot be conducted under the rules that govern a deliberative body such as a legislature where there is great freedom of discussion. Courts must have relevancy rules or otherwise an attorney or witness might talk at length on issues that have no bearing on the case, and which might be prejudicial to the defendant. When counsel asks a witness if he were at a certain place at a designated time, the witness is expected to answer "yes" or "no." Neither the lawyer nor the court wants the witness to launch into a recital of his daily activities, his state of health, or his philosophical or political beliefs.

An irrelevant or immaterial remark or comment is ordered stricken from the record, and the jury is instructed to disregard it. The remark may be good news and the reporter may dash to a phone to give it to his office in time to make an edition. While he is absent, the remark may have been stricken from the record. When the reporter resumes his seat, he should check with a colleague to see what happened in his absence.

Remarks stricken from the record are presumed never to have been said. Therefore, they carry no privilege. The only defense a reporter would have either in a libel or contempt action, would be to plead that mechanical problems prevented the paper from killing the item. If the paper were just locking up when the reporter's phone call came with the new lead, the next edition might be run off before the court strikes out the statement. The statement, however, should be taken out of the next edition and not used thereafter.

Sometimes a remark made is not ordered stricken until the next day's court session. The assumption is that the first printing carries qualified privilege because when it appeared in the paper it was still a part of the official proceedings. But no privilege would attach to it if published after the court's order is made.

Often when a remark is made, the judge may say he will permit it to stand subject to a motion by counsel to have it stricken. That should be a warning to the newspaper that it should handle that statement cautiously.

The more important the case the more likelihood the coverage will be easier because the judge recognizes the great interest in it and sets about to establish liaison with the press. This is particularly true of cases that attract many out-of-town reporters.

The judge may meet with press representatives himself or appoint a liaison man, usually a newspaperman he knows. The judge tells reporters of the conduct he expects from them, what privileges they will have, what restrictions, and also about taking photographs. A violation of any of these rules may bar the offending reporter from future sessions and also lead to his citation for contempt.

Most courts frown on pre-trial conferences between press and lawyers if for any other reason than to be filled in with background. It helps a reporter to understand the future testimony of a witness if counsel explains just what he hopes to develop. Many lawyers go beyond that and attempt to get a favorable press by disclosing that they have a witness who will prove certain points or by revealing the results of investigations conducted under their direction. Such statements are on the borderline, and the reporter should be wary of his use of them.

It is not uncommon for counsel to contend that publication of such statements prejudiced his case. If the court agrees and orders a mistrial, the newspapers which printed them are not likely to escape unpunished. Trials must be conducted in the courtroom and not in the press.

One Iowa newspaper discovered how closely counsel will work with the press, especially local papers. A trial was attracting nation-wide attention with the result that dozens of out-of-town reporters were there. The local paper discovered that most of the readable news came after it had locked up its last afternoon edition. As a result, a morning paper in a nearby city was able to flood the local community with more "real news" than the home-town paper published.

After several days of seeing a morning paper get all the play, editors of the local paper had an informal talk with state and defense counsel. From then on, headlines were made early enough for the local paper. If the judge were aware of the new procedure, he gave no official inkling. Since the material was to be presented anyhow, the defendant did not suffer.

On an important trial, attorneys for both sides may have copies of their closing summations made for the press although most lawyers like to speak extemporaneously in order to press to the fullest any favorable reaction they sense on jurors' faces. The judge, since his charge to the jury must be exact and precise to avoid having it cited as one ground for an appeal, usually reads it from a prepared manuscript. He generally will have copies for the press because a reporter has difficulty grasping the legal technicalities by merely hearing them.

The summation of the state pictures the defendant as a man too dangerous for society to permit to roam among it. The defense, on the other hand, pictures him as anything from the victim of mistaken identity to a man around whom circumstances have woven dastardly a "plot." Since this summation is part of the proceedings, the press may print it although it should give both pictures.

The jurors are the persons who must pass on the guilt or innocence of the defendant, and the reporter, when the jury files out, should not speculate on what the verdict will be. The jury deliberates in secrecy and any attempt of a paper to establish a "pipe line" into the jury room may be held to be contempt.

Reporters frequently have attempted to establish signals with a bailiff so that when the jury files in with its verdict that official, by pulling an ear, twitching his nose, holding up one or two fingers, or maybe coughing, tips off the verdict. The verdict is generally written and handed by the foreman to the clerk of the court for passing up to the judge. Bailiffs are not supposed to know what the verdict is until it is read, but most of them have mysterious ways of discovering the jury's decision before it comes into court.

In the trial of Bruno Richard Hauptmann for the kidnaping of the Lindbergh baby, it is generally assumed that press services made arrangements for a tipoff. The Associated Press, however, flashed the verdict as life imprisonment when it actually was death.

A paper which makes such advance arrangements and gets mixed up in signals may have to pay for its folly. Should it appear on the streets with a story that the defendant was found guilty when actually he was acquitted, he probably has a good case in libel. The paper could not depend upon a defense of privilege because in the eyes of the court the tipoff was just the "gossip" of a private citizen.

A convicted man has the right of asking for a new trial and then appealing to a higher court if it is denied. It may be a year or two from the time the verdict is returned until the case is settled finally. For that reason, the paper assumes some risk in calling a man a thief or murderer because the jury found him guilty. If he wins a new trial, he may be acquitted and therefore is not a thief or a murderer. Until all avenues of appeal have been lost, the safest reference for a newspaper is to say only that he was "convicted on a charge of ...." The only safe time to call a man a slayer or murderer is in the story of his execution.

Civil Suits

Since a civil suit is a dispute between private persons and not between the state and an individual, the coverage of such cases differs from that of a criminal trial.

The actual courtroom privileges are the same. But a civil suit starts with the filing of a complaint or a petition and not with an arrest. The moot question in law is how much privilege, if any, attaches to the complaint and the answer.

An individual in his complaint sets forth certain allegations or grievances which he says he has suffered at the hands of the other. Perhaps he is a store owner and charges a customer has failed to meet payments on an article. Or one motorist charges another wrecked his car and will not pay for repairing it. One corporation may want damages from another for a wrong it alleges the defendant corporation did to it. The causes of a civil suit are as numerous as the activities of man.

The complaint is filed with the clerk of the court or with the court official designated to receive such papers. The defendant is given a specified number of days to answer or suffer judgment against it by default.

The defendant in his answer may say the charges are too general and ask for a bill of particulars. The plaintiff then must file these details. Again, the defendant is given time to answer them. He may deny them or admit they are true but that they do not constitute any grounds for action. In legal language, he demurs, and the court must pass upon it. If the court agrees, the case is dismissed with or without prejudice.

If dismissed without prejudice, the plaintiff usually has the right to file a new complaint if he wishes.

All this maneuvering is called pleadings. The purpose is to cut away all extraneous problems so that the trial can be held upon pre-determined issues. It's expensive and time consuming to conduct a trial, and the courts want to be economical of both, as well as to expedite justice.

The general rule that a proceeding becomes privileged only when it "comes to the attention of the court" is not of much help to the reporter because jurisdictions differ on the interpretation of that clause. Moreover, in the past ten or fifteen years some courts seemingly have reversed earlier stands.

The federal courts hold that the filing of a complaint is a judicial proceeding and entitled to qualified privilege. A paper, therefore, may print all allegations set forth.

Courts in Nevada, Pennsylvania, and perhaps Kansas and Kentucky, have indicated they regard pleadings as privileged. Ohio and Georgia have statutes conferring privilege, and a Texan law seems to have the same effect. New York courts apparently have swung away from an earlier stand that denied privilege to these reports. (6)

Colorado, Louisiana, Massachusetts, Michigan, Minnesota, and Rhode Island, at least on the basis of early decisions, deny privilege to pleadings. A plaintiff and defendant, in all jurisdictions, are held to be addressing themselves to the court, and therefore, they have privilege in their complaints and allegations. Many times, these pleadings contain sensational and even reckless charges since the parties want to "put their best foot forward." The tendency seems to be that many jurisdictions are coming around to the viewpoint that qualified privilege should be accorded to pleadings, but as in most all phases of law, this trend is advancing slowly.

In a jurisdiction where qualified privilege is denied or in doubt, a reporter may print that "John Jones today filed suit against Robert Smith for $25,000 damages for injuries Jones said he suffered in an automobile accident." He might go on to give the reported time and place of the accident. But if the complaint says "Smith was driving while drunk" or "was driving in a reckless and negligible manner" the paper which prints it, in absence of specific protection, should be prepared to prove it. And a paper seldom can do that.

If the defendant files a demurrer, and the court sustains or overrules it, the case is now a judicial proceeding and may be reported. Safety, then, comes when a judge acts in the case.

Juvenile Court

One of the innovations in our legal system in recent years has been the establishment of separate courts to deal with boys and girls. In small counties with only one judge and probably only one courtroom, the same man presides in juvenile court, but the procedure is vastly different from that of an ordinary criminal or civil trial.

In jurisdictions large enough to warrant a separate judge for juvenile court, he is chosen largely because of his friendliness and sympathy toward young people rather than for his ability in law. Society is concerned more with preventing a youth from blighting his whole life with one misstep rather than with meting out punishment.

Juvenile court sessions are usually more informal than other trials and may even be held in the judge's chambers. Many states, by law, as will be pointed out later, restrict the publication of names of offenders below a certain age—generally 16 years old. The press often is barred from juvenile court sessions or if permitted to be there, is circumscribed in its reporting. The custom is for the press to be permitted to publish nothing but the disposition of the case. If a paper obtains testimony given in a juvenile hearing and publishes it despite a statute or judicial decision to the contrary, it is open for a citation for contempt. Should the testimony be defamatory, it has no defense but truth.

Divorces

Publication of divorce proceedings is a moot question in many jurisdictions. Some states, by law or judicial interpretation, restrict the printing of charges filed in a divorce petition or the testimony given at the hearings. The awarding of a decree, however, becomes public property.

Many contested divorces are heard by special masters appointed by the court. A lawyer, sitting as a special master, has most of the prerogatives of a judge on the bench. He can maintain decorum through use of the contempt power and may summon witnesses by having the court issue subpoenas. If law or judicial decision bars reporters, the special master can prevent their attendance.

Testimony drawn from divorce witnesses, especially salacious statements, may later be impounded by the court along with details of property settlements and other material relating to the case. The clerk of the court, or any designated official, keeps this information under seal and it may not be examined without permission of the court. Only the attorneys or interested parties are likely to receive permission to examine these records.

In some states, the laws or decisions regulating divorce hearings, are so general as to lead to disputes in their interpretation. For example California has a law which seems to prevent publication of both pleadings and testimony. (7) Despite this law, the press seems to suffer no handicap in reporting divorce hearings of actresses who elect to receive their decree in California. A Superior Court judge in Los Angeles refused a request of the plaintiff that the hearing be closed to the press. (8).

Wills

In most states, wills become public property as soon as they are filed for probate. The next of kin or the family lawyer takes the will to the division of court variously known as orphan's, probate, or surrogate's court. A will usually names an executor whose duty is to see that provisions of the document are carried out. If the deceased left no will, the courts will appoint an administrator to settle the estate and see that it is divided according to the statutes governing such cases.

In large estates, or in estates in which heirs or creditors are disputing claims, the executor or administrator may file periodical reports with the court to show what he has done. The executor or administrator is discharged when the court accepts his final report.

These periodical or final reports also may be published. A few states, notably Colorado, restrict this information until admitted in open court. (9)

Other Court Proceedings

Besides ordinary criminal, civil, and juvenile trials, courts, as indicated earlier, hear equity suits, contests over wills, guardianship cases, and a variety of other legal actions.

Much of the time of the courts also is taken up with arguments, motions, and other activities. Sometimes these actions are more newsworthy than an actual trial.

One murder trial produced stories that rated only inside pages. But after the defendant was convicted, counsel charged that one juror, when he received a letter to report for duty, had expressed publicly his pleasure because he wanted a chance to hang that fellow. The hearing on this charge made front page news.

Most arguments and motions are made in open court. The only people present, however, may be the judge and the lawyers. But as far as the press is concerned, it is a hearing and may be reported with qualified privilege. The judge who in his chambers signs a decree or grants a motion is engaged in a "legal proceeding." Counsel for a man convicted of murder or other felony may visit a judge at his home or his vacation resort and obtain a writ staying execution or taking jurisdiction in the case. No matter where the judge is at the time, his action is effective and the press can report it.

The lawyer can hope for such a writ or stay only if he can show sufficient reasons. Usually this reason will consist of some new evidence that just came to the lawyer's attention. It may be evidence that another person committed the crime charged against his client.

If the judge releases details from the petition, they, too, may be printed. In rare situations the petition might be of only a general nature, but later the attorney may tell a reporter that evidence shows another person committed the crime. Should the paper print this fact along with the person's name, all of which it obtained from the attorney, it could not claim privilege since this information was not in the petition submitted to the judge. Privilege is possessed only by the material upon which the judge has acted.

Court Records

Most states by law have designated court records as public. These statutes apply to completed records such as judgments and decrees handed down, and the verdicts in trials. The docket on which is listed coming trials also is public.

The transcript and record of a case received by a federal appellate court for review are considered public. Most state jurisdictions do not go this far, but generally the briefs filed by counsel in an appeal to a higher state court may be printed. From the petition filed with the original court in support of a motion for a new trial and from subsequent briefs filed with the state appellate court, a reporter as a rule obtains all the "news" of the proceedings.

For Further Reading

For the classification of federal judiciary records as public, see:
United States Code Annotated, Title 28, 16:556.

COURT DECISIONS

For decisions in cases where the press exceeded its privilege, see:
Evening News v. Bowie, 141 A. 416.
Conroy v. Pittsburgh *Times,* 21 A. 154.

For privilege in a justice of the peace court, see:
Conner v. Standard Publishing Co., 67 N.E. 596.
McBee v. Fulton, 47 Md. 403.
Flues v. New Nonpareil Co., 135 N.W. 1083.

For exceeding privilege in a justice court, see:
Bathrick v. Detroit Post and Tribune Co., 16 N.W. 172.

For privilege when only a warrant has been issued by a justice and a trial not yet held, see:
Beiser v. Scripps McRae Publishing Co., 68 S.W. 457.

CHAPTER X

"Limits of Criticism – Public Officials and Performances"

The Right to Comment and Criticize

Foreign writers and lecturers, after visiting the United States, have never ceased to marvel at what they term the "outspokenness" of Americans. In all age, income, and educational levels, Americans show little hesitancy in expressing their views, comments, and opinions.

While the athletic board of a midwestern university was seeking a new football coach, one wag suggested that it hire the man who had sat back of him all season.

"He not only knew more than the coach, but he made sure everybody around him realized it," this wag wrote.

Some writers have called America a "land of gripers and complainers," but probably a more exact description is "a country of individual argufiers." Every citizen seems to know more about managing the country than either the President or Congress, and every sports fan considers himself more adept than the team manager or coach. Sophomores generally consider themselves more fitted to operate the university than the deans and president, and they often let the officials know about it in the college paper.

Whatever may be the merits of this American trait, freedom of the press would be a misnomer if newspapermen and the public were not permitted to express their views. News and information alone are not enough to permit a democratic government to function. It would be an anomaly to insist that although people choose their own officials, they must abide in silence by any actions or decisions of those officials.

Robert M. LaFollette, Sr., frequently expressed this concept in his oft-repeated "slogan" that "the will of the people shall be the law of the land." Courts, in many decisions, have recognized this right of the people to express their opinions.

Justice Learned Hand summed it up this way:

"... right conclusions are more likely to be gathered out of a multitude of tongues, than through a kind of authoritative selection. To many, this is, and always will be, folly; but we have staked upon it our all." (1)

The Supreme Court, speaking through Justice Black, has said: "... that (First) amendment rests on the assumption that the widest possible dissemination of information from diverse and antagonistic sources is essential to the welfare of the public, that a free press is a condition of a free society." (2)

Many have held it to be not only the right but also the duty of the press to comment and criticize. Justice Frankfurter once held:

"... The press does have the right, which is its professional function, to criticize and to advocate. The whole gamut of public affairs is the domain for fearless and critical comment." (3)

Earlier, the Supreme Court of Kansas, not only expressed the same view but put its opinion into effect by reversing a $1,700 libel verdict obtained against a Manhattan, Kansas, newspaper by a former mayor of that city. The former mayor sued for a story printed during his campaign for street and safety commissioner. Said the Kansas Supreme Court:

"In connection with the coming municipal election, it is the right, if not the duty, (of the paper) to call to the attention of citizens, facts which he (the editor) honestly believed to be true, together with such comment as is reasonably connected therewith, for the purpose of enabling the voters to vote more intelligently.

"And if done in good faith, the publication is privileged even though some of the statements may be untrue or derogatory to the character of the candidate." (4)

From street commissioner to President or Chief Justice of the United States, no American public official is presumed to be exempt from the withering rays of criticism. Those holding no office but who, nevertheless, come to public attention through works or deeds must expect their activities to be scrutinized by their fellow-men.

The right to comment and criticize, like all rights of self-expression, must be construed as neither absolute nor as unbridled license. As Justice Frankfurter has said:

> "But the public function (of criticizing and advocating) which belongs to the press makes it an obligation of honor to exercise this function only with the fullest sense of responsibility. Without such a lively sense of responsibility a free press may readily become a powerful instrument of injustice." (5)

Through a sense of fair play and the necessity of maintaining order in society, Americans either have drawn up, or by implicit understanding, have adopted "rules" to govern this right to speak one's mind about the actions or works of another. The purpose of this chapter is to examine those "rules."

Criticizing Public Officials

The man (or woman) who accepts a public job through appointment or election, finds himself living in a "goldfish" bowl. The law presumes no official, not even the robed judge on the bench, is infallible. The official is permitted as many errors in judgment as the voters will tolerate.

If there is one general rule governing criticism of all officials, that rule is: *the comment must assume the mistake or action was prompted only by an error in judgment or by the official's own conception of how he should have performed that particular act. The criticism must not charge or imply that the action was prompted by dishonesty on the part of the official unless the one who says so is prepared to prove his assertion.*

The courts, too, draw a sharp distinction between opinions and facts although, unfortunately, they have never been able to define the terms with preciseness. Probably the simplest test is: will the reader know that the statement is the opinion or comment of the writer or will he conclude, from the wording, that a fact has been stated? Opinions usually may be defended as fair comment on a matter of public interest; a fact, in most jurisdictions, must stand or fall on the simple test as to whether it is true or false.

If the city council decides to re-locate a street, my paper may accuse members of lack of vision, short-sightedness, misinterpretation of the wishes of the people, or of errors in judgment or planning.

My paper could print:

"In the face of a state survey showing that within three years Main Street will be the principal arterial highway of the city, council last night voted to spend all this year's repair money on improving Second Street. This short-sighted policy of council will cost taxpayers a goodly sum when heavy traffic starts rolling along Main Street."

At the most, council members are accused of lack of vision or errors in judgment. If my paper says, or implies, that the decision was prompted by "little gifts" to each member from the Second Street Improvement Association, the story is libelous.

If county commissioners decide to paint the courthouse white, and my paper believes the color should have been brown, it may say so. But it cannot intimate the vote was prompted by the fact that one of the commissioners (or all of them) had relatives who sell only white paint.

If the chief of police begins a drive against punch boards, my paper can be for or against the anti-gambling crusade. But it cannot say the chief acted in a fit of temper because he failed to win a prize on a board.

Although more leeway is granted by law to criticism of public officials than against those who hold no office, only under a few circumstances can the private life of the official be brought into the story. Even then those facts about his private life had better be true if the paper wishes to avoid trouble.

If the wife of the mayor divorces him, the decree becomes a public record and may be printed. But my paper cannot comment: "The mayor sits at City Hall trying to operate the municipal government and deal with citizens when he cannot even manage his own home."

If the mayor daily fines residents who fail to obtain licenses for their dogs, it is of public interest to know that his own pet roams the streets without a tag. But it is the mayor's private concern whether he permits his dog to romp in the house or keeps him tied on the back porch.

When a man becomes a candidate for a public office, the citizens should have all information necessary to assay his qualifications for that job. If true, it is pertinent for a paper to let readers know the candidate for city treasurer was twice convicted on embezzlement charges. A conviction on reckless driving charges, however, has nothing to do with his qualification for treasurer.

A candidate for liquor law enforcement officer has little ground for complaint if voters are told he was convicted a number of times on charges of drunkenness. But if a candidate for sheriff likes to "take a nip" now and then, it's his own business unless he is campaigning in a dry county.

The *mores* of the community may be broken by a school teacher who spends some of his time in a tavern, but that is not a crime. The school board, however, can take cognizance of the teacher's habits when his contract comes up for renewal. But a paper would have no license for saying the teacher lost his job for intemperance.

The problem of how much latitude to permit in the criticism of public officials, including candidates for office, finds the several states sharply divided into what is popularly known as the "majority and minority schools." The majority school, in general, holds that comment and criticism of a public official is no different from remarks against an individual. If the defamatory statement is false, the official (or candidate) has cause for action.

The late Chief Justice Taft once summed up the majority view: ". . . if privilege is to extend to cases like that at bar, then a man who offers himself as a candidate must submit uncomplainingly to the loss of his reputation . . . with every member of the public, whenever an untrue charge of disgraceful conduct is made against him, if only his accuser honestly believes the charge upon reasonable ground. We think that not only is such a sacrifice not required of everyone who consents to become a candidate for office, but that to sanction such a doctrine would do the public more harm than good . . . the danger that honorable and worthy man may be driven from politics and public service by allowing too great latitude in attacks upon their character outweighs any benefit that might occasionally accrue to the public from charges of corruption that are true in fact, but are incapable of legal proof." (6)

Another federal court, in deciding a similar case, has made plain just what judges in the majority jurisdictions regard as beyond the bounds of permissible criticism.

". . . the distinction must be drawn between comment and criticism, and untrue charges of facts constituting a crime or disgraceful conduct. It is one thing to pass severe criticism upon, or to draw even extreme inferences from acknowledged facts, or to indulge in intemperate denunciation, even though bitter, and quite another thing to assert existence of particular acts of criminality or of shameful misconduct upon the candidate's part." (7)

The majority school, however, does not insist that newspapers turn out "poker face" comment or editorials. As a New York court has said:

"Mere exaggeration, slight irony or wit, or all those delightful touches of style which go to make an article readable, do not push beyond the limitations of fair comment. Facts do not cease to be facts because they are mixed with the fair and expectant comment of the story teller who adds to the recital a little touch by his piquant pen." (8)

Maine courts, apparently, have extended the majority viewpoint to its widest latitude. They have held:

". . . any voter or other person having an interest in the election may fully and freely comment and criticize his (the candidate's) talents and qualifications mentally and physically, for the office he seeks . . . . Even his faults and vices, insofar as they necessarily affect his fitness for the office, may be investigated and commented upon. His private character, however, is only put at issue so far as his qualifications and fitness for office may be affected by it." (9)

The majority viewpoint, then, can be summed up as requiring: (1) the facts be true, and (2) references to the candidate's private life, true or false, must have a direct bearing on his fitness for the office he seeks.

Jurisdictions generally classified as being in the majority school are: Alabama, Arizona, Delaware, the Federal jurisdiction, Florida, Georgia, Illinois, Kentucky, Louisiana, Maine, Maryland, Massachusetts, Michigan, Mississippi, Missouri, Nebraska, New Jersey, New York, North Dakota, Ohio, Oklahoma, Oregon, Rhode Island, South Carolina, Tennessee, Texas, Virginia, Washington, West Virginia, and Wisconsin.

The minority school believes that the newspaper should have privilege for comments based on probable cause although they may not be true. Privilege, however, is destroyed if the paper's motive is other than a desire to enlighten the electorate.

Newspapers in the jurisdictions which permit such privilege should have a reasonable belief that the charges may be true. The press owes that responsibility to its readers despite any legal protection it may enjoy for untrue statements.

The minority school feels that often the newspaper comes into possession of facts which it believes are true but which it cannot substantiate by legal proof. These facts may be of vital public concern, but the community never would learn about them if fear of libel prevented their publication. This is true especially of reports that circulate during election campaigns.

A California court has expressed it this way:

"Under proper circumstances the interest and necessities of society become paramount to the welfare or reputation of a private individual, and the occasion and circumstances may for the public good absolve one from punishment for such communications even though they be false." (10)

Another California court, in finding for the newspaper in a libel suit growing out of a cartoon depicting a police chief said:

"If the publisher of a newspaper honestly believes that a public officer has committed a crime of a nature which would indicate that he is unfit for the office he holds, we think he is not liable for damages under the code (California Civil Code), in a civil libel action, when, without malice, and so believing, he publishes a statement to that effect to the community served by the officer." (11)

States grouped with the minority school are: California, Georgia, Iowa, Kansas, Minnesota, New Hampshire, North Carolina, Pennsylvania, South Dakota, Utah, and Vermont.

Recent changes in Georgia press laws make it doubtful whether that state should continue under the minority group or be returned to the majority school. Therefore, pending a court decision, it is listed with both groups.

In the minority jurisdictions, then, the requirements to establish privilege are:

(1) There should be reasonable evidence for assuming the charges are true, (2) publication must not be prompted by spite or a mere desire to "smear" a candidate or official, (3) the story should be such that, if it were true, it would be fair comment on a public matter and hence entitled to privilege.

A summary of some decisions will show how the two schools operate. In an Eastern state, a nominee withdrew a few days before election, leaving his party without a candidate for that office. The state chairman of his party said the sudden withdrawal had the "earmarks of another Jones affair." Many reporters failed to look up the "Jones affair" in their files before printing the chairman's statement.

About 25 years before, another nominee of the same party also had retired from the race suddenly. Later, it was proved he quit after the candidate of the other party had promised him a certain job if he withdrew. Comparing the new case with the "Jones Affair," implied that the candidate this year had "made a deal" with the opposition. Such an action is repugnant to the American mind and in the majority states, to accuse a man of "selling out" is libelous. Action, however, was started against only one paper which settled out of court. Had the same story been printed in a state adhering to the minority rule, the paper could have defended it.

Arizona courts held libelous a story falsely imputing a criminal offense to a public official. (12) An Oregon paper which called a political leader a "double crosser" also lost a libel action. (13)   A Michigan court, in deciding for the plaintiff in a libel suit, held: ". . . this privilege (to comment or discuss public questions) is limited, and does not extend to protect against false statements, unjust inferences, or imputations of unworthy motives." (14)

On the minority side, a charge in a newspaper that a city treasurer, then seeking re-election, had failed to account for some city funds and a hint that embezzlement was involved was held not libelous although later the accusations were proved false. (15) A North Carolina paper won a suit based on its story, mostly false, that a school board chairman was misusing school funds. (16)

Drunkenness is a difficult charge to prove legally.   Even so-called experts on the subject fail to agree since the amount of liquor that makes one man intoxicated may only "mellow" another.   A Pennsylvania paper, however, which charged a police chief with being drunk while on duty, won a libel suit in which the court said it was not liable "if there was probable cause for their comments and no proof of express malice, even though the statements are not strictly true in all respects." (17)   Another Pennsylvania case involving drunkenness of an officer was dropped before going to trial.   The story said the chief had been shot in a taproom brawl.   He vigorously denied it and demanded a correction.   The next day the paper had a head: "Chief not shot, but half shot."

Although public officials are fair game for comment and criticism, the newspaper must not regard them as "sitting ducks." Fair play and a sense of responsibility must guide the editor.

Persons in Public Life

Under the American political system, a number of men and women exercise power without holding office.   Political bosses, for example, may never go before the voters, yet their influence may sway elections.

Other men and women are quasi-public figures and almost like "officials without portfolio."   A man who heads the principal industry in a city, a woman active in club or civic affairs, the non-paid chairman of the Community Chest, and others, all may exercise considerable influence in public affairs without holding office or being formally affiliated with a political party.

In a third class of these public figures are women such as Mrs. Eleanor Roosevelt or men such as former President Herbert Hoover. Or Bernard Baruch, for years considered the "elder statesman" adviser to administrations of both major parties. Below them, on regional, state, and community levels, are many similar men and women.

An interesting legal problem is how do these men and women fit into either majority or minority rules governing criticism of their actions and talks? The trend is for the courts to regard these men and women as having a quasi-public character. But this tendency is not yet so general nor so pronounced as to warrant a paper printing defamatory statements about them. Their actions, however, if not their motives, can be criticized freely.

If a man in public affairs, advocates spending more money to help post-war Europe, my paper can freely comment adversely on the proposal. But I could hardly defend, except on ground of truth, a statement that he favors more aid for Europe solely because he expects his company to "unload" on the government for delivery to Europe some products it cannot sell in the domestic market. I can mention that he suggests the United States should send more soap to Europe and that he heads a soap manufacturing company. But I must not pry too deeply into the probable motives for his suggestion.

A man who proposes that the community install parking meters must expect his suggestion to be criticized. My paper, however, must not infer that he is interested only because he holds, or hopes to obtain, a franchise to sell meters.

A club woman who by speeches and letters to the editor campaigns to have a new school building located in a certain section of the city should not be surprised if some citizens or the newspaper disagree with her and tell her so. Such comment should not carry the implication that her principal motive stems from her ownership of the only suitable tract of land in that section. The story could mention, however, that she owns a desirable plot in that area, and school directors could be interviewed to see if she had made overtures to sell it. If so, these facts could be reported but without any inferences. After

all, she may be a public-spirited woman and may sell the plot
below its real value.

The distinction that must be made between facts and conclusions may be illustrated roughly by an incident during World
War II. After the Allies broke out of the Normandy beachhead
and General Patton started his famous sweep, one dispatch
said he was heading for Paris. The censor ordered this sentence killed. But he permitted a revision which merely mentioned the General's last reported location and said simply:
"180 miles to the east lies Paris."

Most of the recent court decisions on these quasi-public
figures concern principally men and women holding political
party offices or closely allied with political organizations. As
one court said:

> "The interest which every citizen has in good government
> requires that the right be not unduly curtailed to express his
> opinions of public officers and political leaders, to seek and
> convey information concerning their plans and purposes and
> to freely criticize proposed methods and measures." (18)

The Supreme Court of Missouri, however, held there was
privilege in a story which reported that a minister had lost his
pastorate because of a girl who "couldn't resist his eyes." In
reversing a $25,000 verdict won by the minister against a St.
Louis paper, the Supreme Court said:

> "Everyone who assumes the responsibility of leadership,
> either in politics, in religion, or in thoughts, puts in issue to
> some extent his ability and his sincerity. Furthermore, these
> qualities thus become of importance and interest to all other
> citizens and any newspaper has a right to fairly and reason-
> ably discuss them." (19)

A simple rule for the newspaper in handling criticism of
public figures who hold no office, is to confine itself to commenting only on their suggestions or proposals. There should be
no excursions into their private lives nor into their motives although, as will be pointed out later, it is permissible to review
their technical or other qualifications to permit an evaluation
of their suggestions.

Plays, Books, Movies, Concerts, and Public Performances

When an individual offers himself or his works in a public performance, the phrase "in the limelight" takes on legal meaning. Regardless of whether the offering is a poem the individual reads before the Parent-Teachers Association, a motion picture in which he stars, a book, a painting, or a new type of electric outdoor sign, the public has the right of freely criticizing and commenting.

A manufacturer who brings out a new product also must take his chances with a public whose tastes and standards at times can be fickle. The public may not like the new soap with the secret cleansing ingredient nor the cigarette made by a new mysterious process.

For those who "click" with their offerings, the financial or self-satisfaction rewards may be great; for those who find the public apathetic or hostile the results may be only heartaches and embarrassment. But in all cases, the author or creator loses his right to anonymity.

It's a tradition of the theatrical world that 12 New York critics can "make or break" any play. Only a few plays have gone on to successful runs after this unofficial "jury" has rendered unfavorable verdicts. A few other plays which have won favor at the hands of these critics have proved financial failures.

But so influential is the power of these critics that many producers have closed their shows within a few performances after press notices were unfavorable. They did not want to risk possible further losses. Movies have exaggerated only slightly the scenes in which they show producers and actors scrambling for the first editions of New York morning papers to read the verdict of these critics.

Even the daughter of the President of the United States learned that social position does not save a performer from the caustic criticism by professional critics. One critic advised her to hurry and enjoy her singing career while her father still was in the White House, and another suggested she get married and confine her vocal talents to lullabies.

Numerous court decisions have established a general rule for comments on public performances: *any criticism, no matter how caustic or bitter, is permitted provided no reference is made to the private life of the performer.*

A concert artist may come to my city with an international reputation in music circles. The 5,000 people in the concert hall may stand and applaud vigorously and call him back for half a dozen or more encores. Yet, I may with legal safety say it was a miserable performance, that his voice seemed to break on high notes, and that he and his accompanist at times went their separate ways. The public, if it disagrees with my comments, may stop buying my paper or write nasty letters to me, or the publisher may fire me on the ground I am incompetent, but the artist has no legal recourse. Legally, he still is helpless if my criticism should result in poor attendance at his concerts in other cities, or even cancellations.

But I cannot say his miserable performance was due to his carousing the night before. Nor may I say that on the stage he has a "sweet personality" but at home has the manners of a beast. His private life is no part of the performance and must not be mentioned.

This book will be reviewed and criticized by others in the field. Their verdict I must accept but, if they say it is filled with errors and fallacious reasoning because the author got all his legal knowledge from comic strips or motion pictures of court scenes, I do not have to sit in silence.

I may even call any literary work just plain gibberish. But I cannot say or imply that the author stole his material from others. I must respect both the author's personal life and his professional integrity.

A college paper once referred to the lectures of a certain professor as being so dry the classroom had to be sprinkled to keep down the dust. The editorial may have been reflected later in the writer's grades, but not in any courtroom. The professor, however, would have had a case if the editorial suggested that all his ideas were obtained from "picking the brains of others."

As a sports writer, or just a fan, I can say with impunity that the manager made a bone-headed decision when he instructed the batter to bunt instead of permitting him to take a full swing at the ball. But I cannot imply that the manager was "bought" by the rival team nor that he was trying to lose the game because he was angry at the "front office." *Criticism must never imply unethical, improper, or illegal conduct.*

Probably no more harsh criticism of a performance ever has been written than that by an Iowa newspaperman who reviewed the act of the once famous Cherry sisters. He called one of the sisters an "old jade," another a "frisky filly of 40," and the third "a capering monstrosity." He further described them as "spavined, stringhalt," and with "legs and calves as classic in their outlines as the curves of a broom handle."

A paper which reprinted this review was sued, but a court held the comments were not libelous. (20) In its reasoning, the court said: "Fitting strictures, sarcasm, or ridicule, even, may be used, if based on facts, without liability, in the absence of malice or wicked purpose." (21)

Another court held it is not libelous to say a cartoonist ". . . evidently has run out of ideas . . . and is not willing to attempt something new." (22)

A high school football coach lost a suit against a paper which said his team "is in dire need of a good drill in the rudiments of the game," that it had been furnished a "paucity of plays," and that plays and formations used were "antiques." (23) Some alumni or townspeople may have concluded from the article that the coach was incompetent but the editorial cannot be construed as making this charge.

Personal references are permitted if they are connected with the performance or if these comments are made merely incidental to the review. If a lecturer bills himself as "the man who has built more engineering marvels than anyone else in the world," I can point out, if true, that the only construction projects of his that are on record are a bridge across a Montana country creek and a silo on an Iowa farm. It is not libelous to tell the reader that the psychologist who will speak tonight on "Ten Ways to Rear a Child" is a bachelor.

It was not libelous when some critics said Margaret Truman's voice showed she was not ready for the concert stage, nor is it libelous when a sports writer says a player isn't of major league caliber. The qualifications of a public performer are always open to examination.

The author of a non-fiction book should tell, or at least indicate, the sources of his material. Should he fail to do so, a reviewer, if he knows, may pass along this information in order that the reader may better judge the merits of the book. If my book is "The Inside Story of Life in Tibet" the reviewer may note that I have never been in that country. If my book was based on interviews with people who have visited Tibet, I should have indicated it.

A court, however, held it to be libelous to say, among other things, that a farm lecturer did such a poor job on his own farm that "if everyone farmed as he did, there would be no need to talk about curtailing production because there'd be no production to curtail." Further on, the writer implied that the speaker fitted into the political slogan that "if Mendota (the state mental hospital) doesn't get 'em, Madison (the state government) must." (24)

Sometimes a performer's personal life may result in public indignation to such an extent that major criticism is directed against him and not against his work. Sections of the press, pulpit, and public condemned the showing of a film starring Ingrid Bergman after she bore a child to her Italian film director. Those who believed her film should not be exhibited because of this incident could freely express such opinions because their comments were based on a provable fact. But if she merely had been seen in company with the director, a paper would have had no liberty to accuse her of any transgressions nor campaign to have her pictures barred from exhibition. The sexes mingle freely these days and just because a married woman is seen in public with another man is no justification for intimating her conduct is improper.

Singer Paul Robeson aroused much wrath for his outspoken friendship for Russia. My paper was free to advocate he be barred from the concert stage of my home city. The test is: Has the artist conducted himself in a manner repugnant to the mores of the community? It would be an anomaly to contend that my paper cannot criticize a local club's action in engaging Public Enemy No. 1 to lecture, or the action of a local group in bringing in an advocate of "free love" to talk to high school boys and girls. A public figure is expected to show good morals and be law abiding.

Criticism of products is fraught with the added danger of possibly libeling the manufacturer or seller personally. The company which brings to the market a new breakfast food cannot expect everyone will like its taste, the color of the package in which it is wrapped, or the methods by which it promotes sales.

A manufacturer once marketed penny candy by using different colors for the center piece. A particular color entitled the one who got it to a certain prize, usually more candy free. Some newspapers attacked the selling method on the ground it encouraged children to "gamble." That was a matter of opinion and could be expressed.

But to say that the candy itself was harmful to children or that the manufacturer was "preying" on youth, would have been libelous. I may not like the taste of that new breakfast food, but I cannot say that it is injurious to health. If I believe it is harmful, I might ask the government, under the authority of the Pure Food and Drug Act to investigate and then publish the findings.

In the past few years, several drug manufacturers have used paid advertisements to notify the public that a harmful ingredient was accidentally placed in some of their products and that packages bearing a certain number should be destroyed or returned to the seller for a refund. My paper editorially might suggest the firm be more careful but it could not infer that all the company's products were harmful and should be boycotted by the public.

Public Institutions

An institution, supported entirely or partly by public funds, or an organization or corporation seeking public patronage, is open to criticism just the same as an individual.

My paper editorially may declare the curricula of the local school system are not fitting the pupils for real life situations, that the bus line fails to provide accommodations for the rush hours, that train service is inadequate, that the state university emphasizes theory and neglects the practical, or spends too much money on athletics and not enough on academic equipment, that the Community Chest is wrong in the method by which it allocates funds to its various agencies, that local banks are handicapping merchants and customers by closing on Saturdays, and that the local hospital should have added more beds instead of building a new nurses' home.

A paper, carrying on a campaign against a traction company, declared it proposed to abandon several lines on parallel streets just to avoid paying its share of repaving those streets.   It charged, furthermore, that the company hoped the money it saved could now be paid out as dividends to stockholders. The traction lawyer threatened the paper but did not follow up with any action.   Apparently he had looked into court decisions on questions of fair comment.

Privilege extends if such criticisms are published as comments and not as statements of actual fact and are printed without malice.

Criticism, then, of public offerings— from art to institutions and commercial products—is accorded privilege only if it is fair and made without spite or a desire to vent a personal grudge. It should be confined to the performance only and should not (except under circumstances already noted) delve into the personal life of the performer.

Legally, the word "fair" is construed broadly. As a rule, the courts permit a reviewer his opinion no matter how extreme and unreasonable it may be as compared with the beliefs of others. To the courts, "fair" means simply that the reviewer had facts upon which to base his judgment.

Since spite or personal feelings (legally known as malice in fact) is difficult to prove, the reviewer, in effect, has more legal protection in the publication of criticism than in the printing of any other material that goes into a newspaper or magazine. A reviewer who runs afoul of the law is usually one who has a "chip on his shoulder" and goes out looking for trouble. Even then he may be forced to meet it more than halfway.

For Further Reading

Cooley, Thomas M., *A Treatise on the Law of Torts,* (2d. ed.), Chicago; University of Chicago Press, 1930, p. 246.

—"Fair Comment," in Washington University Law Quarterly, February, 1942.

—"False Imputation of Authorship," in 72 *United States Law Review,* September, 1938.

Ford, James L. C., "Fair Comment in Literary Criticism," *Notre Dame Lawyer,* March, 1939.

Mendez, Manuel J., "Libel of Public Executive Officers," *George Washington Law Review,* June, 1942.

Outland, Ethel R., *The "Effingham" Libels on Cooper,* Madison; the University of Wisconsin Press, 1929.

Smith, Jeremiah, "Disparagement of Property," 13 *Columbia Law Review,* January-February, 1913.

COURT DECISIONS
(Other than those cited in the text)

Permitting wide lattitude of criticism of public officials:

Jones v. Express Publishing Co., 87 Cal. App. 246.

McIntosh v. Williams, 160 Ga. 461.

Coleman v. MacLennan, 78 Kan. 711.

Sternburgh v. Anderson, 250 Mich. 126.

Williams v. Standard-Examiner Co., 27 P. (2d.) 1.

Davis v. Ferguson, 246 Ill. App. 318 (publication other than a newspaper or periodical).

See also *Editor and Publisher,* January 7, 1950, for a discussion of comment on public characters.

Limiting criticism of public officials:

McKillip v. Grays Harbor Publishing Co., 100 Wash. 657 (paid political advertisement in a newspaper).

Commercial Tribune Publishing Co. v. Haines, 228 Ky. 483.

Sweeney v. Baker, 13 W. Va. 158.

Burt v. Advertiser Newspaper Co., 154 Mass. 238.

Langer v. *Courier News,* 46 N. Dak. 430.

Oklahoma Publishing Co. v. Kendall, 96 Okla. 194.

Limiting criticism of political figures other than public officials:

Field v. Magee, 122 Mich. 556.

Sanford v. Rowley, 93 Mich. 119.

Cook v. Globe Printing Co., 227 Mo. 471.

Edwards v. San Jose Printing Co., 99 Cal. 431.

Barr v. Moore, 87 Pa. 385.

Favoring criticism of political figures other than public officials:

Duffy v. New York *Evening Post,* 109 N. Y. App. 161.

Barr v. Providence Telegram Publishing Co., 27 R. I. 101.

Sullivan v. Illinois Publishing and Printing Co., 186 Ill. App. 268.

Criticism of public performances:

Cleveland Leader Printing Co. v. Nethersole, 84 Ohio 118.

Dowling v. Livingstone, 66 N.W. 225.

Dooling v. Budget Publishing Co., 10 N.E. 809.

Battersby v. Collier, 54 N.Y.S. 363.

CHAPTER XI

"Limits of Criticism – The Courts"

Of all public officials, the one who is criticized least is probably the judge. Reporters who freely turn out caustic comments about mayors, county commissioners, governors, members of Congress – and even the President – usually experience sudden chills at the suggestion that a court decision be criticized because the opinion seems contrary to the public will.

The reluctance of newspapers to indulge in legitimate criticism of the courts stems from a number of reasons. Many veteran reporters hold the judge in as much awe as does the cub. Part of this fear has a good basis because the judge is unlike other public officials. Their chief remedy against unwarranted criticism is a suit in libel. A judge has the additional power to cite for contempt of court and this prerogative has been used for good and bad down through the years.

Newspapers are reluctant to criticize the courts, also, because many fail to grasp the legitimate function of the judicial system. It is simply one branch of government and it cannot claim special privileges except those necessary for carrying out its work. Every branch of government is subject to the will of the people despite any talk among the judiciary of inherent rights, privileges, and power. A democratic society cannot tolerate any branch of government that presumes to have power independent of the fountainhead of all authority—the people themselves. Free people do not create Frankensteins to destroy them or to thwart their will.

The Constitution of the United States sets up only one tribunal—the Supreme Court, and even for it, Congress prescribes the number of justices, their salaries and various regu-

latory procedures.   All other federal courts are the direct creation of Congress which may add to or subtract from them as it
pleases.   All federal judges—from district to Supreme Court—
are appointed by the President but must be confirmed by the
Senate.   Thus Congress retains a negative power over appointment and through impeachment it may remove a jurist.   Even
the power of the Supreme Court to annul an act of Congress
is more an historical growth than constitutional permission.

State courts follow the same general pattern although most
state judges are elected for specified terms instead of the life
tenure given to federal jurists.   The governor usually has the
power to fill vacancies only until the next general election.
Since most state judges are elected, the legislature has no negative power through confirmation in the filling of seats on the
bench.   But the legislature controls the creation of new courts,
salaries, many procedures, and also may impeach.

The nature of its work takes the court out of the usual "rough
and tumble" of interplay between officials and people that other
branches of government experience.   A judicial system cannot
function without more stability than that enjoyed by the legislature and the executive.   Judges seldom feel the wrath of the
voters as much as members of the legislature or the executive
branch.   For one thing, most people have a magical conception
of the legal system.   For another reason, terms of judges are
usually longer than those for other officials in order to remove
them from political influence.

But, nevertheless, a judge is no more immune from criticism
than the most humble courthouse or city hall clerk.   The robe
the judge wears enhances the dignity and prestige of the court;
it does not confer upon the wearer any miraculous powers of
infallibility or omnipotence.   As Justice Holmes has said: ". . .
courts are subject to the same criticism as other people . . ." (1)

The newspaper owes to the court perhaps more respect than
it does to other branches of government because the courts are
not concerned with "day-to-day" policy making.   Courts are
more "preservers" of liberties than "propounders" of them.

But a newspaper owes a duty to its community not to remain silent if it believes a court has misused its power or has

departed from a reasonable concept of justice. It need not keep silent, either, if it differs from the court in the interpretation of some basic freedom or right.

In March, 1950, a murder trial in Iowa City, Iowa, attracted nation-wide attention. On the opening day, the judge issued instructions for the guidance of reporters and photographers. As part of the same statement, the jurist expounded at length on the philosophy of the rights and responsibility of the press and expressed the opinion society would be served better if this particular case were not reported. (2)

Portions of his statement aroused considerable resentment among certain sections of the press, and at least a few newspapers wanted to answer the judge. They were restrained by fear of a contempt citation since a trial was in progress.

It was proper for the judge to lay down rules for the press, radio, and photographers since he was charged with seeing that the defendant received a fair and impartial trial. And reporters had to abide by his instructions or face a contempt charge.

But when the judge used his podium to expound his philosophy of the press in modern society, he left himself open for any comments a newspaper wished to make. That part of his statement was merely the expression of a private citizen. And he who speaks his opinion must expect that others may differ with him.

As a matter of fact, the press could have commented temperately on the rules the judge laid down, but it could not have started agitation for their modification. For a judge to assume that his lecture on the press and society could not be commented upon would be equivalent to a notice that he believed the judiciary is above criticism. All the evidence and decisions of American courts are against that premise.

The public acts of a judge are the same as those of any official. A newspaper once was cited for contempt for saying it believed an administrator the court appointed for an estate was not qualified for the job. The judge, holding the editorial was a reflection on the integrity of the court, cited the paper for contempt. An appellate court overruled him with a strong reprimand and suggested his only possible remedy was a suit in libel. The newspaper would have been in contempt if it had suggested the appointment was dictated by motives other than the court's good judgment. There is no more room for a bully on the bench than in any other department of government.

A judge who sentences a man to penitentiary for stealing a loaf of bread and then puts on probation the banker whose $100,000 defalcations wrecked his institution, has no justifiable complaint if a newspaper thinks the decisions are "out of line." In fairness, the newspaper should seek out the reasons for the sentences. The bread stealer may have had a long criminal record despite many opportunities to reform. The banker's crime may have been more from loose bookkeeping or poor judgment than of criminal intent. Had the paper suggested, however, the banker was put on probation because the judge had received numerous loans from that bank, a contempt action may have followed.

During prohibition, a county judge threatened with contempt a newspaper which dared print a state police report that thieves had made off with some "prizes" from his liquor cellar. The newspaper replied by printing in an open letter to the judge the text of the prohibition amendment and the Volstead act. Public opinion did the rest, and the judge wisely decided not to run for a new term.

An eastern newspaper incurred judicial wrath by listing how many receiverships, with lucrative fees, went to relatives of the judge. Here was a matter of great concern to the public. To each judicial threat the newspaper stood its ground. A few years later the judge resigned just as impeachment proceedings were getting underway. It was a newspaper, too, that started a federal circuit court of appeals judge on his way to prison for dispensing "cash register" justice.

The public relies chiefly on the press for its appraisal of how its judicial system is working. No judge, not even one still steeped deeply in the ancient traditions of the old Star Chamber or early English courts, would deny the public the right of making that assay. The courts cannot conduct trials as one judge did during territorial days in the Southwest by refusing to permit defense counsel to present his case on the ground "it would just confuse the jury."

Although criticism of the courts is governed by the same general rules which apply to all public officials, the peculiar nature of the judiciary imposes several additional restraints. In general, these rules apply:

1. Criticism must not impair the dignity of the court by holding up either judge or court to ridicule or scorn because the injury, then, in all likelihood would be suffered not by an individual but by the legal system as a whole. Intemperate stories seldom correct any condition but usually add to the grievance.

The editor of the Cleveland *Press* and three staff members were fined for contempt after they had slipped through the court a faked divorce petition. The purpose, the *Press* said, was to reveal the "slipshod operations of an overburdened divorce court." (3)

The divorce petition was filed on behalf of a make-up editor and his wife who permitted use of their names. The court reporter for the *Press* prepared a journal entry and an official court decree and placed them among other papers awaiting the judge's signature. When the court signed it, the *Press* published the story of what had happened. The Cleveland Bar Association called it a fraud on the court and contempt citations were issued.

Before the contempt proceedings were heard, the court refused to vacate the faked divorce decree and the make-up editor and his wife were remarried. Later, the court annulled the decree.

In court, the editor of the *Press* disclaimed any intention of bringing the court into disrepute but admitted he had used improper methods to bring about the reforms it favored. The day after the fines were imposed, the *Press* announced it was continuing its campaign against "assembly line justice." (4)

2. Criticism or comment must not interfere with nor obstruct the administration of justice. A brazen suggestion that witnesses or jurors should not show up for the trial because the judge will permit lawyers to "browbeat" them certainly

would hamper the judicial process. To implant in the minds of the jurors or the public the intimation that the judge was making unfair rulings during the trial also would obstruct justice. And the same effect would come from an editorial declaring the jury had the duty of finding the defendant guilty. (5)

3. Criticism should not be made while the case is pending. Appellate courts, however, from time to time have been obliged to define "pending" as will be pointed out in the discussion of constructive contempt.

4. Aside from criticism or comment, a seriously false report of a trial also can lead to contempt. (6)

The conduct of a trial is governed by such a pattern of procedures, rules, and precedents that only the most experienced court reporter should feel he is qualified to criticize it. The reporter of lesser experience may decide there is too much bickering over minor details. The veteran reporter, however, can fit each detail into the legal pattern.

Some writers in fields affected by law, but not directly allied with it, have called attention at times to what they describe as "legal maneuvering." One such writer, for example, criticized a court for spending half a day in determining whether the article the defendant was accused of stealing was worth only $1.95 as he contended or $5.95 as the prosecution claimed. The exact value was pertinent. The smaller sum meant the defendant should be charged with petit larcency with relatively minor penalties. But $5.95 was above the sum arbitrarily set by statute as grand larceny. The difference between sending a man to prison for three months or for three years can hardly be dismissed as quibbling.

Charges must be specific for the defendant's protection. For that reason, errors in indictments which may seem trivial to the layman assume great importance in law. The admission and presentation of evidence follows rigidly prescribed rules. As Justice Frankfurter has said:

> "A trial is not a 'free trade in ideas,' nor is the best test of truth in a courtroom 'the power of the thought to get itself accepted in the competition of the market.' . . . It (a court)

is circumscribed in the range of its inquiry and its methods by
the Constitution, by-laws, and by age-old traditions. . . . They
are so circumscribed precisely because judges have in their
keeping the enforcement of rights and the protection of liberties . . ." (7)

Only the veteran reporter who understands these rules can
appreciate their significance. Judges frequently are reversed by
appellate courts for "errors" during the conduct of a trial. Perhaps the judge admitted evidence the appeals court thinks
should have been barred; or he may have rejected testimony
that should have been accepted. He may have erred in some
of his statements to the jury; or his mistakes may have come
at any part of the trial. If judges and lawyers cannot agree on
these questions the reporter, untrained in law, is optimistic to
assume he is qualified to criticize them.

For this reason, the scope of reasonable criticism and comment on the actual conduct of a trial is rather limited for the
sincere newspaper. If it does feel obliged to comment on this
phase of the case, it must not imply that any ruling from the
bench was prompted by the judge's partiality toward either side.
A statement that "the defense was 'hamstrung' because the court
refused to permit two 'key' witnesses to testify" might be both
contemptuous and libelous. For in many sections "hamstrung"
connotes a deliberate attempt, either illegally or unethically,
to prevent a certain act.

Rather than assuming to sit as a judge, the newspaper serves
a better purpose if its criticism is directed only at more tangible
actions. In one jurisdiction, all motorists convicted of drunken
driving were sentenced to spend a day in a hospital visiting
victims of traffic accidents. The judge hoped the sight of these
patients would make a drunken motorist realize what misery
he might have caused.

A newspaper was within its rights in questioning whether
such a punishment really served the purpose for which society
has devised its penal system. Judges have sentenced men to
go to church, to refrain from attending certain public events for
a specified period, to write essays on highway safety and even
to kiss their mothers-in-law. None of these unusual punishments is prescribed by statute and the press may properly question whether they may be imposed by the judiciary.

One judge sentenced all motorists convicted of speeding to one day in jail. By statute, in his state, time spent in court is counted toward any jail sentence imposed. Each convicted motorist was free when court adjourned without having seen the county jail. The judge was irritated when a paper commented that these sentences resulted more in publicity than in results. But in all of these unusual sentences a judge has no legal ground for complaint if editors or the public disagree.

To prevent the impairment of the dignity or effectiveness of the court, to insure an orderly and fair trial, and to prevent any obstruction or interference with the administration of justice, the courts, then, have a powerful remedy at their command—contempt. Contempt is of two kinds—direct and constructive. Of the two, constructive contempt is of far greater concern to the press.

Direct Contempt

When President Andrew Jackson exclaimed in a fit of anger that, "Well, John Marshall (Chief Justice) has made his decision; now let him enforce it," (8) he was speaking as the leader of a political faction embroiled in a state's rights argument rather than as a chief executive cognizant of the duties of his office. (9)

In practice, if an order of a court requires physical force, it could not be carried out effectively should the executive branch refuse to provide that compulsion. For if one branch is in such open rebellion against another, government cannot function.

Sometimes resistance to courts is more subtle. During prohibition, prosecutors often found that juries failed to convict, despite the evidence, because members were not in sympathy with the law. A county judge who sentenced every drunken driver to ninety days in jail, in disregard of any extenuating circumstances, soon discovered juries were reluctant to return guilty verdicts. To prevent a total miscarriage of justice, the judge had to modify his policy.

But courts, the same as all agencies of government, cannot carry out their work unless they have some authority. For courts this authority is two-fold. The courts must be able to maintain order for their own self-protection and to conduct trials. They also must have power to enforce their decrees, judgments, and rules.

During the depression of the 1930's, some groups in Iowa threatened a judge with physical violence if he continued fore-closures on farms. In a normally functioning government, how-ever, the courts experience no difficulty. When the judge mounts his bench, he is master of his courtroom and unless his acts are arbitrary and capricious, his word really is law.

Reporters are concerned with direct contempt chiefly through courtroom conduct. Certainly good manners, aside from jour-nalism training, tell a reporter he cannot dart about to inter-view principals, talk loudly, wave to friends among the spec-tators, approach a juror, cause a disturbance as he goes out to telephone to meet a deadline, or light up a cigarette. If the judge rules the defendant may not be interviewed during the trial, a reporter who sidles over to the defense table during a recess has only himself to blame for any punishment meted out to him.

Although trials usually are presumed to be public, the judge in his discretion may bar both press and spectators. Young people often are prohibited from listening to sex cases. (10) Individual reporters may be barred for gross inaccuracies or for violating a court order. The barred reporter who sneaks back in lets himself open for contempt.

Although direct contempt applies to acts committed within the courtroom or immediate environs, there can be no strict geographical limitation. A reporter who accosts a juror on the way to resumption of the trial is just as guilty of contempt as though he approached the juror in the courtroom.

The late Harry F. Sinclair, oil magnate, was jailed for con-tempt for hiring detectives to "shadow" jurors during his trial in connection with oil lease frauds. The jurors were not mo-lested and probably few of them knew they were being "shad-owed." The court ruled, however, that the activities of the detectives held the threat of intimidation, mental at least if not physical. To say that the judge had no power beyond his court door, might easily lead to interference with justice. A juror who goes home each night and reads daily accounts of the trial can be held in contempt although he may live miles from the courthouse.

Sometimes as the jury files in with its decision the judge not only warns against any demonstration by spectators but also orders the doors locked until after the verdict is read and entered. A reporter who tries to run this "blockade" to get a "flash" to his paper also may find himself in trouble. Calling out an open window to a colleague may be classified as a "disturbance."

Ordinarily what a reporter prints is not direct contempt but constructive contempt as discussed in a following section. Since most reporters know how to conduct themselves, few become involved in direct contempt. But their colleague—the photographer—often becomes embroiled with the judge. (11)

Photographers and Contempt

Sometimes a photographer flagrantly violates a rule in order to get his picture. Many times, however, the trouble stems from the wrong interpretation of the judge's orders.

If the judge simply rules "no pictures," the cameraman should ask for a clarification. Does His Honor mean no pictures while the court is in session, no pictures at any time in the courtroom, or no pictures of the defendant in particular, during the trial, no matter where they are taken?

Once the picture order is made clear, does the ruling also apply to sketches? Some judges have no objection to an artist sketching provided his work does not cause spectators to crane their necks or shift in their seats to watch him. Other judges, knowing an artist can hardly work without attracting attention, include sketches in their order against pictures. The judge may include sketches also to shield the defendant.

When a judge rules no pictures or sketches, it doesn't matter if the taker uses an unobtrusive candid camera or if the artist sketches on a pad on his knee and neither are observed by the court or spectators. Publication of the pictures still is in contempt.

The judge acts on the principle that the prisoner is in the "protective custody" of the court who will look out for his rights. A man brought handcuffed into the courtroom is in no position to resist having his picture taken, especially since the officers guarding him seldom are reluctant to see their own photographs in the paper.

Probably the leading precedent for control of photographs in and out of the courtroom is a Baltimore case decided in 1927. Five photographers and newspaper officials were adjudged in contempt for taking and publishing pictures during the murder trial of Richard Reese Whittemore that attracted national attention. A photographer snapped Whittemore as he was entering the lockup of the courthouse and the popping of the flash bulb attracted the judge in his chambers.

The judge summoned the cameraman and ordered him to give up the picture. Unfamiliar with the technique of news photographers, the judge was unaware that the cameraman had the exposed plate in his pocket. The photographer handed him a blank plate from the camera. The Baltimore News printed the forbidden picture. (12)

When court convened, the judge read an order against pictures and mentioned that he already had confiscated one. In his order he said:

". . . The prisoner is in the precincts of the court, under the protection of the court, and is not able, therefore, to protect himself, and he will be protected by this court from any publicity of that character." (13)

Meanwhile, another photographer with a small camera sat at the press table and snapped pictures unobserved by the judge. Some of these pictures were published by the Baltimore American.

The two issues thus presented were: (1) Can a judge prohibit the taking of photographs in the environs of the court and before a formal order has been handed down against them? (2) can the court prohibit the use of cameras in the courtroom although the photographers are creating no disturbance and, in fact, are working without attracting attention from the bench?

The court disposed of the first question by declaring:

". . . The liberty of the press does not include the privilege of taking advantage of the incarceration of a person accused of a crime to photograph his face and figure against his will."

On the second issue, the court said: "It is essential to the integrity and independence of judicial tribunals that they shall have the power to enforce their own judgments as to what conduct is incompatible with the proper and orderly course of their procedure. If their discretion should be subordinated to that of a newspaper manager in regard to the use of photographic instruments in the courtroom, it would be difficult to limit the further reduction to which the authority of the courts would be exposed. . . . The ability of a photographer to take pictures in court without noise or distraction and without the knowledge of the judge is not a reason why he should be at liberty to ignore positive judicial order forbidding the use of cameras at the trial." (14)

Presumably, under the ruling on the first issue, an artist could not attend court and later sketch from memory without, what the court also said, "unauthorized invasions of his (the defendant's) personal rights." Some papers have tried this method without the court taking judicial notice. One judge, however, reprimanded the managing editor for using such a sketch, but later privately told the newsman that action was "for the record only" because defense counsel had protested. The paper refrained from printing more sketches.

Since the Baltimore decision affords the court a means of preventing all photographs of the defendant, no matter where taken, many jurisdictions now follow that precedent. Four years after that decision, a New York judge went a step further and presumably added "other litigants and witnesses" to the court's protection. He ruled: ". . . prisoners being brought to court are under the protection of the court and are entitled to be brought to court without molestation and disturbance . . . other litigants and witnesses have a right to come into court without being molested." (15)

By adding "other litigants and witnesses," the New York judge has complicated the problem still further. In addition his language is indefinite. Does he mean the courts will afford witnesses the same "protective custody" as defendants or does he mean witnesses merely should have that right? If he means the former, how far will "protective custody" extend in jurisdiction?

The extreme view would place a witness under court protection from the time he steps out his front door although he may intend to take a long detour on his way to court. Many witnesses are agreeable and even eager to have their pictures taken, for it may be their one claim to "glory" in all their lives. Can a judge, then, forbid pictures of witnesses although they may be willing to pose? Or did the court just mean that if a witness requests it the judge will protect him from photographs? And, if so, did the judge mean only within the environs of the court?

There have been no cases growing out of the authority of a judge to forbid "portal to portal" pictures of "witnesses and other litigants."

Even where the judge has made strict orders against photographs, witnesses have been snapped on courthouse steps, pavements, and corridors. Until a case comes before a court, the protection to be afforded witnesses will remain undetermined. But for a judge to insist upon such sweeping power as to forbid photographs of witnesses anywhere, seems valid in neither law nor logic. The more reasonable assumption is that the judge meant witnesses will be protected from "annoyances" as they enter and leave court. But how far down the street the court's protective mantle will follow the witness remains unanswered until the courts speak further.

A number of newspapers, knowing that the trial of a certain defendant will attract much attention, fortify themselves against judicial ban on pictures by photographing the prisoner in many different poses, when he is arrested, at his preliminary hearing, in his cell (if the warden permits) and in other places. They also photograph other principals in the case.

Many of these pictures are filed in the morgue. When the trial opens and photographs are banned, these papers draw upon their unused supply to provide day-to-day art work. A picture editor who is keenly aware of court procedure often can store away photographs that serve almost as well as if they were taken in the courthouse. A judge cannot prevent publication of pictures taken before he assumed jurisdiction in the case.

All judges, however, are not opposed to pictures. Some permit pictures to be made at all times except when the court is in session. Others grant this permission only if the principals consent. Still others permit photographs outside the courtroom.

Some judges ask the foreman to poll the jurors to see if they object to posing for a photograph. If none objects, the court arranges for a setting under the supervision of bailiffs or deputies to make certain no one takes advantage of the situation to converse with the jurors.

Should the jury be taken to the scene of the crime, some judges have no objection to photographers going along and also reporters, provided the press corps speaks only to the bailiffs or officials in charge. The reporter covering such a mission should not print what he may overhear one juror tell another although courts who have granted such permission seldom object to stories that the jurors asked about specific things. In such instances the court may instruct photographers what they may take and reporters what they may print.

At the trial of Bruno Richard Hauptmann for the kidnapping of the Lindbergh baby, photographers operated without much restriction. One of the best pictures, from a news angle if not from a legal sense, was that of Charles A. Lindbergh sitting on the witness stand and looking at the man accused of kidnapping his child. So many flash bulbs were popping most of these pictures looked as if they were taken on a hazy morning.

A Michigan judge overruled the objections of a juror who complained he was annoyed by flash bulbs. The judge told the juror: "I am tolerating this situation (the taking of pictures) because of the legitimate interest of the people of this state and nation in the conduct of this trial." (16)

A Florida judge not only permitted pictures any time court was not in session, but called frequent recesses during the taking of testimony. Each time he left the bench cameramen were free to snap pictures of witnesses, lawyers, defendant and even spectators. Before the trial started, the judge asked the jurors to pose for a photograph and they consented. (17)

A Minnesota judge, presiding at a murder trial, reserved seats for photographers as well as reporters and even permitted radio men to use tape recorders. Public address systems carried the proceedings to people jammed in the hall and across the street to an auditorium where an overflow crowd of 600 followed the trial.

Flash bulbs were permitted only during recesses, but at other times the only additional restriction was that the cameramen must not interfere or disconcert the proceedings. (18)

An editorial writer, defending the court's action against criticism by lawyers, stressed that the judge had visited German courtrooms and:

". . . He believes American courts give the best and fairest justice in the world and the story of our court procedure should be carried to the people whom they are expected to serve. Of course, he realizes this must be kept within good taste and common sense." (19)

The reporter and the photographer, then, must keep in mind that the judge controls both his courtroom and the conduct of the trial. Obedience to court instructions is good journalism ethics and also good law.

For Further Reading

(Since criticism and comment on the courts, together with the court weapons of direct and constructive contempt are tightly interwoven few authorities attempt to separate them into "water-tight" compartments. For this reason, reading references for both Chapters 11 and 12 are given at the end of Chapter 12.)

CHAPTER XII

"Limits of Criticism – Constructive Contempt"

Down through the years, the principal disputes between the press and the courts have been over constructive contempt. Although bench and bar do not agree upon definitions of constructive contempt, much less on the theories and principles centering around it, the newspaperman can consider it as improper acts committed outside the environs of the court.

For the press, these acts usually consist of publication of certain types of stories, articles, editorials, cartoons, etc. Contempt by publication may be a better term for journalism than constructive contempt.

The problem is acute for journalism because:

1. The judge becomes accuser, prosecutor, and then judge of the very proceedings he institutes. (Sometimes the Bar Association initiates the contempt action with the approval of the court.) A judge who feels his dignity and prestige as been challenged scarcely can bring the offender before him and then acquit him. On the other hand, if the case were tried by a jury the "12 men tried and true" might feel the judge had just been oversensitive.

2. Truth is not always a defense. This reasoning follows the old theory of criminal libel in which the axiom was: "The greater the truth, the greater the libel," since it would tend to incite people more to commit a breach of the peace.

3. Many cases revolve around an interpretation of "pending" and courts have no uniformity in their definitions.

4. Constructive contempt, or the mere threat of it, may operate as negative censorship to prevent papers from making needed criticism or comment. An editor who believes a judicial situation needs correcting may hesitate for fear of

being cited for contempt and fined and imprisoned. Appealing to higher courts requires time and money, and the editor may not be in a position to sacrifice either one.

5. Although the federal jurisdiction and at least 36 states have attempted to define exact limits of constructive contempt, courts, in general, have resisted all efforts to limit their powers. Any situation that cannot be corrected readily through legislative action is of serious concern to a society which wishes to govern itself.

In a discussion of constructive contempt, the word "stories" should be construed as including articles, editorials, cartoons, sketches, pictures, letters to the editor and all material published in any form. The press is involved particularly in these areas of constructive contempt:

1. Stories which obstruct justice or present a "clear and present danger" to the administration of justice. (See Chapter 11).

2. Stories which impair public confidence in the court or scandalize the judge or hold him up to ridicule or scorn. (See Chapter 11.) A cartoon was held to be contemptuous for depicting a judge watching the scales of justice tip because money had been placed on one side.

3. A false report of a trial which reflects on the judge. A story would be in contempt if it read: "The witness easily could have settled the issue by positive identification of the defendant, but the judge, yielding to objections, refused to permit him to continue his testimony."

4. Stories prejudicial to the court or to either side. An editorial would be in contempt for saying: "It's just a waste of the taxpayers' money for the defense to prolong the trial because every fair-minded person is convinced by this time that the defendant is guilty."

5. Stories attempting to influence the judge, directly or by implication. A story of this type would be: "The judge's duty in this case is plain even to a layman and, with election coming on, he had better act or the voters will."

6. As shown previously, certain "pre-trial" stories may be in contempt, especially if their purpose seems to be to inflame public opinion against the defendant.

Among many American authorities, contempt by publication is disputed or accepted reluctantly because historically it is linked closely with seditious libel, treason, and prior licensing and other restrictions on freedom of expression which were rejected in the adoption of the Constitution of the United States. (1)

The famous English writer on law, William Blackstone, whose name is as familiar to bench and bar as that of Hippocrates is to the medical profession, is credited with providing the justification for summary punishment for contempt. There is evidence that Blackstone himself leaned heavily upon a judgment prepared by Justice Wilmot, but never delivered, in the case of a London bookseller charged with publishing seditious literature. (2)

Both the federal jurisdiction and at least 36 states have tried to deal with the problem by statute, but the courts have counteracted some effect of those laws by tenaciously asserting a doctrine of "inherent powers" or by broadly construing provisions of the acts. (3)

Congress made its first statutory attempt to limit constructive contempt in 1831 soon after impeachment proceedings against Judge Peck lost by one vote in the Senate. Among the charges against him were his summary punishment of critics.

Some authorities maintain Congress hurried through the law to prevent its verdict from being construed as an approval of Judge Peck's use of the contempt power. (4) Others have maintained that Congress had a broader purpose and support this claim with evidence that the House instructed its judiciary committee "to inquire into the expediency of defining, by statute, all interferences which may be punishable as contempts of courts of the United States." (5)

The law, known as the Act of March 2, 1831, limited contempt to ". . . the misbehavior of any person or persons in the presence of the said courts, or so near thereto as to obstruct the administration of justice." (6)

Federal courts seized upon the phrase, "so near thereto," to practically nullify the intent of Congress, and continued to adhere to the old narrow English tradition they had followed prior to passage of the Act. The heat of agitation in the growing conflict between the North and the South and the war itself virtually completed destruction of the law. That courts during this period were guilty of excesses in using their contempt power will be denied by few authorities today. "So near thereto" in court language meant, in effect, any activity the courts seized upon.

The trail of contempt by publication in the United States is blazed by many landmark cases down through the years. Paradoxically, the justice who affirmed the contempt powers in one famous case was also the justice who later showed the wind was about to shift. In 1907, Justice Holmes spoke for the United States Supreme Court, in upholding a contempt action against a Denver editor who had written, in part, that two state supreme court justices had been placed on the bench in a "deal" to seat certain Republican candidates. (7)

Justice Holmes, in his opinion, said:

"... When a case is finished, courts are subject to the same criticism as other people, but the propriety and necessity of preventing interference with the course of justice by premature statements, argument, or intimidation can hardly be denied." (8)

This case also re-stated the old principle that truth is not always a defense in a contempt proceeding. Justice may be hindered by the truth spoken at a certain time as well as by falsehood.

In 1918, Justice Holmes, in dissenting in another famous case, not only indicated the wind soon might shift but also struck at the crucial issue of permitting the same man to be accuser and judge. He said:

"When it is considered how contrary it is to our practice and ways of thinking for the same person to be accuser and sole judge in a matter, which, if he is sensitive, may involve strong personal feeling, I should expect the power (to cite for contempt) to be limited by the necessities of the case 'to insure order and decorum in their (the courts') presence'..." (9)

His implied suggestion that judges should not sit in actions affecting them still must await legislative action with no assurance that the courts will relinquish what they have held to be their inherent powers.

Although Justice Holmes' dissent foreshadowed things to come, the majority of the court in Toledo Newspaper Co. v. United States clung to the old narrow view. The case grew out of a dispute in Toledo over the street railway franchises. When the railway company's franchise expired, the city council decided to renew it on a temporary basis and also passed an ordinance reducing fares to three cents. The Toledo *News Bee* vigorously supported the city's action and demanded the ordinance must not be upset by the courts in legal action the railway company then was preparing.

Stories, articles, and cartoons were published from March through September in 1914. After a federal court granted an injunction against the three-cent fare, one cartoon depicted the railway company as a sick man who had found a "friend" in the judge. In September, the judge cited the paper for contempt and imposed a fine and included among his charges material that had been published six months previously.

The majority of the Supreme Court, in affirming the sentence, laid down what may be termed a "reasonable tendency" theory, by saying:

". . . Not the influence upon the mind of the particular judge is the criterion (as to whether an article is in contempt), but the reasonable tendency of the acts done to influence or bring about the baleful result, is the test." (10) In dismissing the contention that the articles were only comment on a public issue, the court said:

"The safeguarding and fructification of free and constitutional institutions is the very basis and mainstay upon which the freedom of the press rests, and that freedom, therefore, does not and cannot be held to include the right virtually to destroy such institutions." (11)

This "reasonable tendency" theory, in effect, wiped out the last restraint of the Act of March 2, 1831, and, in effect, was notice by the judiciary that it was going back to the old English tradition. (12). It was to be 23 years before the dissent of Justice Holmes was to be written into judicial law.

The New Trend

A series of cases, the first decided in 1941, has swung the courts back sharply to the intent of the 1831 act, but in the face of strong disagreement on the part of some justices. And one question that still may arise is the need for a clear-cut definition on "pendency." Courts, as a rule, take a more severe attitude toward criticism and certain comment if the case under discussion is still pending. But what does pending mean?

The strict legal view is that a case still is pending until the judicial process has run its full course. That means, in theory at least, until the last avenue of appeal or action is closed. But that might require months to years. The Toledo Newspaper Company case, for example, began in 1914 but it was not decided by the Supreme Court until 1918. A newspaper which must refrain from commenting for months or years will find little practical value in discussing the case at all.

At the other extreme, is the opinion that a case for purposes of comment and criticism loses its pendency when a verdict or judgment is rendered. Under certain circumstances this may be too narrow a view, but the determination of a "middle ground" acceptable to courts and feasible for the press remains largely for the future.

This problem of pendency received judicial attention as the Supreme Court began to shift the principle of contempt back to what Congress had in mind in 1831. In the first of these cases, Bridges v. California, (13) in 1941, the court recognized that there is a timeliness in the discussion of public issues which is destroyed if criticism and comment is held until cases no longer are pending in the strict use of the term. Two cases actually went before the Supreme Court in 1941—Bridges v. California and Times-Mirror Company v. Superior Court—but the decision in the former also covered the latter case. For that reason, the case is commonly known only as Bridges v. California.

The cases grew out of a series of editorials in the Los Angeles *Times.* By nothing more than a coincidence, Harry Bridges, a fiery west coast labor leader, and the *Times,* which was critical of some labor activities, both found themselves appealing to the

Supreme Court on the same issue. Bridges was cited for contempt for publication in the newspapers of a telegram he sent to the United States Secretary of Labor declaring that the attempted enforcement of a state court order (a motion for a new hearing was pending) preventing a local from transferring to Bridges' union would tie up the whole West coast in a strike. He also declared his union did not intend to permit state courts to override the majority vote of union members in choosing their own labor affiliations. Although the telegram was published in the press, no newspaper was cited on this count.

The *Times* was cited for editorials on a variety of subjects. Two charges were dropped by the trial court and the California Supreme Court threw out two more. Three charges were left for the appeal to the United States Supreme Court. One of those charges was based on an editorial in which the *Times* declared that political reasons had motivated the conviction of a woman on a bribe-taking indictment. The other two editorials dealt with labor subjects. One was on terrorism by sit-down strikes, and the other with the heading "Probation for Gorillas?" informed the court that it would make a "serious mistake" if it granted probation to two men then awaiting sentence after their conviction on charges of beating non-union truck drivers.

The Supreme Court agreed unanimously that two of the editorials were permissible. But "Probation for Gorillas?" was approved only by the sharp division of five to four. Although the decision was hailed by many sections of the press as another "great victory for freedom," the result of the moment was unsatisfactory. The deeper significance springs from the fact that in later cases the court seems to have gone more strongly toward the majority position.

Speaking of the principle of preventing comment on pending cases, Justice Black, in the majority opinion, said:

"Since they punish utterances during pendency of a case, the judgments below (of the California courts) therefore produce their restrictive results at the precise moment when public interest in the matters discussed would be naturally at its heighth. Moreover, the ban is likely to fall not only at a critical time but upon the most important topics of discussion." (14)

On the specific issue of pending raised by these cases Justice Black also said:

".. . we are all (majority members) of the opinion that, upon any fair construction, their (the editorials') possible influence on the course of justice can be dismissed as negligible, and that the Constitution compels us to set aside the convictions as unpermissible exercises of the state's power." (15)

Thus, the majority opinion not only restated the "clear and present danger" theory but also applied that principle to pending cases.   The court recognized the two dangers which contempt power is expected to cure.   One is a disrespect for the judiciary. On this, the court said:

"The assumption that respect for the judiciary can be won by shielding judges from published criticism wrongly appraises the character of American public opinion.   For it is a prized American privilege to speak one's mind, although not always with perfect good taste, on all public institutions.   And an enforced silence, however limited, solely in the name of preserving the dignity of the bench, would probably engender resentment, suspicion, and contempt much more than it would enhance respect." (16)

On the other evil for which contempt is relied on as the cure —disorderly and unfair administration of justice, the court said:

".. . (it) is more plausibly associated with restricting publications which touch on pending litigation.   The very word 'trial' connotes decisions on the evidence and arguments properly advanced in open court.   Legal trials are not like elections, to be won through the use of the meeting-hall, the radio, and the newspapers.   But we cannot start with the assumption that publications of the kind here involved actually do threaten to change the nature of legal trials." (17)

Justice Frankfurter, in dissenting, did brush aside the theory that the determination of *pending* is a technical problem for lawyers only, but he contended the test was that the publication must refer to ".. . a matter under consideration and constitute in effect a threat to its impartial disposition.   It must be calculated to create an atmospheric pressure incompatible with rational, impartial adjudication.   But to interfere with justice it need not succeed . . . the states should be able to proscribe attempts that fail because of the danger that attempts may succeed." (18)

Of criticism of judges themselves, without an attempt to interfere with justice, Mr. Frankfurter was as firm as the majority in upholding the right of comment. He suggested judges should not forget "their common human frailties and fallibilities and said:

". . . courts and judges must take their share of the gains and pains of discussion which is unfettered except by the laws of libel, by self-restraint, and by good taste." (19)

The Bridges' decision has another importance that is self-implied but sometimes overlooked. Before 1941, the United States Supreme Court seldom interfered with a state's interpretation of "freedom of press" as it involved contempt of court. The highest court of each state, in effect, was the sole guardian of that state's interpretation of obstruction or interference with justice, the definition of "pending," and all the problems that go into contempt by publication.

In the Bridges' case, the United States Supreme Court was carrying into another field the broad policy it had been slowly applying to federal jurisdiction of many activities through the Fourteenth amendment to the federal Constitution. It now served notice that any suppression of freedom of expression by a state is a federal concern. For that reason, a detailed study of state cases alone in recent years is more a scholarly than a practical pursuit because a publisher anywhere now has constitutional grounds for appealing to the highest tribunal in the nation. The Fourteenth Amendment, prohibiting states from abridging the privileges and immunities of citizens, has draped its protective mantle over the press in its contempt disputes with the courts.

Five years later, vitality was pumped into the Bridges' decision by another landmark case—Pennekamp v. Florida.

John D. Pennekamp was associate editor and editorial writer for the Miami (Fla.) *Herald*. In an editorial protesting delay in action on some rape cases, he also denounced what he termed general delay and confusion in the state's legal system. But in another case, he contended there had been too much haste and that, as a result, a padlocked night club reopened when another judge suddenly sat on the case.

Pennekamp was cited for contempt and the Florida Supreme Court upheld the lower courts in a decision declaring ". . . it is utter folly to suggest that the object of these publications was other than to abuse and destroy the efficiency of the court." (20)

The United States Supreme Court, in reversing the Florida court, said: "To talk of a clear and present danger arising out of such criticism is idle unless the criticism makes it impossible in a real sense for a court to carry on the administration of justice. That situation is not even remotely present in this case." (21)

Justice Reed, delivering the majority opinion, agreed the cases were pending but that ". . . we think the specific freedom of public comment should weigh heavily against a possible tendency to influence pending cases." (22) He suggested that if the judges believed they were defamed they should, as other public servants, seek damages in libel rather than punishment through contempt.

Justice Frankfurter contributed another statement on pending by holding that "the decisive consideration (in determining if a case is pending) is whether the judge or jury, is, or presently will be, pondering a decision that comment seeks to affect." (23)

The final case worth noting in this new trend toward limiting contempt by publication came in 1947. (24)

The publisher, managing editor, and a reporter for the Corpus Christi (Tex.) *Caller-Times* were adjudged guilty of contempt for stories and editorials growing out of a dispute between a soldier then overseas and the owner of a building housing a cafe which the serviceman was operating through an agent. The court ruled the rent had not been paid and that the building should revert to its owner.

Twice the jury refused to sign such a verdict, although locked up all night. Finally, the jury signed with a statement that it was doing so under coercion and against the "consciences" of the members.

The case inflamed the community. The *Caller-Times*, besides its news stories, editorially urged a new trial. Two days before the judge denied a new trial, he cited the three newsmen and they spent several hours in jail while an appeal motion was being drawn up.

The Texas Supreme Court, faced with the Bridges v. California decision, contended that ruling did not apply since this was not a discussion of public issues but of a private lawsuit. The United States Supreme Court reversed the Texas tribunal in a six to three decision.

Speaking for the court, Justice Douglas said:

"A trial is a public event. What transpires in a courtroom is public property. . . . Those who see and hear . . . can report it with impunity. There is no special requisite of the judiciary which enables it, as distinguished from other institutions of democratic government, to suppress, edit, or censor events which transpire in proceedings before it." (25)

The court found inaccuracies in the newspaper stories but said that ". . . inaccuracies in reporting are commonplace. Certainly a reporter could not be laid by the heels for contempt because he misses the essential point in a trial or failed to summarize the issues to accord with the views of the judge who sat on the case." (26)

Speaking of the editorials, the court "assumed" they were unjust criticism, but declared:

". . . a judge may not hold in contempt one who ventures to publish anything that tends to make him unpopular or to belittle him. . . . The law of contempt is not made for the protection of judges who may be sensitive to the winds of public opinion. Judges are supposed to be men of fortitude, able to thrive in a hardy climate." (27)

The majority opinion pointed up another significant observation for the press. It declared that the public was stirred up by what the court did and not by the newspaper stories. For the people, sympathizing with the soldier overseas, had started circulating a petition for a new trial.

Said the court:

"Whatever might be the responsibility of the group which took the action (circulation of the petition), those who reported it stand in a different position. Even if the former were guilty of contempt, freedom of the press may not be denied a newspaper which brings their conduct to the public eye." (28)

In dissenting, Justice Jackson argued that publicity about pending cases ". . . can hardly help affecting the way a judge makes up his mind." He contended that this affect may come either because a weak judge may yield or a strong one may hold more firmly to his views just to show he cannot be bullied. He propounded the question as to whether the majority justices, so far removed from this Texas incident, would have felt the same way if the same kind of criticism were directed at them. (29)

Other Contempt by Publication

The key cases just discussed concern contempt by publication chiefly from the viewpoint of comment and criticism. The courts have been concerned at times with "pre-trial" stories which they believed tended to interfere with the administration of justice.

The situation in Baltimore, as described in Chapter 9, dealt with stories of crimes from the moment police were called in to make arrests or investigations. But our discussion here is concerned with stories appearing as the trial draws near.

One of the most persistent complaints of courts about "pre-trial" stories is that a crime, particularly in small communities, may receive so much publicity that public opinion is inflamed to the point where it weighs against the defendant. The usual procedure is not to take action against the newspaper, but to grant a change of venue to transfer the trial to another county or area.

One judge, however, in denying a request for a change of venue, said that ". . . the apparent unusual interest displayed by the public in this case is not due to any ill will or animosity toward this defendant, but is occasioned by a natural curiosity to hear and read the spicy details of a case of this character." (30)

Disposing of the claim that since the public read the defendant's confession, people called for jury service could not erase it from their minds, the court said:

". . . we must bear in mind that so long as such material has news value the papers are going to print it wherever this case might be tried so that prospective jurors of another county would be in no different position than those in Butler county." (31)

A district attorney in Denver, Colorado, on behalf of a defendant in an impending murder trial, asked for contempt citations against several executives and newsmen of the Denver *Post* for their pre-trial stories. The judge dismissed the action with the comment the petition contained ". . . a great many conclusions and opinions."

The judge continued: ". . . American newspapers are not bound down by the strictness of the English courts. A newspaper has the right to print facts." (33)

A Philadelphia judge refused to grant a citation for contempt against the Philadelphia *Inquirer* for articles about proposed impeachment proceedings against a city official. Attorneys for the official wanted the publisher cited for contempt after failing to have him enjoined from printing further articles on the ground they tended to "bias the minds of the public, officials, and witnesses." (34)

The judge dismissed both actions. In refusing an injunction, the court ruled it would be ". . . an unwarranted infringement of freedom of the press." (35) It also held that the press has the right to bring to the public, news and proper comment and also ". . . to make its proper and thinking effort and contribution toward the preservation of the purity of community institutions." (36)

In refusing a contempt petition, the judge referred to United States Supreme Court decisions as meaning there must be a "clear and present danger" to justice before such action is permissible. (37)

Another Philadelphia judge asked newspapers there to withhold the verdict in an extortion case until another defendant was tried on a similar charge. The court expressed fear the prospective jurors might be influenced by the verdict in the first trial.

The papers refused the request, one editorially expressing puzzlement as to how a verdict delivered in open court could be kept from the public. The judge then in a lengthy statement explained to the second jury that it would be locked up because the papers refused his request.

He told the jurors he was ". . . shocked at such indifference on the part of the press . . . to help in the administration of justice. Especially," he said, "when the newspapers have complied in the past with similar requests from the police department." Later he commended a paper which had printed his lengthy statement to the jury. (38)

A Texas paper won an appeal after being cited for contempt for publishing testimony the court had ordered withheld because the same evidence was to be used in two other cases. The court feared prospective jurors for the succeeding cases would be influenced by reading certain testimony given at the first trial.

After declaring that intelligent people keep up on the news, the appeals court said their reading would not necessarily result in an opinion ". . . so fixed as to render them incapable of forming an impartial judgment from hearing the evidence revealed by a witness, under oath, in a given case." (39)

The Bar and Contempt

Down through the years, lawyers have filled their legal journals and reviews with articles treating the whole broad scope of the power of the courts in contempt. (40)

Although on many issues the press and the bar have been far apart, with neither apparently being able to see the viewpoint of the other, many writers in these legal journals have argued for a definition of publication by contempt that would have the effect of giving wide latitude to criticism and comment by newspapers. A number of these articles appeared before the turning point in Bridges v. California.

The *Yale Law Journal*, in 1950, went so far as to suggest only acts that actually cause intimidation or violence be punished through the contempt power. (41)

After a survey in 1950, it concluded it is doubtful if newspaper and radio comments actually affect the outcome of a trial. (42)

The article called upon the federal jurisdiction to make binding on state courts the ban against contempt by publication, in order that ". . . newsmen, like other persons, will be guaranteed a jury trial, for out-of-court activities alleged to be illegal, and the standard of guilt will be a concrete one of direct and tangible obstruction." (43)

The *Journal* called "dangerously vague" any rule which permits a judge to restrict press comment whenever he believes it might affect the outcome of a case. For, then, a publisher "must guess whether or not his story will bring down the wrath of the court."

Speaking of trial coverage, the *Journal* points out that impartial verdicts "are supposedly assured by examination of jurors, instructions from the judge, and, in the last resort, power to declare a mistrial. If devices such as these fail to neutralize the predisposition of jurors, the fault lies not with the press but with the system as a whole." (44)

Further, it says, "press comment makes its strongest impression when conforming to the pre-existing stereotypes in the public mind; hence it tends to follow rather than cause bias." (45)

The *Journal* concludes that ". . . there seems to be no justification for punishing press and radio reports unless they actually cause intimidation or violence." (46)

Resumé and Analysis:

The power of a court to conduct its trials in an orderly manner and to compel obedience to its rules, judgments, and decrees is admitted to be a necessary part of our legal system.

This power, functioning through the judicial authority to cite for contempt, is, as Chief Justice Taft once said, ". . . important and indispensable. But its exercise is a delicate one and care is needed to avoid arbitrary or oppressive conclusions."

As the Chief Justice continued: ". . . This rule of caution is more mandatory where the contempt charged has in it the element of personal criticism or attack upon the judge." (48)

The Chief Justice further suggested that where practical, or where delay would not injure public or private right, the judge who is the victim of a personal attack ". . . may, without flinching from his duty, properly ask that one of his fellow judges take his place." (49)

So far, there has been little tendency upon the part of the judges either to take the Chief Justice's suggestion or to arrange for a trial by jury.

Direct contempt, acts committed within the court or its environs, should concern the newspaperman but little since good reporters conduct themselves like gentlemen in court and in all public and private meetings.

The principal dispute between court and press concerning direct contempt is over pictures. Only an actor portraying a news cameraman in a movie would insist he has the right to stand up in court and pop flash bulbs at will. But the actual news photographer cannot always see the reason for prohibiting the taking of pictures outside the courtroom, especially if none of the principals objects. Pictures no longer are mere illustrations but a vital and independent part of news coverage. Bench, bar and press, taking cognizance of the society's interest in some trials, should work out a uniform practice to guide photographers and at the same time serve public interest and protect the necessary rights of court principals.

Contempt by publication, however, has been a real threat to the American concept of freedom of press. Some judges in the past have subverted this concept by using the contempt power as a virtual censorship. Recent decisions of the United States Supreme Court indicate that courts in the future must measure with a yardstick more workable than individual judge's ability to withstand the winds of public opinion.

The contention of some courts that pre-trial stories jeopardize the rights of defendants through inflaming public opinion does not seem to be borne out in most cases. As Patterson says:

". . . American judges and even juries, though forced to perform their duties under the spotlight of publicity and comment, have displayed rare intelligence and courage in deciding cases and in the rendition of judgments and verdicts that have not always met with popular approval. Even prolonged and organized propaganda has often proved unable to influence them." (50)

The newspaperman should realize he is in court to report the case and not to try the defendant nor to outguess the judge and counsel. On the other hand, bench and bar, which have been free with charges that the press has turned trials into circuses, might do well to look first at themselves. No reporter who covered the Hauptmann trial (for the kidnapping of the Lindbergh baby) will contend there was any apparent strenuous effort to curb antics of either press or some of the attorneys. (51) By way of contrast, a "front-page" trial later in a little Pennsylvania town was conducted with fitting dignity and decorum by both press and attorneys. The judge, although he presided in a business suit instead of a robe, made it clear at the outset there was a woman on trial for her life and that she was not an incidental participant in an affair arranged for the edification or glorification of either press or bar. At the same time, the judge expressed his appreciation of the intense public interest in the case. At the conclusion, a committee of reporters waited upon him to let him know they regarded his dealings with them as fair and dignified.

The judge, like the host at a social gathering, sets the pace. If the host throws a bottle through a window he cannot complain if guests imitate him. The judge who is firm and fair seldom finds reporters "get out of line." Should one do so, he receives no support from his colleagues. But the judge who believes his bench is in the skies, scarcely can complain if the press thinks it rests on more earthly foundations. The judge may like to commune with the ghosts of the eighteenth century, but the press must work amid the demands of a twentieth century mass society that believes it should and must be informed about public events.

Both bench and press must keep in mind their dual responsibilities. The judge is charged with the duty of seeing that a defendant gets a fair and orderly trial. The press has the obligation of respecting that constitutional provision. And both must realize that society has a right to know how its judicial system is functioning.

But neither courts nor press must interpret their responsibilities as licenses. The judge must not use his courtroom to build up his omnipotence nor his omniscience. And the newspaper must not use the courtroom as the vehicle for a public circus.

For Further Reading
(Chapters 11 and 12)

Chafee, Zechariah, Jr., *Government and Mass Communications*, Chicago; University of Chicago Press, 1947, Vol. 1, chap. 15.

Deutsch, E. P., "Liberty of Expression and Contempt of Court," 27 *Minnesota Law Review*, February, 1943.

Fox, Sir John Charles, *The History of Contempt of Court*, Oxford; The Clarendon Press, 1927.

Gerald, J. Edward, *The Press and the Constitution, 1931-1947*, Minneapolis; the University of Minnesota Press, 1949.

Herman, R. E. (and others), "Recent Limitations on Free Speech and Free Press," 48 *Yale Law Journal*, November, 1938.

Nelles, Walter, and King, Carol Weiss, "Contempt by Publication in the United States," 28 *Columbia Law Review*, April, 1928. Also May number.

Patterson, Giles J., *Free Speech and a Free Press*, Boston; Little, Brown and Company, 1939, Part IV, Chap. 1.

Sullivan, Harold W., *Contempts by Publication*, New Haven; private printing, 2d. ed. 1940.

The Los Angeles *Times* case (Bridges v. California) has been discussed widely in legal and journalistic journals. See: *Chicago-Kent Law Review*, June, 1940; *Columbia Law Review*, December, 1939; *New York University Law Quarterly Review*, March, 1942; *Iowa Law Review*, March, 1942; *Journalism Quarterly*, March, 1939; *Cornell Law Quarterly*, February, 1942; *Rocky Mountain Law Review*, April, 1942 and for rebuttal, June, 1942.

COURT DECISIONS
The leading cases already cited in the text should be read in their entirety. Many other decisions run the gamut of state and federal court view on the whole broad problem of contempt. These cases cannot be listed chronologically because judicial views have fluctuated, and a mere compilation by years may be confusing. In reading them, however, the dates should be noted in order to obtain a better historical perspective.

State v. Morrill, 16 Ark. 384.
United States v. Providence Tribune Co., 241 F. 524.
Froelich v. United States, 33 F. 2d. 660.
Graham v. Jones, 7 So. 2d. 688.
Statter v. United States, 66 F. 2d. 819.
In re: Pacific Telephone and Telegraph Co., 38 F 2d. 833.
In re: San Francisco *Chronicle*, 36 P. 2d. 369.
Tate v. State ex. rel. Raine, 177 S.W. 69.
State v. Breckenridge, 258 P. 744.
In re: Breen, 93 P. 997.
Craig v. Hecht, 263 U.S. 255.
Nye v. United States, 313 U.S. 33.
Pendergast v. United States, 317 U.S. 412.
Sullens v. States, 191 Miss. 856.

CHAPTER XIII

The Right to Print the News

A concomitant of the arbitrary definition of freedom of the press adopted in this book—no prior licensing or censorship—is the proposition that *the newspaper remains the sole judge of what it will print*. Neither a court nor a government agency —state or federal—can compel publication of either news or advertisements if the paper elects not to print them.

Of the material it chooses to use, the paper is the sole judge as to how those items will be displayed and on what page. It may choose to print a paragraph or a column. If a number of people participate in an event, the paper may decide to publish the names of some and ignore the others. But the only compulsion that can be brought to bear is public opinion or an appeal to the editor's fair-mindedness.

In recent years, several types of "news" have caused disputes between sections of the press and other businesses. Some newspapers, believing radio is a competitor at least for the advertising dollar if not for audience, have refused to print program listings of local stations. Most papers which do print the programs list them by names of the stars or under general headings such as "variety," "music," "news," etc. with no identification of commercial sponsors. There is something besides editorial whim behind this policy because a number of surveys have shown people identify programs more from content or star than from sponsor.

From time to time certain radio stations have feuded with newspapers for barring their program listings and several have threatened court action. Such threats were dissipated quickly after station managers talked with their attorneys.

Regional managers of state and federal civil service commissions at times have been aroused when newspapers refused to print announcements of coming examinations on the ground the material was advertising and not news. Several of these federal regional managers, who, no doubt, were more learned in personnel management than in law, have talked with postmasters in the apparent belief that a newspaper, accepted for mailing at a special rate, owes an obligation to print government announcements. The postmasters, no matter how sympathetic, were forced to tell these zealous officials that their only chance of obtaining space was to establish rapport with editors.

Courts many times have ruled that newspapers have no obligation to accept paid advertisements, but only a few cases involving news have been adjudicated. One of these involved a candidate for judge in Illinois. Although the newspaper printed a list of those seeking office, his name was not among them. He sued on the ground his candidacy had been damaged.

The court, in pointing out that the candidate had no legal remedy said:

"... (a newspaper) is the sole judge of the value of news as such. A newspaper must remain free to publish such matters as it regards as possessing news value . . . it must be the judge . . . of the news which it prints." (1)

To claim that a newspaper must print certain types of news, is just a step removed from classifying the press as a public utility with all the attendant regulation to which utilities are subjected. Such a status would destroy the American concept of a free press. Moreover, there is a legal problem, too. In the section on libel, it will be seen that a newspaper is responsible for everything it publishes. To say, then, that a newspaper must accept certain material against its will and also be responsible for it produces a jeopardy that should find no place in society as a whole or in its legal system.

Letters to the Editor

Letters to the editor present several problems: (a) The obligation of the paper to print such communications; (b) the right of correspondent to refuse permission for publication even if the editor wanted to print it; and (c) the actual ownership of the contents of the letter if the sender is not the author.

The first problem can be dismissed readily. Letters to the editor impose no legal obligation of publication, wholly or in part. For, as has been stated, the newspaper is the sole judge of what goes into both its news and advertising columns. The other problems are complicated since in several aspects law is intertwined with custom in an imperfect blending.

Legally, the contents of a letter belong to the writer. The receiver may retain physical possession of the paper and envelope, but can make no use of the contents without permission of the writer.

The law is clear where the letters involve "literary property." A poet who sends his verses to an editor for appraisal only can sue for infringement if the newspaper prints them, for publication gives them to the world and destroys their subsequent commercial value. Publication of even the outline of a proposed feature article also would deprive the author of his common law copyright. (2)

A reporter in writing a feature article or biography of a person may discover that some relatives have letters he has written. Before using them, the reporter should assure himself that he has permission from the actual owner. When the person who wrote the letters still is living, he retains the right to the contents and permission should be obtained from him. If he is dead, the question of ownership may be involved because the person who has the letters may have no publication rights in them.

Almost every year, some one unearths a hitherto unpublished letter written by Lincoln or other prominent figure of a past era. Those letters generally are valuable, and a newspaper should not rush into print with them until it determines who owns the rights. (3)

A newspaper which writes to a person for his views on any subject should make certain he understands the information is wanted for publication. A scientist, for example, in reply to an inquiry from a newspaper might write at length about "flying saucers." Perhaps, he is preparing an article on the subject and may want to retain publication rights. His reply to the newspaper, then, must be considered as merely the imparting of private information which the editor may use as guidance in determining how future stories about the "saucers" will be handled in his paper. The newspaper never will go wrong by having an explicit understanding in writing that material it receives by mail is intended for publication.

The borderline cases are those in which the writer is discussing a general topic and marks his letter "not for publication." An ethical newspaper would respect the writer's wishes, but if it inadvertently or intentionally disregards the request, what legal remedy has the author? This is a question the courts have not determined.

A possible remedy might be a suit by the writer for invasion of his privacy, for a person's thoughts and ideas may be kept to himself if he desires. But it seems presumptuous to maintain that a man who writes about downtown parking meters or the city garbage collection has either literary value or precious thoughts. A man who puts into writing thoughts which he feels may embarrass or damage him is just as foolish as the one who gossips to a friend and then cautions: "Now remember, not a word of this to anyone."

Until the courts rule, however, the newspaper should print no letters marked "not for publication." If the subject matter is of sufficient interest, the newspaper should try to convince the writer the public desires his thoughts.

On many papers, "letters to the editor" are welcomed as an expression of community opinion. Unfortunately, some publicity agencies have learned that most papers will print communications from readers, and they attempt to "plant" stories they otherwise could not get printed by having the material appear in a letter signed by a bona fide resident of the community. It is not unusual to find a local reader's letter discussing industrial, social, economic or international affairs in terms the signer probably doesn't understand. For that reason, a number of newspapers are scrutinizing letters more closely. (4)

Ownership of News

Although, as has been pointed out, news is free to everyone who sees or hears about it, the assembling of news costs newspapers and press associations millions of dollars yearly. The courts therefore recognize that it is unfair for one newspaper or press association to "cut corners" by "lifting" the news of a rival.

Because news is free and also perishable, protection cannot be afforded to it satisfactorily under copyright laws which safeguard literary productions and creative efforts. Since the compiling of news is an undertaking that requires initiative and expense, courts will protect it under the principle of unfair competition or trade practices.

If one press association pays to maintain correspondents at a state capital or other strategic news center and another does not, it would give the latter an unfair advantage to simply "pirate" the material it did not develop itself. Many papers have two or more wire services and it is not too difficult for one press association to check on another before any papers appear on the street.

A newspaper which employs thirty reporters does not want to see a rival with only two reporters equipped with scissors and paste pot clip freely as soon as the first paper comes out with an edition. It, too, is entitled to some protection for its enterprise.

Newspapers and press associations, however, do draw upon each other for "tips." Each major press association has a "code word" for its rivals. Telegraph editors often see coming over the wire a message from one press association bureau to another tipping it off that a rival service has a story from that area which it has missed. The delinquent bureau then goes into action to round up a story of its own.

The United States Supreme Court took cognizance of this practice of newspapers and press associations on obtaining tips from each other.

". . . both parties avowedly recognize the practice of taking tips, and neither party alleges it to be unlawful or to amount to unfair competition in business." (5)

Only in metropolitan centers, do newspapers which publish only in the morning or afternoon, maintain around-the-clock staffs. In smaller cities, each morning or afternoon paper depends upon the other, by tacit custom, to develop for both papers the routine news during its normal working hours. Although journalism does not consider it either unfair or unethical for one paper or wire service to extract "tips" from another, the wholesale appropriation is neither ethical nor legal.

The United States Supreme Court had to pass on this question for the first time in 1918. The Associated Press charged its news was being taken by International News Service in three ways: (a) Employees of certain Associated Press member papers were paid by INS to take news as it came over the AP's leased wires; (b) certain member papers were violating AP by-laws by permitting INS access to their local news before publication; and (c) INS was taking news from early editions of AP papers and from bulletin boards.

The first two questions presented no difficulty for the court. But the third issue revolved around the rights retained by the Associated Press in its news after the first moment of publication. (6) On this problem, the justices found no precedents. (7) The court, five to three, settled the issue by assuming a quasi-property right in news until its commercial value has passed away. The court, thus, arrived at a definition that is indecisive because no one can say when that time limit has expired. News flashed into a newspaper office in the morning may retain commercial value in that community until the paper appears on the street in the late afternoon, although with radio now, such a situation is unlikely. What the court did, then, in effect, was to rule that in news gathering there is a legal concept of unfair competition.

The problem for a time threatened to become acute as radio started its phenomenal growth. In the early days, many radio stations compiled newscasts by merely going to the corner news stand as fast as editions appeared. The news often was read over the air several hours before home subscribers saw the paper.

Again, the Associated Press acted to prevent such unfair competition. It lost its case purely on procedural grounds but the court did say:

"Common sense compels us to agree with the complainant that the purloining of complainant's fresh news and its circulation in KVOS's 'Newspaper of the Air' are both elements of a business of publication for profit. . . . Complainant's news is not only made stale to those of their readers who first have access to the 'Newspaper of the Air,' but also is made free, while still hot, to their readers who pay a usual subscription price for their papers. . . . We are unable to see . . . (it) can be called anything but 'unfair competition'." (8)

This case originated during the so-called "radio-press war." (9)

Necessity and ingenuity combined within a few years to resolve the dispute over news. Newspapers bought radio stations and broadcast their own news. Other stations devised their own local coverage. Press associations employed separate staffs and set up wires for radio stations only. News now is a substantial part of practically every station's programming.

Copyright Protection for Newspapers

The average newspaper seldom can profit from the advantages of statutory copyright. For its day-to-day stories are matters of public knowledge, or as the Supreme Court has said, a record of the history of the day. (10) The element of news in any event cannot be protected.

An eastern newspaper which first hit upon the identities of four dead children in what was being called nationally the "babe in the woods murder case," copyrighted its story. But as soon as it appeared on the streets, rival papers and press associations used the story as a "tip" to develop their own accounts. The copyright notice may have impressed some readers, but its value was scarcely worth the fee. (11)

To secure a copyright, the requirements of the law must have been met at publication time. A paper is afforded no protection by simply printing a copyright notice. In fact, if it does and fails to complete the necessary requirements, it can be fined.

Some publishers copyright the paper as a whole, but here again the fee and trouble are seldom worth it. The "news" element cannot be protected. The non-local features are copyrighted by the syndicate that supplies them, and that leaves the average paper with little other material that can be protected or which is worth protecting. Besides, each edition requires a separate copyright.

Newspaper material which may be copyrighted are stories developed by initiative and enterprise and from sources not generally available. Columns, feature stories not based directly on news, maps, cartoons, puzzles, certain photographs, etc., also may be protected.

A newspaper which sets a reporter to work on an investigation can copyright his story if it is not tied too closely to an event of the day. A paper might comb through records and documents, interview generally inaccessible people, and come up with an expose of the mayor's office. This story could be copyrighted but a rival paper, if it thought the expose worth delving into, may call up the persons named in the article for their comment, affirmation, or denial. In no time, it would have its own version.

A paper, such as the New York *Times*, which helps underwrite explorations or expeditions, can copyright its dispatches from the South Pole. If my paper finances a round-the-world record plane flight, it can copyright the stories from the crew, but at every place the plane lands, rival reporters can write their own versions of what they can observe.

Should the plane get into difficulty and radio for help or ask different airports for weather or landing information, its messages become "news" and may be printed by all who obtain them. The real news of such a trip would be the elapsed time between airports, and that, too, is public. The only protected information are stories from the crew as to how they were eating, sleeping, or passing the time and probably would excite few readers.

Press associations and newspapers copyright stories from foreign correspondents provided the dispatches are not merely reports of an event. A riot in the streets of Paris is public, but a personality sketch of the riot leader may be copyrighted. If the leader is named, any paper can look in standard reference works or other documents and fashion a story of its own. (12)

A reporter who takes the first trip to the moon in a rocket ship can copyright his story upon his return. No other paper may use it without permission. If the reporter, however, says he found human life on the moon, my paper can have a scientist comment on whether he believes that is possible.

A newspaper column may be copyrighted since it usually is considered to be a literary effort. If the copyrighted column, however, says a heavyweight prize fighter is going to retire from the ring, my paper again could call him, or some of his friends, for affirmation or denial.

Since radio has doomed the "scoop" and exclusive stories have a way of being disclosed through contact with the principals by rival papers once the first account is published, the average newspaper does well to concentrate on developing news rather than to worry about protecting its transitory value.

An average newspaper may find that for it, exclusive photographs are more susceptible to copyright protection than stories. Most photographs are taken of an event that is fleeting. A group of bankers, lawyers, executives and other business and social leaders in an eastern state once built a raft to re-live their boyhood days on the river. They planned a 100-mile trip downstream. The second day out, the raft struck a bridge pier and seven of the prominent men were drowned. A news photographer stood on the bridge and snapped the only pictures taken of the men struggling in the water. By the time other cameramen arrived, the bodies had been taken from the river. The first photographer protected his pictures by copyright.

When the liner Vestris foundered off the Virginia Capes with the loss of more than 100 lives, an amateur cameraman stood on the sloping deck, taking pictures. Again, he had protection through copyright. The Atlanta photographer who snapped a picture of a woman jumping from the window of a burning hotel also had an exclusive picture that he could guard.

Of course, any other photographer who happened to be there could have taken either the Vestris pictures or the woman leaping from the hotel window. A newspaper that uses "art" photographs in its rotogravure or Sunday section may copyright them. But if the picture depends, for example, on the special pose of a baby, any other cameraman can obtain a baby model and photograph him. Ideas cannot be copyrighted.

The ownership and use of pictures will be discussed more fully in a later chapter. But unless the newspaper has an exceptional and exclusive photograph of a person or a situation that cannot be duplicated, it will fare better by passing up a copyright and using that fee to buy more plates or developers. Newspapers grow more through day-to-day good work than by spasmodic flashes of genius or luck.

Copyright as a Limitation on Newspapers

Congress had a two-fold purpose in setting up the copyright laws:

(a) Authors are entitled to reap the rewards of their endeavors. The composer of a literary piece should profit from his work and ingenuity as much as the carpenter who builds a house.

(b) The "useful arts" can be advanced only if the public shares them. Progress is not attained by having authors bury their works in bureau drawers nor more than mankind profits if inventors refuse to market their devices.

For that reason, Congress has insisted that statutory protection begins only with publication. Once it is obtained, copyrighted material can be used only by permission of the owner.

The few exceptions include books. A newspaper reviewer under common practice may quote such sentences or even paragraphs as he believes necessary for an intelligent understanding or appraisal of the work. The newspaper, however, cannot reprint a "substantial amount" without infringing upon the copyright. While admitting there is no precise definition for "substantial amount," courts generally hold it to mean any portion that tends to lessen the commercial value of the original.

A book, *A Trip to the Moon*, may contain only three chapters dealing with the actual time the author spent on the planet. The remaining chapters may detail his advance preparations and his feelings when he returned to earth. The three chapters about his experiences on the moon are the heart of the book. Reprinting of one of those chapters certainly reduces the sales value of the book and reproduction of all three chapters may destroy it.

Reproduction of a copyrighted cartoon, photograph, song, lecture, sermon, map, etc. certainly reduces their commercial value, especially in the area where the newspaper circulates. But the ordinary talk a speaker delivers before a convention, club, or organization cannot be copyrighted. Such speakers are not concerned with protecting their talks, but on the contrary, they expect newspapers to give them publicity.

Press associations frequently carry stories beginning: "The New York *Times* (or other paper) tonight in a copyrighted story says, etc." Those stories are used by arrangement with the paper quoted. If used without permission, the fact that the originating paper is given full credit does not eliminate the liability for infringement should the paper desire to bring action.

Material from reference books in the newspaper morgue cannot be used verbatim should the book publishers object. Newspapers, however, usually buy such books solely for the information they contain. An ethical and also a prudent newspaper gives credit to the source which in most cases is satisfactory "payment" for use of the material.

A copyrighted article, cartoon book, map, photograph, etc. is just as much a piece of property as a house or an automobile. The certificate of copyright is just as valid as a deed to real estate. A newspaper should use no copyrighted material unless it first obtains permission. The careful newspaper moreover insists upon having that permission in writing.

For Further Reading

Cormack, Joseph M., "Newspaper Copyright," 18 *Virginia Law Review*, March, 1932.

———"Property Right in News," 22 *Virginia Law Review*, March, 1936.

———"Right of Newspaper to Enjoin Broadcast of News Published," 44 *Yale Law Journal*, March, 1935.

Thayer, Frank, *Legal Control of the Press,* Chicago; The Foundation Press, 1944, Chapters 4 and 14.

17 *United States Code Annotated,* par. 5 (list of subject matter which can be protected by copyright).

COURT DECISIONS

Tribune Co. v. Associated Press, 116 F. 126.

Altman v. New Haven Union Co., 254 F. 113.

Warren v. Pulitzer Publishing Co., 78 S.W. 2d. 404.

Public Ledger Co. v. New York Times Co., 275 F. 562.

Atlantic Monthly Co. v. Post Publishing Co., 27 F. 2d. 556.

Journal Publishing Co. v. Drake, 199 F. 572.

Public Ledger Co. v. Post Printing and Publishing Co., 294 F. 430.

CHAPTER XIV

"Protecting the Sources of News"

In the relatively few areas in which bench, bar and press remain far apart, none looms larger than the question of granting privilege to a reporter and his news sources. (1) Privilege for the press means a confidential status between a reporter and his news source which no court or state agency can compel him to reveal. Statutes permitting this status are commonly called "shield laws."

The first shield law was enacted in Maryland almost without notice in the press elsewhere. (2) A Baltimore reporter in 1896 went to jail for contempt of a grand jury because he refused to disclose the source of his information that enabled him to predict accurately a pending indictment. The Baltimore *Sun* immediately began an editorial campaign to confer privilege upon reporters and a few months later the law was on the statute books of Maryland. (3)

Bench and bar were quick to denounce the new Maryland law. One lawyer wrote:

"In Maryland, they have a statute making the most irresponsible tramp reporter a privileged person in the matter of communications the same as doctors and lawyers." (4) As late as 1940, John Wigmore, whose works on evidence are standard, called such laws "legislative novelties." (5) The bar has grown even more unrelenting in recent years.

The question of privileged communications is old in law. A confidential status between lawyer and client was recognized back in the reign of Queen Elizabeth. Common law also recognized the same privilege between husband and wife. Now by statute or otherwise, practically every jurisdiction in the United States extends privilege to these classes as well as to priest and penitent, physician and patient, and informer and government. A few states have added other classes. (6)

It was 33 years after Maryland enacted its shield law that another such statute went on the books. This one was adopted in New Jersey. Two concerted drives have been made by the press to extend these laws. The one campaign—beginning in 1935—had mild success but a drive in 1948-50 met with only one gain.

Associations of newspaper publishers, newspapermen, and Sigma Delta Chi, journalism fraternity, joined in the 1935 campaign after Martin Mooney, a reporter for the New York *Journal-American*, was sentenced to 30 days for refusing to disclose the source of his information upon which he based a gambling expose. The court of appeals, in affirming Mooney's sentence, said: ". . . in general, the mere fact that a communication was made in express confidence or in the implied confidence of a confidential relation does not create a privilege." (7) Furthermore, the court continued:

> "No pledge of privacy nor oath of secrecy can avail against a man for the truth in a court of justice. The policy of the law is to require the disclosure of all information by witnesses in order that justice may prevail." (8)

Mooney's name is not alone on the list of newspapermen who down through the years have gone to jail or been fined or threatened with such action for refusing to betray a confidence. A New York *Tribune* city editor in 1913 was cited by a grand jury for failing to disclose his source for an expose of frauds in the customs house. Prodded by the jury, he finally invoked constitutional immunity on the ground "it might tend to incriminate me," hinting, in effect, that to reveal the information would be giving testimony against himself. Of course, no one believed he was involved in any way in the frauds, but his plea stymied the jury since no person is forced to testify against himself. The federal attorney then tried a new approach. He had a presidential pardon prepared absolving the editor of any crime in connection with the case. The newspaperman countered by rejecting the pardon. The United States Supreme Court upheld his right to refuse a pardon on the ground it implied a crime with attendant disgrace. (9) The jury finally abandoned its attempt to get the information from him.

The following year, two reporters for the same paper were cited for refusing to name the jewelry smugglers who had provided the information for a series of articles. This time, the reporters came up with a new legal angle. In their appeal, they cited a clause in a federal law which forbids the disclosure of customs house news without the express permission of the Secretary of the Treasury. The appeals court accepted this plea.

Two Washington, D. C., reporters in 1929 went to jail rather than tell the names of some capital bootleggers about whom they had written. That prompted Representative LaGuardia, New York, and Senator Arthur Capper, Kansas, to introduce a bill in Congress to grant privilege to newspapermen. Although the bill failed, Congress, as it was pointed out in an earlier chapter, has shown no inclination in recent years to compel reporters to disclose their news sources.

In 1948, a news editor and a reporter of the Newburgh (N. Y.) *News* refused to disclose where they had obtained information on gambling. A judge, who said he did it reluctantly, sentenced them to ten days in jail. (10)

Frank Gannett, head of the company which publishes the *News*, said he was "proud" of the two men for "acting in the best newspaper traditions." (11)

A Tennessee judge cited a reporter for failure to disclose his source for articles charging that state highway patrol officers protected bootleggers transporting whiskey from wet to dry counties. But in addressing the reporter, the judge said:

"I take my hat off to the newspapers, but I don't think it is fair to the attorney general to withhold information. You do the courts more harm than good when you quote these things and won't tell who the people are." (12)

After a Providence, R. I., Grand Jury criticized newspapers for printing an affidavit obtained about gambling instead of turning it over to police, both the Providence *Journal* and *Bulletin* replied editorially:

"From a practical standpoint, the obvious objection to having our reporters give evidence of illegal gambling to police is the danger that the police themselves may suppress or misuse such information . . . the press has a public function. If

it is the function of the state to give the people police protection, it is equally the function of newspapers to give people
information about how the police are performing. . . . To the
extent that we 'cooperate' with public authorities, we compromise our right to report and criticize their activities. . . .
Our real purpose is to protect the right of the people—the
right to be informed about their government through sources
independent of that government." (13)

In 1950, the editor of a Florida weekly was sentenced to
30 days for keeping in confidence the source of a story about
an attempt to bribe a councilman. (14)

A survey in 1950 disclosed this status of privilege between
the press and its news sources in the several states:

Privilege granted by statute: Alabama, Arizona, Arkansas,
California, Indiana, Kentucky, Maryland, Michigan, Montana,
New Jersey, Ohio, and Pennsylvania.

Privilege by unofficial belief of attorney general: Oklahoma
and Utah. (15) These unofficial opinions were based on court
decisions.

Presiding judge determines: New Hampshire. (16)

Possible protection: South Carolina (17) and Georgia. (18)

Privilege denied by court decisions: Colorado (19) and New
York. (20)

A newspaperman and radio commentator served a term in
the Thurston County, Washington, jail for refusing to disclose
his sources for comments about a grand jury investigation of
state affairs. The case was not appealed and therefore, the question in Washington remains indeterminate.

In all other states, there is neither statutory nor judicial
authority. Attorneys general of many of these states reported the
problem had never been presented to their supreme courts.

Although New Jersey was the second to adopt a "shield"
law, the scope of its protection has been placed in doubt by a
decision of its Supreme Court in 1943, ten years after the statute
was enacted. (21)

The New Jersey law, the model for many of the later statutes,
reads:

> "No person engaged in, connected with or employed on any newspaper shall be compelled to disclose in any legal proceeding or trial, before any court, before any grand jury of any county or any petit jury of any court, before the presiding officer of any tribunal or his agent, or before any committee of the legislature, or elsewhere, the source of any information procured or obtained by him and published in the newspaper on which he is engaged, connected with or employed." (22)

Although the intent of the legislature seemed clear, especially to publishers and newspapermen who led the fight for the law, the supreme court came up with a novel interpretation. In effect, the court said three Hudson county editors could not be forced to tell the sources for their information but must disclose who brought that information to their newspaper offices. The case revolved around statements from certain unnamed city officials.

The subversion of the intent of the law is quickly seen by recognizing that if the editors told who brought that information to them, the messenger could be questioned and forced to tell where he had received it. Eventually, the trail would lead to the officials who gave out the information, and the whole purpose of the law would be defeated.

The court also ruled that the law does not prevent a reporter from disclosing his source if he wishes to do so. Newspapermen had interpreted the law to mean they had the same status as attorneys who are forbidden to divulge communications entrusted to them by clients.

A lawyer who sponsored the law in the assembly said the court's interpretation renders the statute "useless and meaningless." (23)

There have been no recent cases in New Jersey to clarify this doubtful status of the "shield" law.

In 1949, when most legislatures were in session, 18 states considered "shield" laws but Michigan alone enacted such a statute. Four states — Alabama, Arkansas, Indiana and Maryland—amended their laws to place radio reporters under the same protection.

Illinois, which passed a "shield" law in 1935 that fell before a gubernatorial veto, tried again in 1949 without success. Certain sections of the press editorialized against it. (24)

New York, in making another attempt in 1949, received a favorable report from the Codes Committee of the senate, but a number of powerful papers opposed the bill because it offered only limited protection. Under the proposal, supreme court justices could compel a reporter to testify "in the public interest." Obviously, such a phrase can be interpreted to include practically every situation. (25)

Legal periodicals are filled with articles opposing "shield" laws for reporters. Newspapermen and others have written extensively in favor of such laws. On the basis of this voluminous material, arguments on both sides may be summarized as these:

Opposed

1. Courts fear their authority will be weakened if necessary evidence is excluded, and fair trials will be impossible.

2. A sensational press may extol criminals.

3. Public officials could be held up to ridicule and distrust by a newspaper which thus would be relieved of any responsibility to remedy the situation it exposed.

4. Newspapermen would be turned into detectives or might effect alliances with the underworld.

5. In all classes of privilege, the identity of both parties is known, but "shield" laws conceal one party. Therefore, it could not be determined if such a relationship actually existed.

6. News sources are not endangered without such a law because only a small percentage of news is obtained from sources reporters want to protect.

For

1. Disclosure of sources shuts off further news.

2. Disclosure of crime or "unhealthy" civic or political associations, aids justice.

3. Newspapermen can tap many sources which are reluctant to talk to police or authorities.

4. Printing of news is a public service.

5. Libel laws assure adequate protection against reckless publication.

6. The reporter's relation with his source is the same as that of a lawyer with his client. (26)

For legislative guidance, the Law Revision Commission of New York retained a Cornell University law professor to make a survey of the states having "shield" laws. His report concluded that available data ". . . certainly give no indication that in the states where privilege statutes exist, the administration of justice has suffered because of their presence." (27)

The sponsor of a privilege law in the 1949 Tennessee Legislature, declared: "We want to encourage our press constantly to expose the corrupt." (28) The bill failed of passage.

For newspapermen, accustomed to campaigning for many issues on behalf of others, the record of obtaining only one new "shield" law in 1949 in eighteen states, is an indication either that the press, like old Miles Standish, cannot speak effectively for themselves or that bench and bar have erected formidable opposition to extension of privilege.

Protection Against False Information

Despite the care with which a good newspaper scrutinizes the copy that flows into its editorial rooms daily, erroneous stories do find their way into print. A reporter who errs can be disciplined, but what about the false story the paper accepts in good faith from an outside source who may even be a reputable person known to members of the staff?

An error may lead to an expensive libel suit because proving that the story came from a "usually reliable source" is satisfaction only for the editor's soul and not for a jury. Every good society editor, for example, learns quickly that she cannot print a birth announcement until it has been verified by a call-back to the family because some practical jokers with a perverted sense of humor delight in phoning in such announcements about their friends who may have been married only a short time.

Aside from defamatory stories, there are many items which, if untrue, may not seriously damage the affected person but may cause him annoyance and embarrassment to say nothing of the paper's reputation for veracity. Sometimes false items are brought or sent in to a paper to vent a personal spite. A bobby-soxer brought to one paper a prepared engagement announcemen of a popular high school athlete. Unfortunately, the first convenient office was that of the sports editor and because the youth was a three-letter winner, the sports department used the story instead of turning it over to the society desk.

In investigating the youth's complaint the next day, the managing editor discovered the bobby-soxer had hoped the athlete would take her to the senior prom. When he showed no such inclination, she revenged herself by announcing his engagement so that no other girl would accompany him. It is not libelous to say that two eligible persons are engaged, but the story proved embarrassing to the parents of both boy and girl and also the school.

Sometimes the practical joker poses as the secretary of an association or club and sends in an announcement of an important meeting. Then he gets a chuckle standing in front of the hall and checking how many gullibles show up. Or a press agent may go far beyond the bounds of "permissible puffery" with claims that make the paper later appear foolish. (29)

Few states have attempted to deal by law with such situations and in several of these jurisdictions the statutes apply only to libelous stories. New York pioneered such laws by enacting a statute in 1890 making it a misdemeanor to give wilfully a libelous statement to a newspaper. (30) In 1920, New York amended the law to include "any untrue statement of fact with the intent that it be published." (31)

New York newspapers have invoked the law on a number of occasions. In 1945, a man walked into a Utica newspaper and dictated an obituary of his mother. Friends who called at the house the next day with messages of condolence were greeted by the woman herself.

The man told the court he had been drinking and had squandered most of his week's pay. He thought the obituary would create sympathy from a creditor who had been pressing him.

Calling the case the most unusual that ever came before him, City Judge Walsh, sentenced the man to 30 days in jail and told him:

"We have come to rely upon our newspapers as the greatest source of truth in our democracy, a truthful medium of facts. In perpetrating this hoax, you have worked deliberately to destroy the faith we have in newspapers.

"In order that the public will know that the Court places a great reliance upon our newspapers, you will have to be dealt with severely. . . . It (the sentence) is a warning to you, and more important, it is a warning to everyone else, that they cannot give false information to the newspapers and escape punishment." (32)

A survey of the states shows the following protect the newspaper against false news through criminal penalties against the informers:

Penalties for any false information: Arizona, Maine, Minnesota, Montana, New York, Ohio, (33) Utah, and Virginia.

Penalties only if information is libelous: Nevada, North Dakota, Pennsylvania, and Washington.

Penalties for false births, marriages, and deaths: Rhode Island.

North Carolina provides penalties for "false *and* libelous" information but there has been no judicial determination whether the story must be both. (34)

All states, however, have statutes providing criminal penalties for circulating false stories about the condition of banks, trust companies, building and loan associations, and other financial institutions. If the false story concerned a bank, presumably both informer and newspaper could be penalized.

Since the statutes treat such offenses as misdemeanors, the penalties usually range from fines of $100 to $500 and prison terms of 30 days to 11 months. (35)

The legal crux of these laws centers around the requirement that the purveyor of the information must know that it is false. That suggests only a jury can determine if the purveyor knew it was false or if he merely repeated a rumor or an opinion as a fact.

A Canadian court was presented with an unusual case of a man who confessed to newspapermen that he had committed two murders. In the absence of a specific statute, the man was arrested on a charge of obstructing justice when his story was found to be a hoax. But the court ruled that since newspapermen are not officers of the law the man was guilty of no crime. (36) In effect, the ruling also was notice to reporters not to be so gullible and print confessions before they learn if there have been any murders.

During the depression of the 1930's, there were a number of cases of men in one part of the country confessing to murders and serious crimes in another section of the United States. When they were returned by officers, it was readily ascertained they could not have been involved. Apparently, they merely wanted free transportation to that section.

Since these confessions were made to policemen and not to reporters, newspapers, even in states having laws against false information could bring no action. Police might have charged them with interefering with justice but there is difficulty in proving that a confession is a pure hoax rather than the trick of an overwrought mental state or imagination. Besides, police in most cases were quite willing to forget their blunders if the public would do likewise.

Sometimes the hoaxer, if he hurts no one in particular, is regarded by the newspaper as merely the source of interesting feature material. Some youths at Cornell University once arranged an elaborate 90th birthday celebration for a mythical pioneer iron and steel manufacturer. Messages of congratulations poured in from governors, industrial leaders, and a host of other prominent people whose rewards for kindly thoughts were only red faces when the hoax was exploded. University of Pennsylvania medical students had a national publication accept their favorite skeleton as one of the outstanding college men of the year. The skeleton received a certificate and a highly complimentary letter from the editor.

In 1950, some officials of the United Nations were chagrined when nominations came in for cities in which to hold an inter-

national parley on tariff. One of the suggested cities was Pif-
fleheim and the name was solemnly sent around for member
nations to vote upon. Finally, some one suggested to the secre-
tariat that it look up the American meaning of "piffle."

Stories of flying saucers from other planets were printed
freely in 1949 and 1950 and probably the most fantastic was
that about a Los Angeles man who had seen a wrecked saucer
in the Mexican mountains and in it a 22-inch midget, presumably from another world. When scientists began writing on the
subject, no newspaper then could be certain if the subject be-
longed in the news or feature sections.

Presumably, in states which have statutes against false information, a newspaper could ask for criminal action against
its own reporters for a hoax. During prohibition, an overly-
imaginative New York City reporter hoaxed his own paper with
a story about a palatial liner anchored off Sandy Hook on which
nattily-dressed men and women in evening gowns drank and
gambled. The reporter's otherwise brilliant services were dispensed with but the paper took no further action against him.

To some, it may be a paradox that even in states which have
laws against hoaxers, there is no penalty for a paper which of
its own volition prints false stories. Of course, if the stories
are defamatory, the injured party has recourse to libel suits.

In the early days of American journalism, hoaxes helped
build up circulation. Readers of the old New York *Sun* revelled
in the astounding discoveries of human life on the moon, supposedly made by a well-known astronomer, and later, New York
buzzed over stories about the man who crossed the Atlantic in
a balloon but the trip existed only in the imagination of Edgar
Allan Poe.

Even the master showman, P. T. Barnum, was hoaxed by the
petrified man dug up in 1889 at Cardiff, N. Y., and when he
could not purchase it for $150,000, he made a duplicate and
toured the country. As recent as 1917, H. L. Mencken wrote
a faked newspaper article about how America fought the introduction of the bathtub. Some cities, he said, passed ordinances against it and one President ordered a tub taken out of
the White House. Unfortunately, his article now appears in
some authentic history books.

Stories in Indiana newspapers in 1949 sent thousands of people to a small lake to see a giant turtle that started out with a weight of 500 pounds but seemed to grow with each edition. Metropolitan reporters and cameramen who also hastened to the lake were just as disappointed as the spectators when the turtle refused to came up for pictures and interviews.

A statute making a newspaper criminally responsible for false stories (other than libelous articles) would be impractical to enforce, assuredly unconstitutional, no doubt entirely ineffectual, and certainly unnecessary. Every honest mistake which a good newspaper corrects promptly would become a crime, a county prosecutor could become a negative censor, and a jury probably would have to pass on most of the contents daily.

A newspaper's editorial columns may be opinionated and its human-interest features may tickle the imagination, but its news columns are open to no trifling. A newspaper that loses the confidence of its readers goes out of business just as promptly as the store which no longer commands the goodwill of its customers. Even in the so-called "monopoly" cities, where there is only one newspaper, residents can check its accuracy by reading local stories in out-of-town newspapers which may also circulate in that community or by listening to the radio. Few communities today are at the mercy of only one news source.

Court decisions, in cases other than libel, have established that papers have no legal obligation for stories that may prove false. A newspaper's mistake in a recipe may cause many women to throw their newly-baked cakes into the garbage can, but none of them can sue for either the material or time she wasted.

A sports article that misses an important point in its instructions for a trick dive, does not make the paper responsible if a subscriber tries it and hurts his back. A woman who tried a dandruff remedy mentioned in a newspaper article lost both dandruff and her hair. The courts dismissed her claim for damages on the ground the writer had not professed to be a physician but merely had given advice much as would a friend or neighbor. (37) A New Mexico paper printed an obituary of a man which proved to be false. A son had a heart attack when he read of his father's supposed death, but the courts held the paper was not liable. (38)   A New York reader was denied the right of action after he lost money because the newspaper had made a mistake in stock quotations.

In 1938, Orson Welles threw New Jersey into a turmoil by his "invasion of Mars" broadcast.   Thousands of people became panicky.   Some barricaded their homes and others went screaming hysterically into the streets.   The more stalwart grabbed guns and went out to defend their state.

No one had any legal remedy, no matter how much anguish he may have suffered, but the Federal Communication Commission could reprimand the originating station.   Further such scripts no doubt would have been figured in the station's license renewal.

The Newark (N. J.) *Star-Ledger*, during the "flying saucer" excitement published an imaginary interview with the pilot of a saucer who was supposed to have landed on the roof of the newspaper building.   The paper planned it as a fantasy, but many people apparently didn't stop to ask themselves such obvious questions as how the "flying saucer champion" of Mars happened to speak such good English.   To allay fears, the paper the next day explained the story had been a hoax.

At least one man said he had to call a physician to quiet his wife's nerves.   Another woman also complained of being so upset she became ill.   But in neither case would the sufferer have a legal remedy against the paper. (39)

To say that a newspaper should have no liability for a false story but that a person who deliberately gives faked news to it, should be punished is not paradoxical.   A newspaper is a responsible business institution; a practical joker or the person bent on spite or revenge is irresponsible.   The difference may roughly be compared with that between the established department store which must succeed or fail by community goodwill and the itinerant peddler who drops in to "work" the town and then moves on.

Although relatively few states have statutes against purveying of false information to newspapers, there has been little agitation in press circles in recent years to extend this type of law.

Apparently, newspapers believe that with or without such a law, the best protection is a vigilant news desk.

For Further Reading

Code of Ethics, American Newspaper Guild, Sec. 5 (for Guild's stand on privilege).

"Confidence Laws" in 36 Virginia Law Review, February, 1950.

Corpus Juris (legal encyclopedia) title "Witnesses," p. 377.

Steigleman, Walter, "Newspaper Confidence Laws," 20 Journalism Quarterly, September, 1943.

————, "Combating the Practical Joker," 22 Journalism Quarterly, December, 1945.

Tilbits, Legrand E., "Confidence Laws," 22 Cornell Law Quarterly, December, 1936.

————article on confidence and privilege, 84 University of Pennsylvania Law Review and American Register, December-January, 1935-36.

Wigmore, John, Evidence in Trials at Common Law, Boston; Little, Brown and Co., 1940, Vol. 5.

———— article on confidence and privilege, 45 Yale Law Journal, March, 1936.

COURT DECISIONS

Plunkett v. Hamilton, 70 SE 781.

In re: Grunow, 85 A. 1011.

People vs. Durant, 48 P. 75.

Ex parte: Lawrence, 48 P. 124.

CHAPTER XV

"Photographs and the Law"

Framers of the United States Constitution could not foresee that one day technology and inventiveness would combine to produce photography, radio, and other devices to confound their direct and concise command that freedom of the press must not be abridged.

Long after photography had passed from the novelty stage, many newspapers still had not appreciated that pictures, instead of being mere illustrations or "fillers," might be used as an almost independent branch of reporting. The reputed Chinese axiom that "one picture is worth 10,000 words" has made a great impression today on most newspaper editors.

The delay of the newspaper in utilizing the full effect of pictures was due to several causes. Technological development was necessary to permit picture-taking to be adapted to the speed of newspaper production. Some of the lag was due also to the high cost of the whole process from snapping the picture to reproducing it on the newspaper page. But editors cannot discount their own lack of vision as another contributing factor in the delay. (1)

Today, by wire, cable, and radio, pictures are flashed from one end of the world to the other, and even the smallest papers seem to have become "picture conscious." The reader has come to expect not only the latest news but also pictures to show him what the "cold type" cannot describe.

Pictures always have presented legal problems, but the development of the so-called candid camera accentuated them. Although that fad seems to have diminished, for a number of years amateur photographers bobbed up in meetings, theaters, and other gatherings. Railroads once ran special trains through scenic country with frequent stops to permit the "shutter bugs" to climb down and start shooting. A man trying to regain his equilibrium on an icy pavement or enjoying a hot dog in front of a roadside stand was never sure that his antics would not bob up in a newspaper or a photography magazine.

In his relations with the law, the photographer differs from the reporter in several ways. For while news is free, pictures involve three essential legal points:

1. The right to take the picture.
2. The ownership of the picture.
3. The right to publish the picture.

In each point, legal questions arise that may trap the unwary cameraman.

The Right to Take Pictures

An old general rule was that a photographer may take a picture of anything he can see, even if he has to stand on tiptoes.

But this generalization needs some clarification because two conditions are involved. The photographer must stand only where he has a legal right to be, and the subject matter should be in a public or semi-public place.

The cameraman's legal right to be in a particular place must not be a restricted one. A student who complies with university regulations may attend certain classes, but he has no right to take pictures in those meetings without the instructor's permission. The instructor may not have the right to grant such permission if general university rules forbid it. An individual may have permission, if not a right, to attend court sessions but that again doesn't include the privilege of taking pictures. Visitors at times are permitted at military installations but may not violate rules against photographs.

There is no conflict over the proposition that any photographer standing in a public place can snap pictures of events occurring in public places. A cameraman can shoot a picture of a traffic accident in the street. Pictures can be taken of the Easter parade as the promenaders stroll along the boulevard. A man chasing his hat along a windy street can be photographed although the picture may embarrass him. A picture, taken in a public place, then, is no more different than a news item obtained there. The subject of both picture and news story forfeit their anonymity by being there.

A difficulty arises in situations where the cameraman is in a public place but the subject matter is on private property. The president of an eastern college was accustomed during the summer months to work in his office in a bathing suit. He refused to permit his photograph to be taken, and a cameraman had no right to barge into his office to snap it.

One photographer, however, stood on the sidewalk bordering the campus and snapped the president as he walked from one building to another. The educator attempted legal action but was advised he had no remedy since he had exposed himself to public gaze. It would seem paradoxical to contend that although anyone walking on the public pavement might see him he still was protected from pictorial reporting.

The rights of a photographer in such cases are interwoven with other problems, both legal and practical. The newspaper is concerned primarily with pictures that are "news" and the intangible element of judging when an event is of public interest often conflicts with strict legal theories.

If a man practices yogi rituals, the newspaper may feel he is of sufficient news interest to warrant a story and pictures. The newspaper may regard the article as purely an entertainment feature, but some readers may be glad to learn about new methods for relaxation or concentration.

When the yogi practices on his front lawn, he seems to have little ground for insisting upon privacy since all who walk by may stop and watch. But where he confines the ritual to his living room, passersby may not sneak up to a window for a peep, and neither may a photographer take a picture.

Should the yogi display be limited to his hedge-lined back yard, the assumption is the man desires privacy as well as fresh air. How much of the former he gets, depends upon the height and thickness of the hedge and also upon the number of stories of adjoining buildings. For no law prevents an individual from looking out his own windows or even inviting friends to share the vista if it is interesting or pleasing enough.

On the question of photographing the man in his back yard, law becomes involved with the practical work-day world. A photographer could not step into the yard to take a picture. But, if given permission, he could stand on the balcony of the house next door.

The right to publish such a picture, however, brings up several legal questions, one of which—privacy—will be discussed fully in a succeeding section. And privacy is a subject on which the several jurisdictions do not agree.

Although the law assumes a man's house is his castle, he cannot do exactly as he pleases. He cannot annoy his neighbors with loud talk, or noise, or pummel his wife and children, or set fire to the building. The law even prescribes the minimum amount of clothing he may wear in front of his children.

A man's immunities become fewer as he steps into his yard. If he wears less clothing than society regards as the minimum for outdoors, he can be arrested for indecency although he walks only in his fence-enclosed yard. In many communities he cannot build bonfires without obtaining a permit, raise pigs or goats, or carry on experiments that may harm or annoy neighbors or endanger other property.

So the principle that a man's house is his castle admits of many exceptions. And his activities in his own yard are subject to even more social control. But society's concern over enforcing these limitations does not mean that the public in general should have an equal interest in everything the man does in his own yard. The question, then is: Does the public have enough general interest in his yogi tricks to entitle it to read about them and see photographs?

In states recognizing the principle of privacy, the yogi might make good his claim that publication of photographs invades his right to be let alone. The courts, of course, would have to decide whether, since neighbors and probably passersby could see him, he didn't forfeit his protection of privacy. In jurisdictions where privacy is not recognized, he undoubtedly would have to prove he was damaged by the pictures. In both jurisdictions, however, the newspaper should be aware of the possible risk involved in the publication of such photographs.

A more practical problem, which has been faced by at least several newspapers, is the right to photograph such an event as a wedding reception if held in an enclosed lawn or yard. A marriage license is a public record, but the marriage ceremony and reception are private.

The only two afternoon newspapers in an eastern city were denied the right to photograph such a wedding reception of the daughter of a state official. The family had contracted with an out-of-town commercial studio and insisted the newspaper must use its pictures. The studio wanted $10 a print which the newspapers felt was not a fair price.

In a plot adjoining the enclosed lawn, a contractor was excavating for a new house. He permitted cameramen to stand on a steamshovel and obligingly moved it to a position where the wedding reception could be photographed almost as well as from the lawn. The bride's father talked of legal action if the pictures were published but did not follow up his threat. The legal questions, therefore, remained undetermined. But the community apparently enjoyed both the pictures and the story of how they were obtained.

In such cases, however, the paper has a practical solution if not a legal one. It can refuse to print the commercial pictures and insist that either it takes its own photographs or the reception gets no publicity. Few brides hesitate when such a choice is laid before them.

Accidents occurring on private property present a less confused issue because, for one thing, public interest in them can be justified more readily. Train wrecks and airplane crashes are news, and both have a way of happening mostly on private property. To snap train wrecks a photographer usually must stand on the railroad's right-of-way or on adjoining private property. Either the railroad or the land owner may arrest the cameraman for trespassing, but in practice this is seldom done. The owner of the private land in most cases, if he is on hand, finds it more interesting to cooperate with a news photographer than to insist upon restrictions favoring the railroad.

Railroad detectives, however, have dispersed photographers from the right-of-way and also have tried at times to confiscate the plates. Since any damage in pictures is generally not from the taking but from the publication of them, a photographer can bring in an assault and battery charge against a railroad detective who forcibly takes plates from him. A photographic plate is just as much a piece of property as an automobile, and a railroad detective can't seize it or break it any more than a traffic policeman can wreck an automobile which is parked illegally.

Plane crashes also occur mostly on private property, but unless they are military planes, cameramen, as a rule, experience no difficulty. A photographer, however, cannot interfere with rescue attempts just to get a better picture.

Many legal writers, stressing the strict interpretation of law, emphasize the necessity for the event to be on public land. But some courts apparently have come to the conclusion that picture taking should not be too different from news reporting of outdoor events. If a reporter can be there to gather facts for a story, the cameraman should have the same privilege.

In Philadelphia, two guards employed by a private corporation attempted by force to prevent a photographer from taking a picture of an outdoor accident at the company plant. The two private policemen were indicted for assault and battery but the complaining newspapers later refused to prosecute after an assistant district attorney and judge had reprimanded the guards.

The assistant district attorney said:

"The Commonwealth takes the view that whether news photographers take pictures on public property or on private property, makes no difference, so long as the occurrence is of public concern; that under the circumstances even though the photographers may have been on private property, their basic right of taking pictures should have been in no way impeded." (2)

While the guards were "roughing up" one cameraman, a second photographer took a picture of them. Shown this picture, the judge commented:

"This case expresses one of the very fundamental principles of law. And these men (the guards) ought to know that this was an assault on the newspaperman's basic right to take photographs, assuming there was no abuse of that privilege, because they have a right to print freely.

"These defendants ought to be taught that they challenge the very basic right of a newspaper to print the news, and they just cannot use their arms and hands, as is shown in this photograph, when these photographers are taking pictures." (3)

A photographer taking pictures of an accident at a midget auto race in Massachusetts had his plates seized by a track official. A judge held the track official under $1500 bail. (4)

An Alabama governor was billed by a Columbus, Georgia, paper for film holders which the paper said an aide of the official had destroyed at the chief executive's order during a football game at Auburn, Ala. The photographer rescued one plate showing one of the governor's aides lunging at him, and the paper not only used it but made it available to other newspapers. The governor apparently objected to being photographed while he held a paper cup in his hand. (5)

A news photographer driving back from an assignment noticed some excitement at a pool on a private estate. He climbed the fence and got to the pool in time to take pictures of rescuers dragging from the water the bodies of two drowned boys. The estate was owned by a lawyer who threatened action if the picture were used. The paper countered by admitting the cameraman had trespassed but declared it was willing to have him pay the nominal fine that goes with that offense. It published the photograph, and the lawyer took no action.

What the courts would have done is problematical. Although the event was on private land, it certainly was affected with public interest. And the coroner's report on the accident was a public record.

The right to take pictures in semi-public places brings up at once the difficulty in defining "semi-public." Such a definition is as ineffectual as those which try to distinguish private from public meetings.

The eccentric millionaire who stood on his head in the lobby of the Metropolitan Opera House in New York, during the intermission, received wide pictorial publicity. Photographers had a field day, too, with the woman who propped her feet on a chair in the same lobby and started puffing on a cigar.

An actress, working the minor vaudeville and supper-club circuits, showed up at a theater a few days after her marriage with a badly swollen black eye. A newspaper learned she had sworn out an assault and battery charge against her bridegroom, but she refused to be photographed. The managing editor sent a cameraman to the theater. As she appeared on the stage, the photographer stood up and snapped her picture.

Patrons in turn applauded her unladylike tirade and the action of the cameraman in taking a picture of her demonstration. She demanded the photographer be evicted, but as he was leaving under the friendly propulsion of two ushers, the theater manager stuck a $5 bill into his hands and whispered:

"Be sure I get two good prints."

Undoubtedly, the photographer could have been arrested on a disorderly conduct charge brought by the theater manager. As a matter of practical business, few theater managers would risk antagonizing a local newspaper for an incident that their showmanship tells them will pack the house for future performances.

The actress did not make good her threat of suing for invasion of privacy. An old New York decision suggests she may have had a case, but in view of today's wide use of pictures, an actress who performs before all who have the inclination or the admission price to see her, might have trouble convincing a jury she suffered any damages. As a matter of fact, the publicity brought her engagements in theaters and clubs which in the past did not feel she was a sufficient drawing attraction.

A Los Angeles judge, in a suit brought by Movie Star, Robert Mitchum, gave an unusual twist to cases involving actors. Soon after Mitchum was convicted of possessing marihuana cigarettes, a woman, in offering a sofa for sale, advertised that "Robert Mitchum Sat Here." The court dismissed his suit on the ground that movie stars make their living selling themselves to the public and therefore, have very limited claims to privacy. (6)

A railroad station, ship pier, hotel lobby, office building lobby, and similar places where people come and go freely, may be considered as semi-public. If people there are newsworthy, the photographer can take their pictures but he cannot force them to pose nor create a disturbance.

When Al Capone was released from federal penitentiary, a newspaper sent three cameramen to a railroad station on a "hunch" that the gangster might board a train for Chicago. The first photographer was instructed to snap Capone, the second was told to start shooting if anything happened to the first man, and the third was ordered to watch for anything the first two missed.

As Capone swung up the concourse steps with two body-guards, the first cameraman fired away. One of the body-guards lashed out and knocked the camera from the photographer's hands only to see the second take a picture of the action.

The other bodyguard then complained to a station policeman that "passengers were being annoyed." The officer promised to look around and if he saw any disturbance to quell it. Just as the Capone entourage started down the steps to the train shed, the third photographer called to them and snapped them as they turned around. That completed the series.

A man who is greeted with a kiss from a girl as he emerges from the train gate has no legal remedy although the picture may prove embarrassing. If he thinks he has news value he should either reconcile himself to the possibility of having his picture taken or else caution his female friends not to be so demonstrative in public.

Ownership of Pictures

The newspaper owns the photographs which its cameramen take. But it does not always own the pictures it acquires by other means.

Commercial and portrait studios take pictures on order. The negatives they may keep in their files but a studio legally cannot give nor sell a print for publication without the consent of the party who paid for the sitting.

This picture is somewhat analogous to the letter. The letter writer retains the thoughts and ideas; the receiver owns the paper and envelope. The studio owns the negative but the sitter controls the use of the prints.

The doctor who X-rays your chest and the dentist who takes pictures of your teeth, own the negatives. You pay for the service and not for the negatives. But you control all publication rights and if pictures of your chest or teeth bob up in a medical or dental journal, you have a right of action against the doctor or dentist. And neither man may make prints and show them to colleagues at the next meeting of his professional society.

Pictures, of course, can be copyrighted, and the copyright owner then controls publication as much as the author does of his literary work. Many newspapers, especially in smaller communities, arrange with commercial studios to furnish pictures for publication. Many papers use this method for obtaining photographs of weddings or anniversaries, high school or college graduates, business and civic leaders, and in general, of people who are of permanent or transitory news value in the community.

Technically, the newspaper should have permission of the subject before the picture is used. It is unlikely, however, that a bride or a businessman just elected chairman of the Community Chest will object to publication of their photographs. Many studios build up their business on the strength of their ability to have the local newspapers publish the pictures.

Where a crime is involved, the situation is different legally but confusing from a practical standpoint. The news of the man's arrest may be the front page banner. To include a photograph of him, although obtained from a source not authorized to give it, certainly cannot damage him further except to enable more people to recognize him.

If the crime is particularly newsworthy, the newspapers probably will take his picture as he posts bail, enters jail if bond is denied, goes to his preliminary hearing, or at any other step in the proceedings. In view of such pictorial possibilities, the legal question is: In what way has he actually been injured by the

studio picture? And what remedy does he have? It's too late
to enjoin publication of the picture, he hasn't been libeled unless the caption infers he is guilty and later he is acquitted, and
his privacy was lost legally by his arrest.

It doesn't seem logical, therefore, to permit him to collect
damages for the studio picture when later the newspaper may
publish as many photographs of him as it cares to take. On
the other hand, there was a definite breach of contract when
the studio turned over his photograph for publication.

Such questions, unfortunately, have not been judicially construed for the guidance of newspapers because practically all
suits over photographs have involved unauthorized use in advertisements or violations of copyright. In these cases, the law
speaks plainly.

The Right of Publication

Publication of pictures, then, involves these factors: (a) Ownership of the picture; (b) contract existing between subject and
photographer; (c) libel; (d) pictures which the law will not permit to be used; (e) invasion of privacy.

A newspaper, it has been pointed out, cannot legally use a
picture which it does not own unless it has acquired publication
rights. As one court has said the rights belong to the individual
who pays for the photograph. (7)

The presumption is that a person who engages a photographer has a contract with him. The photographer breaches the
contract when he supplies a print to a third person unless the
sitter approves. Newspapers, however, want photographs only
of people in the news. If the subject is in the news, his chief
claim to legal protection—privacy—already is in doubt because
of his participation in an event of public interest.

A woman did win a suit because a studio gave to a newspaper a print of the picture it had taken for her of her dinner
party. But even legal journals criticized that decision, for it
was published in connection with a news story. (8)

If an explorer is financed privately, his backers may send
photographers along and take exclusive pictures which can be
copyrighted. But since the expedition must load somewhere,

any newspaper can take pictures of those preparations as well as at any stops the party makes enroute. A newspaper, if it wished to spend the money, could have a cameraman at the North Pole or in the jungles to await the arrival of the exploring party. It could not go among the expedition members without permission nor could it "shadow" the party as it proceeds with its actual work.

Such an expense would seldom be warranted because the supporters of the expedition probably want to sell pictures to newspapers and press associations to help defray expenses. For a few dollars a newspaper thus would obtain rights to as many pictures as it wished.

The problem of the contract between sitter and photographer usually resolves into a practical working arrangement. The other factors—privacy, libel, and forbidden pictures, admit of real danger to the newspaper.

Libel in Pictures

In succeeding chapters, libel in stories will be dealt with at length. It is sufficient here to define libel in pictures as any picture which defames the subject by damaging his reputation or holding him up to scorn, contempt, or ridicule. The most common form of libel in pictures is wrong identification. The photograph purports to be that of an individual in the news but through an error, it is actually the likeness of another person who may have no connection with the event described.

A Chicago paper lost a libel suit because a photograph purporting to be that of a girl mentioned in a suicide story was actually the likeness of another girl. (9) The New York *Herald* in a feature story on a notorious Italian bandit, quoted him as saying he planned to visit the United States. The illustrative photograph was not that of the bandit but of a man living in New York. The courts held it was libelous. (10)

A Denver paper in a story about a girl making an appeal to the governor to save her father from the gallows for killing her mother inadvertently used the wrong photograph. This also was held to be libelous. (11)

Numerous other decisions support the conclusion that a wrong photograph, no matter how innocent the error, is libelous if used in connection with a defamatory story.

Cartoons also may be libelous if defamatory. But a caricature in itself is not libelous. The law recognizes that caricatures, especially of public figures, depend upon the exaggeration of features, stance, or actions.

If the cartoon, however, infers the subject is guilty of illegal or unethical acts, it is libelous. (12)

In Arizona, police raided a studio and confiscated pictures of female models who had been photographed in the nude. A newspaper printed just the heads of these photographs. Six models sued for libel and for invasion of privacy. The privacy count was dismissed but the jury awarded each one $500 for libel. (13)

Pictures, which standing alone are permissible, may be rendered libelous by wrong or defamatory cutlines. Two jurisdictions have ruled that to falsely call a man a Communist is libelous. If the Communist party holds an outdoor rally, all who attend may not be Communists because undoubtedly curiosity seekers will drop around. A man in a clearly recognizable position might be libeled if the caption merely said: "Communists Whoop It Up."

A minister, wearing an ordinary business suit, stopped to watch prisoners caught in a gambling raid being taken from the patrol wagon into the city jail. The caption indicated every one in the photograph was under arrest. The minister had a few solemn moments explaining to parishioners that he was just a spectator. He, too, might have had cause for action had he chosen to bring it although the picture was taken on the sidewalk.

A mayor of a midwestern city, elected on a reform ticket, was forced as part of a club initiation, to play a slot machine. A journalism student snapped a photograph and had it on the way to a picture magazine before he checked the legal implications. To members of the club, the mayor was just contributing to the evening's fun. To outsiders, however, he might have appeared in a different light had the photograph been published.

It takes clear and clever cutlines to erase the sting of such pictures, for a man whose reputation is injured through a joke suffers just as much as one hurt intentionally. A careful editor does not live in a year-round atmosphere of April Fool.

A church deacon coming out of a state liquor store with a package under his arm may be photographed. But the caption may make the picture libelous. The deacon may have stopped in the store to chat with a church member or a relative who works there. The package he is carrying may be a pair of shoes or his lunch.

All persons entering or leaving a strike-bound factory may not be labor "scabs." Persons not connected with the strike or the factory, may have legitimate business there.

A state senator, popularly known as the "father of the prohibition law" (in that state) was photographed as he sat whistling at his desk in the chamber. The cutlines said he was whistling "How Dry I Am." The senator the next day maintained the photographer was "tone deaf" because the tune actually was "How Firm a Foundation." The correction made even a better news story than the original item, and the senator was satisfied.

The danger of libel lurks in illustrations for exposes, no matter if the subject is violation of the all-night parking ordinance or butchers who cheat by putting their hands on the scales. A paper joining in a campaign against owners who leave their cars parked on principal streets all night, took pictures at random. One automobile pictured, with license plates showing plainly, was that of the chairman of a citizens' traffic committee which had initiated the drive. He was on an emergency trip to a drug store whose owner opened out of hours to fill a prescription for him. He was damaged by this unfair insinuation that he was violating the rules he was campaigning to enforce. Law sometimes may not give such a man relief but ethics should.

Exposes are illustrated more safely by posed photographs with the models clearly understanding and agreeing to what is expected of them. For the photographer should realize his camera must be aimed as carefully as a loaded gun.

Forbidden Pictures

States have laws against publication of obscene photographs and the federal government prohibits their circulation through the mails. "Obscenity" is another word that defies precise definition.

A magazine devoted to the serious study of art may contain pictures that in another publication might be classified as obscene. A working definition, therefore, depends upon the circumstances.

Metropolitan art centers frequently send exhibits on tour so that more people may learn to appreciate good paintings. If the exhibit contains nudes, the editor, with the awareness that his is a family newspaper, must let his own judgment dictate which pictures he will reproduce. For the law permits him to reprint art works if intended as such.

A Milwaukee, Wis., judge ruled that photographs of nude women on the covers of match boxes were obscene. The judge said that while such pictures could be displayed properly in an art gallery, the saloon in which police found the match boxes, could not be classified as such, despite some paintings on the walls. (14)

The law places no restrictions on gruesome photographs of mangled bodies or of the body of a dead person lying in state. Again, the editor is limited only by his own conception of his readers' wishes. If he has even a rudimentary sense of good taste, he should never become involved with the laws governing obscenity.

Laws also prohibit the reproduction of money, postage stamps, securities, and other financial notes. But the law is not too meticulous. Coins were eliminated from the law in 1951.

Such statutes have two purposes: (a) To lessen the chances of counterfeiting, and (b) to prevent the passing of the reproduction as genuine.

Stamps may be pictured generally if the size is smaller or larger than the original and in black and white. Christmas and Easter seals look like postage stamps, but certainly the only persons who can be fooled by them are probably those who still persist in mailing letters in fire alarm boxes.

It is far-fetched to maintain that a picture of a pile of money seized in a gambling raid lends aid to counterfeiters or permits a reader to cut out one of the bills and spend it with even the most gullible storekeeper.

A paper with a series on how prominent people of the community made their first dollar started out to illustrate it by having each subject hold up a dollar bill. The legality of the picture, since it was in black and white and the bill appeared much smaller than its original size, does not seem to be as open to question so much as the editors' news sense, for the photographed dollar had at the most only symbolic significance. But undue apprehension over the law, finally induced the editor to change illustrations which probably relieved the readers more than the government.

Before reproducing any stamps, money, bills or financial papers, the editor should ask himself if the newspaper picture is likely to fool anyone or if counterfeiters might be able to use it. In practically all cases, he can answer the question himself readily.

Privacy in General

Although the privacy of an individual may be invaded in the news columns as well as in pictures, the principal concern to a newspaper is in photographs. For many times a newspaper may use a picture of a subject which has little news appeal aside from the illustration.

In no area of law of the press, is there as much confusion as in the doctrine of privacy. Only a few states have dealt with it by statute, and some jurisdictions even deny there is such a right.

A dozen courts may have just as many definitions of privacy but for practical purposes it may be considered as "the right of each individual to be let alone or not to be dragged into publicity." (15)

The assumption, then, is that every person may keep his private affairs to himself. He loses that right, of course, by participating, voluntarily or involuntarily, in a public act. A man, for example, may keep to himself his views on all subjects, but if he answers the question of an inquiring reporter on the street, his opinions become subject to discussion by the paper or any readers. His daily normal routine also is private although when he steps from his front door he is out in public and his actions can be observed.

If a newspaper decides to award him a prize for being the most careful pedestrian in town he may modestly decline or ignore the honor, but he can hardly complain his privacy has been invaded. However, if a newspaper without his consent enters him in a contest to choose the most popular man in town, he may object legally.

Although some legal writers attempt to trace the doctrine of privacy back to early eighteenth century England, the first detailed espousal of it in the United States came in 1890 in an article written by Louis D. Brandeis and his law partner, Samuel D. Warren. The two, apprehensive of the rise of "yellow journalism," advocated damages or injunctions for violations of ". . . the right of each of us to keep his private life in private." (16)

But in only one area did the doctrine take very firm hold New York, Virginia, and California, by statute, and about 11 other states definitely support the right of privacy for unauthorized use of names or photographs for trade purposes. A number of other jurisdictions have tended to swing in that direction.

When the doctrine is applied to news, the shadowland grows large. Besides the varying definitions of news, there are also elements of time and relevancy. Is an event that happened 50 years ago news today merely because a paper decides it is and revives it? If years after a man drops from the headlines a paper looks him up to report what he is doing now, is that legitimate news?

These are questions which courts have faced. A New York court ruled that an erstwhile child prodigy was not damaged legally when years later a magazine checked into his whereabouts and wrote an article about his then rather humdrum life. (17)

Said the court:

"Regrettable or not the misfortunes and frailities of neighbors and 'public figures' are subjects of considerable interest and discussion to the rest of the public. And when such are the mores of the community it would be unwise for a court to bar their expression in the newspapers, books, and magazines of the day." (18)

Two Alabama sisters sued a radio station for broadcasting a story about the disappearance of their father 43 years previously. There were no new developments in the mystery, but the court ruled that ". . . the right of privacy is supported by logic and the weight of authority . . . but in the face of legitimate public interest it has to give way." (19)

A studio to advertise a motion picture featuring a "girl who had a way with men" penned notes in feminine handwriting on tinted stationery and mailed them to men whose names were obtained from directories and other sources. The notes, signed by a girl who called herself "your ectoplasmic playmate," asked the men to meet her in front of a downtown theater and said to recognize her they should "just look for a girl with a gleam in her eye, a smile on her lips, and mischief on her mind."

One paper, believing the note was news, reprinted it. A girl in the community with the same name as the signer of the note sued for invasion of privacy although she elected to proceed against the studio and not the newpaper. The studio won in the lower courts but on appeal the decision was reversed in favor of the girl. (20) Presumably, the girl also could have sued the newspaper.

A Texas paper was named in a suit brought by a woman whose husband was killed in an automobile accident. The paper identified him as one of the men who had been indicted some months before on charges of stealing grain. The widow contended the reference invaded her privacy and that of a minor son. (21)

In the face of other decisions in Texas and elsewhere, it doesn't seem likely that the widow can make the action good. The decision in the case of the child prodigy already discussed suggests the courts do not attempt to prescribe a time limit on news.

The courts have never been required to pass on the permissible use of a past crime when reprinted in such columns as "25 years ago today." The erstwhile criminal, having paid his debt to society, may still be living in the community with only a few people aware of his past troubles with the law.

Does such reprinting, for no apparent purpose other than to revive memories of readers, invade his privacy? In view of the child prodigy decision, it is only problematical that he would have a cause for action. In 12 states, however, he might be able to try an additional remedy, for in those jurisdictions, truth, to be a defense in libel, must have been published "with good motives and for justifiable ends." A court would have to rule if a "memory column" met those requirements.

In any event, this question should remain purely hypothetical. For an editor with a keen sense of fair play and good taste will eliminate such items from the column.

In news matter, then, invasion of privacy is encountered infrequently for the simple reason that people get into print only when they do something. And what they do, usually, is news which destroys a claim to privacy. A hermit is entitled to his seclusion, but even he has no legal complaint if people think his peculiar way of life is of sufficient interest for a feature article.

As one lawyer has said:

"A man's only hope of exercising his right of privacy is to live a happy humdrum life and stay out of the way of newsmen." (22)

Privacy in Pictures

In handling pictures, the newspaper is more likely to run into limitations of privacy than in news matters. But here again, the only well-defined boundaries are those pictures used for trade purposes, particularly advertisements.

The editorial side of the newspaper probably is concerned with advertising in this sense only if it handles promotion or circulation-building "stunts." Courts may regard such promotions as advertisements rather than news.

But even here there are border cases. As a circulation boost-er, a paper took closeup photographs of crowds at the local ball park. Each day, the paper awarded a money prize for the fan displaying the most enthusiasm. It made its selection by circling one fan who received $10 when he called at the news-paper office and identified himself. Obviously, the picture would have been of less value had not part of the crowd been shown.

A man three seats from the encircled winner threatened ac-tion on the ground his privacy was invaded. His real reason, it developed, was the fact that he was supposed to be home sick.

Although the picture was for promotion purposes, and there-fore, in effect, an advertisement, a judge said privately he saw no cause for legal action. Men who play hookey from work apparently may not attend public exhibitions without the risk of their sins finding them out.

New York, California, and Virginia, by statute, and many other jurisdictions by judicial decisions, permit damages for un-authorized use of photographs in advertisements. All the weight of logic is behind this reasoning. Otherwise, a man might find his picture in all types of advertisements from breakfast food to cowboy suits or pogo sticks and discover because he once sampled a particular whiskey he now is a "man of distinction." And a girl might discover she is featured on the jacket of a book "The Confessions of a Private Secretary." (23)

Few cases involving news pictures have gone to the courts for an interpretation of privacy. A woman taxi driver made good her claim against a magazine which used her picture to illustrate an article purporting to show that drivers take ad-vantage of visitors' ignorance of zoning laws to overcharge them. The woman driver complained that, although the article did not specifically accuse her of overcharging passengers, read-ers would get that impression from just seeing her picture with it.

In news pictures, the mere fact the subject does not wish to be photographed is not sufficient grounds to maintain a suit for invasion of privacy. In Minneapolis, a father in court for a custody suit against his divorced wife, sued for $20,000 because a news photographer had taken a picture of him and the chil-dren during a court recess. In dismissing his suit the court said:

". . . He (the father) probably does not fully appreciate that through the force of circumstances, he was required to throw aside the mantle of privacy. . . . But the undeniable fact is that he has made public the most intimate and indeed scandalous occurrences of his domestic life and had them spread on the public records of a court of his own choosing." (24)

A Los Angeles paper which used a photograph of a woman who had committed suicide won a suit brought by the husband for invasion of privacy. The court ruled that there was no violation because the woman was the principal in an occurrence of public interest. (25)

Although the law is willing to extend its protection to those having a just claim, it does not try to make itself ridiculous. A school superintendent in a town of 12,000 once retained a lawyer to study action against a newspaper in a neighboring city which had printed the educator's picture with brief cutlines announcing that he was spending the summer at the seashore. When the superintendent returned home late in August, he found his apartment bare. Thieves had driven up a moving van and had made off with all his furnishing, including floor rugs.

The superintendent maintained the thieves would have been unaware of his absence had not the paper invaded his privacy by printing "an unauthorized picture and story." The lawyer advised him that such a claim, put into a legal proceeding, would produce nothing but a laugh from both the judges and community at large. Furthermore, it was explained to him, a newspaper needs no permission to print such stories and pictures.

The proprietor of a second-rate apparel store once contended a newspaper had invaded his "business privacy," which is a novel twist to the already unstable doctrine of privacy. What perturbed the merchant was that in its pictures of a fire at his store, the newspaper had estimated damage at $25,000 while he already had contracted for a "double truck" advertisement to announce a "gigantic $75,000 fire sale." No lawyer took him seriously enough even to threaten action. Two days later he contracted for additional advertising space, so apparently the community was unaffected by the discrepancy.

The state of Washington, in effect, denied the principle of privacy in a decision finding a minor daughter was not damaged by publication of a family picture when her father was arrested on a charge of fraud. The justices even held that publication of the photograph might bring sympathy for the child.

Here is one instance in which many newspapers would not care to claim their legal right to publish such pictures. Mention in the news column that the accused man had a wife and daughter would be justified by many newspapermen; but many would reject the use of the picture which enables the child to be singled out for possible scorn and ridicule at school or among neighborhood children. Photographs usually produce more lasting impressions than the printed word.

There are times, then, when legal rights should be balanced against social responsibility. Like the dead pedestrian who had the right of way, a newspaper gains little from exercising its legal rights if the community disapproves.

Resumé and Analysis:

The growth of pictorial journalism has produced additional legal problems for the press as well as developing new aspects of old questions. The use of the camera differs from news reporting because pictures involve the right to take them, their ownership, and the right of publication.

A general rule is that a news photographer from a public or semi-public place may snap what is happening there. The photographer, however, may not violate any law in order to get his picture.

If the subject is on private property, a problem arises but a good assumption is that when the subject is performing an act that passersby can see, he has little complaint if he is photographed. It is not good logic to assume that while a crowd might gather to watch a man standing on his head to mow his front lawn, a photographer canot snap a picture of the performance.

The general principle of ownership of a picture is that it belongs to the person who paid for having it taken. A commercial studio may not sell or give out for publication a picture for which someone else paid. In practice, many studios at least technically violate the law but since the pictures are generally used in laudatory publicity, there seldom is any legal complaint. The safest method is for a newspaper to obtain releases from the subjects on all pictures it does not take itself.

Courts are leaning to the principle that pictures of "news events" may be taken and published even if the photographer were on private property. But the photographer may be arrested for trespassing.

A photographer cannot compel any person to submit to having his picture taken, no matter if that person is participating in a news event. The subject always can cover his face or call upon an officer for protection against annoyance. But few people, other than criminals, seem to object to having their pictures published.

A picture may be libelous in itself, or a non-defamatory picture may be made libelous by its cutlines or caption. Sometimes a picture may be both libelous and an invasion of the subject's right of privacy.

Privacy is an "elastic" principle of law not accepted in all jurisdictions. In general, it affords an individual the right to live his life in anonymity, if he so chooses. The advertising worker is more concerned than the editorial man about privacy since most jurisdictions recognize an individual's name or picture must not be used for trade purposes without his consent.

Fewer cases involving invasion of privacy have arisen on the editorial side because a newspaper seeks stories or pictures only from those people who are in the news. While privacy is a problem which the newspaperman, especially the photographer, must consider, it need not be the bugaboo some writers have attempted to create. The right to gather news now generally includes pictures because of the universal interest in them.

Dawson, who said a man's only hope of exercising his right of privacy is to stay out of the way of newsmen, might well have added: "And also of photographers." (26)

For Further Reading

Bartenstein, Fred J., "Right of Privacy," 2 *Washington & Lee Review*, Fall number, 1940.

Brandeis, Louis D. and Warren, Samuel D., "The Right to Privacy," 4 *Harvard Law Review*, December, 1890.

Cole, George, "Libel by Publication of Pictures," 2 *Ohio State Law Journal*, May, 1936.

Davis, Norris G., "Recent Developments in the Law of Photographs," 19 *Journalism Quarterly*, September, 1942.

Doan, Edward N., "The Newspaper and the Right of Privacy," 5 *Journal of the Kansas Bar Association*, February, 1937.

Green, Leon, "The Right of Privacy," 27 *Illinois Law Review*, November, 1932.

Ludes, Francis J., "Right of Privacy" in *Corpus Juris* (legal encyclopedia).

Nizer, Louis, "Right of Privacy: a Half Century's Developments," 39 *Michigan Law Review*, February, 1941.

————"The Right of Privacy," 22 *Kentucky Law Journal*, November, 1933.

COURT DECISIONS
(other than those noted in the text)

Almind v. Sea Beach Co., 141 N.Y.S. 842.

Petransky v. Repository Printing Co., 200 N.E. 647.

Munden v. Harris, 134 S.W. 1076.

Kunz v. Allen, 172 P. 532.

Bazemore v. Savannah Hospital, 155 S.E. 194.

Jones v. Herald Post Co., 18 S.W. 2d. 972.

Jeffries v. Evening Journal Publishing Co., 124 N.Y.S. 780.

Myers v. Afro-American Publishing Co., 5 N.Y.S. 2d. 223.

Jackson v. Consumers Publications, Inc., 256 N.Y. App. Div. 708.

Heymann v. Dodd Mead & Co., 260 N.Y. App. Div. 573.

SECTION III

"Restrictions on the Press"

CHAPTER XVI

"The Origin and Nature of Libel Laws"

Of all the restrictions which society has placed upon the press, none is more important than that imposed by the laws of libel. For society, through such laws, has endeavored to set definite boundaries between the private rights of its citizens and the public interest. That those boundaries today are not defined as exactly as both the newspaper and the courts might wish is the fault, not of the laws, but of the changing view of society toward the free exchange of ideas, facts, and opinions.

The libel "codes," like so many of our laws, have been amended and added to, until in places the original foundation looks too insecure to serve the needs of modern communications. For man today seems not to want to limit himself to being his brother's keeper but also likes to set himself up as his judge and critic. Mass communication in a mass society is too complex to rely solely on theories, principles, or even laws, of the more compact and leisurely world of the past. Today's newspaper reader not only wants to survey the whole world at his breakfast table but also demands he share the gossip, rumors, comments, opinions, and criticism of all those who want to express themselves on any subject, complete with pictures.

The newspaperman, who in certain moments of his daily work, may believe libel is merely a legal device to thwart his constitutional freedom to print everything that comes to his attention, may take some comfort in knowing that the problem is as old as mankind itself.

In effect, libel is simply a legal concept of the principle expressed popularly by Shakespeare when he wrote: "Who steals my purse steals trash, but he who filches from me my good name, robs me of that which does not enrich himself and makes me poor instead." (1)

Shakespeare was not expressing a new idea, for long before the dawn of literate history, man was more concerned for his good name than for his physical being. From primitive tribes to modern society, reflections on a man's good name were regarded as being so serious as to require action by the group as a whole and not by the defamed individual alone. An "eye for an eye" or "a tooth for a tooth" was satisfactory revenge for physical wounds but not for an injury to the reputation.

Thousands of years ago, an individual whose good name was sullied asked the group to remove the blemish by punishing the offender. It was not sufficient that he become his own avenger. Today when a man goes into court to sue for libel, although his action is against an individual, his primary purpose is to ask society to restore his previous good reputation. He wants to regain approval of the community.

On the banks of the Ganges and along the sweep of the Nile, years before the Christian era began, the lowliest toiler and the Pharaoh alike, called upon the sun goddesses to be their witnesses, that, while they may have sinned, they had never slandered a man—friend or foe—by speaking evil of him.

The early Greeks and the Romans, and even the Germanic hordes that once overran most of Europe, recognized that injury to the reputation was such a grievous wrong it must be dealt with by the group. Often the offender had his tongue clipped, an eye gouged, or a brand applied to his face or forehead so that all might know he had spoken evil of a fellowman. Sometimes he was banished as being unworthy to associate with the group although his spear or knife may have helped many times to fill the tribal larder or to repel a common enemy.

When Moses came down from Mt. Sinai, he brought with him perhaps the first "written" recognition by the new religion that to "bear false witness against thy neighbor" was to break a law from which there was no appeal.

The early Saxons collected damages for slander, and, moreover, the one who uttered the words had to admit publicly that he had lied. Before the first newspaper appeared in England, men there were writing books on slander.

Libel, besides being a form of social control, is a real financial hazard to the newspaper. Alfred McClung Lee reports that the New York *Graphic*, in its comparatively brief career, is reputed to have been sued for $6,000,000 to $8,000,000 in libel actions, although it is believed to have paid less than $6,000 in judgments and out-of-court settlements. (2)

The old New York *World* is reputed to have had a $250,000 "revolving fund" set aside to contest libel suits. Many of those suits were invited, or at least expected, during the *World's* numerous crusades.

Few newspapers escape libel suits or the threat of such suits. Some of these actions have resulted because the newspaper put its responsibility to the community ahead of possible financial risk to itself. Others have come about through ignorance on the part of the editorial staff of the basic laws of libel.

The concept of slander has come down through the centuries relatively unchanged except that today slander (and libel) is regarded as a civil wrong rather than a crime. But the distinction is chiefly one of procedure, for society still insists that among the individual's most cherished rights, none is more important than that which permits him to keep his good name.

Libel Defined

Definitions of libel are as numerous as the writers upon the subject. All of them have as their base the word "defamation" which the dictionary says is ". . . a bringing into disrepute, dishonor, or disgrace." Or, as an Iowa court defined "defamation," it is ". . . the taking from another his reputation." (3) *Any word, or act, then, that detracts from a man's good name or reputation is defamation.* If the defamation is oral (except by radio) it is slander. When written, defamation becomes libel.

The law concerns itself with reputation and not with character. In other words, law is not interested in what an individual actually is but only in what the community thinks he is. When a newspaper story causes an individual's friends or neighbors to think less of him, the law says real damage has been done.

Although it is customary to think reputations can be ruined only by defamatory stories, it is possible to commit libel in a highly laudatory article. A paper by attributing to a physician the discovery of a cure for the common cold or cancer might cause him to lose prestige among his professional colleagues and the confidence of his more intelligent patients.

A psychologist who developed a machine to measure what the paper called "brain waves" felt he was damaged by both the "too-loose" description and also by the fact that the article failed to state he had patterned his device after a model originally made by an European scientist. He felt colleagues might assume he was claiming credit for a device he had not perfected himself and in scientific circles that would result in loss of prestige. He was satisfied when the newspaper published a correction.

An army colonel sued a radio network because he claimed its dramatic presentation of an episode in which he had taken part had made him out a braggart, and gave the impression that he had won the war almost single-handedly.

Slander today is a minor offense because the possibilities of damage by word of mouth are slight as compared with the harm the printed word can do. The spoken word passes quickly, but the printed word may endure and be circulated for years and to an audience that cannot be counted.

In defining libel, "writing" must not be construed narrowly. A cartoon containing no words, a photograph, a sketch, or even letters placed in the sky by puffs of smoke can be just as libelous as the most aesthetically printed page.

Types of Libel

Modern society recognizes two types of libel: Criminal and civil. For any act to become a crime, as has been pointed out, it must injure society as a whole. Criminal libel, then, is a libel that affects the public in general rather than specific persons although it may be directed at individuals.

Criminal libel is encountered infrequently by newspapers. Any story, article, editorial, etc. which causes, or tends to cause, a breach of the peace, may be criminal libel. Any article that may tend to incite people to insurrection against their government is criminal libel. In time of war, and perhaps in peace through the Alien Registration Act of 1940, an article that betrays security secrets or interferes with military operations may be criminal libel.

An article criticizing a conscription law in peace times or demanding a reduction in the armed services is permissible opinion. But if the article urges youths not to register for the draft or to desert from the armed services as a peace gesture, it would be libelous. Writers may appeal for a change in government by any constitutional means they favor, but advocating use of force to bring about the changes is libelous.

An editorial suggesting the community organize a lynching party and steal a prisoner from the county jail to save taxpayers the expense of a trial, is libelous although no mob forms. For there is a reasonable assumption that the article might provoke violence.

To urge that citizens take into their own hands the job of seeing to it that a local club no longer remains as "a den of vice and immorality" is certainly an invitation to them to commit mob violence. Any article purporting to give arguments in favor of atheism is not libelous but a scurrilous attack on the Deity might be.

Many states also classify as criminal libel any unwarranted villification of the dead. Since all right of civil action dies with the person injured, attacks on the memory of the dead must be dealt with by the state.

The law recognizes, however, there is a place for legitimate criticism of men and women now dead even if the article "debunks" many prevalent beliefs about them. Sanctity is not gained by death alone. For each generation may change its historical perspective of both its dead heroes and villains.

In most states, prosecutions for many types of criminal libel can be maintained only if there is an evil motive behind the purpose of the writer. And intent and motive are elusive problems in law.

Since newspapers are seldom involved in criminal libel, the major emphasis should be on civil injuries.

Civil libel, as has been stated, is a tort. *A tort is a wrongful act done by one individual to another, and the party injured may sue for damages.* (4)

As in all civil wrongs, the state is not a party to a suit for civil libel. It is up to the individual to bring his suit, prove his injury, and collect his damages.

Determining Libelous Words

At one time, the courts made a sharp distinction between words that are libelous in themselves—*libel per se*—and words whose connotations when applied to particular circumstances might be libelous—*libel per quod*. Today this distinction has been abandoned generally by writers on law.

The reason these two sharply defined categories have been pretty well eliminated is three-fold:

1. Language is dynamic and both intrinsic meaning and connotation of words change rapidly. In the days of George Washington, for example, a gentleman of good breeding paid the highest respect to another of his rank by referring to him as a "character." Today the term "a character" implies the individual to whom it refers is a possible candidate for a psychiatric ward. At one time or another in the past, courts have held it to be libelous *per se* to use such expressions as "rascal," "rotten egg," "hypocrite," "glib tongue," "gave it to him in the neck," "blackballed," "a publican," "political henchman," "has a peculiar sense of the truth," "character assassin," "racket," "had brainstorms," "cashiered," "racketeer," "tool of Wall Street," "derelict in his duties," and many other words and phrases that today pass almost without comment.

2. Some words are considered part of the "give and take" of everyday life when applied to certain classes of people but may be libelous when hurled at others. The word "liar" is bantered about frequently today, especially in public life. Practically every person has at least one friend whose statements he discounts because of his friend's known inability to distinguish clearly between fact and fantasy, even in matters in which truth is most desirable. As the mother said to her little boy who insisted the horse out on the street was an elephant: "I've told you at least 40 million times not to exaggerate."

Newspapers, with pretentious modesty, once disguised "liar" under such modest statements as: "He hurled an ugly word at him." Today "liar" not only enlivens some public disputes but also fits well into a headline.

But if "liar" is hurled at a minister, it may be libelous because of the respect in which most people hold the clergy. To refer to a man's ancestry as being definitely of canine extraction, was once libelous *per se*. But not too long ago a President of the United States applied the term to a newspaper columnist. They still may be "fighting words" but libelous only under special circumstances.

3. Maintaining a distinction between *per se* and *per quod* may be unfair to the individual who is libeled because a jury may feel there is also a difference in the injury. Libel *per quod* may cause as much damage to a reputation as libel *per se* just as a pedestrian struck by a licensed driver may be as badly injured as if he had been hit by a man without an operator's permit.

Although the distinction of *per se* and *per quod* is neither too valid nor too useful, it is well to keep in mind that some words are libelous in themselves. It seems hardly necessary, however, to compile a list of words that are actionable in themselves because they damage reputations. Every newspaperman long since has been aware of most of them. He knows such terms as thief, quack, shyster, prostitute, pervert, forger, blackmailer, debaucher, fire bug, etc., as well as any word that would make people think less of the individual to whom they are applied, are libelous when uttered falsely.

He should know, too, that a story appearing harmless on the surface, may be libelous if the facts are wrong. A newspaper may publish the announcement of a woman's engagement as legitimate news. But if the woman is married already, the story attributes to her an act which is repugnant to society and which, if she went through with it, would be criminal.

Therefore, it is libelous to print that a married woman has become engaged to another man. Movie actresses sometimes announce the name of their next husband before they are legally free of the current one, but, if true, it is not libelous to say a woman intends to seek a divorce in order to marry another man. However, an unverified rumor about a woman not in public life may be libelous. (5)

Birth announcements if untrue are a constant source of potential libel because to say a woman married only a few months has had a baby implies she was guilty of unchastity.

A newspaper columnist once said that a song, then popular, had actually been written by a youth who had sold it for a mere $200. Again, this statement of itself is not libelous, but the effect of the story was to charge dishonesty against the men whose names were on it as composers. They sued for libel and won. (6)

Some words admit of two different interpretations even when applied to the same class of people. One businessman may be flattered if he is called "sharp." Another may feel he has been libeled.

To the one businessman, "sharp" may mean he watches the market carefully, buys raw material at just the right time, processes just the right amount of goods, and sells when demand is at its peak. It may also connote for him that he uses modern accounting methods, keeps his inventory fluid, doesn't overextend his credit, or a score of other things that may spell the difference between profit and loss.

The other businessman, especially if he is a banker, may believe "sharp" accuses him of "bending" the law when it suits his purpose but never breaking it, and of engaging in possibly legal but unethical practices. Only a jury could determine if "sharp," then, is libelous. Few businessmen, however, would object to being called "astute."

A newspaper was sued for libel because a deskman changed around a court reporter's story. The reporter had written: "At this time, he denied he had re-labeled the packages." The copy reader, either because he wanted to add more "punch" to the story or else in the interest of better sentence construction, changed it to: "He denied re-labeling the packages at this time."

The reporter wanted to indicate the question was asked and answered at a particular period of time in the proceedings because the man had made several appearances on the witness stand. The witness, in his libel suit later, contended the change had him admitting he had re-labeled the packages at some time which he denied and which had not been proved. The paper lost the suit.

Instead of classifying words as libelous *per se* and *per quod,* the more practical procedure is to assume that certain words are actionable in themselves and that the intended meaning of other words must be construed from the special circumstances surrounding their use. But if adjudged libelous, the cost may be the same to the paper in either event.

Or stated another way: Certain words of themselves detract from a man's reputation, hold him up to scorn, contempt, or hatred, or damage his social or business position. Certain other words tend to have the same effect, but the determination of whether they actually do, is for a jury to decide.

Courts not only recognize that language is dynamic but also that the same word may have additional meanings in different localities. Lawyers have a 14-volume work on "Words and Phrases" to help them determine the legal sense of many expressions that to a layman seem common enough. A judge may use 1,000 words in his opinion to define one word or phrase.

Justice Holmes expressed one court's views on changing connotations this way:

"A word is not a crystal, transparent and unchanged; it is the skin of a living thought and may vary greatly in color and content according to the circumstances and the time in which it is used." (7)

The dictionary does not help the newspaper too much because courts have held that "dictionary meanings are not conclusive."

The publishers of one dictionary, in the preface, said: "The editors believe that from the point of view of modern linguistic science we must discard the all-too-prevalent assumption that 'the dictionary' is the final authority and its pronouncements are valid for all time." (8)

Since the dictionary, the right-hand tool of newspapers, is not of too much help in determining doubtful words, how can their actual meaning be ascertained? The courts give some clue by telling how they determine meanings.

Courts have said:

"A newspaper publication (story) must be measured by its natural and probable effect upon the mind of the average lay reader." (9)

"In determining whether words are libelous, they are to be given their ordinary and popular meanings; and if they are susceptible of two meanings, one libelous and the other innocent, the former is not to be adopted and the latter rejected as a matter of course, but it must be left to the jury to determine in what sense they are used." (10)

"In construing words alleged to be libelous we cannot travel into the realm of conjecture, but must confine ourselves to the natural, ordinary and commonly-accepted meaning of the words themselves, considered in connection with the other facts alleged in the complaint." (11)

"In deciding whether words will bear an innocent meaning, a writing must be construed as a whole without taking any word or phrase out of context, or placing undue emphasis upon any one part." (12)

"But words are not always used in their correct sense. Some persons, in a forced attempt at colorful expression, indulge in ill-advised use of inaccurate terminology; and an article written in that manner may or may not be libelous, depending upon the occasion and circumstances and how it is understood by those reading it." (13)

"If language is capable of two meanings, one of which would be libelous and actionable and the other not, it is for the jury to say, under all circumstances surrounding its publication, including extraneous facts admissible in evidence, which of the two meanings would be attributed to it by those to whom it is addressed and by whom it may be read." (14)

"It is inconsistent with a due regard for the protection of the public from libelous attacks that obsolete or antiquated and practically unused meanings of words should be searched for and studied out, to show that at some remote period of history they were not approbrious." (15)

"The question is not what the writer intended the words to mean, but what they would be understood to mean by the ordinary reader." (16)

". . . one assaulting the reputation . . . of another in a public newspaper cannot justify it upon the ground that it was a mere jest, unless it is perfectly manifest from the language employed that it could in no respect be regarded as an attack upon the reputation . . . of the person to whom it is addressed." (17)

"English is not a dead, but a virile language, flexible, progressive, continually being enriched from all sorts of sources, its common speech made piquant and interesting by slang and jargon, often better understood by the man in the street than the classic diction of its great masters." (18)

"A writing is a libel if, in view of all relevant circumstances, it discredits the plaintiff in the minds of not the court, nor of wise, tolerant and thoughtful men, nor of ordinarily reasonable men, but of any considerable and respectable class in the community." (19)

The meaning and connotation of words not only changes down through the years but they also differ by geographical areas. To call a man in the Harlem district of New York City "a friend of the negro" might send him to the state legislature or Congress; to use the term in the "solid South" might be libelous. In some sections of the West, "horse thief" might still be a "fighting expression" and libelous; but in the East the best of friends often greet each other with: "How are you, you old horsethief?" But automobile thief probably is libelous everywhere in the United States. In some dairy states, an epithet of scorn is to say a man uses oleomargarine although it is a legal product. Probably, the expression is not serious enough to be libelous but it does harm one's social position.

In some sections, calling a butcher a "seller of horse meat" is no more libelous than saying he handles Grade A beef. In other areas, it is libelous, depending upon how those communities regard horse meat as human food.

Another court, besides the one already noted, in Arizona, had to let the jury pass on whether "racket" still retained its one-time "sting." The newspaper contended it meant simply a "trick or scheme," but the plaintiff maintained it accused him of making money unethically, if not illegally. (20)

The word "Communist" shifted in the courts several times within a few years. In 1940, a New York court, reasoning that the Communist party was on the state ballot, held the word was not libelous in itself. (21) The following year, a court in the same state, held it was libelous. (22) Then, came the war, and Russia became associated with the nations fighting Germany. It is unlikely that during the war years, a man would have been libeled *per se* by being called a Communist although in some sections the word never was in good repute.

In 1945, a New York federal court held Communist was libelous and within several years, a number of other jurisdictions had reached that conclusion. (23) Another federal court in holding the word to be libelous in 1947 said:

"Concededly, the word (Communist) is carelessly and perhaps indefinitely used today. Nevertheless, there can be no denial that its appearance as a characterization in a newspaper political editorial is sufficient to destroy a person's presumably good reputation with the public." (24)

Such words as "screwball" and "souphead" are not libelous, a Maryland court decided in 1948, and neither do they constitute "indecent language."

In analyzing the meaning of screwball, the judge concluded it could mean:

(a) A peculiar or eccentric person, like crackbrain, crackpot, crank, queer duck, queer fish, nut, queer potato and queer specimen, or (b) a stupid or insane person like batty, bughouse, crazy, boob, dippy, screw-loose, and soft-head. (25)

Said the court:

"There can be no denial that the word screwball is an epithet of disparagement. But there's nothing much you can do about it." (26)

From these, and other decisions, some general observations can be drawn up. They would include:

1. Certain words, most of which should be obvious to any newspaperman, are libelous in themselves.

2. Other words may be made libelous by the circumstances in which they are used.

3. Dictionary meanings are not taken by a court as conclusive.

4. Words and phrases are not to be taken out of their context in order to determine if they are libelous.

5. Authorities on semantics are not called upon by the courts to help in libel suits because words often are not used in their correct linguistic sense. The damage in libel is not always done by the precise and exact meaning of words but by the interpretation which the newspaper reader places upon those words.

6. If words have two meanings, the jury must decide which was intended by the newspaper. Slang and jargon further complicate the ordinary usage of many words.

7. The "sting" in libel comes not from what the newspaper meant to convey but what the reader understood from the words.

8. Since the English language is dynamic and flexible, words and meanings may change from year to year. Radio, theater, movies, popular music, sports pages, feature columns, and comic strips probably add more new words to the language than good literature. Even more effective is the seeming ability of these popular sources to shift the connotations of many standard words. Some librarians still post: "Only low conversation permitted here," and then look startled when college students read the signs and go into hysterics.

Drew Pearson, Washington columnist, reports that when the United Nations decided to include in its new headquarters building a room where delegates could sit in quiet meditation, the United States delegates suggested it be named "The Temple of Prayer." Trygvie Lie, Secretary-General, thought the name too formidable and suggested "Rest room." (27)

The new words or connotations derived from popular sources often are readily accepted by the "man in the street."

9. The meanings and connotations of some words varies also in different geographical areas so that a word might be held to be innocent in one jurisdiction and libelous in another.

10. A jury is the final authority for deciding what the ordinary, average person in that particular community takes the words to mean despite pronouncements by semantics authorities, dictionaries, or users of precise English.

For Further Reading

Angoff, Charles, *Handbook of Libel*, New York; Duell, Sloan and Pearce, 1946, has a summary of the basic libel laws of the several states.

Wittenberg, Philip, *Dangerous Words*, New York; Columbia University Press, 1947, contains a chronological chart of words that have been held libelous at various periods of time.

Thomas, Ella Cooper, *The Law of Libel and Slander*, New York; Oceana Publications, 1949, contains a brief chart of actionable words arranged by states. Also a chart of defenses against libel in the several states.

Newell, Martin L., *The Law of Libel and Slander*, Chicago; Callaghan & Co., 1924 (4th ed.).

33 *American Jurisprudence* (legal encyclopedia), p. 38, sec. 3, for generally acceptable legal definitions of libel.

Prosser, William L., *Handbook on the Law of Torts*, St. Paul; West Publishing Co., 1941, Ch. 17.

Practically every law journal or review has delved deeply into the subject of defamation.

LIBEL IN ENGLAND

Ball, William Valentine, and Browne, Patrick, *The Law of Libel and Slander*, London; Stevens & Sons, 1936, 2d ed.

Button, Wilfred Alan, *Principles of the Law of Libel and Slander*, London; Sweet & Maxwell, 1935.

IN OTHER EUROPEAN COUNTRIES

Rothernberg, Ignaz, *The Newspaper—and Its Laws*, London; Staples Press Limited, 1946. Also United States edition, New York; Staples Press, Inc., 1948.

CHAPTER XVII

"Intent and Responsibility in Libel"

"Honest Mistakes"

An "honest confession" may be good for the soul, but an "honest mistake" can be ruinous to a newspaper.

Unless a newspaper is embarking upon a crusade or an expose, with all the attendant dangers in such articles, it becomes involved in libel most times through the best of intentions. Often the libelous story is about an individual of whom the newspaper never heard before the particular event that gave rise to the offensive article.

A partner in a law firm which has defended a number of newspapers in libel suits once listed what he thought were the chief reasons his clients got into trouble. In order of importance, his list was: (1)

(a) *Taking the obvious for granted.* In one city, a man well-known in the community because of his support of all amateur and professional athletic events, was called Dan Jones by everyone. When he was arrested in a shady real estate deal, one paper referred to him as Dan Jones and the other as Daniel Jones. Both gave his address as of the 400 block of Third street.

When a Dan Jones of that block sued for libel, the papers discovered for the first time that the sports enthusiast was not Dan Jones but Harold Jones. Moreover, he never lived in that block because the address was that of a specialized sporting goods store where he usually received his mail. Even the chief of police was amazed that the man's name was not Daniel, until he recalled that as a high school athlete Jones had been dubbed "Dandy" which the community had shortened to Dan.

The actual Dan Jones operated a small loan and real estate rental agency, and he had no difficulty proving he had been damaged. It cost one paper, $2,000 and the other $2,700, besides court expenses, for taking for granted the obvious.

(b) *Carelessness by both reporter and copy reader.* The reporter's notes may read "Harry Jones" but he inadvertently types "Henry Jones." Or the article may correctly say one man was arrested and a second questioned, and the copy reader, daydreaming at his work, makes the head: "Pair Arrested."

(c) *Failure to check thoroughly.* Sometimes the reporter does his work slovenly or takes the line of least resistance; at other times he may be reliving the days of the "story-book newspapermen" and pound out an item hurriedly to obtain a "scoop." During the enumeration of the 1950 census, some midwestern papers blossomed out suddenly with stories that farmers in a certain section were refusing to fill out their blanks and had destroyed them. To charge a man with defying the law, is a serious offense.

A check with the district census headquarters later disclosed that the wrong blanks had been sent to the farmers and they were asked to destroy them since regathering would have cost more than the amount of paper saved. Since none of the farmers was identified sufficiently, there was no libel, but no newspaperman who handled the story can be proud of such work.

(d) *Too much reliance on "friends" instead of ascertaining the facts independently.* In early 1941, when national defense had become a paramount concern in the United States, the general manager of a large department store called the two afternoon newspapers in his city to tell them that his neighbor, the owner of a commercial studio, had just been whisked away by two Federal Bureau of Investigation agents on a charge of espionage. There was no FBI office in that city with which to check the story.

The manager said as he was coming out of his house, he saw the FBI agents escort the neighbor to a car and that the neighbor half whispered to him: "Well, the FBI caught up with me." He was being taken to a city about 90 miles away.

A call to the man's wife brought the information that he was away and she didn't know when he would be back. The first newspaper, with an edition coming up, used the story with a lead: "It was reported etc."

The city editor of the second paper suddenly recalled there was a state photography convention in the city to which the studio owner was being taken. While the reporter who was to handle the story chafed at missing an edition, the city editor asked a press association to check. In half an hour, back came the answer that the suspected espionage agent was at that moment reading a paper before the convention.

When the studio owner began legal action, the store manager admitted he had not seen the incident but that another neighbor had witnessed it and had told him. The other neighbor insisted, however, his facts were correct. And on the surface, they were. Two FBI agents had picked up the photographer, but they had been his college chums and were just giving him a ride to the convention city.

The photographer said what he had whispered was: "These are FBI men," and that he made no reference to being "caught." His intention, he said, was to impress his neighbor about the kind of friends he had.

After hearing that the men were FBI agents and seeing them help the photographer into the car, the neighbor's imagination had done the rest. Since stories of the arrest of "spies" were beginning to creep into the newspapers, the store manager not only accepted his neighbor's version but embellished it and adopted it as his own.

The newspaper settled out of court for a reported $5,000 and also for the first time agreed to use photographs of weddings and parties taken by the studio.

Although the photographer himself contributed somewhat to the misunderstanding, the newspaper could not justify publication on those grounds. The studio owner probably suffered even greater harm because he was of German extraction.

The courts, time and again, have ruled that "honest mistakes" do not excuse libel. The legal reasoning is sound because damage to reputations may be just as serious from "honest mistakes" as from any other cause. (2) Since most libel suits originate through mistakes, to excuse them would, many times, deprive a defamed individual of the redress due him.

Typographical Errors

The newspaper whose reporters and copy readers are constantly on the alert, sometimes finds its good work nullified by the slipping fingers of a linotype operator or by a make-up man who gets a corrected line into the wrong place.

On many papers, the type is already in the forms before corrections are made. Sometimes the linotype operator may hand the corrected line directly to the make-up man, and no one sees the corrected form until the paper has rolled. Such a procedure may save a few precious minutes in the composing room, but the newspaper may find the practice is expensive.

A Pennsylvania newspaper paid $7,500 because through such a composing room procedure, a corrected line inserted in the wrong place in an editorial caused it to read that a state official had lauded a man convicted of vice and liquor law violations. The corrected line actually belonged two paragraphs down, but the make-up man put it in the first place where a turned rule indicated there was an omission.

The newspaper was permitted to bring a composing room form into court and show the jury how such corrections were made. It also placed into the record evidence that the mistake had been caught and the page re-plated after only 1,000 papers had been run off. But the jury made its award and the verdict was upheld by the state supreme court. Two years later, the paper was caught in the same kind of mistake, but this time the jury denied damages to the injured man.

A Texas paper was sued because a guide-line slug got into print in the midst of a list of men re-classified by a draft board. Under the name of one man appeared the slug: "Pg 2 Pro-Nazi." The man asked for $25,000 but the jury gave him only $100. (3)

Several papers either have been involved in libel suits or have been threatened with such action, because facetious notes written by a reporter at the end of his story got into print.

A Pittsburgh paper escaped with a red face and an apology after such a note appeared in bold face type at the end of a list of names of those attending a business dinner. The reporter, uncertain if one man invited actually had appeared, wrote at the bottom of his copy: "Don't include Jones among the guzzlers until I check."

Smart reporters learn early that notes to the city editor should be written on separate sheets.

Errors in Wire Stories

Every newspaperman with a sense of responsibility concedes it is his duty to check thoroughly all stories originating in his community. But no newspaper, no matter how keen its sense of fair play, can check on the thousands of words that come to it over press association wires. And from the smallest daily to the largest metropolitan journal, newspapers are dependent in varying degrees upon press associations. (4)

As a practical working method, two factors are involved in the handling of wire stories. One is the handling of wire stories mentioning local persons. If the story that originates from a distant city mentions an individual from the paper's community, the newspaper has an obligation to check with local sources. The wire service, also, cannot supply all the details which may be available locally to round out the story.

If the wire story, for example, says a local man is involved in a crime in a distant city, the newspaper certainly can check whether the man is absent from home. Should the crime be in Seattle and the man's wife says she just had a card from him from New York, only a careless newspaperman would print the press association account without further checking.

The second factor concerns wire stories that do not involve local personalities. A newspaper must trust its press association to deliver a fair and accurate account. The law approaches the ridiculous when it assumes, as most jurisdictions do, that a paper should have verified such stories before publication.

But the general principle is that a newspaper is responsible for libel in press association dispatches. To be safe, then, a New Jersey newspaper, receiving a wire story about a San Francisco man involved in a crime there, should make its own check with police officials or other sources on the coast. Such a procedure is impractical from both time and expense angles.

Fortunately, most libel cases involving wire dispatches have been stories about people from the newspaper's own community. The newspaper which fails to check them is not on too firm ethical grounds when it attempts to exonerate itself for publishing them. And it has little justification for complaining the law denies it protection on such stories.

An important case illustrating this point is that of a North Carolina paper which was advised by a local FBI agent that he "thought" a man arrested that day in New Jersey in a vice raid had once lived in the paper's community, and moreover, had been convicted there of a similar charge. A reporter recognized that a man of that name had once been connected with a local theater and had been convicted of a vice charge. The name was not in the city directories for the past few years but had appeared in an issue five years previously. Without checking at either the theater or the address given in the old directory, the newspaper printed a story headed: "Vice Ring Man Is Known Here." It identified him as formerly connected with a local theater, and mentioned his prior conviction on a vice charge.

The theater man later was discovered to be living in another state and was neither the person who was arrested in New Jersey, nor the one who had been convicted previously. (5)

The newspaper later printed a correction which the courts held was not in the form required by the state's "retraction" law. The jury awarded compensatory damages but denied punitive damages.

In affirming the judgment, the state Supreme Court said:

> "The failure to go to a known and easily available source of information . . . constitutes more than a scintilla of evidence tending to show that in publishing the article the defendant acted with reckless disregard of plaintiff's rights and is sufficient to support submission of an issue of punitive damages. This is all we are required to determine." (6)

This legal, but in a practical sense, narrow view, has been summed up by one court this way:

> "The law does not recognize as privileged the repetition of an untruthful and libelous statement on the ground that it

was communicated to the person making the statement by an authority having a reputation for truth and accuracy. While the Associated Press no doubt deserves all that is said for it as being a truthworthy, honest, and accurate newsgatherer, a newspaper, in publishing Associated Press news reports, cannot justify itself as publishing a privileged communication, or otherwise, on the ground that the Associated Press is a trustworthy, reliable and truthful organization for the gathering and dissemination of news." (7)

In Florida, however, the courts have recognized that strict common law theories do not fit well into the production of the modern newspaper. It denied damages to a man who maintained a wire story libeled him. (8)

The Florida court made a distinction between a press association dispatch and what it called "the original and voluntary composition" of the local newspaper. It reviewed at length the common law principle that an individual is liable even though he merely prints what he has heard, names his authority for the story, and has no intention to cause the reader to believe it is true.

But, said the court,

". . . the legal premise upon which the modern rule of actionable liability rests is that a person who repeats a slander or libel is presumed, by his reiteration of it, to indorse it, and make it his own." (9) Publication, however, of a press dispatch, the court held, cannot be presumed to be an indorsement of it by the paper.

About wire dispatches, the court said:

"No newspaper could afford to warrant the absolute authenticity of every item of its news, nor assume in advance the burden of specially verifying every item of news reported to it by established news gathering agencies, and continue to discharge with efficiency and promptness the demands of modern necessity for prompt publication, if publication is to be had at all.

". . . To hold otherwise, would mean that newspapers at their peril publish purported items of news, against the falsity of which no ordinary human foresight could effectually guard and at the same time keep up the prompt daily service expected of present day newspapers." (10)

Calling upon the judiciary to take note of how modern newspapers must depend upon wire services, the court further said: ". . . the courts must apply to the new conditions which the practice (publication of wire dispatches) has brought about, a rule of reason with respect to legal presumption that would otherwise flow from the publication of libelous matters such as occasionally creep into the best regulated agencies for collecting and disseminating the news." (11)

Although the Florida decision has been hailed widely in journalism circles as exonerating newspapers from responsibility for wire news, a more sober reading of the opinion does not justify such ultimate optimism. True, it does seem a large step forward. But the court seems to be making clear it had in mind only those dispatches on which the local paper could not reasonably check. When a local person is mentioned in a press association story, the newspaper does well to check all possible local sources for verification.

Malice

Although an injured man is entitled to redress, the law recognizes that there should be a distinction between the individual hurt inadvertently and the one harmed deliberately. The man who is injured intentionally may not suffer more than the one harmed by mistake, but the deliberate offender should be taught that he cannot vent his spite at will. Unfortunately, the law makes the distinction by the use of the same word—malice.

Since the law uses "malice" both in its ordinary meaning and in a legal sense, the word sometimes causes confusion. The ordinary meaning of malice is spite or evil intent. Law calls this meaning "malice *in fact*."

In a strict legal sense, malice simply means a wrongful act has been done. It is called "malice *in law*." Malice *in law* is presumed in all defamatory stories because a wrong has been done to the individual offended.

If it can be proved that the defamatory story was published by the newspaper to injure the individual deliberately, or that it was giving vent to spite, the permissible damages usually are greater. Since malice in fact figures so seldom in libel cases, some confusion is avoided by dismissing attempts to distinguish between the meanings. If the story is libelous, there is malice in law. The plaintiff would have to prove malice in fact.

As an Iowa court has said:

"Legal malice in the publisher of a libel is not inconsistent with honesty of purpose and good motive. Whoever gives currency to libelous matter must be prepared to prove its truth, if he would avoid liability to the party injured." (12)

Another court, in discussing the same question, said:

"The plaintiff makes a complete case when he shows the publication of matter from which damage may be inferred. The actual fact may be that no malice exists or could be proved. Frequently, libels are published with the best of motives, or perhaps mistakenly or inadvertently but with an utter absence of malice. The plaintiff recovers just the same." (13)

Except, then, in infrequent cases in which spite is alleged, the courts do not look into the intent of the publisher. The best of motives and the most honest intentions do not prevail when an individual has been injured. As one court has said:

". . . the law looks to the tendency and consequences of a publication, rather than to the intention of the publishers." (14)

Who Is Responsible?

Since the nature of the two offenses is different, the law distinguishes between the liability for criminal and civil libel.

In criminal libel, it is necessary to determine responsibility in order that the state may know whom to punish. The company or individual owner of a newspaper is liable by statute in a few states for all criminal libel and in other jurisdictions only if the company or owner authorized the story or was aware that it would be printed. Executive officers, including editor or managing editor, have the same responsibility as the company or owner. Where statutes make an executive responsible for all libel, the presumption is that if that official were absent when the story originated, he would not be held. (15)

The reporter, copy reader, and any departmental editor who authorized or worked upon the story in any form, can be held for criminal libel. In actual practice, the executives are usually cited for criminal libel, along with the company, which may be fined.

In civil libel, the general rule is that all who had a part in the dissemination of the story are liable. Technically, a defamed individual could sue the newsboy who hawks the papers, the linotype operator who set the story, the pressman who turned out the copies, the reporter who wrote it, the copy reader who passed it, and up the line to the president of the company.

The layman, imperfect as his knowledge of the law may be, seems aware, however, of the axiom: "Sue the man who has the money."

Since civil libel is a suit for damages, it would be foolish to sue a newsboy whose only assets may be a bicycle and a few spinning tops or yo-yos. Or a linotype operator who may have to borrow between pay days.

A Pennsylvania resident did bring suit against a "news boy." During a hot political fight, a newspaper ran off an extra with sensational charges. The paper was owned by two partners. One of them grabbed a bundle of papers and sold them in front of an election precinct. He was sued for libel but the plaintiff later dropped the suit and then proceeded against the paper as a partnership.

The owner of the paper, individual, partnership, or corporation, is customarily named the defendant in a civil libel suit. The one who sues then knows he has a reasonable chance of collecting any damages the jury may award him.

Who May Sue for Libel?

Any individual who thinks he has been defamed may sue for libel. A minor may sue through his parents, guardian, or "next of kin." All an individual has to do is to go to the courthouse (or the place provided by his laws for beginning damage suits), fill out a complaint, and the action is begun.

If his state has a so-called "retraction law" (to be discussed later), he may first serve written notice upon the newspaper, state the true facts, and ask for a correction. Such a procedure may mitigate damages but does not absolve the newspaper of all liability.

As a general rule, only the party actually injured may sue for libel. If a second party is not named but the implication is such as to identify him in the community, he also may sue.

One newspaper, in reporting that a woman postal clerk had been arrested for pilfering from the mails, said some people believed she stole "that she might help others." Her brother, the postmaster, sued and won on the ground the community identified him as the "others." Had the story merely mentioned that her brother was the postmaster, it would not have been libelous. (16)

A defamatory story about a man may mention that he has a wife and two children, and their humiliation and mental anguish may be as great as his, but they have no cause for action. Should the story, however, charge or infer that either the wife or children were involved in the crime they, too, could sue.

To permit wives and children to sue for damages because the husband and father was libeled would be contrary to logic and soon lead the law far afield. The next logical step would be to include all relatives, down to distant cousins, especially if they had the same surname. In some cases they might actually be damaged by the story, but the law gives them no redress.

Under the peculiar status in which society places women, husbands in some jurisdictions may sue for a libel on their wives. The wife also may sue in her own name or jointly with her husband. The situation is not too flattering to women because the principle goes back to the days when the law regarded a wife as little more than the property of her husband.

Courts justify the principle today on the same grounds by which a man may sue for damages also if his wife is injured in an accident although he may not have been with her at the time. The law says her injuries deprive him of her society and services. Actually, the law is paying tribute to the old theory that the husband is "lord and master."

There is some logical basis to this reasoning, however, because a libel against a woman is usually more devastating than against a man. Although women today move about freely and mix with men in business and social life, a stigma on a woman's reputation will not be condoned as quickly as that against a

man. Women may console themselves that the law gives them
more protection when, in effect, it simply is another manifesta-
tion of the "double standard," which society articulately denies
but to which it silently subscribes.

Libel Against Cities

A political unit of government, such as a city, has no right
of action for libel. The newspaperman, however, must make
a distinction between the city as a corporate unity and the
officials of the city.

If the mayor or any city official or employee believes he has
been libeled he may sue just as any individual. A story that
says the mayor favors parking meters because it will put more
money in the till for him to dip into, is libelous against the mayor.
But if the story says the city is hopelessly in debt and its credit
is in danger of being impaired, the city has no right of action
although the article is entirely false.

This principle was firmly established in a suit brought by
the city of Chicago against the Chicago *Tribune*. (17)

The *Tribune,* in editorials and articles used such terms as:
"the city is broke," "bankruptcy is just around the corner," "(its)
credit is shot to pieces," "the city administration having busted
the city and having reduced it to such insolvency that it is issuing Villa script to pay its bills, is reaching out for the State."

The city charged that the articles caused it provable losses.
Firms which normally sought contracts for providing various
supplies refused to do so because of the articles and the city
estimated it had to pay $7,000,000 more for supplies than had it
been able to obtain competitive bids. It also charged that a
bond issue had to be sold at a discount with another $2,500,000
loss.

Although the *Tribune* admitted some of the material published was false and that the city had suffered damage, the court
said:

"We do not pass upon the truth or falsity of the publications
nor the merits of the political controversy between the parties.
We consider the question solely from the standpoint of public
policy and fundamental principles of government. For the

same reason that members of the legislature, judges of the courts, and other persons engaged in certain fields of public service or in the administration of justice are absolutely immune from actions, civil or criminal, for libel for words published in the discharge of such public duties, the individual citizen must be given a like privilege when he is acting in his sovereign capacity. This action (the suit by the city) is out of tune with the American spirit and has no place in American jurisdiction." (18)

There is no doubt that the same principle applies to all political divisions. A township, county, or even a state cannot sue for civil libel. In effect, to allow such suits would be to admit that a system set up by the people for their own convenience and advantage somehow obtains rights independent of its creators. And such a doctrine is false both to logic and the American way of life.

Chain Libel Suits

Under the common law, each repetition of a libel or slander was cause for separate action. By that theory, a man would have cause for action each time an issue of the offending newspaper was sold.

So again, principles that served a more leisurely era must be re-examined in an age of high-speed mass communications. Legally, a man defamed by a press association dispatch or an item in a syndicated column, still has the right of action against each newspaper that publishes it. Technically, at least, he might institute suits in dozens of cities against as many newspapers.

Some courts, recognizing how news is disseminated in these days, permit a newspaper in defending a libel suit to show that the plaintiff already has recovered damages in the same case against other publications. Such a defense does not eliminate further claims but often tends to mitigate the amount of damages.

The most recent series of libel suits was instituted by Martin L. Sweeney, former Congressman from Ohio. He sued 68 newspapers which had carried in the syndicated column "The Washington Merry-Go-Round" an item which Sweeney contended accused him of being anti-Semitic. (19)

The suits were complicated because Sweeney also claimed that his standing as a lawyer had been injured. Thus, two issues went before most of the courts—the right of a newspaper to comment on public officials and the alleged libel on a man's professional life.

Federal courts, as a rule, follow the laws of the state in which the suit is brought. In some states, it has been noted, falsity alone does not destroy privilege to comment on public officials. Sweeney hardly could have proved malice in fact since the article originated in a syndicated column which the papers used regularly but whose content they do not control.

In three actions in Pennsylvania, for example, the courts ruled there was no libel against Sweeney as a lawyer. On the issue of fair comment, Pennsylvania, which subscribes to the minority view, requires such comment to be libelous must imply that the public official has betrayed his oath of office. Since a Congressman has no prescribed duty to recommend candidates for judges and is accorded that honor by the President only as a courtesy, the article could not have intimated Sweeney had broken his oath. (20)

As an indication of how the courts differed in the cases, it can be noted that the same court in New York came to opposite decisions on two of his complaints. A newspaper argued that Sweeney's complaint was not sufficient cause for action, but an appeals court ruled it was. Later, the syndicate, instead of contesting the sufficiency of his complaint, elected to go to trial and defended on a plea of fair comment. The jury found for the syndicate.

Sweeney appealed on the ground that since the court had found his complaint against the newspaper was good, it should have instructed the jury in the case of the syndicate to find damages for him. This time the same court overruled Sweeney's plea. (21)

A Texas court, in dismissing the complaint, applied as its test the effect upon the ordinary reader in Texas of an article about an Ohio Congressman. Said the court:

". . . It seems to me that this court should not close its eyes to the fact that the 'ordinary reader' of defendant Corpus Christi, Texas, *Caller-Times*, probably never heard of Congressman Sweeney before the publication, didn't remember his name five minutes afterward, and did not care whether he opposed the appointment of Freed (the candidate for judge), or on what grounds. As a general rule, 'ordinary readers' in these parts are fortunately tolerant and skeptical, especially as to political matters. They subscribe to the general principle, recognized by statute and decisions, that newspapers are free to publish and comment concerning a public officer so long as they do not falsely charge him with such conduct as would subject him to removal from office." (22)

All in all, the great majority of the suits went against Sweeney. It cannot be claimed, however, that the results came about solely because courts are not in sympathy with chain suits although that undoubtedly was a factor. The victories can be laid more to the general spirit of the times in which criticism, comment, and opinion find freer expression today than in some past decades.

When Right of Action Ceases

The right of action in libel may be said to die with the death of the individual who was defamed. It has already been pointed out that relatives or friends of a person who is libeled have no right of action themselves unless they were specifically defamed by the same story.

A wife, then, cannot sue for a libel on her husband after he is dead. (23) Neither can a mother begin action for libel against a son after he has died. (24)

The legal reasoning is that libel is an injury to reputation, and one's good name dies with him although his memory may live on.

As one court said:

"The general rule is that a libel upon the memory of a deceased person that does not directly cast any personal reflection upon his relatives does not give them any right of action, although they may have suffered mental anguish or sustained an impairment of their social standing among a considerable class of respectable people of the community in which they live by disclosure that they were related to the deceased." (25)

There are two other bars to actions. A newspaper may always arrange a settlement with the individual who claims he was defamed. If he agrees, he cannot later bring action for the same libel. The newspaper, however, should have such releases drawn up by a lawyer to insure complete protection.

The law recognizes, too, there should be a time limit within which a person may sue for libel. Otherwise, a newspaper might be harassed for years.

The majority of states by statute or court decisions hold that actions must be brought within one year after first publication.

These states are: Alabama, Arizona, California, Colorado, Connecticut, Delaware, Georgia, Illinois, Kansas, Kentucky, Louisiana, Maryland, Michigan, Mississippi, Missouri, Nebraska, New Jersey, New York, North Carolina, Ohio, Oklahoma, Oregon, Pennsylvania, South Carolina, Tennessee, Texas, Utah, Virginia, West Virginia, and Wyoming.—30

Within two years—Florida, Idaho, Indiana, Iowa, Maine, Massachusetts, Minnesota, Montana, Nevada, New Hampshire, North Dakota, Rhode Island, South Dakota, Washington, and Wisconsin.—15

Within three years—Arkansas, New Mexico, and Vermont.—3

Damages

The financial danger to the newspaper in civil libel stems from the lack of mathematical standards to measure damages. Awards have ranged all the way from nominal damages of six cents (which merely vindicated the plaintiff) to the $287,000 given to a southern governor because a national magazine inferred he was indifferent to lynchings in his state. (26)

There are almost as many classifications of damages as there are writers on the subject. Formal names, therefore, are only guides to describing what the damages cover.

Types of damages may be divided into these headings:

General damages—compensation for such intangibles as mental anguish, loss of reputation or loss of social and business positions, physical pain, inconvenience, humiliation, etc. These are the damages the law presumes are in all defamatory statements.

Special damages—compensation for provable losses. If the defamatory article cost the injured individual his job or prevented his being appointed to a new position he sought he has actual damages. If he is a business or professional man, he may be able to prove his revenues declined by a specific amount after publication of the libel.

Punitive damages—sometimes popularly referred to as "spite money" or "smart money" and more formally as exemplary damages. As the name suggests, such damages are awarded as a punishment or penalty against the offending publisher. To receive punitive damages, the plaintiff generally must prove malicious intent upon the part of the publisher. An individual who called the newspaper's attention to a libelous article about him would have a good claim to punitive damages if the newspaper persisted in repeating the libel.

Although the courts generally are in a better position to determine injuries than the average men and women who make up juries, the amount of the award is usually left to the jury. And juries may be influenced by many germane and extraneous matters such as the reputation of the newspaper in the community, the reported wealth of the newspaper, the character of the libelous words, the sex of the plaintiff, especially if the libelous material reflected on the chastity of a woman, the reputation in the community of the plaintiff, the feeling in the community toward the charges made by the article, political sentiments, and many factors that cannot be guessed at, much less given their proper weights.

The trial court has the power to set aside an award or reduce it if the judge believes it is excessive or not warranted by the testimony. Appeals courts usually do not interfere with such action by the trial judge. (27)

Courts, however, have called attention of juries to the fact that a man with an established reputation, especially a business or professional man, is likely to be injured more seriously than if the same libel were directed at one who is just embarking upon his career. (28)

On the other hand, some courts have noted that in recent years "radical changes have taken place in conditions affecting the cost of living. This fact has been recognized by the courts in passing upon the amounts of verdicts." (29) Therefore, verdicts that some years ago would have been held to be excessive, now are permitted to stand. (30)

An estimate of what value courts place upon certain libelous publications may be seen by some verdicts in the past 25 years.

Charging unchastity, $30,000; traitor to his country, $100,000 but reduced to $25,000; competitor is going bankrupt, $100,000; white man had danced with negro women (in South), $10,000; defaming a judge, $20,000; falsifying an expense account, $80,-000, reduced to $20,000; and physician is a drug addict, $10,000.

Settlements out-of-courts seldom are made public. But three newspapers are reported to have paid a total of $100,000 to three men whom they called Communists. A physician, inadvertently listed in an expose of "quacks," is reported to have settled for $20,000.

Every newspaperman should frame the axiom: "He who prints pays." But what he pays many times depends upon a jury, and consistency is not among the major virtues of most juries.

For Further Reading

Davis, Norris G., "The Sweeney 'Chain Libel' Suits," 21 *Journalism Quarterly*, June, 1944.

Outland, Ethel R., *The "Effingham" Libels on Cooper*, Madison; University of Wisconsin Press, 1929 (early chain libel suits).

Weber, Sylvia, "Punitive Damages in the Law of Libel," 10 *Brooklyn Law Review*, March, 1941.

Pollack, L., "Recovery (in Libel) by Surviving Relatives," 26 *Cornell Law Quarterly*, June, 1941.

————"Liability of Newspapers for Libel Transmitted by Press Associations," 15 *New York University Law Quarterly*, May, 1938.

Wittenberg, Philip, *Dangerous Words*, New York; Columbia University Press, 1947, Chap. 7.

Chafee, Zechariah, Jr., *Government and Mass Communications*, Chicago; University of Chicago Press, Vol. 1, Div. A.

COURT DECISIONS

Rights of Surviving Relatives of Libeled Individual:
State v. Haffer, 94 Wash. 136.
Commonwealth v. Clap, 4 Mass. 163.

When second party has right of action:
  Hall v. Huffman, 159 Ky. 72.
  McDavid v. Houston Chronicle Publishing Co., 146 S.W. 252.

"Honest Mistakes":
  Washington Post v. Kennedy, 3 F. 2d. 207.
  Switzer v. Anthony and Denver Express Publishing Co., 71 Colo. 291.
  Walker v. Bee-News Publishing Co., 240 N.W. 579.
  Lundin v. Post Publishing Co., 104 N.E. 480.
  Maloof v. Post Publishing Co., 28 N.E. 2d. 458.

Jokes Do Not Excuse Libel:
  Triggs v. Sun Printing and Publishing Association, 71 N.E. 739.

Claims for Punitive Damages:
  Hall v. Hall, 103 S.E. 136.
  Revves v. Winn, 1 S.E. 448.

Holding paper is responsible for wire news:
  Szlay v. New York American, Inc., 4, N.Y. Supp. 2d. 620.
  Hearst v. New York *Staats-Zeitung*, 71 N.Y. Misc. 7.
  Begley v. Louisville Times Co., 272 Ky. 805.
  Carey v. Hearst Publications, 143 P. 2d. 857.

Holding paper is not responsible for wire news:
  Layne v. Tribune Company, 146 So. 234.

(The full decision should be read in order to understand one court's recognition of modern newspaper problems as well as to grasp the possible limitations on protection against non-local stories.)

CHAPTER XVIII

"The Three Elements in Libel"

What Makes A Libel?

It takes more than mere words to make a libel. For defamatory words, standing in isolation, cannot be a libel any more than a few disjointed and unconnected sentences can be called a story.

A libel has three component parts, and all of them must be present before an individual can maintain any action.

These three essentials are:

1. Defamation
2. Publication
3. Identification

Words, no matter how defamatory, cannot constitute a libel unless they are published. And if the defamatory words are published, they cannot create a libel if they are directed at, or hit, no one in particular.

Each of these essentials, although called by words easily understood, admit of peculiar legal meanings and interpretations.

Defamation

Although the general nature of defamation was discussed in a preceding chapter, there are some other factors to be noted in classifying defamation as one of the essential elements of libel.

The law recognizes a distinction between defamatory words and words which cause damage but do not defame. To the individual who is harmed, the difference may seem purely legalistic, but to the newspaper the distinction is practical and vital.

Defamatory words, as has been noted, are those which detract from an individual's reputation or hold him up to contempt, scorn, or hatred. The words in themselves may cause the damage or the injury may come only from the circumstances under which the words are used or from the meaning which a particular community applies to them.

Some courts include "ridicule" in their definitions of defamation, but since this word has a "double meaning" the law is concerned only with a narrow interpretation. If the ridicule produces only a laugh at the individual's expense, he cannot claim he was defamed although he may have been embarrassed. Satire is a form of ridicule but generally is not a cause for action.

The distinction between libelous and non-libelous ridicule might be expressed in popular terms as the same difference between "laughing at" a person or "laughing with him." Americans, with their reputation for humor, are supposed to enjoy good laughs at their own expense, but they may feel degraded or shamed if they are "laughed at."

Courts have tried to explain the distinction in various ways. One said:

"If its (the libelous word) design be wanton and malicious ridicule, and the tendency of the publication to hold up the plaintiff to the sneers of society, to degrade him, and lesson his standing, an action may be maintained. . . . Terms of mere general abuse, published in a newspaper, are not libelous." (1)

Another ruled:

". . . a degrading imputation must appear on the face of the libel, or by necessary inference from it. Hence, mere scurrility or abuse, without point or specific imputation, is not actionable." (2)

Ridicule may "bite" and "sting" but still not be libelous.

A state senator once arose to tell his colleagues how in his zeal to be at the capitol for a vote on a bill he had driven from his home in less than four hours. A reporter, making some calculations, figured the senator had averaged almost 59 miles an hour although the state speed limit was 50 miles. In a feature article, the reporter propounded the question whether it was proper for a senator to break one law in order to get to the capitol in time to pass another.

Colleagues immediately dubbed the senator "Speedy" and his constituents picked up the name. The senator was so embarrassed that he decided not to run for a second term. Clearly, he had been damaged, but the law could not protect him.

Cartoons, especially, are usually drawn for a laugh but unless they impute to an individual an illegal or unethical act, his best response is to join in the fun. An Alabama traffic policeman who failed to recognize his new car and put a parking tag on it had to endure the jests of fellow officers and citizens until the incident was forgotten. But he had no right to sue the newspaper which came upon the story and printed it.

A state Supreme Court justice in Iowa, who commuted to his office, once had the train wait five minutes while his wife drove home frantically to retrieve his false teeth which he had left on a table. The whole state got a laugh at his expense and when he got his teeth back, he joined in the smiles.

Sometimes the words may produce damages that can be proved but yet may not be defamatory. As already pointed out, caustic reviews of public performances may cause a financial loss to the performer or artist, but he has no recovery.

The words may damage a man in his business. A merchant may advertise that his wares are the most durable and the cheapest of any similar products in town, and competitors, because of his claims, may lose business, but he hasn't libeled them.

A merchant who advertises: "Buy one at the regular price and get the second article at only one cent additional" may damage other stores by taking trade away from them. There is no remedy unless the first merchant is dishonest and has raised prices. If an ordinary 25-cent article is increased to 40 cents and then an additional article sold for a penny more, other merchants may ask the Federal Trade Commission to cite him for unfair trade practices. But there is no action in libel.

A vice-president of the United States once said he saw no reason for men to wear hats, and hat manufacturers quickly protested that his statement injured their business. They might have been able to offer convincing proof of loss of sales revenues, but a man has a free choice of wearing a hat or going bareheaded, and he may communicate his views on the subject to anyone who will read or listen. The vice-president later did buy a hat but instead of wearing it, he carried it in his hand. Only he knows what prompted his purchase, but it certainly wasn't through fear of legal action.

A surgeon whose skill with his hands attracts admiration from colleagues and deep respect from his patients may find the same hands produce only monstrosities when he attempts to build a dog house or attach a sun porch to his home. His neighbors may enjoy a good laugh at his handiwork, but they haven't injured him in a legal sense.

In some cities, a society leader may be a virtual "dictator," controlling the fortunes of all those with social aspirations. Her invitation list, when published in a newspaper, may tell the community who has made the grade socially, but those omitted have no right of action although they may be so badly injured they eventually leave the city.

The New York *Social Register* adds and deletes names with every edition. An individual dropped from the *Register* may feel the damage even in his business, but he must bear his burden without relief from the law.

Associations of tailors and dress makers each year select the "ten best dressed men" and the "ten best dressed women" in the United States. In 1950, when the name of the Secretary of State, Dean Acheson, did not appear on the list of "best dressed men" for the first time in a number of years, his personal tailor issued a long explanation to the press. The omission of his well-known customer may have cost the tailor some business, but he, too, was without legal recourse. The law does not concern itself with social position or etiquette.

To an actor, publicity is his "life blood," but none has grounds for a legal complaint if he is not included on the numerous lists of "best actors" or represented on the equally numerous lists of "best performances." Such omissions may cost him a good role if a producer decides his failure to achieve recognition indicates lack of public interest in him.

The omission may be deliberate. One newspaper chain for a number of years refused to mention a particular actor because the head of the organization reputedly felt that a certain movie in which the actor starred was a "takeoff" on the publisher's own life. Few newspapers commented on the incident because it involved an element of publication risk. Readers who depended largely upon those chain newspapers may have concluded that the actor was inactive or had "slipped" and such deductions might have hurt his "box office" appeal. But he could neither compel the chain to mention him nor start an action because it refused.

Some political candidates often complain that public opinion polls are unfair to them, and after the 1948 presidential election there was talk in Congress of investigating the surveys to see if they had been "rigged." Reputable public opinion agencies would not destroy themselves by falsifying returns, but, if any of them did, the most a candidate could claim was that he was the victim of an unethical "trick."

Consumer groups publish bulletins listing "best buys" or "unacceptable," and while no one can measure exactly the influence of their opinions, certainly a product suffers some damage if classified as "unacceptable" or "not recommended." But the law will not aid the damaged company.

A college football star, tentatively offered a good coaching position on the strength that he will be an "All-American," has no legal recourse if the selections later fail to include his name, and it costs him the prospective job.

Defamation is not synonymous with disparagement. It must go deeper. In the case of the football star, he would have had a cause for action if false charges of "dirty playing" had cost him that job.

Neither does the law recognize damage to pride. Ridicule may puncture a man's ego but the law offers him no balm. The community may laugh at him, but embarrassment finds no compensation in money damages.

A newspaper may say falsely that a man has the measles and his friends may josh him about being in his "second childhood." But he either must "grin and bear it" or shun their presence until they find new subjects for their jokes. But if the paper says falsely that he had contracted a so-called social disease, he has a cause for action.

Words that damage, then, may be classified under two headings. In one classification are words that cause harm and damage but for which no legal redress may be obtained. Words, however, that tear away a man's reputation and cause ordinary men to hold him in contempt or to shun him, are defamatory and actionable.

Publication

As far as newspapers are concerned, publication needs little explanation because when defamatory words appear in print they are there for all to see. The newspaper can hardly deny they were published.

To round out the principles of libel, it is well, however, to keep in mind that publication in a legal sense is much more complex. The law distinguishes between publication in civil and criminal libel.

To be published legally, criminally libelous words need be seen only by the individual against whom they are directed. The assumption is that even though he alone sees them, he might be provoked to violence with just as much disturbance of the peace as if the words had been seen by many people.

In civil libel, publication comes only if another party besides the writer and addressee sees the words. The distinction is necessary since civil libel is damage to one's reputation. And reputation, as has been pointed out, is merely what others think of a person. They can hardly be influenced to change their opinion if they never hear of any accusations made against him.

A hypothetical case illustrates the difference. If I write a defamatory letter and mail it to the individual against whom I am inveighing, it is a matter between two persons. He cannot show it to a third party just to have a cause for action. But if a third party inadvertently sees it, there is publication.

Or, after the letter is written, I may stick it in my pocket while I decide if I should mail it. Should I forget it and later employes of a cleaning and pressing establishment find it in my pocket and read it, the man to whom it was addressed has been damaged. Because now others know his reputation has been impugned.

If the letter is stolen from me, and the finder shows it to other parties, then he has published it and I may disclaim any legal responsibility for having it come to light. As one court expressed it more than 100 years ago, when the writer of a libel permits it to leave his control, it is like the arrow shot into the air, for eventually it is bound to hit something when it falls to earth. (3)

Two of the complexities of publication do concern newspapers. If a newspaper submits a galley proof to one outside its employ for checking or other purposes, the individual defamed could claim publication no matter if the paper later discarded the story. There is no publication, however, if the galley proof is submitted to the newspaper's lawyer for checking.

A Pennsylvania newspaper was involved in a suit over "galley-proof" publication. It submitted proofs of a political editorial to a party official for comment. He, in turn, consulted other advisers, and finally the newspaper discarded the editorial as "too dangerous" to publish. But the individual at whom it was aimed obtained one of the proofs and submitted it as evidence of publication. The case was settled out of court.

The second complexity is that publication does not necessarily mean original publication. Newspapers at times reprint editorials or stories from other papers, especially during political campaigns. The one who is defamed may proceed against both the originating paper and the one which reprinted the material.

A press association once was given galley proofs of a story involving charges against several state political leaders. It sent the story over its wires but the originating paper at the last minute decided against using it. The press association made a settlement with the political leaders.

The courts a number of times have upheld actions brought against papers which merely reprinted stories from other publications. In fact, one of the most celebrated of American libel cases was that brought in 1804 against Harry Croswell, editor of a Federalist paper in Hudson, N. Y., for an article he had reprinted from the New York *Evening Post*, attacking President Jefferson. Croswell lost, although his brilliant defense by Alexander Hamilton was one of the steps toward obtaining statutes permitting the jury to pass upon both the law and fact. (4)

A newspaper which reprints a defamatory story cannot escape responsibility by "softening the blow" through editorial comment that it does not believe all the charges. (5)   Otherwise, a newspaper might publish libelous material at will by merely adding such remarks as: "We do not believe there is sound foundation for all these charges."

Identification

If defamatory words are published but refer to no specific individual, there is no libel except under special circumstances dealing with groups or minorities as discussed in a following section.

To be libelous, however, a story need not mention an individual by name.   An innuendo or general description may be just as plain to the community as if the person actually were named.

As the courts have said:

> "Statements are not libelous unless they refer to some ascertained or ascertainable person." (6) And that person must be the plaintiff who brings the action. (7)

The identification need not be by words.   In the section on libel in photographs it was shown that the wrong picture is libelous.   The legal reason is that the wrong photograph is sufficient identification, although the story is not intended to be about the one whose likeness is shown. (8)

A Texas newspaper published a story about General Adolpho Herrera, at that time a figure in Mexican politics.   One Rodolfo Herrera, living in the Texas city, maintained that his friends took the story to be about him although the given name was different and he never had referred to himself as "general." The courts agreed that he had been "damaged." (9)

Although the custom is not as widespread as in books or magazines, some newspapers do occasionally print feature stories with fictitious names for the characters.   If an individual in the community has the same name, or can show he was damaged otherwise by the story, he has cause for action.

For the courts have said:

> "The question is not so much who was aimed at, as who was hit. The fact that the publisher had no actual intention to defame a particular man or indeed to injure anyone, does not prevent recovery of compensatory damages by one who connects himself with the publication, at least, in the absence of some special reason for a positive belief that no one existed to whom the description answered." (10)

Although this court was ruling on a novel, a newspaper using fictitious names in an expose story takes the risk of hitting an actual resident in its territory.

In a previous section, it was shown that a postmaster was able to convince a jury that he was identified by a story of his sister's theft which commented that "some believed she stole for others." (11) But, as also indicated earlier, writing that a man arrested for a crime has a wife and two children, although identifying them by names, is not libelous of them because the story imputes no charges to them.

Sometimes a story is intended by the newspaper to refer to one unnamed person, but the readers interpret it as being about another. The second individual has a right of action, and the contention of the paper that it did not mean him is of no avail.

A number of newspapers have found themselves involved in libel suits because of what may be termed identification by vocation. A defamatory article about a veterinarian, although it does not name him, carries sufficient identification if he is the only one in the city. During prohibition days, a well-known Washington bootlegger was identified frequently in newspapers simply as the "man in the green hat." Actually, several hundred men in Washington may have worn "green hats" but most readers knew to whom the articles referred.

Naturally, the bootlegger himself did not sue because he could hardly have come into court with "clean hands." Other men wearing green hats did not sue because they would have had to establish some reason why they believed the articles were about them. A man hardly cares to go into court to prove there are grounds for his friends believing he is a bootlegger. That particular style of green hat, however, quickly lost its popularity among Washington men.

The case of the North Carolina newspaper which identified a man arrested in a vice raid as a "former theater man in this city" has been cited. Had the newspaper not added the identifying "tag," the second man with the same name as the arrested person probably would have had to prove special damages to recover. (12) At least, the damages would have been mitigated and punitive damages denied.

A California paper paid damages for another "vocation identification." A physician was arrested and committed to an institution as a drug addict. Accepting the word of a police officer, the newspaper identified him as a former football star, who in his athletic days had gained national prominence. The former gridiron star was now a physician and surgeon in Los Angeles. The two physicians had the same surname and the same initials for their two given names. To add to the irony, the arrested physician had succeeded the athlete when he left a hospital staff to enter private practice.

If the paper had used only the two initials it might have escaped by publishing an explanatory story to show there were two physicians with the same surname and initials. But the identification "tag" of "former football star" left no doubt in the readers' minds as to whom was meant. (13)

Frequently, stories appear about old-time movie stars, athletes, or other public figures who now have fallen upon evil days. The newspaper should be wary of accepting such identification. The man who is brought in from Skid Row and charged with drunkenness or vagrancy may give the name of a one-time public figure and even display newspaper clippings about his once prosperous days. He may be the one-time great and then again he may be the victim of his own warped imagination. If the former public idol is still living, he has a case against the paper which accepts the word of the imposter.

A woman was brought into Chicago police court on a charge of petty robbery. It was plain she also was a drug addict. She claimed to be the famous Annie Oakley, once toasted on two continents for her marksmanship with a rifle.

The real Annie Oakley was then living in retirement in New Jersey. She made good her complaint of libel. (14)

A New York paper lost a suit for its story describing how a former street railways president and broker now was reduced to begging money for liquor. It was another case of wrong identification. (15)

Old-time athletes, in particular, seem to bob up in police lineups and slums until further check exposes them as imposters. A pocketful of clippings does not make a derelict a former World Series hero or a one-time All-American football player or the former holder of a world's boxing title. Even the FBI at times learns that it has "agents" whom it hears of for the first time when the impersonators run afoul of real police officers.

These "once upon a time" stories make real human interest reading. But sometimes they can be expensive.

Identification of Groups

In most libel suits involving newspapers, the identification is specific because the defamed individual is named, and his street address also printed. Or if the libel is by innuendo, readers seldom have to do much guessing to figure out whom it hits.

Organizations or groups as a whole may be libeled, it will be pointed out later. But what about cases in which the reference is to a group but only one or two specific individuals actually are meant? For example, a newspaper may charge that one member of the board of county commissioners is profiting through a "cut-back" on materials sold to the county. There are three commissioners. Does one, or all three of them, have a right of action?

Here is another area where the law lacks uniformity among the several jurisdictions. The general rule that if the group is small enough any one can maintain a libel action is not of much help because courts differ on the exact numbers.

One court, in emphasizing there can be no action if alleged libelous words are applied to an "indeterminate class," held:

"But if the words may be a reasonable application, import a charge against several individuals, under some general description or general name, the plantiff has a right to go to trial, and it is for the jury to decide whether the charge has the personal application averred by the plaintiff." (16)

The court was speaking in the case of one of twelve radio editors on New York City newspapers. Comedian Eddie Cantor, nettled by comments in some radio columns, said he had great respect for all radio editors except those in New York City.

"However," he said, "I shall continue to fight those New York radio editors who are experts at log rolling, who use their columns for delving into personalities that have nothing to do with radio, and whose various rackets are a disgrace to the newspaper profession.

"There is but one person writing on radio in New York City who has the necessary background, dignity, and honesty of purpose." (17)

The court ruled that the radio editor who sued had a right to go before a jury to show Cantor's comments were directed at him since he was a member of the group under attack.

"Radio editor" is a rather general description, but the one who sued claimed that it referred to a writer who reviewed performances and programs and that there were only twelve of such men in all New York City.

A story attacking New York City "editors" presumably is too vague to maintain a libel action. For in New York, the word "editor" might include editors, managing editors, city editors, sports editors, departmental editors, trade publication editors and even staffs of press associations.

To presume, however, that twelve is within the permissible limits for individual identification, is not necessarily correct. An Oregon court was faced with deciding a case brought by two radio repairmen who worked for the same firm.

This firm was the only one in the city offering "pick-up and delivery service" on radio repairing. A newspaper said that "a radio repair and pick-up service is not meeting its commitments." The court ruled, however, that the story did not contain a direct reference to the two plaintiffs. What the court meant was that there was not sufficient identification for maintaining a libel action. (18)

One of the 12-man board of trustees of a university collected damages because a newspaper charged the board showed favoritism in appointments and purchases of supplies. (19)

A juror collected damages after a newspaper said a verdict was arrived at through the use of whiskey. (20)

Such vague terms as "city leaders," "civic leaders," "business leaders" or "leading citizens" ordinarily do not admit of sufficient identification. But a New York court ruled that in a town of 4,000 "our officials" is sufficient identification when the community is governed by a mayor and three trustees. (21) The court indicated that cause of the action, a letter to the editor, caustic as it was, might have been justified as fair comment had not the writer charged the officials were dictated to by gangsters. (22)

In Washington, D. C., one man owned nine of the 20 parking lots in the downtown area. There were not more than 12 individual owners of the 20 lots. A Washington newspaper under a heading: "Parking Lot Racket Probe Ordered Here" charged that the parking lots, after motorists had paid and left their cars, moved them into the streets to provide room for other automobiles.

The owner of the nine lots sued, but the court ruled that the article dealt with parking lot owners as a "class" and therefore no individual was "defamed." (23)

As the court explained:

"The courts have chosen not to limit freedom of public discussion except to prevent harm occasioned by defamatory statements reasonably susceptible of special application to a given individual." (24)

A charge that officials of the Workers' Alliance diverted membership fees to pay for Communist propaganda under direct orders from Russia was held not to be libelous of any particular official since the Alliance has many local units, county organizations, and a state-wide council. (25)

The language of the court may be of some help in determining when a member of a group can maintain an individual action in libel.

"The reference to 'their officials' who are accused of diverting membership dues to further Communist agitation, applies no more to the plaintiff than would a similar statement, accusing federal judges of encouraging violations of the import tax laws be made to apply to any one judge. . . . Where a group is very large and nothing that is said applies in particular to the plaintiff, he cannot recover." (26)

A Wisconsin court held there was not sufficient identification when a newspaper printed that a state sanitarium had on its staff part-time doctors who are arrested cases of tuberculosis. The sanitarium employed four part-time doctors. (27)

Numbers alone, then, are not absolute guides as to sufficient identification of individuals when stories refer to more than one person or to a group. But in the absence of more specific criteria, numbers must be taken into account.

Some general observations would be:

1. The larger the group is, the less is the possibility of libel through identification.

2. Identification is more certain among small groups created legally than in more informal groups. Boards of trustees, commissioners, *et al* are set up by law and people know, or may readily learn, who are the members of the boards. The "Citizens' Committee for Traffic Enforcement" is apt to be an informal and loosely-organized group whose membership changes frequently.

3. Such references as "city leaders," "the town's most influential families" and the like, generally are too vague to permit an individual to sue for libel. If by "city officials" the article indicates it means the mayor and three or four trustees or commissioners, it may be libelous.

4. Even when there is a small group involved and the language fails to indicate affirmatively that all members were involved in the charge, it was held that "defamatory words must refer to some ascertained or ascertainable person, and that person must be the particular plaintiff." (28)

Thus, if a county board were composed of five Republicans and three Democrats, and the story charged the majority with graft, none of the Democrats would have a right of action since the accusations involve only the Republican members.

5. If a member of a small group sues and wins damages, the other members do not automatically share in the award nor receive similar payments. Each would have to enter a separate suit although in some jurisdictions there might be a "joint suit."

6. Sometimes even a small group is unintentionally narrowed by a newspaper to the point where an individual has the right of action. A company, employing ten janitors, is robbed, and the president says he believes it was an "inside job" and blames a janitor. None of the ten may have a right of action. But if the president says he believes the robbery must be blamed on a "newly-employed janitor" and only one of the ten has come to work within the past several months, that janitor can claim identification.

7. If the group is not too small, the bromide: "Some of the members" etc. may eliminate possible suits or mitigate damages in event there is an action in libel.

For Further Reading

Burdick, Francis M., *The Law of Torts*, Albany; Banks & Company, 1926, Chap. 2 and 9.

Gatley, Clement, *Libel and Slander in Civil Action*, London; Sweet and Maxwell Co., 1924.

Newell, Martin L., *The Law of Libel and Slander in Civil and Criminal Cases*, Chicago; The Callaghan Co., 1924, 4th ed., Sec. 200.

Thayer, Frank, "The Changing Libel Scene," *Wisconsin Law Review*, May, 1943.

Yankwich, Leon R., *It's Libel*, Los Angeles; Parker & Co., 1950.

COURT DECISIONS
(In addition to those cited in the text)
Defamation:

Dorr v. United States, 195 U.S. 138.

White v. Nicolls, 44 U.S. 3.

Commonwealth v. McClure, 3 Pa. 464.

McFadden v. Morning Journal Co., 28 N.Y. App. Div. 508.

Wolfson v. Syracuse, 254 N.Y. App. Div. 211.

Identification:

Williams v. Journal Co., 247 N.W. 435.

Brown v. Journal Newspaper Co., 107 N.E. 358.

Watson v. Detroit Journal Co., 143 Mich. 430.

Burkhart v. North American Co., 214 Pa. 39.

Lynch v. Kirby, 131 N.Y.S. 680.

Weston v. Commercial Advertiser Association, 184 N.Y. 479.

Barron v. Smith, 101 N.W. 1105.

Publication:

The codes of the several states define "publication" as it applies to libel. California, for example, says:

"To sustain a charge of publishing a libel, it is not needful that the words or things complained of should have been read or seen by another. It is enough that the accused knowingly parted with the immediate custody of the libel under circumstances which exposed it to be read or seen by any other person than himself." . . . Penal Code of California, 1941, Sec. 252.

The majority of the states agree with the California definition but the exact statute in each state may be obtained readily from the code of that state.

CHAPTER XIX

"How the Laws of Libel Operate"

Where Libel May Lurk in the Newspaper

The newspaper, it cannot be repeated too often, is responsible for everything it prints. Libel is committed most often in news stories and editorials, but it may be found lurking also in headlines, pictures, cartoons, syndicated columns, cartoon strips, letters to the editor, and in advertisements, both display and classified.

A newspaper may not sign away its responsibility for libel. An editorial notice, for example, over letters to the editor, may announce that the newspaper is not responsible for the views expressed by the writers, but this is simply evidence that the paper is willing to print all sides of any discussion. If a letter contains libelous material, the paper may be sued although the name and the address of the writer is given.

The inclusive responsibility for its contents is one of the prices the newspaper pays for being the sole judge of what it will print either as news or advertising. If the newspaper were forced against its will to print certain material, it would have just grounds for disclaiming legal responsibility for those items. The law, however, makes the newspaper the sole guardian of its pages and so insists that it must assume all the risk for what it does choose to publish.

In preceding chapters, especially those dealing with the rights of the newspaper to comment and criticize, some aspects of libel have been discussed. This chapter will deal with specific examples of libel in the various sections of the paper.

Libel in Headlines

Writing heads is an art little understood by the layman who cannot seem to appreciate the limitations of space. Some critics of the press, in attacking certain headlines as "misleading" and "unfair" have found they can do no better when confronted with the same situation as the man on the copy desk. Moreover, they can take hours or even days to devise their versions while the deskman may have had only a few minutes to read, edit, and write the head.

Copy deskmen soon learn that reference to "rubber type" may be funny when they gather to talk shop but it is not humorous when they are confronted with an involved economic story that must be explained to the reader in two or three lines of 11 or 12 spaces each. Even staid newspapers which were so prim and precise finally gave up on Franklin D. Roosevelt and joined in designating him as "FDR" or " FR" for headline purposes.

A general rule is that the courts will read the headline and the context of the story together in determining if it is libelous. Obviously, however, there must be many exceptions to this general rule since the headline itself may be libelous although the story may be non-defamatory.

For years, a bugaboo in most newspaper offices was the handling of wire stories on court pleas. Here and there along the line, a day-dreaming telegrapher sometimes forgot the "not" before the "guilty." Most press associations instructed operators to capitalize the "not" to emphasize it for the news editors. Often when both operator and editor were blameless, a linotype operator slipped, and the story still appeared without the "not."

When automatic printers with their all capital letters replaced the manual telegraph, tape punchers spaced out the "n o t" to draw attention to it. But that, too, was not fool proof against the handling of the story in editorial and composing rooms. Now most press associations use "pleaded innocent" although in the court room the plea still is "not guilty."

Courts have concerned themselves with the function of the headline. Said one:

"The headline . . . being so conspicuous as to attract the attention of persons who look casually over a paper without reading all its contents, may itself inflict very serious injury upon a person, both because it may be the only part of the article which is read, and because it may cast a graver im-

putation than all the other words following it. The headlines
. . . may even justify a court or jury in regarding the publication libelous when the body of the article is not necessarily so."
(1)

Courts have recognized, too, that at times the headline writer
in seeking "punch" goes beyond words or the meaning of the
story. If the "punch" is obtained at the expense of accuracy,
it may be libelous.

A Pennsylvania newspaper reported that a bank had obtained judgment on a promissory note against the two co-own-
ers of a hotel. The judgment was a matter of court record and
could be printed. But the headline said the hotel proprietors
were "embarrassed."

One of the owners sued for libel on the ground that "embarrassed" implied he was in financial straits and thus injured
his credit. The court agreed with his interpretation. (2)

Judgments are entered daily in many courts. They do not
always mean that one party is without funds, for often they are
the result of a controversy over goods, services, or amount of
money actually due, and both sides may have agreed to an
amicable suit to permit a court to determine the facts.

A theatrical paper printed a story that two vaudeville acts
had paid $1,000 to obtain contract releases in order to open at
another theater. The article itself was true, but the headline
read: "Shuberts Gouge $1,000 from Klein Brothers."

The court ruled that "gouge" means to "cheat" or "defraud"
and hence is libelous. (3)

Many individuals and corporations often secure a cancella-
tion of a contract by making a financial arrangement with the
second party. Such an accepted business practice cannot be
called a "gouge."

The most common form of libel in headlines is in criminal
news in which the space limitation compels the writer to use
such phrases as: "Kidnaper Held," "Embezzler Nabbed," "Burg-
lar Caught," etc. Such brevity may be expensive since the headline, in effect, says the man arrested is guilty of the charge.

Such headlines come under the ruling of a court which said:

"Even if the matter published is privileged either absolutely or qualifiedly, because it is a report of a public proceeding or even in which the public has an interest, the privilege will not extend to the headline if the headline contains a libelous charge." (4)

As pointed out, it is permissible to say that a man was arrested on a charge of kidnaping if he actually were taken into custody. But "Kidnaper Seized" passes judgment upon him which a newspaper cannot do.

Headlines on stories about judicial proceedings, the courts have pointed out, are not part of the privileged report but merely comments on it. Therefore, they must be a "fair index of the matter contained in the report." (5)

Courts do not strain to read the headline out of context. But they do insist the headline be an accurate, if not precise, reflection of the story.

The New York *Times* was sued for a headline: "David Paris Guilty on Forgery Charge." The facts were that Paris, a lawyer, was suspended from practice for five years after a federal court found that three affidavits he had submitted were forged. The story plainly indicated that Paris was not found guilty of forging the affidavits but merely of submitting them to the court.

In finding for the *Times*, the court said that while the headline was not precise, it could not be called inaccurate when read in conjunction with the article. (6)

Libel of Professional People

The word "profession" is used today rather loosely in designating vocations. Some newspapermen refer to their work as a profession although language purists frown at such a description.

In the chapter on criticism it was shown that there are risks in commenting upon professional men. The danger is so great that it is worth noting here some more exact ways in which a professional man may be libeled inadvertently by a newspaper.

Whether the designation is narrow and exact, or broad and loose, every professional man depends upon the goodwill of the public. Few laymen are competent to pass upon the qualifications of a surgeon or dentist. To the average person, framed diplomas on doctors' offices look pretty much alike and there is little individual distinction in the framed pictures of the medical classes with which the doctors were graduated.

The community judges its doctors and dentists by word of mouth on the most superficial of standards. The doctor who led his class in scholarship may struggle to build up a practice while the student who several times was placed on scholastic probation may attract patients from the first day he hangs up his shingle.

Before World War II, when many young doctors started out with lean years, a physician beginning practice in a small community, quickly established a business by his insistence upon a complete physical check-up for every one who came to the office, no matter if the patient were suffering from a sprained wrist or a fallen arch. He later told a reporter privately that he did it to while away time and to keep in practice, but publicly he professed his method was part of his "preventive illness" policy. Soon the community was saying that "the young doctor certainly knows his business," and patients of the other physician long-established there began switching to the newcomer.

It would have been libelous for the reporter to print what the young doctor told him because it would have injured his professional reputation. If the remark were published, the young physician probably would have denied making it, and a jury, with ordinary men and women who in general respect for the medical profession, no doubt would have taken his word against that of the reporter.

Of other professions, such as architect and engineer, the public is even less qualified to pass judgment. Some professions, or so-called professions, are more sensitive to public opinion because the work they produce can be evaluated more readily. Every person who pays 50 cents to see a movie can pass on the merits of the play, the cast, and the photography, although his judgment may be simply a statement that he liked or did not like it. Every reader of a book can pass judgment on the author by the same means.

In the chapter on criticism of plays, books, concerts, movies, and other public performances, it was shown that a reviewer is permitted his opinion no matter how contrary it might be to the views of the audience as expressed in applause or calls for encores. The reporter, unless he is an experienced critic, may have no more sound basis for his opinion than the layman in the audience.

The reviewer can pass on the qualifications of the performer and need be wary only of delving into his personal life. In statements about some professions, such as medicine and law, the lay critic, including the reporter, is handicapped not only by lack of experience but also because the state through licensing such men, already has endorsed their competency. Therefore, to call a doctor a "quack" is libelous while an actor may be called a "ham" with no more repercussions than the ruffling of his pride and dignity.

Doctors

The doctor is granted considerable protection in his private practice although he can be sued for mistakes, and a paper, if it wishes, can call attention to his wrong diagnosis as long as it does not infer the error was due to incompetency. If the doctor, however, endorses a cigarette or a mouth wash, he must expect that certain sections of the public may not approve of his "extra-curricular" activities. A psychiatrist who testifies in a court trial cannot expect every person will agree with his findings and recommendations.

Courts have held to be libelous these comments about doctors.

"has a general want of professional skill." (7)
"profiteered on post-mortem examinations." (8)
"unworthy to retain his diploma." (9)
"used unprofessional methods." (10)

And, as it has been cited previously, a laudatory article may be libelous if it causes the physician to lose prestige among his colleagues or draws him a rebuke from his medical society. A Louisiana surgeon made good his complaint against a newspaper which praised some of his operations. The surgeon contended the article had the effect of advertising, which the medical world frowns upon. (11)

When a doctor or a professional man is arrested, the newspaper, of course, may print the news no matter how damaging it is to his professional standing. A physician, acquitted of an abortion charge, may still find his practice is ruined but he has no legal remedy against a paper which confined itself to printing only the permissible news in the case.

Ministers

There is no general term of derision for ministers, such as quack and shysters for doctors and lawyers, but because of the high respect in which society holds clergymen, they can be libeled by words that may be harmless when applied to other people. Ministers may be "mistaken" in print but never "liars."

What a minister actually thinks when another motorist crumples the fenders of his new car is between him and his conscience. But to say falsely that he was profane would be libelous. An ordinary motorist is permitted such language when his new car is damaged. (12)

To call a minister "discourteous and ignorant" is libelous. (13)

To infer that a minister is too attentive to women parishioners is libelous. (14)

A minister who takes part in public affairs, however, can be criticized, for then he is stepping out from his pastoral duties and becoming an ordinary citizen. (15)

Lawyers

The lawyer with his client has a position in law equivalent to that of a doctor and patient. The law regards these relationships as confidential and protects him. For that reason, a libel on a lawyer not only may injure his ability to make a living but also may harm his relationships with clients.

"Shyster" and "ambulance chaser," of course, are words no newspaper uses in speaking of lawyers unless it wishes to part with a substantial sum of money.

A newspaper found it was libelous to call an attorney "a puny little lawyer." (16) It also is libelous to say an attorney is "tricky." (17) A newspaper cannot say a lawyer took a case ᴏnly to get a fee. (18) It is also damaging to say a lawyer started a suit for damages without being authorized to do so by the injured person. (19)

Attorneys may be disciplined by their association or by the court. If an attorney is suspended from practice for a definite period it is libelous to print that he was disbarred. A disbarred lawyer is like an unfrocked minister; he has been ruled out of his profession. (20)

A New York court, however, ruled it is not libelous to print that parents of a youth involved in a morals case had petitioned the governor to appoint a "competent lawyer" to investigate. The district attorney claimed the words "competent lawyer" inferred he was not capable of handling the case. In dismissing the protector's suit for $100,000, the court said the parents were exercising their constitutional right of petition. (21) And the newspaper, the court held, was exercising its right to comment on a public issue." (22)

This case, however, must not lead to the conclusion that it is permissible to charge or infer that a professional man is not competent. The paper was safe because it wisely adhered without additional comment to the language of a petition filed with the governor. Readers may have interpreted the story as a charge of incompetency against the district attorney but, as has been said, courts do not strain to seek harm in a phrase that is capable of a non-defamatory meaning.

Educators

Charges of incompetency against a teacher may cost him his job and reduce his chances of further employment just as a similar accusation against a professional man may lose him patronage. School boards, and even university trustees, either through a careless disregard of the actual meaning of the word or in an effort to win public support, have dismissed instructors for "incompetency" when, in fact, the dismissals were due to other causes. Clashes of temperament, disagreements over methods of conducting classes, or displeasure over the instructor's "outside activities" are frequently disguised under the loose term "incompetency."

Many college professors who are international authorities in their fields are dismissed or resign because of clashes with colleagues or administrative officials, and the disputes in no way involve "competency." The reporter should use "dismissed for incompetency" only when he has that charge in an official written statement from the school board or trustees. A public school teacher who is discharged because he refuses to assume any out-of-classroom work, such as chaperoning social events, or who is dismissed because he objects to the required textbook or the schedule of classes, or because he and the principal disagree generally on education views cannot be called "incompetent."

A music teacher, dismissed for a variety of reasons, made good her complaint against a newspaper which, without any such formal charge from the school board, said she had been ·dropped for incompetency. The court agreed with her contention that the reader would assume she lacked the ability to perform her job. (23) It is not libelous, however, to say a university dropped a professor because it had "good and sufficient grounds" and that he no longer was "a useful member of the faculty." (24)

The story, however, wisely refrained from indicating that the professor was not qualified to teach the subject.

To say that a girl caused a scandal among the faculty by working in a professor's office without pay is libelous. (25)

Authors, Editors, and Others

Although a reviewer of a public performance may not delve into the performer's private life, he is permitted to assay that individual's qualifications. Unlike law or medicine or a few other professions, the state does not pass upon the qualifications of those offering works for public approval. Any one with a typewriter and a ream of paper can write a book, any one with a paint set and an easel can dabble on canvas, and any one with sufficient nerve can go out on the stage and sing or dance or tell jokes. The public then will express its opinion, good or bad, without fear of legal action.

It is libelous, however, to say that an author pirated his material or that he is offering the works of another as his own. A newspaper settled out of court for intimating that the sketch of an architect must have been done by one of the young men in his employ because it looked "too sane" to be his own work.

Although this seems to be the age of the "ghost writer" a woman author collected from a columnist because he inferred her book had to be rewritten before it could be published. The author contended that the statement damaged her reputation as a professional writer.

A man who makes his living, or part of it, writing or lecturing has a case if a "faked" or "garbled" interview quotes him as making statements that learned people in the same field would regard as absurdities. An Italian Count who lectured before lay audiences and learned societies sued on the ground that an interview attributed to him had him telling about adventures in Africa which were fantastic. He contended the story lowered his prestige among learned men and damaged his ability to command audiences for his lectures. The courts ruled his complaint was good. (26)

Sports figures, accustomed to the "give and take" of criticism as the fortunes of the game make them in turn "hero or goat," can be libeled. To accuse an athlete, professional or amateur, of "throwing a game" is defamatory.

A New York paper, in an article on evolution, proposed the thesis that a modern wrestler is not much different in physique from a gorilla. It was illustrated with pictures of a gorilla and of a then well-known professional wrestler. The courts held it to be libelous. (27)

A man who was able to show extensive formal training in criminology, and also that he had written widely on the subject, complained of libel because a letter to the editor called him a "humbug," and a "pseudo-scientist." The courts ruled he had a case. (28)

A newspaper found itself in a suit for saying that the roof of a new high school building was sagging and in danger of collapsing and that it "didn't speak well for those who designed and built the school." The architect sued and his complaint was held to be good. (29)

Even an editor may be libeled. The editor of a daily news-paper sued because a handbill distributed around the city charged that ". . . his (the editor's) hat covers the worst corruption in the entire town." It also accused the editor of "villifying" people who drank while he ". . . punishes more fire water than any gut-ter pup ever known." The handbill suggested the best thing that could happen would be to have the editor tarred and feath-ered and carried out of town on a fence rail. (30)

Using either a strict or a broad interpretation of "profession," professional men and women may be libeled by stories charg-ing:

1. Incompetency or lack of proper qualifications for their work.

2. Unfitness either through lack of sufficient training or in their general methods of procedure or professional conduct.

3. Lack of professional integrity which may include every-thing from gossiping about patients or clients and asking exorbitant fees to "blackmail" or "bribery."

Incompetency is one charge that a newspaper seldom will be able to prove if it wishes to rely on truth as a defense in libel. A doctor, lawyer, or even a teacher, has a state certificate to prove that an examining committee found him to be qualified and competent. One doctor may privately criticize another, but he shrinks from repeating that criticism from the witness stand.

Doctors may differ in their diagnosis or prognosis but who can prove where truth lay even if the patient dies? Every day patients die of diseases that others are able to overcome and fight their way back to health. Treatments to which one patient responds produce no improvement in another.

The only way to prove incompetency is through testimony of others qualified in the same field. And men of the pro-fessions and of the sciences just do not go around testifying that certain of their colleagues are unfit. The newspaper, realizing that, steers clear of any inferences about the skill or ability of these men. It confines its comments and criticisms of these persons to their public acts where the opinions of the layman, in the eyes of the law, carry as much weight as those of the learned man.

Libel of Public Officials

(See Chapter 10 on "Limits of Criticism — Public Officials and Performances.")

Libel of Public Figures

(See Chapter 10 on "Limits of Criticism — Public Officials and Performances.")

Libel in Photographs

(See Chapter 15 on "Photographs and the Law.")

Libel of Groups

One of the new dangers in libel is the growing recognition by the courts that an entire group may recover for defamatory statements made about it. Formerly, the theory was that libel could damage only the reputation of an individual. But a group or organization may suffer just as greatly from a libelous statement as an individual.

The question which the courts faced, and which in some jurisdictions has not yet been answered definitely, is: If a group (or organization) is damaged, should the remedy be a charge of criminal libel brought by the state or should the group be permitted to seek damages?

Some groups or organizations cannot be libeled. An editorial charging that one of the major political parties is a "tool of Wall Street and the enemy of labor" may hurt that party at the next election, but law offers no remedy. For one thing, the American government functions through political parties and no issue is imbued with more public interest than an election. To stifle criticism of political parties is, in effect, to restrict the citizen's right to discuss freely his government and its functioning.

For another thing, a political party is a rather nebulous organization. A certain number of Americans relish "being born a Republican (or Democrat) and dying a Republican (or Democrat)." But countless numbers adhere only loosely to party principles and shift their allegiance frequently as new issues arise. A Republican voter in Kansas certainly cannot claim that he was injured by a scathing editorial in a Democratic paper in New York which attacked the Republican party in general.

Sometimes size mitigates against actions in libel. An atheist journal may charge in each issue that the church is mislead-

ing the people. But who or what is the church? Exposes have
been written about doctors, lawyers, ministers, advertisers, businessmen, and practically every vocation, profession, or calling.
An article about unethical practices of doctors is never interpreted by the reader to mean that all physicians are guilty of
the same improper conduct.

Even if it were, no individual doctor could maintain an
action. The American Medical Society, unless it were accused
of unethical practices as an organization, would have no grounds
for a suit. The law, then, would be unable to determine who
really was harmed by the article.

Many articles have spoken unfavorably about education and
educators, but who are they? Every teacher from kindergar-
ten instructor to college professor is referred to at times as an
"educator." Clearly, the category is too broad for any one of
them, unless specifically named, to claim he was damaged.

The problem is no simpler if more specific terms are used.
The Republican party and the Protestant church are still too
large, and too loosely organized, to claim damages.

But a group or association, that has a definite membership,
may be libeled. A particular church, a veterans' organization,
a labor union, a fraternal society, a farm organization, or any
well-defined group can be harmed by defamatory statements.
The libelous article may cause the organization to lose members,
or through loss of public esteem, nullify the objectives for which
it was founded.

Few major cases have arisen in which such organizations
have sought damages. Usually, an article about such associations will mention one or more officers by name, and these
men have a right of action.

One of the few cases is that of the National Maritime Union
which sought $1,000,000 damages from a press association and
also $1,000,000 from a chain newspaper named as co-defendant.
The case grew out of a story in 1943 that a National Maritime
Union crew had refused to unload a ship at Guadalcanal on a
Sunday and that sick marines had to take over the job to get
the war cargo on the docks promptly.

The case finally was settled in 1949 with the press association paying $7,500 to the union and the chain newspaper, $1,000. The press association also sent out a corrective article on June 2, 1949, almost six years after the original story was published.

Three other suits brought by the union, against individual newspapers a year after the story first was printed, were dismissed. (31)

An electrical workers union sued a newspaper for statements which the union claimed damaged its interests and also its credit. The court ruled its complaint was good, and said:

". . . the usefulness of labor unions depends largely upon their reputation for honesty, fair dealing, and a sincere effort to improve the standards of labor. Insofar as the first cause of action (in this particular suit) alleges injury to the business and credit of the union by reason of publication of the defamatory words, it states a good cause for action in favor of the union." (32)

The newspaper, of course, can criticize freely all public activities of the union, and in event of a strike, it can remain neutral or take either side it chooses. The courts are concerned primarily with stories that injure the union's business and more especially, its credit. (33)

A corporation, in the eyes of the law, is a person, and hence, it may sue for libel. This right is generally conceded to the corporation whether it is a regular business concern or one devoted to charity or other non-profit activities. Presumably, the right extends also to partnerships or to firms which are nothing more than individuals carrying on business under a trade name.

A corporation does not have a character or reputation in the same sense as an individual although the law does regard it as a "person." A corporation, then, to maintain an action in libel, as one court said, must prove the words "attack the company's methods of doing business, accuse it of fraud, or must attack its financial position." (34) If the defamatory words attack the reputations of officers or employes of the corporation, the company cannot sue, but the individuals named may bring action. (35) For a statement charging a corporation president with fraud does not necessarily accuse the company of any illegal or unethical practices.

Carelessness in identification has brought a number of news-papers into court. Companies, at times, sublet part of their office or warehouse space, and some even rent desk space. One wholesale grocery company rented part of its space to a pack-ing firm. When the packing firm was raided and hundreds of pounds of horse meat labeled "Grade A beef" were confiscated, a paper used the name of the grocery company which was the only name appearing on the warehouse. Police had reported merely that the raid was at the warehouse. The newspaper settled out of court.

A Wisconsin paper was sued because it said that police had confiscated obscene postcards in a raid on a novelty company office. The company named had sublet space to another con-cern which was the one raided. A Pennsylvania newspaper paid for a story that two officers of a real estate company had been arrested in a "phony land deal." Police had told a re-porter they made the arrests at the real estate office. A check of the city directory showed the two men had offices where the police had served the warrants. But the real estate com-pany had rented desk space to promoters of a new cemetery and the realtors were not involved in the land deal.

A non-profit corporation, such as a church, hospital, college, etc., usually meets part or most of its expenses by financial aid from public-spirited citizens. An attack upon such an organiza-tion may cause a drop in revenues or may even compel it to be liquidated. In permitting such a non-profit corporation to sue for libel, a New York court said:

"Their (non-profit corporations) usefulness depends largely upon their reputation for honesty, fair dealing, and an altru-istic effect to improve social conditions. . . . The number and amount of . . . contributions would necessarily be affected by the publication of false and malicious articles to the effect that it is engaged in illegal and reprehensible conduct in the man-agement of its affairs." (36)

Criminal Libel of Groups

Although corporations both profit and non-profit, and small and well-defined groups or organizations, may be able in some instances to maintain actions in civil libel, the so-called "minority groups" have no such legal recourse. These groups include racial and religious minorities. The law is expressing increased concern for them but just doesn't quite see how to protect them.

The problem is the ever recurring one of freedom of expression balanced against the protection of the citizens or, in this case, a group of citizens bound together by some common characteristic, racial, religious, fraternal, etc. A newspaper or periodical which attacks such a group may cause harm to every member of it, yet no individual could come into court with sufficient ground to claim damages.

Several states have tried to deal with the problem by making it a criminal offense to libel people of a particular race or religion. Some of these statutes resulted from the agitation produced by a number of organizations which flourished in the last few years before the United States headed into the Second World War. In 1953, the United States Supreme Court upheld an Illinois law which provides punishment for the circulation of canards against minority groups.

States without specific statutes sometimes have relied on the general rules of criminal libel on the ground that such attacks tend to cause a breach of the peace. A publication which attacks a certain minority may help to foster a race riot or other disturbance or, at least, lend comfort to it.

Congress several times has considered a bill to impose criminal penalties for distributing in interstate commerce any material which might tend to incite disturbances through attacks on ethnic or religious groups. In 1949, such a bill was backed by the American Jewish Congress.

Explaining the purpose of the bill, an official of the Jewish Congress said:

"Libelous attacks on ethnic or religious groups as such touch and concern each of their individual component members. . . . Over and above the personal injuries inflicted, they have nourished and sustained ethnic and religious discrimination, contributed to civic dissension, and enfeebled the nation at large. Undismayed by these consequences, ethnic and religious hatemongers of all types not only peddle with complete immunity their poison but are abetted in their efforts by the availability of mailing privileges." (37)

The bill permitted truth, or reasonable and honest belief in the truth of the statments made, to be absolute defense.

Few people, according to comment at the time, quarreled with the objectives of the bill but many expressed doubts on the practical application of it without infringing upon the First Amendment.

The danger is that under such a bill some one must decide on the publisher's "reasonable and honest belief." It is possible that under such a law the author of a textbook might find himself embroiled in a suit because he attempted to give both sides to arguments over ethnic and religious issues. Or a newspaper might be sued for merely mentioning that a certain undesirable situation was brewing in the community. Identification of a man as a member of a particular group, although it might be a legitimate part of the news story, might be grounds for other members claiming the group was being attacked.

Editor and Publisher, in pointing out some of the possible dangers in the application of such a law, suggested:

"Rather than put a weapon on the statute books that could be misused, we believe it would be safer, saner, and more effective to continue attacking the problem through public education on the meaning and value of tolerance." (38) The bill did not pass.

The federal government charged a New York sculptor with mailing postcards containing "scurrilous and defamatory matter about Jews." The court, noting that Congress had failed to deal with the problem, dismissed the complaint on the ground that at present the law prohibits only mailing "scurrilous" material about an identifiable person, not about a group. Of course, had the language been obscene, the statutes on obscenity could have been invoked.

Criminal libel has been charged against publications for articles attacking specific organizations. A Chicago German-language newspaper charged the American Legion was an "instrument bought with British money to suppress the truth, to gag the freedom of conscience, to beat down every free expression of opinion, and to betray organized labor." It further harangued the Legion as having on its rolls two classes of members: Those who volunteered in the First World War and were, the paper said, "the refuse of the nation," and draftees who had to serve in the army through compulsion and who in no way "showed any patriotism." (39)

The man held responsible for the article was sentenced to six months in prison. The state Supreme Court, in affirming the sentence, said:

"A libel upon a class or group has as great a tendency to provoke a breach of the peace or to disturb society as has a libel on an individual and such a libel is punishable even though its application to individual members of the class or group cannot be proved." (40)

Affirming a conviction for criminal libel for a story about the Knights of Columbus an Oklahoma court said:

"The law is intended to, and does, protect the self-respecting law-abiding citizen against these calumnies, whether made against an individual specifically, or a class of individuals collectively." (41)

A New York man who printed a scathing attack on Roman Catholic priests was acquitted of a charge of obscenity but the court pointed out he could have been charged with criminal libel. The court said:

". . . The foundation of the theory on which libel is made a crime is that by provoking passions of persons libeled, it excites them to violence and a breach of the peace. Therefore, a criminal prosecution can be sustained where no civil action would lie, as for instance, in this very case, where the libel is against a class." (42)

Such statutes and court decisions, however, do not mean an organization or a class of people cannot be criticized. The law deals only with scurrilous attacks that tend to provoke the peace or which hold up all of the group to contempt or hatred.

Papers at times have complained because delegates to national conventions of some organizations have "roughed up" the city by throwing bags of water and other articles from hotel windows, annoyed pedestrians, blocked streets to normal traffic, or damaged public and private property. Some cities forbid certain organizations from bringing their conventions back.

A newspaper is within its rights in criticizing such extensive "horse play." There is no libel on the organization even if the paper suggests the national officers should control delegates more firmly. An ordinary reader assumes that "rough house" tactics is not the official policy of the organization and that convention officials cannot control boisterous delegates as well as a college dean can discipline students.

Trade Libel

A product may be libeled just as a corporation or an individual may be defamed. In most cases of so-called trade libel—or libel of a product—the company also is damaged and it prefers to sue for injury to its reputation rather than for harm to its product alone.

A paper which says a grocer sells moldy bread defames the grocer, for the bread originally was an edible product and it was not baked moldy. If a paper, however, says a certain soft drink is poisonous, the product has been damaged.

Usually, a company whose product has been libeled must prove malice in fact and also that it actually has suffered financial loss through the publication.

One court explains what is actionable in trade libel this way:

"To maintain an action for slander of property it must be shown that the words were false, maliciously published, and special damage, proximately, naturally, and reasonably resulting to the owner of the property." (43)

The owner of a building might be able to prove damages if a story said the house was "haunted." Even in this age, many people have no desire to consort with ghosts. If the property owner were unable to dispose of the building, or forced to sell far under the market price, he could prove the ghost story caused damage. Whether he could make good his claim for damages, however, is doubtful since the newspaper could show the story was printed only for the public interest which the ghost reports aroused.

In Albany, N. Y., a newspaper printed a series of stories that two cases, and possibly three, of tuberculosis had been discovered among state employes quartered in the basement of a private downtown office building. The owner of the building sued on ground that the stories damaged the building and would have an effect on future rental possibilities.

A South Dakota paper won a suit filed by a packing company which contended its products had been damaged through articles pointing out the danger to health of eating beef if the animals had died of starvation or exposure. A Providence, R. I., paper was sued for a series of articles about the quality of milk sold in the city. The articles were based on a study made by a dairy specialist from the University of Connecticut.

Libel of the Dead

Dead men neither tell tales nor sue for libel. Libel, as has been pointed out, is an injury to the reputation, and the law says a man takes his reputation with him to the grave although the memory of his good life and worthy deeds may inspire generations yet unborn.

A man's survivors, no matter how closely related by blood or law, cannot collect for libel unless they, too, were specifically defamed by the article. As has been indicated, to permit damages for a libel on a dead person would lead to suits by every distant relative, no matter if the relative had never met the deceased.

Many suits have been brought for civil libel of a dead person, but the courts have been unanimous in denying damages to any survivors. A court in Iowa reported:

"We have not been cited to an authority, and, after a diligent search, we have been unable to find one, which authorizes a recovery in such a case." (44)

A mother sued because a newspaper said her daughter died during an abortion. The mother contended the story also damaged her reputation, but the court held that the only injury was to the dead girl. (45)

By statute in most states, and under the common law in all, criminal libel proceedings, however, can be instituted for a deliberate villification of the memory of the dead. The state Supreme Court of Washington in 1916 affirmed a criminal libel conviction against a man for his attack on George Washington. (46)

The state however must prove that the article was inspired by ill motives. This restriction protects the historian or the feature writer who comes upon some new evidence about the life of a past hero or villain. An article which "debunks" a past hero is not libelous; it is criminally defamatory if it "blackens his memory" for no other purpose than sheer spite or the intentional desire of the writer to attract attention to himself without regard for truth or facts.

A living man, as it was shown previously, is not libeled if a newspaper inadvertently prints his obituary. An obituary, as a New York court has stated, is an item that states ". . . that an event has come to pass which is looked for in the history of every man, is regarded as beyond his control, and, therefore, does not permit the inference that the man has done any act which he could not have done or which he need not have suffered." (47)

"It is no dishonor to die," said a Montana court in dismissing an action for an erroneous obituary. (48)

Although it is no dishonor to die, an erroneous report of a "dishonorable death" is libelous. If the premature obituary said the man committed suicide, he would have a case because society disapproves of self-destruction. (49) It would be libelous, too, if the false story said death occurred in a place indicating a criminal or disgraceful element such as a house of prostitution or a gaming parlor. If the erroneous obituary were printed for the purpose of gain, such as the hope for quick profits from buying or selling stock in the company which the man headed, or to damage the man's business, it also would be libelous. But such situations are not likely to confront a newspaperman who feels a responsibility towards his job.

For Further Reading

Kerr, James M., "Criminal Libel, Libeling a Class," 86 *Central Law Journal*, May, 1918.

"Libel on Physicians," in 38 *Michigan Law Review*, April, 1940.

Merryman, John H., "Defamation of a Group," 21 *Notre Dame Lawyer,* September, 1945.

Pollock, L., "Defamation of the Dead," 26 *Cornell Law Quarterly,* June, 1941.

Riesman, David, "Control of Group Libel," 42 *Columbia Law Review,* May, 1942.

"Right of a Union to Sue," in 41 *Columbia Law Review,* May, 1941.

Smith, Jeremiah, "Disparagement of Property," 13 *Columbia Law Review,* January-February, 1932.

COURT DECISIONS
(Other than those cited in the text)

Quinn v. Sun Printing and Publishing Association, 109 N.Y.S. 1143.

Curry v. Journal Publishing Co., 68 P. 2d. 168.

Finnish Temperance Society v. Sovittaja Publishing Co., 238 Mass. 345.

DuPont Engineering Co. v. Nashville Banner Publishing Co., 13 F. 2d. 186.

Bee Publishing Co. v. World Publishing Co., 59 Nebr. 713.

McAllister v. Detroit Free Press Co., 48 N.W. 612.

Eagles et al v. Liberty Weekly, Inc., 244 N.Y.S. 430.

State v. Levland, 37 Wyo. 372.

Jerald v. Houston, 261 P. 851.

Brinkley v. Fishbein, 8 P. 2d. 318.

Van Lonkhuyzen v. Daily News Co., 161 N.W. 979.

Lyman v. New England Newspaper Co., 190 N.E. 542.

CHAPTER XX

"Defenses in Libel"

The Three Principal Defenses

Up to this point, the situation seems rather hopeless for the newspaper charged with libel. A newspaper cannot print an edition free of all defamatory matter because people commit crimes, do things that draw censure from other segments of society, and make charges and counter-charges in freely discussing public matters.

A newspaper free of criticism, censure, and even defamation would be, in all probability, spineless and of little service to the community. The practical goal of the newspaper should be to rid itself of actionable defamation while at the same time exercising a spirit of fair-mindedness in fulfilling its obligation to its readers.

Although a story may contain the three essentials of libel—defamation, publication, and identification—it does not follow necessarily, that in printing it the newspaper is without any legal support.

The three principal defenses a newspaper may offer to a charge of libel are:

1. Truth.
2. Qualified privilege.
3. Fair comment on a public matter.

None of these defenses is an absolute protection in all jurisdictions, for often other factors intervene to nullify, or at least, modify them. Clarification of these factors is the aim of this chapter.

Truth

When Cicero wrote: "Great is the might of truth . . . (for) she will with ease defend herself," he was not setting forth a legal principle. For Truth often finds, as she proceeds through the courts, that the path contains pitfalls.

A courtroom is not an open forum in which ideas, opinions, and even facts, are argued until truth shines through. Truth in a courtroom is established only by the weight of admissible evidence.

Or, as a United States Supreme Court justice has expressed it: "A trial is not a free trade in ideas . . . the range of the inquiry and methods are circumscribed precisely because judges have in their keeping the enforcement of rights and the protection of liberties." (1)

Every reporter comes across stories which all his experience and judgment tell him are true, but he dares not print them because his deep-seated conviction and logical conclusions cannot be offered into evidence in event of a suit for libel. The court wants provable facts, not deductions, no matter how sound their basis.

Proving facts is not so simple as it may sound. In one state, a truck slipped from its parking place on a hill while the driver was in the rear sorting packages. It crashed into a store window and injured several persons. The driver was charged with failure to have his truck under control. But a magistrate dismissed the charge because no one could prove the defendant was the driver. His company, of course, was responsible for the damage.

Every police chief knows all the vice dens in his city, but obtaining legal evidence to suppress them often is impossible, especially since the customers won't testify. New York City police once raided a horse-race parlor which they had "spotted" for several weeks. Before they were able to break into the room, employes and customers threw betting slips and form sheets down an elevator shaft where a janitor quickly hurled them into a furnace.

Police found about 15 men sitting around a table reading the *Racing Form*. A spokesman said it was a literary club and that the subject for discussion that day was horse racing. The court, albeit reluctantly, was forced to accept the explanation since police admitted they had uncovered no evidence of gambling.

The men were released and presumably went back to resume their interrupted literary discussion.

New reporters assigned to the court beat soon became impressed with the meticulous efforts of the prosecution to show a crime was committed before coming around to the defendant. A man cannot be convicted of stealing money before a theft has been established.

What is truth, then, that will stand the newspaper in good stead in a libel suit? By truth, the newspaperman must understand, is meant the truth of the charge that was printed. A newspaper which says flatly that a cashier stole $5,000 must prove: (1) that the money was stolen, and (2) that the cashier stole it. It cannot offer as a defense the fact that it obtained the information from a "reliable source." It said the cashier stole the money and that is what it must prove.

The burden of proof is on the defending newspaper. The cashier, who brings the libel suit, need not show he did not steal the money. In fact, if the newspaper fails to prove he did steal the money, the cashier may insist that the newspaper's attempt at establishing truth was, in effect, a re-publication of the libel or evidence of malice in fact. (2)

Many cases lead to some conclusions as to what the courts regard as proving the truth of printed charges. A New York newspaper, in a story about a couple who had separated, said the wife, longing for love she did not receive, had found consolation elsewhere, and that he was giving her a divorce to prevent scandal from touching the innocent head of their child.

The court said it would have been permissible for the paper to say the two had separated, that the husband had consented to a divorce, that the husband had neglected his home for his work and even to give incompatibility as the cause. But the phrases "found consolation elsewhere," and "scandal touching their innocent child" imputed unchastity to the woman. This charge, the paper could not prove. (3)

Another New York paper called a man a "Rogue's Gallery man." Although police had his picture, it was not on display in the room commonly referred to as "Rogue's Gallery." His complaint was held good. (4)

While the law is exact it is not picayunish. Minor errors will not prevent a charge from being substantiated if the degrading part is proved. A story that a teller took money from the trust funds of his bank could be substantiated with proof that he actually stole from the mortgage account. If the story, however, intimated he was able to steal because of the laxity of his superiors, the mistake might infer that the bank trust officer was derelict in his duties and might be libelous of him.

The law's concern for truth is expressed by a New York court this way:

"When the truth is so near to the facts as published that fine and shaded distinctions must be drawn and words pressed out of their ordinary usage to sustain a charge of libel, no legal harm has been done." (5)

A newspaper, however, which says a man was arrested, cannot defend on ground of truth if a warrant was issued but never served. (6) It could print that a warrant had been issued.

Domestic tiffs are frequent causes of such mistakes. After a quarrel, a wife may hurry downtown and fill out a warrant, charging her husband with assault and battery or other crimes. By the time she returns home, her desire for legal revenge may have cooled, and she withdraws the complaint before the warrant is served. Newspapers should be wary of stories about warrants until they are actually served because until then, in most jurisdictions, a man is not arrested.

But even if a newspaper can prove its charge, it may find truth is not a complete defense to civil libel. Some states require that the story be printed "with good motives and for justifiable ends."

In states having this requirement there are some dangers of truth being libelous. In the previous discussion on "memory columns," the possible danger was pointed out of re-printing years later an item about a crime, especially if the defendant served his time and now is back in good standing in the community. The courts would have to determine if a "memory column" is a "good motive" or a "justifiable end."

Ordinarily, in these states a paper has little trouble proving its good motives. If the story were printed as a news event and handled in the customary manner such articles are treated, the plaintiff probably would have to prove malice in fact before the newspaper can be charged with bad motives.

Under the common law, truth is a valid defense against a civil libel. Some states, however, by constitutional provision, statutes, or court decisions have modified this principle to require expressly that the truth must have been printed with good motives and for justifiable ends.

A number of states are silent about truth in civil libel but permit it to be offered in evidence in criminal libel. The presumption is that in civil libel these states are following the common law principle. All state constitutions contain declarations for a free press and this freedom hardly could be said to exist if truth were not accepted as a defense in civil libel.

On the basis of constitutional provisions, statutes, decisions, and common law principles, the several states have set up these requirements on truth as a defense in civil libel:

Truth as a defense: Alabama, Arkansas, California, Connecticut, Georgia, Indiana, Iowa, Kansas, Kentucky, Louisiana, Maryland, Michigan, Minnesota, Mississippi, Missouri, Montana, New Jersey, North Carolina, Ohio, Texas, Utah, Virginia, Washington, and Wisconsin.—24

Truth with good motives and for justifiable ends: Arizona, Colorado, Delaware, Florida, Idaho, Illinois, Maine, Massachusetts, Nebraska, Nevada, New Hampshire, New Mexico, New York, North Dakota, Oklahoma, Oregon, Pennsylvania, Rhode Island, South Carolina, South Dakota, Tennessee, Vermont, West Virginia, and Wyoming.—24

Since criminal libel is directed at possible breaches of the peace rather than injuries to individuals, fewer states permit truth only as a valid defense. The majority require that the publication be prompted by good motives.

The several states, in criminal libel, permit:

Truth as a defense: Arkansas, Colorado, Indiana, Maryland, Missouri, Ohio, Tennessee, and Vermont.—8

Truth when published with good motives and for justifiable ends: Arizona, California, Delaware, Florida, Idaho, Illinois, Iowa, Kansas, Louisiana, Maine, Massachusetts, Michigan, Minnesota, Mississippi, Montana, Nebraska, Nevada, New Jersey, New Mexico, New York, North Dakota, Oklahoma, Oregon, Pennsylvania, Rhode Island, South Carolina, South Dakota, Tennessee, Texas, Utah, Washington, West Virginia, Wisconsin, and Wyoming.—34

Truth permitted to be introduced into evidence: Alabama, Connecticut, Georgia, Kentucky, and Virginia.—5

The constitution and statutes of New Hampshire are silent about defenses in criminal libel. The constitution, however, is emphatic in declaring that "the liberty of the press is essential to the security of freedom . . . (and) ought to be inviolably preserved." (7) A newspaper should be able to use this constitutional provision to advantage in a suit for criminal libel.

Qualified Privilege

(See chapters on news coverage of various governmental bodies.)

Fair Comment and Criticism

(See chapters on criticism of public officials, public figures, and public performances.)

Although qualified privilege and fair comment and criticism were discussed in detail in previous chapters, it may be well to note here the conditions under which these two defenses will not avail. Both qualified privilege and fair comment and criticism are lost to the newspaper as defenses *if:*

1. The story is grossly inaccurate.

2. Publication was inspired by "spite" or a desire of the newspaper to get "revenge" upon the person mentioned.

3. The story includes additional material not a part of the proceedings.

4. The story is impartial by failing to include both sides. In court stories, the only news one day may be defamatory material about the defendant, but the newspaper later should see that testimony favoring him also receives a good play.

5.   The comment is about "private" matters, or the "private life" of public performers.

Newspapers are accorded qualified privileges in order that public matters may be discussed freely. Proceedings of legislative, executive, and judicial agencies could not be printed if the publisher were held liable for all statements made as part of the official records.

One writer explains it this way:

"A newspaper publisher, confronted with the choice of publishing or withholding matters of general interest and concern in his community, may be deterred from publishing such matters by fear that if a libel action ensues he will have no defense of privilege. In such cases, liberty of the press would be throttled quite effectively as it would be by the same publisher's fear of losing his printing privileges under some law licensing newspapers.

"If it is necessary to progress in democracy that the press should be jealously guarded against all acts of the government which would prevent or limit the free discussion of matters of general interest and concern, it is no less important that such discussion be recognized as qualifiedly privileged in libel action brought by individuals." (8)

In demanding accuracy of newspapers, courts do not insist upon scientific precision, but they are concerned with substantial correctness and with fairness. One of the best evidences of fairness is the fact that the newspaper printed both sides of the story.

Retraction Laws

Although damages are presumed to vindicate an individual's good name, society is more interested in restoring his previous reputation than in the amount of money he can win from a jury in a libel suit. For that reason, a retraction or apology may be offered in most jurisdictions in mitigation of damages.

Some states, by statute, have set up rules governing retractions. An apology or retraction usually eliminates punitive damages. A few jurisdictions permit an apology to eliminate all but actual damages, but this broad provision is open to constitutional doubts.

One authority on newspaper law reports that in states having these so-called retraction laws, he has found publishers who believe that an apology averts all liability of the paper. (9)

Such a belief has no foundation in law. It is comparable to saying that a motorist who unintentionally runs down a pedestrian can dismiss his liability with: "I'm sorry. Please excuse me."

A man who is injured has a right of redress which cannot be taken from him. Retraction laws void punitive damages and may mitigate other claims, but they do not dissolve all liability. Actual damages, which are permitted under the retraction laws, at times may be costly to the paper. A New York assemblyman was awarded $100,000 actual damages because a newspaper accused him of taking a bribe. (10)

In states which have no retraction law, newspapers generally are permitted to introduce evidence of their good faith and lack of malice in fact in printing the offending article. The jury then decides what effect such plea will have on its award. A retraction could be offered as evidence of "good faith."

In all states having retraction laws, two types of libel are dealt with separately.

1. Reflections on the chastity of a woman are not covered by the law. The newspaper which makes such implications or charges cannot by law mitigate damages through a correction or apology.

2. Charges against a political candidate must be retracted within a definite period—usually three to five days—before the election. The reason is obvious. The most abject apology is no good to the candidate after the voters have gone to the polls.

Each state having a retraction law sets forth in detail the rules which must be observed before the paper can plead the law as a partial defense. In some jurisdictions the newspaper must take the initiative; in others the person libeled must serve notice upon the newspaper, set forth the true facts, and formally ask for a correction. Only then, in some jurisdictions, can an individual file suit. Of course, if the newspaper ignores the demand, the defamed individual can sue and offer the refusal of a retraction as one evidence of malice in fact.

The correction must be asked for within a specified time, ranging from several days to a week or 10 days after publication. An individual who needs more than 10 days to make up his mind if he has been libeled certainly cannot have suffered too much injury. In some cases, however, the defamed individual may be out of the city when the article is published and under other circumstances the real "sting" of the article may be delayed. But newspapers cannot be put in the position of one Pennsylvania paper which was asked to correct an item 60 years after it appeared. A man, living in retirement in Florida, found a copy of an 1889 paper among his effects and noted that in the story of his high school graduation his name had been listed incorrectly. (11)

In all jurisdictions, the courts make these stipulations about retractions:

1. The apology must be frank and straight-forward. It cannot be disguised under stories beginning: "Further developments in the First National Bank embezzlement case today indicated that Cashier Robert Jones was not the man referred to by the district attorney, etc." The paper must say plainly that it made a mistake and it should offer its regrets.

2. The apology need not be approved by the defamed person before publication, but it does give the paper more safety if it obtains such approval. If the defamed person approves in advance the wording of the retraction, he is in no position later to contend that the apology was unsatisfactory. If he does not pass upon it, the jury must decide if the retraction is a sufficient apology.

3. The retraction must be displayed as prominently as the original article. Again, the courts do not insist upon technical precision. If the original article were a page one streamer story, the apology need not carry an eight-column banner. A two-column box, prominently set out at the top of the page, should satisfy the court that provisions of the act were carried out.

A page one libelous story, however, is not retracted if the apology is buried inside. It is not retracted either if the newspaper uses most of the space to justify the reasons for the original publication. One court set up this rule for determining if a retraction meets the legal requirements:

". . . it (the law) does require a full and fair correction, apology, and retraction which must clearly refer to and admit the publishing of the article complained of and directly, fully and fairly, without an uncertainty, evasion or subterfuge, retract and recall the alleged false and defamatory statements and apologize therefore." (12)

The court rejected as insufficient the paper's correction which said:

"This newspaper was informed Wednesday that the Harry Roth, arrested in vice raids in New Jersey, was not the Harry Roth who some years ago was connected with the Palace Theatre, as was stated in the article in yesterday's paper. The Harry Roth who was engaged in business here was a much younger man, it was said, and he was a young man of exemplary habits and character, according to citizens who were personally acquainted with him.

"The statement (original story) was based on information that the prisoner, following his arrest in New Jersey, had indicated to officers he was at one time in the movie business here." (13)

Speaking of this correction, the court said:

"It neither retracts nor apologizes therefore, but merely states that the defendant (newspaper) is then in possession of information contrary to that contained in the original publication." (14)

Retraction laws are not new. Alabama and Virginia adopted a form of retraction laws almost a century ago. Michigan adopted one in 1885 which set the pattern for other states. Three years later the state supreme court declared the statute unconstitutional, but since then Michigan has passed a new law. (15)

In 1904, the Kansas Supreme Court declared a similar statute unconstitutional in that state. That state still is without a statute. (16)

There are two general classes of retraction laws. In one group, are those statutes which eliminate only punitive damages. The other group permits recovery of actual damages only.

This latter group—permitting only actual damages—seems to bear the chief criticism of the courts. Both Michigan and Kansas Supreme Courts objected to their state statutes on the ground ". . . it is not competent for the legislature to give one class of citizens (newspapers) legal exemptions from liability for wrongs not granted to others." (17)

The *Harvard Law Review*, however, more than 40 years after the Michigan decision, expressed the opinion that ". . . It is no innovation to restrict recovery to actual damages, where good faith is shown." (18)

Besides inferring that retraction laws are "class legislation," the courts also have held that damages for injuries to reputation are, in effect, a property right of which an individual cannot be deprived. The loss of reputation, the courts say, is a substantial loss. Therefore, a defamed person should be permitted to recover substantial damages.

With the first group of statutes—those denying only punitive damages—the courts do not seem to have much quarrel. Such laws have been upheld in Alabama, Minnesota, New Jersey, North Carolina, and North Dakota. (19)

Ohio permits a defamed person to elect if he wishes to ask for a retraction or to proceed under the old law. On that basis, a court held the retraction statute was constitutional. (20)

In California, a district court ruled a section of the retraction law was unconstitutional because it limited recovery to special damages and thus set up a privilege for one class of citizens (publishers and radio station owners). (21)

A California publishers' group succeeded in winning a rehearing (22), and in May, 1950, the Supreme Court reversed the district court and held the section was constitutional. The court said that, "as between the interests of the defamed and the interests of the public in the dissemination of news or the avoidance of dangers in excessive general damages, it (the section of the law) is constitutional." (23)

The suit was against two newspapers which had printed a press association story that a former city attorney had been convicted of a felony. The last two paragraphs, which the papers did not use, explained the conviction had been set aside by the state supreme court.

The papers retracted with a page-one box in the same position and of the same size type as the original story. Besides affording a test of the retraction law, the case affords a good lesson in news writing and in copy reading. A man whose conviction is reversed by an appellate court legally has not been convicted at all, and a good news story certainly should make that fact apparent in the lead.

Georgia had a retraction law which was more favorable to newspapers than that of any other state. But in 1949, Governor Herman Talmadge, whom a majority of newspapers opposed in his campaign, succeeded in getting the law repealed.

States which eliminate only punitive damages through retraction laws apparently give the press little more protection than those having no such statutes. For in most jurisdictions, the defending newspaper can offer evidence of "honest mistake," and "good intentions" and "absence of malice in fact." Juries seldom award punitive damages in the face of such evidence.

One writer on law believes such statutes—denying only punitive damages—makes no significant changes in the measure of damages for inadvertent libel. (24)

Retraction laws are on the statute books of these states: Alabama, California, Connecticut, Delaware, Florida, Indiana, Iowa, Kentucky, Maine, Massachusetts, Michigan, Minnesota, New Jersey, North Carolina, North Dakota, Ohio, Oklahoma, South Dakota, Texas, Utah, Virginia, West Virginia, and Wisconsin.

The Right of Reply

In certain quarters, there is agitation for the United States to adopt some form of the "right of reply" which is used in a number of continental European countries.

Although the laws vary in the several European countries, the general provisions give to the victim of a defamation or error the right of setting forth the true facts which the offending newspaper must print. In some countries, the individual is permitted to use in his reply twice as much space as the original article. In some cases, he may write as much as he wishes, but all over twice the amount must be paid for at regular advertising rates.

Only one American state—Nevada—has such a law. Although it was placed on the statute books in 1911, a search of Nevada reports shows no cases in which the courts dealt with the law, either to force its application or to pass on its constitutionality. There have been no studies either to determine if the law has attained any of the objectives which sponsors hope from such statutes. From reported cases, the libel situation in Nevada follows the pattern of most of the other states. (25)

The Nevada statute, in part, reads:

"If in any newspaper or other periodical published or circulated within this state any matter is published regarding a person named or otherwise designated in such a manner as to be identified therein, it shall be the duty of the editor . . . to publish gratuitously any denial or correction of the matter so published that may be received from the person so named or designated when the denial or correction is signed by the person so making the same." (26)

The person who desires the correction must submit it within one week after publication of the original article. Failure of the editor to comply with the law is punishable by fines of $100 to $1,000, or six months in prison. (27) If the reply exceeds the length of the original article, the excess must be paid for at regular advertising rates.

The Commission on the Freedom of the Press recommended that the right of reply should be carefully considered in the near future. Zechariah Chafee, Jr., in his section of the Commission's report, called the right of reply the best alternative available in libel actions. (28)

Chafee's arguments for, and against, the right of reply, may be summarized briefly as: (29)

For:

1. It gives any citizen a cheap, expeditious, and convenient method of combating misstatements about himself in the press without waiting for vindication through a libel suit.

2. A libel issue going to court is complex, but a dispute over the right to reply would be narrowed simply to: (a) Did the original article name or designate the plaintiff? (b) did the newspaper actually refuse to print the reply? and (c) was this refusal excused by the nature or length of the reply?

Against:

1. It will impose serious and novel burdens on newspapers and judges.

2. The remedy can be circumvented because the newspaper can still keep "one jump ahead" of the individual by making new statements as fast as the old ones are corrected.

3. Establishment of an unprecedented legal remedy runs the risk of demoralizing existing desirable practices.

Although some legal writers and critics of the press may feel the right of reply is the remedy for newspapers' mistakes and libel, newspapermen can see practical defects which more than outweigh the usefulness of such proposals.

Confining the compulsory replies to libelous material only would be confusing enough because the courts then would be as involved in determining what is defamatory as they are now in regular libel suits. If the proposed remedy is to include all misstatements, and apparently the person named or designated will have sole power to determine if the article is in error, the situation looks rather hopeless.

The constitutional aspects alone are grave. When a court can compel a newspaper to print one type of article, what will limit its power to order publishing of other types? There is no freedom of the press once any authority can force publication. A Massachusetts court was on better constitutional grounds when it refused to compel publication of a retraction but instead instructed the plaintiff that his remedy lay in an action for damages. (30)

If the reply, which the paper is forced to print, mentions another individual, he, too, then, must be given space to answer. If the article a newspaper is compelled to print defames another individual, who will take the responsibility for it?

Supporters of the right of reply do admit that "cranks" may find it a convenient way of getting into print. But dismissing "cranks," let's turn to more substantial citizens.

If "innocent people" only were permitted to correct mis-statements or errors, no newspaper would object seriously be-cause every reputable paper now speedily rectifies its mistakes. When a staff member catches an error, it usually is remedied before the individual mentioned has time to ask for a correc-tion. In addition most newspaper open their columns to letters on matters involving opinion as well as facts.

Despite some critics who insist that a newspaper will correct only libelous matter, in 22 years of newspaper work, I have found no newspaper which did not freely and promptly rectify its mis-takes. A newspaper, however, does not waste space on frivolous corrections. A lodge secretary who complains that while 125 people actually attended the annual picnic the paper had said "about 100" may not find the newspaper devoting space to his wailing. A minister once demanded a correction for a story which said he had addressed an association. He contended that what he had done was to "read a paper." Speeches and papers have some significant difference in scientific and learned circles, but the average newspaper reader knows nothing of the dis-tinction and cares less.

The United States is inhabited by "argufiers, press agents, publicity seekers, and space grabbers." Certain classes of peo-ple would seize upon reply statutes to have a "field day" until the paper was burdened with "equal space or twice as much." Such statutes are tailored for public relations experts, ordinary press agents, public officials, and public figures of all types.

A deposed European monarch, to curry American favor, re-tained an expensive New York public relations agency. The agency professed to be aghast when newspapers said its job was to prepare a favorable press for the former monarch's pro-posed visit to the United States and enlist sympathy for a move-ment to have him returned to the throne, with the hope of an eventual money loan from America. It maintained it had been retained only as a "personal consultant" to inform the former king about American customs. To force a newspaper to devote equal space to such a naive explanation is repugnant to both paper and readers.

General Franco of Spain hired an American public relations firm to erase some of the "sting" the American press was putting into its articles about him. This firm, too, insisted it was not Franco's press agent but, by a coincidence, "news" favorable, to Franco began coming out of New York.

When an American heiress was preparing to sail for Europe to marry a count, some newspapers reported she was giving up her American citizenship. She denied it vigorously, and of course, would have been entitled to equal or twice as much space. A week later she cancelled her American citizenship and sailed. One reporter, whose paper ran a corrective story, radioed her at sea a one-word message: "Liar."

Still more dangerous is the proposed inclusion of public officials under the right of reply. Each newspaper that was critical of a public official would be forced to give him space the next day to lull the citizens back to slumber. Newspapers have exposed graft and corruption in city, county, state, and even national administrations. It cannot perform such public service if compelled to give equal space for a reply.

To avoid using all its space in replies, the newspaper probably would give up its inquiry into the administration, and the community would suffer. A public official now has the right to sue for libel, and that knowledge makes a newspaper check carefully before printing.

Within little more than a week in 1950, the American public was treated to the spectacle of the two top men in national defense contradicting themselves. While the Secretary of Defense was declaring the United States "could lick Russia within an hour if she started anything," the Chief of Staff was deploring the fact that the country was not prepared for war. A newspaper which used the Secretary's statement probably would have had to print any replies leaders of the service branches wished to make since they were "designated" if not actually named.

The Secretary of State denied the United States had "written off" China to the Communists while a press association was even then distributing to its newspaper clients the text of such a memorandum the department had sent to its consuls abroad. Readers would give up in disgust to find the Secretary's reply in one column and the department's memorandum in the other.

A newspaper once reported on wire tapping activities of the Federal Bureau of Investigation. The Bureau, at first, denied any such activities. The newspaper refused to retract its story, and the Bureau finally revised its statement to admit it had used wire tapping in "about 170 cases" but had made no "wholesale" use of the method. Whether wire tapping is justified in certain cases was not the point at issue. The newspaper was not passing on motives but simply stating what it believed to be a fact. Under the right of reply, the Bureau would have been entitled to an answer and there the matter would have ended with the reader assuming the newspaper had been reckless in making such a statement.

In one state, two men with medical degrees operated a diabetes clinic where treatments, especially diets, were contrary to the accepted methods of the best hospitals and specialists. As a result of the newspaper's expose, the two men went to prison. If the men had been injured falsely, they had a remedy in libel. Under the right of reply, they would have rebutted the article, and the newspaper would have ended the series to avoid devoting more space to answers. The medical association was the first to laud the articles and commend the newspaper for breaking up the clinic.

Any faker who moved into town with a cancer "cure" would be entitled to space if the newspaper even intimated that people should be cautious about the remedy. The reply probably would spur more people to try the "cure."

Congressmen often use voice or division votes to dodge being put on record on particular bills. Good reporters, however, size up the Congressmen's true sentiments. But they could not tell readers their honest opinion of the Congressmen's actual stand without being forced to give them equal space. It is no coincidence that few Congressmen have ever disputed publicly that the newspaper was wrong in such stories.

It would be a poor press agent who couldn't keep his client constantly in the news if equal space were devoted to replies.

The first story he "planted" would contain just enough errors to obtain him space for his "correction." "Space-grabbing" is a practice familiar to all newspapermen. The right of reply would dignify it with legal sanction.

In a state, dominated for years by one political party, a split among leaders developed into a "dog" fight. One group by a sudden "coup" seized party control and gave the titular leader the alternative of resigning or being ousted.

He entrusted the preparation of his letter of resignation to a political reporter on an afternoon paper. An editor of the morning paper, published by the same company, learned of the story and printed a report that the party leader was being forced out.

The party chairman demanded an "immediate retraction of such a scandalous story." The editor countered by offering not only to retract but also to buy the chairman a dinner if the party leader was still in his post by the end of the month.

Two weeks later, the party leader resigned "due to ill health" and promptly accepted a commission in the navy. Washington reporters found no difficulty "reading between the lines" of some of those "It is with deep regret that I accepted your resignation" letters written by the late President Franklin D. Roosevelt.

A newspaper which reported that a large manufacturing company was about to close its local factory was roundly rebuked by the parent company for spreading such "gossip." The newspaper obtained its story from some top officials of the local factory who were carrying in their pockets their notices of transfers to the company's other plants.

Since about 500 employes were involved, the story was of vital concern to the community. What further confidence would readers have in the newspaper had it been required to print in equal space the company's denial? For within three weeks, the factory closed.

Lesser public figures would find the right of reply tailored to their measure. A Midwestern football coach was still denying that he had resigned on the day a rival school was announcing he had signed a five-year contract with it. Being forced to print the coach's reply on the same day it prints the announcement of his new job is not the way to build newspapers which can best serve a community.

Few newspapermen would quarrel with the objectives of a reply law, but they readily see the abuses of such statutes. Most newspapers not only give both sides of the story but also are just as prompt to correct substantial non-defamatory errors as they are to rectify mistakes that may cost them money damages.

Here and there, exceptions appear upon which many critics pounce upon gleefully to generalize. There are newspapers of which not even their own staffs are proud. Newspapermen deplore them as much as any critic. But newspapermen ask that something be said also for the hundreds of newspapers that, day in and day out, go about their job with a keen sense of community responsibility and fair play.

If newspapers generalized with the same type of arguments as some of their critics they could condemn whole professions as being corrupt, because newspapers have printed stories of doctors indicted for receiving financial "kickbacks" from optical companies, of lawyers disbarred for embezzling their clients' money, and of ministers jailed for affairs with their choir singers. Newspapers do not judge a whole profession by the malpractices of some of its members, and in turn, feel they should be accorded the same courtesy.

In many communities, especially medium-sized cities, there is a new type of "ambulance chasing" lawyer. He examines closely each issue of the newspaper and then glibly assures certain individuals that they have "a good chance of collecting a lot of money." Seldom does he have a case that the law would even entertain.

One newspaper sent to the bar association a list of complaints with documented evidence that the individuals had not been offended by the articles and had not thought of even protesting until assured by the lawyer that they could collect money. The bar association took no action.

This newspaper, tired of being harassed, found an effective remedy was to tell the receptionist not to admit the lawyer but to suggest to him he walk across the street to the court-house and begin legal action. After several such challenges, the lawyer ceased to annoy the newspaper. Although this news-paper believed the bar association should have looked into its complaints against the "ambulance chaser," it still did not condemn the whole legal profession because of his antics.

A newspaper is handicapped because, unlike most profes-sions, its national associations do not exert disciplinary control. Such control is not easily administered to a group working with as pliable a material as truth, comment, and opinion.

The newspaper, too, would like its critics to peep out from behind books written a quarter of a century ago. The news-paper has advanced far in the past 25 years, and nowhere is the improvement more noticeable than in the new type of newspaperman. A large percentage of present-day staffs are college graduates, not only trained better in public affairs and in the arts and sciences to interpret the changing world, but also inculcated with a sense of social responsibility.

"Sex, sin, and excitement" has long since been abandoned by the reporter as his working formula. He now writes of political, social, and economic events with the facility that old-time newspapermen once devoted to sensational news. The hope for even greater newspapers tomorrow seems to be in better hands when left to such men than if the law is relied upon to effect doubtful "reforms."

The right of reply might lead to even greater harm. The press is accused frequently of denying a voice to minorities al-though statistical studies never seem to bear out such generaliza-tions. It is not unusual for a statistical study to show, for exam-ple, that a newspaper devoted the most space to the political party whose adherents are loudest in their complaints that their side was refused a hearing.

In one state election, a newspaper assigned two veteran re-porters to cover the three gubernatorial nominees whenever they appeared in the paper's circulation territory. Since only one nominee was there at a time, the newspaper had two sea-soned reporters at every meeting.

When the nominee of a minority party, which had no hope of winning, spoke in that area, he complained bitterly that his speech had been "warped" by the two veteran reporters. The managing editor polled rival reporters who agreed that his two men had written a fair and accurate account. To be fair, the editor permitted the minority nominee to answer in a "letter to the editor." The letter occupied a column and a half and was devoted exclusively to developing points which the nominee had not touched on in his speech. The paper had given him space to correct what he said were mistakes in the coverage of his speech. Instead, he devoted the space to new material. When pressed for specific examples of how the original story was in error, he hedged.

The day after his letter appeared he insisted upon publication of a second letter. This letter was devoted to an attack on the lethargy of local voters who had not shown enough interest to turn out to hear him.

When the election was over, the editor sent queries to all three nominees, asking what criticism they had of the paper's coverage of their campaigns. The winning and losing major nominees said they regarded the paper as having been most fair to them. The minority candidate again took the paper to task for inaccuracies and unfairness.

In the 1948 presidential election, many newspapers discovered no matter how much they tried to be fair and accurate, the followers of a certain minority nominee berated them.

If a newspaper, operating under the right of reply, knew that no matter how much it tried to be fair to a minor candidate that still the next day it would be compelled to devote the same space, or even more, to that nominee's shadowy complaints, it would be forced, in self-defense, to ignore that candidate entirely. Political reporters know there is no greater pest than a minor candidate imbued with the persecution complex who never will concede he has been treated fairly.

In municipal elections, especially, minor candidates often make wild and reckless charges that the laws of libel will not permit to be published. How could a newspaper handle them, for if it printed as much permissible material as it could extract from their speeches, they would take advantage of the reply law to compel publication of lengthy answers with possibly libelous material? The only alternative to expensive litigation would be to ignore them entirely.

Every newspaper "spots" those people in the community whose influence is in inverse proportion to their lung power. A paper generally is willing to give them reasonable space although it knows that whatever it prints will be followed by a barrage of letters, complaining of mistakes, insufficient space, or inadequate headline treatment. Sincere men, with something to offer the community, make such complaints only when the paper has committed a substantial error.

College newspapers find that certain cliques of students are perennially complaining of persecution through being misquoted or denied ample space. Half a dozen students attempt to create the illusion that they are speaking on behalf of "a cowed and intimidated student body."

Here and there, are minority groups which deal fairly. They concede that reporters are trained to cover events and to judge news. The editor welcomes their views as much as those of other groups.

But the practical effect of a reply law would be that editors, to save themselves grief and space, would simply ignore those groups who are never satisfied until they can read a deep plot into the most active news story.

Another proposed change in the libel laws was advocated before the National Conference on Editorial Writers by Morris Ernst, widely-known for his writings on journalism. Ernst proposed that a complete retraction eliminate all libel damages unless malice in fact were proved. (31)

The proposal met with little response from the editorial writers. A Washington (D. C.) *Post* editorial writer suggested that such revision might be an invitation to mere labeling campaigns which would not be particularly helpful. (32) To call a man a Communist now is libelous and a newspaper must be sure of its ground before it makes such a charge. But if the only penalty were a retraction, the newspaper could make the charge and trust readers would not accept the retraction dictated by the defamed individual. The following day the newspaper might admit the man was not an actual member of the Communist party but that he had Communist sympathies or leanings. No retraction could mitigate the harm that story would do to the individual.

Criticizing the Ernst proposal, one publishers' journal said:

> "Newspaper workers have become educated in their obligations regarding the law of libel. The majority of editors and newspaper workers have arrived at an understanding of their responsibilities and their liabilities. These have become incentives in the production of better newspapers. To tear it down would be lowering of standards which have taken years to establish." (33)

Fred S. Siebert believes that "libel laws as they exist today are an invitation to the unscrupulous to harass the communications media and at the same time are an effective barrier against those individuals whose rights have been seriously injured." (34)

Of the right of reply in continental European countries, he says: "Unfortunately neither the French nor the German remedy has proved any more successful than our own libel laws."

What we need, as he sees it, "is to throw out the 17th. century English libel laws which we have inherited and, with our traditional ingenuity, invent a new remedy which will fit American conditions and American needs." (35)

Sponsors of proposed changes in the libel laws have done a service by bringing sharply into focus the newspaper's responsibilities. Every good newspaperman will profit by the discussion and criticism of these advocates of new laws. As a matter of practical solution, however, the newspaperman has cause to doubt if the proposed remedies are cures for the complaints which gave rise to them.

The essence of the present situation is: Every reputable newspaper promptly corrects its mistakes. In matters involving only opinion, most of them are willing to give space to both sides.

An individual who thinks he has been harmed has the right to seek vindication in the courts. The newspaper does not relish an expensive law suit any more than does the individual.

Most newspapermen will concede that the laws of libel are not perfect for either the newspaper or the individual. But they seem to work better than to set up by law such farces as compelling a newspaper to deny a story that time soon will confirm.

A Simple Test for Libel

Libel need not be a bugaboo to the newspaperman. When in doubt about a story, he can subject it to a simple test. First, he should ask himself:

1. Is there publication? If he uses the story he knows it will be published.

2. Is it defamatory? If it holds up the individual named to contempt or hatred, or charges him with a crime or illegal or unethical act, it is defamatory.

3. Is there identification? If it names the individual, the identification is certain. If it mentions no names, are there inferences that readers will readily grasp as applying to a particular individual in the community?

The first "no" answer to any of these three questions classifies the article as non-libelous, and the remaining questions can be dispensed with.

If all three answers are "yes," then the newspaperman should ask:

1. Is the story true? The question is not: "Did I get these facts from a reliable source?" but: "Do I have proof that a court will accept?"

2. Is there qualified privilege attached to this story? Is the story a fair and accurate report of a judicial, legislative, or other official public proceeding?

3. Is it fair comment and criticism of a public matter?

When the newspaper gets the first "yes" answer to this series of questions, he need go no further. The story, except under unusual circumstances, may be published with the knowledge that the paper can defend it in any court action.

For Further Reading

Chafee, Zechariah, Jr., *Government and Mass Communications*, Chicago; University of Chicago Press, 1947, Vol. 1, Chap. 8.
Daitch, J. I., "Fair Comment, Privilege," 4 *Georgia Bar Journal*, November, 1941.

Dawson, Samuel A., *The Legal Doctrine of Qualified Privilege*, New York; Columbia University Press, 1924.

Donnelly, Richard C., "The Right of Reply," 34 *Virginia Law Review*, June, 1948.

Freedman, Marvin, "Right of Fair Comment on Matters of Public Interest," 10 *Southern California Law Review*, June, 1937.

Hall, John M., "Preserving Liberty of the Press by the Defense of Privilege," 26 *California Law Review*, January, 1938.

Harrington, J. Ross, "Truth as a Complete Defense in Libel," 4 *Notre Dame Lawyer*, April, 1929.

Heath, S. Richard, "Privilege," 9 *Wisconsin Law Review*, June, 1933.

Ray, Roy, "Truth—a Defense to Libel," 16 *Minnesota Law Review*, December, 1931.

COURT DECISIONS
(Other than those cited in the text)

Truth:

Gardner v. Self, 15 Mo. 480.

James v. Powell, 152 S.E. 539.

Quaid v. Tipton, 51 S.W. 264.

Skrocki v. Stall, 110 P. 957.

McCue v. Survey Associates, Inc. 106 N. Y. Misc. 161.

Block v. Nussbaum, 160 N. Y. App. Div. 633.

Privilege:

(See cases listed at end of chapters on qualified privilege.)

Fair Comment:

(See cases at end of chapters on Fair Comment and Criticism.)

CHAPTER XXI

"Restrictions on the Use of Names"

Journalism, nurtured on the slogan that "names make news", is finding that the law limits publication of names under certain circumstances.

Some restrictions have been pointed out in the discussion on privacy and libel. In advertising, most jurisdictions permit the use of names only when specifically authorized by the individuals themselves.

But there are additional limitations. As one court has said:

> "Nothing so exclusively belongs to a man or is so personal and valuable to him as his name. . . . Others have no right to use it without his express consent, and he has the right to go into any court at any time to enjoin or prohibit any unauthorized use of it." (1)

A person, of course, cannot prevent the publication of his name when he takes part or becomes involved in the news or a public event. At other times, however, his name should be used only with permission.

Petitions, either for placing candidates upon a ballot or to exert public opinion on a public issue, sometimes cause a newspaper trouble. In the 1930's, when Congress was concerning itself with public utility legislation, members were flooded with cards and telegrams.

An investigation disclosed that certain utility companies were responsible for the telegrams and that they had signed them with names taken at random from city directories. A man has cause to complain if his name appears on a petition or is signed to a letter or telegram without his authorization.

If the petition calls for some action which he opposes or which may cost his prestige among colleagues, he has a cause for action. There are no reported cases from which conclusions can be drawn, but presumably he.would have a just complaint against the newspaper which published his name as a signer of the petition. A physician, for example, might be damaged if his name appeared on a petition favoring euthanasia. A minister would be damaged if his name appeared as the signer of a petition to permit the opening of a tavern.

False signatures on letters to the editor also can lead to trouble. The newspaper should verify the signature on such letters before publication. It should also verify any signatures it wishes to take from a petition.

An Iowa columnist received a bad fright after he invented a fictitious character and gave it an unusual name. The columnist represented the character as a despicable person, and kept the myth alive by printing letters signed by him. One day the columnist received a letter from a nearby town. It was signed with the same name as his mythical character and threatened the columnist with an action in libel. The columnist had a few bad moments checking by telephone until he learned the letter was the prank of a friend. It's never wasted time if invented names are checked with directories before use.

States are becoming increasingly concerned about publication of the names of juveniles who are arrested. Special juvenile courts have been set up in many jurisdictions in order that hearings may be more informal than regular court sessions and to prevent one mistake from ruining a juvenile's life.

Seven states by statute, and a number of others by court decisions, prohibit the use of names of juveniles involved in crimes. Some jurisdictions permit publication only if the crimes are felonies or if the youths had been arrested previously.

By statute, these states prohibit publication of names of juveniles arrested—Arizona, Arkansas, Colorado, Michigan, Nevada, New Hampshire, and North Dakota. It is impossible to list states where such publication is prohibited by court decisions because of the varying manner in which those rulings are made effective. In some states, it is virtually on an "unwritten agreement" basis only. In others, the courts settle the question by hearing juvenile cases in chambers and releasing no information.

In addition, many newspapers long since have adopted a policy of printing no names of juveniles on the principle that every youth is entitled to "another chance." But statutes, decisions, and newspaper policies are likely to be ineffectual in murder or felonies because the community will learn about them from other sources. Sometimes by a straight statement of facts in such cases the newspaper serves public interest better than by a policy of voluntary or involuntary censorship.

A newspaper which does print the name of a juvenile runs all the risk of libel as if the article were about an adult. At what age a child can be libeled has not been determined by the courts although one judge did say that "an infant at the breast of his mother" can be libeled by publishing that he has a "loathsome or permanent disease, or a private and humiliating physical malformation." (2) The court expressed this opinion in holding good a complaint in libel filed on behalf of a boy of five years.

To charge falsely a boy or girl with theft or other crime, or hold them up to scorn and hatred, is just as actionable as if the article were about adults. The parents would have no right of action unless the defamation also mentioned them or as, for example, in the case of a child movie star, the article deprived them of the value of his services.

Birth records, once they are filed, are kept secret in fourteen states to protect adopted and illegitimate children. (3) The press has little quarrel with such laws because the newspaper seldom wants to consult such records. In fact, many newspapers have led fights to abolish the practice of some states of noting illegitimacy on any birth record at any time.

Unfortunately, illegitimacy sometimes is news as the world discovered when a well-known movie actress bore a son whose paternity was admitted by her director. Births and deaths are natural events that cannot be concealed by statute or custom. Adoptions are news usually only when the foster parents are public figures, and in those cases the principals themselves seldom seem adverse to publicity.

However laudable may be the purpose of sealing birth records, society does not gain as much by such laws as it would by statutes forbidding such references on the certificates in the first place. At times society seems to take peculiar means of arriving at its desired goals.

The increasing number of so-called sex crimes has led to some efforts to curb the names of victims. In some nineteen states, by statute or decisions, names of girls or women victims of sex attacks may not be published. The law is concerned for two reasons: (a) to save the victims from embarrassment, and (b) to be assured of their help in convicting perpetrators of such attacks, for women are reluctant to make a complaint or testify if they know their stories will be given publicity.

Both of these reasons undoubtedly are well-grounded in social values. But newspapers are not raising phantom cries of "freedom of the press" in questioning some of the statutes.

When a rape victim goes into open court to testify how is the case to be reported? If the paper is forced to pass up the court case entirely, is the community served better by not knowing at all what is transpiring? All defendants in rape cases are not guilty, but how is the public to judge if justice has been done if it is denied access to the facts? Absence of regular news coverage may lead to perfunctory trials in which the defendant is deprived of the well-established legal principle that he is innocent until proved guilty beyond a reasonable doubt.

If the newspaper disguises such cases under innocuous references such as "a serious charge" who in the community will be fooled for long? "Criminal assault" may sound better than rape but the public will use its own terminology. The victim will not be less embarrassed by any attempt to disguise the charge.

A more serious aspect comes in those rape cases in which the victim's escort is murdered. If the name of the girl is not published at the time of the crime, how can her identity be kept from the murder trial when the perpetrator is arrested? By that time the community knows the real facts, and the mere mention that the girl testified tells the public she was the rape victim. How could a murder trial be reported at all if the newspaper is not permitted to name the principal witness?

Wisconsin, which in 1925 prohibited publication of the name of a rape victim, discovered when the statute was tested in 1948 there were many ramifications that the legislature had not considered. This test case is an example, too, of how hurried zeal to correct a situation often leads to confusing and impossible conditions.

The original law said newspapers could not print the name of any victim of rape. Legally, therefore, a press association story originating on the West coast and about people there, could not be printed in Wisconsin if the charge were rape. It's one thing to try to shield a community resident from embarrassment and another to tell a newspaper it may not print names involved in certain crimes, no matter where they happened. An even greater defect was the failure of the Wisconsin law to include radio stations.

The test came in a criminal suit brought against a Madison editor for printing the name of a coed who had been raped after her brother-in-law had been slain. The editor had identified the girl as the victim of "criminal assault." Strangely enough, another paper in the same city called the coed a rape victim, but no action was taken against it. The test case, then, was suspect from the start. (4)

The defense challenged the constitutionality of the law as well as raising the practical question of how the story of the man's murder could have been treated without bringing in the girl. The principle constitutional pleas were on abridgement of freedom of the press and denial of equal protection since publishers of the printed word only were to be penalized.

The trial court held the statute was unconstitutional. The state appealed which is an unusual step in a criminal procedure and can be done only when there is a substantial error in the law. The state Supreme Court reversed the trial court and remanded the case for a new trial. The lower court judge, hearing the case without a jury, acquitted the editor. Again, the state appealed, but this time the Supreme Court ruled that any further action would place the editor in "double jeopardy" which is unconstitutional.

As a result of this test, the 1949 legislature made some revisions. The statute now applies only to names of *living* rape victims and also includes radio stations. Another important revision made the statute applicable to crimes occurring in Wisconsin only.

As Thayer points out, the revised statute still leaves open both the question of constitutionality and practicality. He assumes a hypothetical case in which a man is murdered and his wife raped. A newspaper could print that the man was slain and his companion raped. If the reader presumes the "companion" was not his wife both the memory of the dead man and the social prestige of his wife might be damaged. (5)

There is a social problem, then, that cannot be solved satisfactorily by the simple process of dumping a bill into a legislative hopper. A South Carolina case illustrates further some of the complications. A reporter for a newspaper and one from a press association were indicted for stories about the raping of a 16-year-old girl. The perpetrator later was electrocuted. (6)

Although South Carolina forbids publication of the name of a rape victim, the two indictments were not based on direct violations of this law. Stories of the crime and trial were published without the girl's name. But the grand jury held that since the girl was known to those who attended the trial her reputation was damaged. The press association reporter was indicted for writing a death-house interview with the rapist.

The question raised earlier repeats itself in this case. How could a paper have covered the trial and execution without mentioning the crime? How could the girl's reputation have been damaged by publication of facts that any court room spectator could hear for himself and spread by word of mouth? If the trial and execution were not covered, is society served best when a man is brought into court in silence and later executed in the same secrecy?

Many newspapers, realizing the social implications involved, have tried to deal with the problem on their own initiative. Their policy is similar to that of two Wilmington, Del., newspapers which editorially explained why it was not printing the names of two rape victims. Said the papers:

"After a good deal of soul-searching and earnest consideration of the public duty of the press, we have come to the conclusion that the name ought to be omitted when the victim of
a rape is obviously and unmistakably innocent. In such a case,
flaunting a woman's shame and misfortune before the world
can serve no public purpose comparable to the unhappiness it
would cause." (7)

But the papers concluded:

"These papers will continue to follow this policy until and
unless these rape cases are tried in open court and the victims
appear as prosecution witnesses. When that happens, the victims step upon a public stage; their names become a matter of
public record which the press is obligated to print." (8)

Columbus, Ohio, newspapers have adopted a policy of mentioning no victims of sex crimes "unless the crime is one of
particular violence or results in death." (9)   .

The assistant director of the Federal Bureau of Investigation
suggested to New York state editors that newspapers in covering sex crimes "spotlight" the offender and shield the victim. (10) He would have that "shielding" continued even during court trials.

Indiana editors, in considering the problems of both juvenile
and sex crimes, arrived at these observations both for and against
compulsory secrecy:

1. A survey showed the overwhelming majority of the papers did not print the names of juveniles involved with the law
unless the crime was of major importance.

2. No law against publication of names can be absolutely
effective because people will find out the facts. The question,
then, is: Which is better, the probable distortion of facts on
street corners or the publication in a responsible paper of the
actual facts?

3. Consideration must be given to public policy on the
part of the government in exercising its police powers to protect people against unwarranted embarrassment. (11)

The publishers concluded:

"The chief fault to find with such legislation (forbidding publication of names) is that it can be both beneficial and detrimental in that it can serve to curb future crime by some and encourage the habituals. Whether the good outweighs the bad is a factor to be considered before resorting to the extreme of prohibiting publication of the news." (12)

As the Indiana publishers suggest, these types of laws should not be enacted hastily or in a frenzy. The original Wisconsin statute shows how ill-advised it is to enact such statutes without careful thought and discussion.

Every restriction on freedom of the press should be thought out seriously before enacted into law. And the press should be a party to the discussions. Both aspects — legality and practicality — should be explored fully.

On the practical side, if a state forbids publication of certain names how will it control out-of-state newspapers which may have wide circulation in that state? How will it control radio stations which can beam into the state news that local stations and newspapers are forbidden to publish? A community newspaper usually will discuss a crime with caution and restraint but the out-of-state newspaper or radio station sometimes sensationalize in a bid for readers or listeners. Public interest is not served if residents hurry to newsstands or tune in out-of-state stations to hear details of a crime which their own community newspaper dare not print.

If the state forbids publication of names, even during a trial, the next logical step would be to bar spectators. If that is done, what will society gain by the secrecy?

Those who lived through the "dirty 1920's" still have a touch of nausea at the recollection of the "legal blackmail" which passed under the formal title of suits for breaches of promise. A sincere girl who was jilted may have sought advice from a marriage counselor but she didn't go into court and put a cash value on her heart. Society rebelled so much at this "blackmail" that in most jurisdictions so-called "heart balm" suits were outlawed by statute.

If sex crimes are going to be kept secret from commission through trial, who can doubt that another type of "legal blackmail" will spring up? A girl who must face the public is less likely to "trump up charges" than if her only evaluators will be a judge and jury.

A juvenile who makes a mistake is entitled to another chance. But what about the youth whose petty theft leads into grand larceny, armed robbery, and perhaps eventually murder? Somewhere along that trail society, for its own protection, should be informed about him.

A statute, no matter how drawn up, cannot be absolutely effective in keeping certain names out of the newspaper or in preventing the community from obtaining the facts and identities from other sources. If the problem is left entirely to the newspaper, the result also will not be absolute, for some newspapermen, just like some business and professional men, have a dull sense of social responsibility.

But if proponents of a ban on certain names, on the one hand, and the press, on the other, accord to each other an honesty of purpose, the two together should be able to arrive at a workable solution.

CHAPTER XXII

"Post Office Regulations"

What Is Barred from the Mails

It would be an anomaly if Congress which set up the postal system had no control over what material may pass through the mails. Thus the courts from time to time have been called upon to distinguish between mailable and non-mailable matter.

The power of Congress over the mails has been affirmed in a number of court decisions. One court, in speaking of the authority of Congress to set up and maintain the postal system said:

"... that (power) carries with it, as a necessary incident to that power, the right ... to determine what shall be carried or transported by means of such postal system." (1)

In general, the law makes it a crime to mail:

1. Obscene, lascivious, and indecent articles.

2. Any material interfering with the armed forces.

3. Any material advocating insurrection or armed resistance to the government.

4. Lottery information.

Books, magazines, and special publications have run afoul of all these prohibitions, but a "family newspaper" should never become involved in at least the first three.

Definitions of obscenity, indecency, and lasciviousness are mostly subjective. In an earlier chapter it was pointed out that nude pictures do not always come under these regulations since they may be photographs of accepted works of art. "Girl art" and "smoking room humor" are not barred from the mails, the courts have said. (2)

Advice on sex, once frowned upon by the postoffice depart-ment, now goes through the mails unless it can be proved it was written solely for the purpose of pandering to perverted tastes.

In the trial of a sex crime, the newspaper might run afoul of the obscenity law, but there is no reported case of a general newspaper being barred from the mail for printing such testi-mony. The newspaper knows that unless it exercises good taste it will hear more promptly from readers than from the post-office department.

A family newspaper, too, doesn't advocate insurrection. But the lottery statute has caused considerable consternation and confusion among newspapers in the past few years.

The Lottery Law

The history of the lottery law duplicates the story of many criminal statutes. Down through the years, the law was revised, added to, and amended to cope with situations never contem-plated by the original framers of the act.

Lottery once had a definite connotation. It meant a scheme by which tickets were sold at set prices. The stubs were placed in a barrel or drum, shaken up, and a certain percentage of them drawn out. Holders of the tickets drawn received cash. The principal prize usually was an amount of money that made the winner a wealthy man for the times.

Today in some Latin American countries and elsewhere, lot-teries are still operated under the sponsorship of the govern-ments. Perhaps the best known to Americans is the Irish Sweep-stakes. Tickets drawn from the drum represent horses entered in a British race. The ticket on the winning horse once was worth about $100,000 to the holder, but now the amount has been reduced to about half that sum.

Lotteries were used in early American days to finance col-leges, churches, schools, road building, and other public im-provements. Social repulsion against gambling finally led to outlawing lotteries in the United States.

Today the Post Office uses the lottery law to prohibit a vari-ety of activities from advertisements of theater "bank nights" to newspaper guessing contests on football or baseball scores.

The first law to curb lotteries was passed by Congress in 1827. It forbade postmasters from acting as agents for lotteries and from vending tickets. (3)

In 1868, Congress amended the law to include besides lotteries "so-called gift concerts," or other similar enterprises offering prizes of any kind on any pretext whatever. Literature either promoting such enterprises or announcing winners was barred from the mails. (4)

The next step taken by Congress was in 1890 when it barred from the mails announcements of any scheme offering prizes dependent upon chance. (5)

Then in 1909 the law was revised to include any scheme offering prizes depending *in whole or in part* on chance. (6) This is the authority by which the Post Office Department today construes many prize offerings as "lotteries."

The law affects both advertisements and the news columns. At intervals, the post office seems to become increasingly active in combating these schemes and in issuing new interpretations of what constitutes violations of the law.

The newspaper is concerned about the law not only because of criminal penalties but also because violations may lead to revocation of its second-class mailing privilege. The usual procedure is to bar from the mail on the offending edition, but persistent violations can cost a paper its permit.

For a number of years, newspapers printed freely stories of Americans who won fortunes in the Irish sweepstakes, complete with pictures of the celebrations staged by the winners. A few years ago the Post Office Department became vigorous in seeking to bar these stories from the mails. Some newspapers avoided a direct violation of the law by printing stories that certain Americans had receive "awards" of $10,000 to $60,000. The usual "victory celebrations" were described, but there was no mention of the occasion for the "awards." Underneath these stories and separated only by a small dash, the newspapers printed as a straight news story the results of a certain horse race in England.

One of the most peculiar rulings on lotteries came in 1947 from the postmaster at St. Louis. A service club in North Carolina raffled off an expensive automobile. The winning ticket was held by a Negro, but he was denied the prize and another drawing held. Many residents of the community, indignant at this racial discrimination, took up a collection to buy the Negro a car.

Any news story about the raffle clearly violated the lottery laws. But the story of the denial of the car to the Negro and the subsequent action of residents in buying him another was a human interest feature packed with drama. Press associations distributed it widely, and many newspapers printed it on their front pages.

The St. Louis postmaster informed the *Star-Times* that its story violated the lottery law and reprimanded the newspaper. The newspaper appealed to Washington, and the St. Louis postmaster was reversed in an opinion by the Post Office Department's solicitor general who said:

> "Despite the literal wording of the law it was not intended to exclude from the mails publications of such items which have a news value in their own right and in which the lottery element is only incidental to a newsworthy event." (7)

Courts have ruled that a lottery has three elements: (a) a consideration paid, (b) a prize, and (c) the determination of winners by chance alone. (8)

The confusion for the newspaper comes in the "in whole or in part" clause. Merchants frequently give prizes to customers, charitable organizations offer "inducements" for contributions, and fraternal, social, and other organizations award "door prizes" for some of their events. In some sections of the country, the games of "bingo," "screeno," "keno," and "bunco" suddenly became popular. The Post Office Department ruled that such games violate the law.

The mushrooming of "give-away" radio programs with their fabulous prizes, gave a spur to all types of "contests," and the post office had many situations presented to it for interpretation. At various times, the department sent top-ranking officials to conventions of publishers' groups to explain the law in detail, but without too much clarification since some of these executives disagreed among themselves on what constitutes violations of the lottery statute.

A study of the law itself is of little help to the newspaper because its meaning depends upon what interpretation the Post Office Department chooses to make at any given time.

Speaking before the Tennessee Press Association in 1948, the chief hearing judge of the Post Office Department outlined some "schemes" which he said came under the lottery law. They included:

1. Prizes offered by merchants if merchandise must be purchased to receive a ticket. The requirement to buy goods, although at the regular price, is held by the department to be "consideration."

2. Offers of prizes to the first 50 or 100 customers to enter the store on the morning of a sale.

3. Prizes to housewives selected at random from the city directory provided they have in the house a certain product.

4. Tags attached to toy balloons and then released over the city. A particular color of tag entitled the finder to a prize.

5. Any contest in which the money is divided in event of ties. Such contests, no matter what skill is involved, are legal only if they bear the slogan: "In case of ties, duplicate prizes will be awarded."

6. "Bingo" and similar games, and the newspaper cannot disguise them under such terms as: "Party," "Games," etc. (9)

The Department hearing judge listed as acceptable:

1. Contests involving skill (but duplicate prizes must be awarded for ties).

2. Contests involving skill even if a product must be purchased to enter. (10)

The skill in a permissible contest may be of many kinds. It can be writing letters or slogans, identifying pictures, making drawings or sketches, composing or filling out last lines to jingles, or any scheme in which contestants must use ingenuity, skill, and thought. Guessing the number of beans in a jar is not looked upon as "skill," no matter if a contestant "cribs" by filling a jar at home and counting the beans.

At times, the Post Office has sanctioned and in turn frowned upon, guessing contests on election or census figures or football or baseball scores.

In 1949, the Post Office Department made another ruling on football contests. It held them to be illegal if the newspaper printed a coupon or listed the games in such a way as to encourage or permit the contestant to mark his choice in the margin and mail in the coupon or clipping. The Department held that such coupons or arrangements of games "induces" the contestant to buy a newspaper which becomes "consideration." (11) The contest is legal if the newspaper announces that answers need not be scored on the coupon or margin but may be sent in on a sheet of paper.

The newspaper is barred from the mails no matter if the scheme it prints is permissible in the state of publication. Newspapers have tried various ways to make certain contests legal.

In some cities, merchants hold "spring sale days" and "autumn festivals," with free tickets for cash drawings given with all purchases. Some newspapers have made no mention of these prizes in their mail editions but printed the stories only in the paper that was to be delivered by carrier. Until recently, the Post Office Department did not object. Now it holds that such stories cannot be printed in any edition on the theory that a copy with the story might find its way into the mails accidentally. Or a resident, mentioned in the news columns, might mail a copy to a friend or relative in another city.

In several cities, the merchants tried a new tack. Tickets were given out with purchases. But when the stubs were drawn from the drum, the holders did not automatically win a prize. Instead, they were called to the platform and asked a series of questions. If they answered correctly, they won a prize. Since the questions included such "puzzlers" as: "In what direction does the sun rise?" no ticket holder ever lost his prize through failure to give the correct answer.

Although the Post Office has not ruled on this subterfuge, in all likelihood the original purchase still will be considered as invalidating the scheme. Several newspapers handle movie "bank nights" under the announcement: "Surprises are in store for those who attend the show tonight." The Post Office has not as yet ruled on this procedure.

In addressing Indiana publishers, the chief hearing judge of the Post Office Department, explained why charities and fraternal groups come under the ban on contests of chance. He told them:

"Morally, I can see no harm in it (such schemes). The Post Office Department, however, knows it isn't the churches, fraternal, and charitable groups that will do the wrong things and conduct the fraud.

"If the Post Office gives an inch, some chiseler somewhere would take a mile—that's why we're sometimes what you might call picayunish." (12)

A Florida newspaper, in announcing an automobile raffle in its city Christmas week, printed:

"Walter R. Brown hung up a sock in City Hall park which St. Nick at the appointed hour filled with a brand new automobile. Not having a car, Buddy Brown wrote Santa the usual note: 'It was just what I wanted'." (13)

There were no repercussions from the Post Office Department.

The only guide for the newspaper is to determine whether any contest offered it as a news item or an advertisement is based, in whole or in part, upon chance. If it is, the contest is illegal. Where prizes are determined by skill alone, the contest is permissible.

But with the actual law of little help, with the Post Office making and revising interpretations frequently, and with each postmaster assigned the task of being the initial judge on non-mailable matter, the general counsel of one state press association was not amiss when he philosophized:

"The most that can be said for the postal rules and regulations is that they are highly confusing." (14)

For Further Reading

Chafee, Zechariah, Jr., *Government and Mass Communications,* Chicago; the University of Chicago Press, 1947, Vol. 1. Consult index.

Deutsch, Eberhard, "Freedom of the Press and of the Mails," 36 *Michigan Law Review,* March, 1938.

Gerald, J. Edward, *The Press and the Constitution, 1931-47,* Minneapolis; the University of Minnesota Press, 1948, pp. 129-36.

"Postal Power and Its Limitation on Freedom of the Press," in, 28 *Virginia Law Review,* March, 1942.

Rogers, Lindsay, *The Postal Powers of Congress,* Baltimore; Johns Hopkins Press, 1916, p. 98 ff.

COURT DECISIONS
(Other than those cited in the text)

Ex parte Jackson, 96 U.S. 727.

In re Rapier, 143 U.S. 110.

United States v. Currey, 206 F. 322.

Magon v. United States, 249 U.S. 618.

Swearingen v. United States, 161 U.S. 446.

United States v. Journal Co., 197 F. 415.

Post Publishing Company v. Murray, 230 F. 773.

United States v. Rosenblum, 121 F. 180.

Boasberg v. United States, 60 F. 2d. 185.

SECTION IV

"Advertising and Radio"

CHAPTER XXIII

"Advertising – Rights and Restrictions"

Legal Problems of Advertising

Since advertising provides the greater part of the newspaper's revenues, the press is vitally concerned with advertising.

The legal problems of advertising do not touch too deeply into the editorial side although the newspaper's promotional activities, generally handled by the news department, may come under some of the legal rights and restrictions applied to advertising. Both in those cases, and for a general over-all understanding of the operation of the newspaper, the editorial man should be acquainted with some of the legal problems.

Political advertising and paid statements by industrial firms, groups, and individuals on public issues are on the increase, and the editorial man often is better acquainted with the subject than the advertising department. He, therefore, should know the legal problems involved.

The editorial man should know these principal legal problems of advertising:

1. The right of the newspaper to refuse advertising.
2. Responsibility for errors in the copy.
3. Responsibility for fraud.
4. Responsibility for libel.
5. News "disguised" as advertising.

The Right to Refuse Advertisements

Since a newspaper is not a public utility, it is the sole judge of whom it will serve. It has a free choice in accepting or rejecting either news or advertising.

The courts a number of times have affirmed the right of the newspaper to refuse any advertisement.

The courts, in general, have followed the ruling laid down in 1918 by an Iowa court:

> "The newspaper is an ordinary business. . . . If a newspaper were required to accept an advertisement, it could be compelled to publish a news item. If some good lady gave a tea, and submitted to the newspaper a proper account of the tea, and the editor of the newspaper, believing that it had no news value, refused to publish it, she, it seems to us, would have as much right to compel the newspaper to publish the account as would a person engaged in business to compel a newspaper to publish an advertisement of the business that person is conducting . . .

> ". . . the publishers thereof (a newspaper) have a right to publish whatever advertisements they desire and to refuse to publish whatever advertisements they do not desire to publish." (1)

Some states require publication of what newspapers call "legal advertising." Local government units must publish as paid advertisements their budgets, revenues, expenditures, bids for supplies, election notices, proposed bond issues, annual reports of each office, and much material of a similar nature. Statutes generally specify that this information must be inserted in a newspaper in the county affected.

In one Indiana county, the only newspaper there refused these legal advertisements on the ground that the rate permitted by the state was too low. County officers, in order to comply with the law, sought the help of the attorney general to compel publication. He was forced to tell them that the newspaper was within its rights in refusing the advertising. (2)

In his reasoning, the attorney general was following the conclusions of a number of courts. In another Iowa case, the court found that it was within the discretion of the county board to designate an "official paper" for the publication of its proceedings, but that ". . . neither the legislature nor the board could compel any newspaper to publish the proceedings no matter what compensation might be fixed therefore, and if the plaintiff was not satisfied with the rate fixed by the board, he was under no obligation to do the work." (3)

Sometimes a newspaper may contract with an advertiser, and later, for various reasons refuse to publish the advertisements. The advertiser then has a right of action in equity for breach of contract, and also possibly a suit for damages.

A newspaper cannot conspire to suppress competition by refusing to print advertisements of particular firms or individuals. Conspiracies are illegal no matter who engages in them. But conspiracy is usually a difficult charge to prove.

On the other hand, businesses cannot conspire with each other to boycott a newspaper in order to force down its advertising rates. For the function of law is to give equal protection to every one.

Responsibility for Errors

An advertisement is regarded by the law as merely an "invitation to bid." It is not a legal offer in the sense that the contract is completed as soon as a customer comes to the store prepared to pay for the article.

As one court expressed it, the advertisement is simply an announcement by the advertiser that he is opening negotiations. (4) The price quoted in an advertisement, said another court, is a mere announcement of what money value the merchant has placed upon his merchandise, and it, too, is not a legal offer to sell at that figure. (5)

From these decisions, a typographical or other error in the price quoted in an advertisement imposes no legal obligation upon the merchant to sell at that figure. Unless the price error is substantial, some stores, as a purely good-will gesture, will sell at the advertised price although it may mean a loss on the item.

Since the merchant is not compelled to sell at the advertised price, a typographical error, however embarrassing it may be, does not cost the store any actual damage unless it voluntarily decides to sell at the erroneous figure as a good-will gesture. For that reason, the newspaper has no legal obligation for such errors. The customary practice is for the newspaper to print a correction in the next edition. This announcement tells customers that the store was not at fault and is part of good business relations between the merchant and the newspaper. If the error is substantial, the newspaper may reprint the advertisement without charge.

Newspapers have been sued few times for errors in prices in advertisements. In 1949, a Mississippi store was awarded $4,000 damages against a newspaper which inadvertently printed the store's "after Christmas sale" advertisement 10 days before Christmas instead of 10 days afterward as called for by the copy.

The newspaper had been given two full-page layouts at the same time. One was to run December 15 and the "clearance sale—one-half off" advertisement was to appear early in January. The newspaper mixed up the copy and the "sale" advertisement was published December 15. The store went ahead with its "premature clearance," and then sued the paper for its loss.

The state appellate court, however, reversed the verdict and held the newspaper, although clearly negligent, was not liable. The court brought out the points already discussed, (a) an advertisement is only an invitation to the public and, (b) if the store elects to sell at the erroneous price it must stand the loss. (6)

A Georgia court in 1949 arrived at the same decision in a suit brought by a store to compel a newspaper to pay the difference between the erroneous price of $5 for fur scarfs and the actual figure of $15. The court rejected the store's claim against the paper. (7)

A Midwestern weekly newspaper faced the same situation when a typographical error in a food advertisement quoted the price of bologna at 29 cents a pound instead of the correct 39 cents. While the publisher was seeking legal advice on his liability, another merchant, seeing the "cut price," hurried in with an advertisement holding bologna at 27 cents a pound. A third grocer, getting wind of what was happening, came in with an announcement that his bologna was 25 cents a pound.

For the next several issues of the paper, bologna was one of the principal items advertised as store keepers kept reducing prices to meet competition. By "mutual consent" the merchants finally pegged the price at 19 cents.

The "bologna war" gave the publisher about 200 extra inches of advertising. Apparently, the first merchant was so wrought up by the "war" that he never noticed the paper had made a mistake in his original advertisement. The publisher, torn between good business and good business practices, discreetly kept quiet.

The newspaper, however, is responsible if typographical errors destroy the usefulness of the advertisement. If it inadvertently placed the Ford dealer's signature on a Chevrolet advertisement, the Chevrolet dealer certainly has reason to refuse payment or to demand the advertisement be printed again — and correctly.

Responsibility for Fraud

The general rule is that a newspaper is not responsible for fraud in an advertisement unless the publisher knew the announcement was fraudulent. Various governmental agencies deal with fraudulent advertising, and, in addition, individual newspapers, publishers' associations, advertising agencies and the journals of these fields have worked together to clear up fraudulent and misleading advertisements.

Since proving a publisher knew an advertisement was fraudulent is usually difficult, the publisher's interest in honest statements is just part of good business practices. False or misleading advertisements make no friends for the newspaper.

The advertiser, of course, is always responsible for his advertisements.

Libel in Advertising

The principle of "he who prints pays," it should be repeated here, extends to advertisements as well as to news. Fraud in an advertisement is one thing; but libel is the responsibility of the publisher although the advertiser also may be sued. All the principles of libel in the news columns apply also to advertisements.

Libel in advertising is most frequent in paid political announcements or statements issued in connection with disputes, and in pictures through the use of the wrong photograph. The correct photograph, if published in an advertisement without permission, may lead to an action for invasion of privacy. A false or unauthorized testimonial also may be libelous if it quotes a living person as endorsing the product. (8)

A magazine lost a libel suit for printing an advertisement offering for sale a booklet on the experiences of a "giddy typewriter girl in New York." The advertisement suggested the nature of the contents by saying: "Good is no name for it. Sent in plain wrapper."

The advertisement was illustrated with the picture of a young woman. She had no connection with the booklet or the contents, and the court held it was libelous *per se*. (9)

The reading matter of an advertisement may be libelous for the same reasons any news story may be held defamatory. Or the headline alone of the advertisement may be libelous. (10)

Advertisements Disguised as News

Congress, through its power to control the mails, has made it a criminal offense to print any "editorial or reading matter . . . for which money or other valuable consideration is paid," unless it is plainly marked "advertisement." (11)

Although some publishers believed this statute was another abridgement of freedom of the press, the United States Supreme Court held the law was constitutional. (12) Many newspapers, especially the smaller ones, print "readers" on the same page with movie advertisements and "puffs" for industrial firms on special pages such as "business pages." Most of this editorial matter is about firms which also have advertisements on the page.

Although some writers on law believe "readers" may violate the statute against "paid editorial matter" no newspaper has been sued for printing such material as "news."

The statute was enacted at a time when advertising was extravagant and flamboyant. Reckless claims for patent medicines and similar nostrums, for bogus or doubtful stock, and for other desirable goods and products were inserted in the news columns and carried with them all the prestige of the newspaper. These are the abuses the law was designed to correct.

Many small newspapers substitute movie "readers" for reviews since their staffs are neither large enough nor properly trained to write dramatic critiques. Although the "readers" are mere "plugs" for a picture, most of them do tell about the experiences during the shooting of the film or little incidents involving the stars. The reader who is an avid movie fan may find them more to his taste than any review such papers could write.

There seldom is a definite understanding and never a contract between the newspaper and the theater that its "readers" will match the size of its advertisements. Most advance "news" stories about circuses or touring sports attractions, such as a professional tennis troupe, are nothing more than "clippings" from publicity books.

Smaller papers which at times carry special sections devoted to gardening, baby-week, clean-up-and-paint-up week, county fair week, and such occasions would be hard pressed to obtain enough pertinent editorial matter to make the section of general interest if business firms did not supply it.

Industrial firms also often contract for a page or even a section to celebrate an anniversary, the completion of a new building, or the addition of a product to their regular line. Such occasions, too, often have news value.

Other firms buy space to explain their side of a labor dispute, to comment on pending legislation affecting them, and to discuss other issues on which they want to emphasize specific points. In most such cases, the subject matter of the advertisements also is worth a news story.

Under a broad interpretation of the statute, all these stories might be classified as "paid editorial matter" in the sense that they were "inspired" at least by the subject matter of the advertising. But the 50th or 100th anniversary of the town's leading industry or business is certainly a news event, too.

The statute, then, seems to have been aimed at a deliberate attempt to pass off an advertisement as a news story in order to lend the paper's prestige to it. When confined to this narrow interpretation, the law serves a good purpose.

For Further Reading

Chapman, Clowry, *The Law on Advertising*, New York; Harper & Bros., 1929.
Finkelhor, Francis, *Legal Phases of Advertising*, New York; McGraw-Hill Co., 1938.

"Right to Refuse Ads," in, *Editor and Publisher*, March 10, 1945.

Handler, Milton, "False and Misleading Advertisements," 39 *Yale Law Review*, November, 1929.

COURT DECISIONS
(Other than those cited in the text)

The Right to Refuse Advertisements:

In re Louis Wohl, Inc., 50 F. 2d. 254.

Mack v. Costello, 143 N.W. 950.

Lake County v. Lake County Publishing Company, 117 N.E. 452.
    Responsibility for Errors and Fraud:

Lovett v. Frederick Loeser Co., 207 N.Y.S. 753.

United States v. Staples, 45 F. 195.

Georgian Company v. Bloom, 108 S.E. 913.

Meyer v. Packard Cleveland Motor Company, 140 N.E. 118.
    Libel and Privacy in Advertising:

Pavesich v. New England Life Insurance Company, 50 S.E. 68.

Foster Millburn Company v. Chinn, 120 S.W. 364.

Munden v. Harris, 153 Mo. App. 153.

Burton v. Crowell Publishing Co., 82 F. 2d. 154.

Barber v. Time, Inc., 159 S.W. 2d.

CHAPTER XXIV

"Radio – Rights and Restrictions"

How Radio Differs

Most of the material in this book applies to radio as well as to the press. In many chapters, "radio" may be substituted for "newspapers" without any change in the text. For in the actual gathering and writing of the news, the radio reporter differs from the newspaperman principally in the techniques peculiar to the preparation of information for broadcasting rather than for the printed page.

Legally, however, the radio presents problems which the press does not encounter, or meets only in modified form. As compared with newspapers, radio, in broadcasting news, has these principal differences or exceptions:

1. No flat constitutional guarantee of freedom.

2. A negative censorship through the right of the Federal Communications Commission to determine if a station is serving public interest, necessity, or convenience.

3. A limited right of expressing its own views.

4. A compelled necessity to present both sides of a public issue. The newspaper is the sole judge of how fair it will be.

5. A conditional right to its broadcasting means (wave length) as compared with the newspaper's outright ownership of all its publication facilities.

6. A negative government control over programs as compared with the newspaper's right to print only what it pleases.

7. A different interpretation of defamation.

8. A different conception of responsibility for defamation.

9. Only a few states have radio retraction laws.

10. Fewer states grant privilege to newscasters than to reporters.

Of these differences and exceptions, the principal ones affecting the news side of radio are those dealing with constitutional freedom, negative censorship, expressing the station's own views, defamation and responsibility for it, defamation defenses, retraction statutes, and privilege.

The Radio and Constitutional Freedom

Although the First Amendment, and the related Fourteenth Amendment, provide for complete freedom of speech, the radio is not included in that provision. Radio stations have taken to the courts their demands for freedom, but the courts have said plainly that there can be no such liberty for broadcasting as there is for the press.

In rejecting a plea that freedom of speech was being abridged by a ruling of the Federal Communications Commission, the United States Supreme Court said:

> "If that be so (that the ruling abridged freedom of speech), it would follow that every person whose application for a license to operate a station is denied by the Commission is thereby denied his constitutional right of free speech. . . . Unlike other modes of expression, radio inherently is not available to all. That is its unique characteristic, and that is why, unlike other modes of expression, it is subject to governmental regulation." (1)

But, as the same court had pointed out a few years earlier: "The Commission is given no supervisory control of the programs, of business management, or of policy. In short, the broadcasting field is open to anyone, provided there be an available frequency over which he can broadcast without interference to others, if he shows his competency, the adequacy of his equipment, and his financial ability to make good use of the assigned channel." (2)

Despite this assurance, however, that radio is "free," complete liberty cannot be obtained by a medium which does not depend alone on the initiative and enterprise of the owner. Any one may start a newspaper at any time in any place he chooses, and the government is not concerned about the publisher's competency, equipment, financial condition, or about the need in the community for another newspaper.

Negative Censorship

Justice Frankfurter chilled some broadcasters by declaring that the Federal Communications Commission not only was to be a kind of traffic officer to police wave lengths and the traffic over them but also had "the burden of determining the composition of that traffic." (3)

Some broadcasters read into this statement an indication that the Commission could, if it desired, determine programs. But events since have not borne out these fears.

The Commission, by law, is denied the power of censorship. The Communications Act of 1934, as amended, says plainly:

"Nothing in this Act shall be understood or construed to give the Commission the power of censorship over radio communications . . . and no regulation or condition shall be promulgated or fixed by the Commission which shall interfere with the right of free speech by means of radio communication." (4)

The same section of the Act, however, did place some restrictions upon "free speech" by forbidding the uttering of "any obscene, indecent, or profane language by means of radio communication." Infractions presumably were to be dealt with through disciplinary measures against the offending stations. In 1948, this provision of the section was repealed and then reenacted as part of the United States Criminal Code. (5)

Penalties now include fines up to $10,000 and prison terms to two years. This provision is comparable to the law forbidding such language in printed form from passing through the mails. Both the radio and the newspaper are left to their own interpretations of "obscene, indecent, and profane." But a newspaper which prints an expletive uttered by a witness or a public figure is less likely to draw a penalty or a rebuke than if the same exclamation were heard on the air. And books have much greater latitude in language than even the newspaper.

The "family newspaper" can be "censored" by the parents before the children read it, but the words coming out of the radio speaker cannot be held back from any who is listening. The newspaper, of course, is no more desirous than the radio of offending "good taste," but the printed story can be handled more realistically, especially if it involves sordid details.

Despite the explicit wording of the law against censorship, the power of the Commission to review programs and to lend great weight to past performances when a station's license is up for renewal, exerts a restraining influence on what is broadcast.

In 1950, while a senate committee was investigating the interstate transmittal of information useful in gambling, the Commission called upon some stations to list all horse race "news" they were broadcasting. Several stations broadcast entries, odds, and other pre-race information and later the results and mutuel prices paid.

The inference was that the Commission would determine if those stations really were serving public interest. (6) The Commission also began lengthy hearings on several west coast stations charged with "slanting" news.

The law, then, forbids the Commission to censor programs. But since it has the power to evaluate how stations are using their facilities, a licensee, if he wishes to continue on the air, has no choice but to abide by Commission regulations or "suggestions." Negative censorship can be just as effective as positive restrictions.

The Right To Express Views

Perhaps no ruling by the Commission has been more bitterly contested than the order that stations may not editorialize on the air. Some have evaded the order by giving time to "public spirited citizens" whose views paralleled closely those of the owners of the stations. Others, by presenting "editorial round-ups" from newspapers, achieve almost the same effect through the process of selection.

The prohibition against station "editorializing" seems hard to justify in the face of sponsored programs of commentators who range far and wide in their comments and criticisms. The situation is not comparable to newspaper columns. A newspaper, if it wishes to be fair, may purchase as many different shades of opinion columns as it wishes to use. The station, which carries a network commentator hostile to labor, may honestly desire to offset him but may not be able to sign up a pro-labor program.

The public, long since accustomed to opinion and comment, might be served better if the station were permitted to broadcast its comments with the identification, probably at the beginning and the end, that "these are the views of this station." Few radio listeners are dependent solely upon one station. As it is, listeners now seek the commentator most nearly in accord with their own opinions. Only a serious student of a public issue looks around for both sides, no matter if the subject is presented over the air or by the printed page. The so-called "round-tables" and "forums" are not exceptions because they command only a select audience. The fact that most of them are broadcast during the less desirable hours should be some evidence that the general listeners do not search too diligently for facts and truth.

The station, however, should be censured for refusing to sell time to responsible groups or people who wish to discuss the other side of an issue. It should draw censure, too, if it permits its comments to be interspersed with regular newscasts. Many newspapers learned by painful experiments that news and comment do not mix. As long as the station keeps news and comments separated and plainly identifies each, it should be permitted to express its own opinions. Denial of the right, deprives stations of some effective community service they otherwise could render and has retarded development of a distinct station "personality."

On June 2, 1949, the Commission decided that station owners could broadcast their own views on public issues, but that "partisanship will be subject to examination at the time of license review." (7)

This ruling was widely interpreted as reversing a decision made by the Commission in 1941 in what has been termed the Mayflower case. In 1941, a station owned by the Mayflower Broadcasting Corporation of Boston applied for renewal of its license. At the hearing, evidence was introduced that the station for the past year had editorially supported certain political candidates and certain public issues with no attempt to be neutral. The Commission, finding the station later had reversed its policy, renewed the license but laid down rules to insure that all sides of public issues would be given time. (8)

Later clarifications have shown that the Commission in its 1949 ruling was not granting free reign to editorial comment on the air. In April, 1950, the Commission said that if a station takes part in a public controversy it "must seek out, aid, and encourage the broadcast of opposing views." (9) It is not enough, said the Commission, that comparable time be made available to the opposition. The licensee (station), it said, must take a "positive role in bringing about a balanced presentation of opposing viewpoints." (10)

The Commission's statement was issued as part of a letter to a New York City station inquiring what positive steps it had taken to present opposition to the series it had broadcast in favor of fair employment practices.

In the same week, a situation in Detroit brought additional clarification from the Commission. An automobile workers' union asked for time to discuss a strike then pending. The automobile company refused to accept time for its side of the discussion, and the station, on the theory that a one-sided presentation was contrary to the Commission practices, refused the union's request. Later, it agreed to make an hour available for joint use by both sides. (11) The company showed no inclination to use any share of the time.

The Commission notified the Detroit station that "it appears your action is not in accord with the principles enunciated in the Mayflower decision." (12)

For the information of the station, the Commission cited this passage from the Mayflower decision:

". . . where the licensee has determined the subject is of sufficient import to receive broadcast attention, it obviously would not be in the public interest for spokesmen for one of the opposing points of view to be able to exercise a veto power over the entire presentation by refusing to broadcast its position.

"Fairness in such circumstances might require no more than the licensee make a reasonable effort to secure responsible presentation of the particular position, and if it fails in this effort, to continue to make available its facilities to spokesmen for such position in the event that after the original programs are broadcast, they then decide to avail themselves of a right of reply to present their contrary opinion." (13)

Although the Commission's statement was called a "clarification," some in the radio industry felt it was confusing. The question is: What is a "positive role" in encouraging presentation of the opposing side? Just how far must a station go in its attempt to roundup contrary views? Who is considered a responsible party to speak for the opposition?

In the case of a strike, the questions are not so pertinent. Any person designated by the union or by the company to present its side is a responsible party.

But confusion seems apparent in many public issues. In one city, a rather informal group began agitating for adoption of the city manager plan. A number of people, through letters to the editor and in public utterances, opposed any change from the commission and mayoralty system.

If the group favoring a city manager were given time who would be the responsible party to speak for the opposition since it was not organized? The organization speaker would come to the microphone well-prepared, presumably after numerous discussions with group members in order to solidify their viewpoints. The opponents, acting individually, would not have the benefit of interplay and discussions, in order to crystallize their group viewpoint. The listening public might hear both sides but the presentations obviously would not be of equal ability.

One writer expressed fear that such a ruling might lead to "shadow boxing." The station might give time to a well-prepared, well-informed, and capable speaker to discuss one side of the issue. Then, to satisfy "impartiality," it could give equal time to an individual whose presentation would be no more effective than that of the average person who hurriedly dashes off a letter to the editor. (14)

Such presentation would be as unequal as if an amateur boxer were matched with the world's heavyweight champion. Public interest is not served by giants battling straw men.

Although political broadcasts usually are paid for and therefore are comparable to advertisements, the Commission forces stations to sell equal time to all candidates. The station is not compelled to sell time to any candidate, but if it permits one to broadcast it must afford equal opportunities to all others. (15) If a candidate is financially unable to buy time, apparently the station has no further obligation. Thus, the community hears only part of the campaign issues.

This situation is not comparable to the press because a newspaper usually devotes news space to all candidates. This doesn't mean that newspapers are more fair than radio but only that the peculiar nature of radio imposes special problems. For the same reason, a newspaper may permit wider discussion of public issues since it can open its columns to individuals, no matter if they are speaking for themselves or for a group.

Radio Defamation

The laws of libel as outlined in this book apply to radio as well as the press although two important legal distinctions are raised by broadcasting.

1. Since radio is oral, is defamation on the air slander or is it libel?

2. Who is responsible? A newspaper is responsible for everything it prints but such an exact requirement in many cases is unfair to a station. A speaker, deliberately or through "mike fright," may blurt out statements he did not intend to make.

These legal questions were presented to the courts very early in the development of radio. The answers, while still not precise, lead to some rather definite conclusions.

Is Radio Defamation Libel?

Radio is an example of what happens when a new invention collides head on with well-established social institutions. Before the advent of radio, the social institution of the law had placed defamation into permanent grooves. Any oral defamation was slander; any written information was libel.

It required no mental gymnastics to adapt the law of libel, from time to time, to new methods of communication such as pictures, billboards, posters, and even sky writing. But radio quickly made obsolete the historical distinction between slander and libel.

Slander today is considered a minor offense and seldom is it encountered in law. Back-yard and bridge table gossip and word-of-mouth whispering are rather limited in the damage they can do. The printed word presents not only the problem of wider dissemination but also of permanence.

The spoken word vanishes into air, and unless one is close enough to the speaker he doesn't even hear it. The printed word is there for all who wish to turn to it repeatedly. And instead of a single tongue, the newspaper speaks with thousands of tongues.

The radio at first presented little difficulty because it was generally considered to be a novelty and purely an entertainment medium. After the famous radio-newspaper "war," news became an important part of programming, and problems arose. (16)

As customary in such situations, the courts and legislatures first began amending and revising the legal system to meet the problems of radio. Now the adjustment is almost one of pure accommodation, with the result that it is completely satisfactory neither to those in the legal field, to the radio industry, nor to society as a whole.

The courts first looked at the new medium and noted that the words were delivered to the ear instead of to the eye. The logical conclusion was that radio defamation, being oral, was slander.

Soon it was discerned that such a definition was unsatisfactory. A newspaper has a defined circulation. More persons besides the buyer may read each copy of the paper, but, in general, the newspaper has a definite and limited circulation. Words go out from the radio station, and no one can tell exactly where they go or who hears them.

Geographical boundaries are no barriers to radio waves. A small weekly newspaper with a circulation of 500 can plot its readership fairly accurately. But a radio station in the same community may spill its sounds into a number of surrounding counties. The possibility of harm from defamation is therefore much greater.

It is true that the newspaper with only 500 circulation may inflict grievous damage because the individual it defames probably will be living in that community. But the radio not only would harm him in his own town but also spread the defamation to the four winds.

A community problem in that small town would be almost in the nature of a "family matter." For that reason, the courts view a story printed in the small weekly differently from the same account published in a paper which has only incidental circulation there.

Although on this point of law, there are no cases involving radio, a Wisconsin court did make this distinction in a suit brought against a Milwaukee paper for an article about the mayor of an upstate small city. It said:

"The general rule . . . may be stated to be: if a newspaper, published primarily for a given constituency . . . has a small circulation outside such constituency, it is not deprived of its privilege in the discussion of matters of concern to its constituency because of such incidental outside circulation." (17)

The court held the Milwaukee newspaper responsible because it had only "incidental circulation" in the small city whose mayor it had criticized. The court indicated that a newspaper published in the small city could have erected a successful defense of "fair comment and criticism," but that the metropolitan newspaper, by spreading the story over its vast circulation area, lost this plea. (18)

The radio station, legally, should be in the same category as the metropolitan newspaper. The problem became more acute when stations began joining networks, making it possible for defamation from one program to spread over the whole country. Such hookups make the possibility of harm unlimited.

The courts soon realized it was unfair to say to the newspaper of 500 circulation that defamation must be paid for by practically any amount a jury will award while the broadcast, heard in several counties, should be subject only to the minor penalties of slander.

The courts, therefore, began to reason on the basis of harm, actual or potential. Since radio words are apt to be disseminated more widely, the penalty should be severe. To aid them, the courts also called upon the fact that most broadcasting is done by script. A script is written and hence subject to the laws of libel.

Such improvised reasoning is no tribute to the legal system. It would have been much better for society had legislatures been deliberate bodies with vision and had set to work at once to meet squarely the challenge of the new medium.

But the reasoning, improvised as it was, arrived at what seems to be the most logical answer. Now, with radio as much a part of communications as the newspaper, it cannot plead for special privilege to avoid its full responsibilities.

An historic case in the United States in deciding whether radio defamation should be libel or slander, originated in Nebraska in 1932. (19) A written speech was broadcast, and an individual referred to in the address sued for libel rather than for slander. The court said:

"It was shown that while the defendant company did not require and did not have a copy of the speech in advance of its utterance, yet its employes in charge of the station did not use or attempt to use means to stop or shut off the speech, though that could have been done instantly by mechanism which is part of the equipment. . . . There can be and is little dispute that the written words charged and published constitute libel rather than slander." (20)

This case raised another question. The defendant company argued that the Federal Communications Commission forbids censorship, but the court held that provision merely prevents the station from censoring political party words and does not mean that it is immune from the penalties of broadcasting defamatory words. (21)

Other courts soon followed the Nebraska decision. (22) If a person prepares a script and delivers it in advance to newspapers but then speaks from memory instead of reading it, it still is libel, according to one court. (23)

It is fairly well-established, then, in law, that if a script is involved, radio defamation is libel. But what about extemporaneous speeches or where the speaker interpolates? Some words may come to the speaker as an afterthought, or, if the broadcast is originating in front of an audience, the speaker may expand his remarks as he sees favorable reaction from the spectators.

On this question, the courts are divided. Some apply the test of wider dissemination doing more grievous harm and call it libel. Others hold it to be slander.

In considering the problem, one court said:

"The person who hears the defamatory matter over the air ordinarily does not know whether or not the speaker is reading from a manuscript. Furthermore, what difference does it make to such a person, so far as the effect is concerned?" (24)

A New York court, confronted with a case in which words were interpolated into a prepared script, ruled that the added remarks must be considered slander. (25)

A Pennsylvania court, surveying the perplexity that radio has produced in defamation, suggests that it might be regarded as a distinct form of action.

The court observed:

"The danger of attempting to apply the fixed principles of law concerning either slander or libel to this new medium (radio) of communication is obvious. But the law is not so firmly and rigidly cast that it is incapable of meeting a new wrong as the demands of progress and change require. In this State, our tort actions are in trespass; the pleader need not lay his cause either in slander or in libel, and as defamation by radio possesses many attributes of both libel and slander, but differs from each, it might be regarded as a distinct form of action." (26)

Frank Thayer suggests that in view of the confusion, uniformity be attained by establishing a new classification in tort, to be called radio defamation. (27)

Despite the confusion, however, it seems definitely established that where a script is involved, radio defamation is libel. For interpolated or extemporaneous remarks, the several jurisdictions differ, but the growing tendency seems to be to recognize the widespread circulation of radio as causing such serious harm that penalties must be more severe than those imposed for slander.

The state legislatures have given little help toward solving this problem. But Louisiana has taken a forward step by replacing its libel and slander statutes with a law of defamation. (28) Such legislation takes the problem out of the realm of legal speculation and recognizes that, after all, the real concern must be for the protection of the individual.

Who Is Responsible?

The second area of confusion in radio is the determination of responsibility for defamation. The newspaper axiom: "He who prints pays" cannot be applied to radio strictly because of the unusual situations that develop.

Under one theory, the station should be responsible for any defamation sent out through its facilities. Such a principle is comparable to the press theory where the publisher is responsible in civil libel for all material appearing in his newspaper.

The radio, however, has some peculiar problems in determining responsibility. They include:

1. Material broadcast extemporaneously or interpolated even where a script has been sent in and approved in advance.

2. "Package" programs in which a radio show is produced, directed, and acted by people with no connection with the station.

3. Network programs which the local station has no way of checking in advance.

4. The regulations of the Federal Communications Commission forbidding stations to censor political broadcasts.

5. Determining the place where the action should be brought in programs that spill across state borders.

Early decisions established the principle of absolute responsibility of the stations, equivalent to the law applicable to newspapers. In Sorenson v. Wood, the defamatory remarks were interpolated into a political speech. (29) Action was begun against both speaker and station. The station set up two pleas: (1) It was a political speech and the Federal Communications Commission forbids censorship of such talks, (2) a radio station is a common carrier, and common carriers by tradition are exempt from liability for defamation.

The court rejected both pleas. It held that a station has the right to compel a script and to insist upon deletion of material it believes to be defamatory. Such procedure, the court held, is not censorship. (30)

A radio station, the court further held, is not a common carrier because it can exercise considerable choice in selecting those to whom it will make its facilities available.

The court also noted that the station did not have a copy of the script and that no effort was made to cut off the speaker.

The same absolute doctrine of liability was arrived at in a case in which an extemporaneous remark was made in a sponsored network program originating in New York City. (31) A Kansas City outlet of the program was sued by the plaintiff who had been called a former convict.

The station maintained there was no way in which it could have known that the remark was to be made and that since its utterance was finished in a few seconds, there was no reasonable method by which it could have been cut off.

But the court, assuming these pleas were true, said:

"The conclusion seems inescapable that the owner of the station is liable. It is he who broadcasted the defamation. He took the utterance of the speaker which came to him in the form of pulsations in the air. Those waves of air he changed into electrical impulses. These he threw out upon the ether, knowing they would be caught up by thousands and changed again into sound waves and into a human voice. He intended to do those things. But for what he has done the victim of the defamation never would have been hurt." (32)

This decision is analogous to those holding a newspaper is responsible for press association copy.

A court in the state of Washington reached the same conclusion on station responsibility when a sponsored local program accused a sheriff of selling confiscated stills at auction instead of destroying them. The program implied the stills later found their way back into the hands of bootleggers. (33)

These decisions were handed down from 1932 to 1935. In 1939, there came an indication that the courts were realizing the impossibility of clinging to a strict doctrine of station responsibility.

A professional golfer, appearing on the sponsored program of Al Jolson, told the singer that his first job was as golf professional at the course of the Summit Hotel in Uniontown, Pa. Jolson quipped: "That's a rotten hotel."

The hotel was awarded $15,000 against the network. The state Supreme Court, in reversing the decision said:

"The important question raised is whether a radio broadcasting company which leases its facilities is liable for an impromptu defamatory statement, interjected 'ad lib' into a radio broadcast by a person, hired by the lessees, and not in the employ of the broadcasting company, the words being carried to the radio listeners by its facilities . . .

"A rule unalterably imposing liability without fault on the broadcasting company under any circumstances is manifestly unjust, unfair, and contrary to every principle of morals. A fair aspect of the harm to the persons injured must be considered as well as the circumstances under which the incident occurred. An essential consideration in formulating a rule is the grave possibility of pyramiding damages as well as establishing criminal responsibility if defamatory broadcasting is treated as libel.

"We, therefore, conclude that a broadcasting company which leases its time and facilities to another, whose agents carry on the program, is not liable for an interjected defamatory remark where it appears that it exercised due care in the selection of the lessee, and, having edited the script, had no reason to believe an extemporaneous defamatory remark would be made." (34)

The court's ruling has since become known popularly as the "reasonable care" theory. Three years later, a New York court followed the same rule in a case involving a political speech. The defendant company brought out that under the regulations of the Commission it could not censor political speeches, and the court agreed that under such circumstances a station should be permitted corresponding privileges. But the principal issue was whether a station which examined a script in advance was liable for interpolated remarks. The court said:

"The physical aspects of radio broadcasting warrant a rule that if the management of a radio station has used due care in the selection of the lessee and its facilities and in the inspection of the script, it should not be liable for extemporaneous defamatory remarks." (35)

The "reasonable care" doctrine, however, would not apply if the interpolation were done by regular employes of the station. If a regular announcer makes the "ad lib," the station is responsible.

Although it is dangerous to make predictions in law, the "reasonable care" theory seems to be growing in favor, both in the courts and the legislatures. A jury in New Jersey, in 1949, after deliberating eight hours, found for a radio station on the ground that it had exercised "reasonable care" in looking over the script of a political speech. (36)

The case had been in the courts for several years. The plaintiff, a deputy secretary of public welfare, first brought action in slander which was dismissed by the trial court. The Court of Error and Appeals, however, reinstated the suit on the ground the complaint was broad enough to set forth a new type of action—defamation. (37) The majority of the court favored the principle of absolute station responsibility and remanded the case for trial. But the jury voted for the "reasonable care" principle.

The "reasonable care" theory, however, in the near future will provide some new problems. For one day, the courts must decide just what is "reasonable care." Does it mean merely the reading of the script by any employe of the station? Or must it be read by a station official, and if so, by whom?

If the situation could be applied to newspapers, would "reasonable care" mean the ordinary work of the copy desk or by some one with the title of "editor," who might be city editor, managing editor, news editor, or editor? Thus, the firm ground toward which the courts seem to be working their way in radio defamation, may prove one day to be only quicksand.

Political Speeches

In political speeches, whether the time is donated or bought, the libel problem is complicated further by the law which says these talks may not be censored. (38) Although some courts have held that the deletion of defamatory material from a political script is not censorship, (39) the Federal Communications Commission has ruled repeatedly that the law is a mandate to the stations not to "blue pencil" political speeches. In what has become known as the "Port Huron case," (40) the Commission in 1948 advised stations they must not censor political talks, and, in turn, they would not be held responsible for defamation. Whether an administrative agency of the government can waive away station responsibility, especially where state laws are in effect, is a question that the courts probably will have to pass upon. After this decision, several attorneys advised their client stations to take out libel insurance or some other protection before permitting political broadcasts. (41)

The Commission itself seems to thwart some possible solutions to the problem. The Commission has called attention to the law which permits stations a free choice as to whether they will carry any political speeches. (42) But if a station does sell or donate time to one candidate, it must treat all others equally. This seems a superficial method of trying to meet the problem. Many candidates may broadcast from scripts free of defamation, but if the last nominee appears several weeks later with a fiery speech what can be done? The Commission says he is entitled to time because others have broadcast. It says further that the talk may not be censored. If the station follows the court ruling in the Volvia case (43) and wants to cut out sentences it believes are defamatory while the candidate insists the script is innocent of libel, who is to be the final judge? The candidate may appeal to the Commission and involve the station in an expensive and time-consuming hearing. If the station yields, it may find itself sued for libel.

The Commission has presented a further dilemma by calling the attention of stations to the importance of political broadcasts as a service to the public in debating public issues. (44) In some radio circles, this "suggestion" has been interpreted as a positive command to permit political talks.

The station, thus, is caught between the law and the Commission. A Philadelphia suit is now pending on this very issue. A federal court, taking cognizance of the Port Huron decision, ruled that a station was not responsible for defamation in a political speech since the law gives it no power of censorship. The plaintiff, a Philadelphia lawyer, is appealing this ruling. (45)

Some legislatures have attempted to deal with the problem. A few of them relieve the station from responsibility for all programs if it exercises "reasonable care" which, presumably, means checking the script in advance and being alert to cut off defamatory words. Other states extend this privilege only to political broadcasts. The states line up this way:

Privilege for all broadcasting: Colorado, Florida, Iowa, Montana, Utah, Virginia, Washington, and Wyoming.

Privilege for political broadcasts: Illinois, South Dakota.

Mississippi simply says the stations must be governed by the federal law on political broadcasts.

Retraction Laws

Indiana and North Carolina have radio retraction laws that operate in a similar manner to their newspaper retraction laws. The correction must be broadcast at the same time of day as the original item "and with the same sending power." (46) Both states include television, and there are some in the industry who are waiting curiously to see the form of the first retraction by television.

Radio Defamation Defenses

The radio may avail itself of the same defenses open to the newspaper. It may plead truth, qualified privilege, or fair comment and criticism of a public matter.

But there appears to be an important exception. A New York court refused to accept qualified privilege as a defense for comment broadcast on a sponsored program. The court held that the discussion was not for public good but for commercial profit. (47)

There is nothing in this case, however, to warrant a fear that a regular news program would not carry qualified privilege if it were sponsored. The court seemed to be objecting more to the nature of the comment since it was an attack on insurance companies who at the time were not involved in the news.

A sponsored program of straight news or commentary on public issues seems assured of receiving the same protection as similar news or articles in a newspaper.

A news program direct from a courtroom was held to be protected under qualified privilege. (48)

Inaccuracies on the air, just as in the newspaper, destroy privilege. A station was asked by a sheriff to broadcast that he wanted to "hold" a car and driver. The station, instead, broadcast that the sheriff was seeking the driver for stealing a car. Apparently, there was a dispute over the ownership of the car between the motorist and a bank. The plaintiff elected to proceed against the bank, but the courts dismissed the complaint with the statement that the station was the party responsible for the mistake. (49)

Who May Be Sued and Where?

Although all disseminators of libel may be sued, the custom among those defamed by the press is to sue the newspaper, on the theory that it is a financially responsible company.

Should the individual defamed by radio sue the station or the network if it is a "chain" program, or should he proceed against the actual speaker or the agency which leased the time?

Until the courts determine definitely the responsibility for defamation, the plaintiff may find his suit dismissed because he has chosen the wrong defendant. From cases already cited, a sponsored network program is the responsibility of the agency which leases the time. The hotel which was denied damages from the network, (50) probably had a right of action against the advertising agency which had purchased the time.

In states adhering to absolute station responsibility, the suit, even for a network program, could be brought against any station that handled the program. In those states following the "reasonable care" doctrine, the suit would have to be brought against the firm which bought the time or perhaps the speaker himself. If the time purchaser, showed that he, too, had exercised "reasonable care," probably the only recourse would be against the speaker who interpolated the defamatory remarks. But this is a question still to be determined definitely.

Once the defamed individual decides upon his defendant, where may the action be brought? A station, especially one located near borders, may cover more territory in adjoining states than in the one in which it is located. If one of these "foreign" states has laws more "favorable" to the defamed individual than the home state, can the plaintiff bring his action where conditions seem to be of the greatest advantage to him? Or if he sues and loses in the "home" state, can he bring further action in an adjoining state? If he is known nationally and is defamed on a network can he bring a series of suits against stations which carried the program although, as indicated in the Sweeney chain libel cases, courts do not look with favor upon multiple suits? These are questions which the courts must face some day.

Contempt of Court

Broadcasters can be held in contempt of court the same as newspapermen and for the same reasons. Judges may be held up to ridicule or to scorn and justice may be obstructed as much by the spoken word as by the printed page. A Los Angeles station owner was cited for attempting to influence a judge. (51)

An Iowa station was censured by the presiding judge at a murder trial for broadcasting a "poll" it had taken regarding the guilt or innocence of the defendant. The jury was not locked up, and it could have heard and been influenced by the broadcast, since those polled were veteran reporters whose opinions might have carried some weight with the jurors. A station risks contempt of court in broadcasting such polls.

Privacy

The radio may not invade an individual's privacy any more than a newspaper, but again, the broadcaster has the same defenses as the reporter. The decision so far by the courts on radio invasion of privacy have been interwoven mostly with dramatizations based on actual events.

In a case free of this complication, the courts held that an individual loses his right of privacy by becoming involved in a public event. Radio Commentator Drew Pearson broadcast that a defendant in a suit attracting nationwide attention was a waiter in a Washington hotel where some government officials, on the prosecuting side of the case, dined frequently. The waiter, Pearson said, was in a position to overhear their conversations. After the broadcast, the waiter lost his job and he brought suit.

The court ruled, however, that the waiter by being involved in a publicized public case forfeited his privacy. (52)

A California man, however, was held by the courts to have a right of action for invasion of privacy because a station broadcast a dramatic sketch of a holdup in which he had been the victim. The station used his name without his permission. (53)

This decision followed the reasoning of a much earlier one giving a ship radio operator the right of action against a motion picture company which made a feature film based on a news event. The radio operator concerned was portrayed in the movie without his permission. The court found the motion picture company at fault because it was using the man's name for trade or profit. (54)

In news and comment, a station may use the name of an individual who figures in a public event. In dramatic shows, despite the two decisions cited above, the question is still open as to whether a dramatization is for "purposes of trade" and thus an invasion of privacy. Some dramatizations may be merely analogous to a feature story in a newspaper. It would seem these types of drama shows are permissible. But when the station profits by selling time for such shows, a new principle intrudes.

The station is on safer grounds when, for such shows, it obtains permission to use names.

Privilege

In twelve states, it has been pointed out, a newspaperman by statute, is protected against forced disclosure of his news sources. Only four of these states, however, have seen fit to grant such privilege to the radio man. Two rejected the proposal during their 1949 legislatures.

Bench and bar, in general bitterly opposed to privilege for newspapermen, seem even more determined to refuse it to broadcasters. Besides all the same objections it has raised to newspaper privilege, the legal profession, in addition, seems to feel that radio still is too "immature" to be granted this privilege.

Privilege is now accorded to radio men in: Alabama, Arkansas, Indiana, and Maryland.

It was denied to them in Pennsylvania and New Jersey.

Seven states, in their 1949 legislatures, defeated bills that would have extended privilege to both newspapers and radio. They were: Connecticut, Maine, Massachusetts, Minnesota, Missouri, New York, and Oregon.

False Information

The states have done nothing to penalize those who provide false or libelous information to radio stations.

Facsimile

The already complicated legal situation in which radio finds itself appears likely to become more confused if facsimile broadcasting ever begins to fulfill some of the promises its proponents hold for it.

The courts will have to determine if facsimile is broadcasting or printing. The "reasonable care" doctrine on responsibility for libel by radio can hardly apply to facsimile, for station editors will have a chance to check copy as carefully as the newspaper. In those states, stations may find themselves in the paradoxical situation of being cleared of responsibility for libel by speech but held accountable when the same story is sent by facsimile.

Television

Television, in all probability, will produce for radio some of the problems that photographs have raised for newspapers. Studio programs will present no difficulties, but when television starts operating as freely and extensively as the newspaper cameraman, invasion of privacy may become an issue.

The same laws and decisions now affecting pictorial journalism may be applied to television. Certainly, an individual taking part in an event worth televising is committing a public act. If he is close enough to get into the range of a television camera, presumably he would have no more claim to privacy than if he had stepped within the focus of a newspaper photographer.

But if the program is sponsored, will the individual be able to maintain in some cases that his picture was used for "trade purposes?"

Facsimile and television strengthen the argument that a new type of tort is needed to cover radio defamation. Otherwise, the courts, already laboring under the impact of radio, may soon find the problems have become so complex that neither the radio industry nor society can be sure of its rights and privileges.

Resume and Analysis:

In the gathering and reporting of the news, the radio man operates under most of the rights and privileges, and also restrictions, of the newspaper reporter. But in addition to the law, the broadcaster is subject also to the administrative rules of the Federal Communications Commission. Sometimes these regulations conflict with the accepted legal principles governing other forms of communication.

The two areas most in doubt are: (1) Is radio defamation slander or libel? (2) Who is responsible for radio defamation?

The courts appear to have swung rather definitely to the theory that radio defamation is libel—or at least must be dealt with by stronger remedies than those provided for slander because of the greater harm from the wider dissemination of broadcast material.

On the question of responsibility, the courts have divided into two schools. The one holds the station, like the newspaper, has absolute responsibility for everything it broadcasts. The other, believing such a position is untenable because of the peculiar nature of broadcasting, has evolved the "reasonable care" principle. Under it, a station is not responsible for impromptu or interpolated remarks, or for network programs over which it has no direct control.

There seems to be some tendency for more jurisdictions to come to this viewpoint. Some newspapers have criticized this doctrine on the ground it gives radio an unfair advantage over the press which operates under the principle of absolute responsibility. (55)

As a practical working matter, the situations are not comparable. The newspaper can read every line of copy and knows what is going into print. A station, no matter how alert its employes may be, cannot blank out a defamatory "ad lib" that takes only a second or two to utter. The newspaper might be on more reasonable ground if it used this radio interpretation to argue for freedom from responsibility for press association copy, since the circumstances are analogous to network programs.

In political broadcasts, stations are torn between complying strictly with the law against censorship and the fear they may be sued for defamation. Clearly, in this area, the law should be more specific.

In general, the radio has the same defenses as the newspaper. But its best defense, the same as that of a newspaper, is an alert staff, accurate and careful in its work, and armed with a knowledge of the legal questions involved.

Laws affecting radio are largely the result of accommodation to a new medium of expression. What is needed badly is the sweeping away of these confusing and sometimes contradictory principles and a general rebuilding upon a new foundation.

What is needed, too, in legal circles is a recognition that radio is a new medium with peculiar problems and not a mere adjunct of old ways of expressing ideas, opinions, and comment.

For Further Reading

Ashbury, Aubrey L., "Legal Aspects of Radio Broadcasting," 1 *Air Law Review*, July, 1930. (For history of early attempts at regulation)

Bartenstein, Fred, Jr., "Defamation by Radio," 1 *Washington & Lee Law Review*, Fall, 1939.

Berry, John L. and Goodrich, Warren M., "Political Defamation: Radio's Dilemma," 1 *University of Florida Law Review*, February, 1948.

Chafee, Zechariah, Jr., *Government and Mass Communications*, Chicago; University of Chicago Press, 1947, Vol. II, various sections discussing radio.

Globensky, J. L., "Liability of Radio Stations for Defamation," 24 *Notre Dame Law Review*, February, 1948.

Moser, J. B., and Lavine, Richard A., *Radio and the Law*, Los Angeles; Parker & Company, 1947, Chapters 8, 9, and 10.

Wittenberg, Philip, *Dangerous Words*, New York; Columbia University Press, 1947, Chap. 13.

COURT AND COMMISSION CASES
(Other than those cited in the text)

Singler v. Journal Company, 260 N.W. 431.

Erie v. Tompkins, 304 U.S. 64.

KVOS, Inc., 6 F.C.C. 22.

Trinity Methodist Church v. Federal Radio Commission, 288 U.S. 599.

Locke v. Benton & Bowles, 2 N.Y.S. 2d. 150.

Lynch v. Lyons, 20 N.E. 2d. 953.

Rutherford v. Daughtery, 91 F. 2d. 707.

SECTION V

"Legal Problems of the Future"

CHAPTER XXV

Conclusion

A book which examines the law as it affects the press must record necessarily some dissension between the legal system and journalism. But only the naive reader will carry away the impression that the newspaper expends most of its energies in a continuous battle to protect itself or society from the encroachment of the law.

That rapidly-vanishing prototype of reporter who persists in looking upon his work as a game or adventure may picture himself manning almost single-handedly the last bulwark of freedom of expression. His more realistic colleagues know that fundamentally the law and the press are serving the same purpose.

Both are social agencies working toward the common goal of helping society to maintain itself and to progress. At times, law and journalism have differed on the means to this goal, and more differences can be predicted for the future, but these conflicts should not be glorified under the name of "war."

Journalism, especially mass communications, being a newer agency and still suffering from growing pains, sometimes is prone to mistake the law's stability, obtained through age, as more of a hardening of the social arteries than as a venerable restraint. On the other hand, law, grown rather rigid and formal through the years, often sees journalism as impetuous and impatient of any control, with a tendency to act before first analyzing the steps it is taking.

As Siebert says:

"Journalism needs the stability which the social experience of the law can contribute; the law can profit from association with so fluid and socially-malleable an instrument as journalism." (1)

Without a rapid dissemination of news and information, a democratic government cannot function. Its operation would be spineless, too, if there were no wide latitude for the free interplay of opinion, comment, and criticism. Although history taught that principle long ago, the peoples of the world discovered it anew in the years leading up to the Second World War. And in some areas of the world today, that principle remains either unrecognized or intentionally subdued.

Never in world history has a nation been provided more adequately with information than in the United States today. And never in world history has a nation done more to encourage the right of the individual to speak his mind.

The American people respect their institutions, but it is a respect arising from the most critical examination of them. Americans reject any theory of veneration or sacredness that discourages a free and open discussion of agencies, institutions, or individuals. Even England knows no such complete freedom of expression because reverence for antiquity often can be more stifling than positive law.

Down through the years, American newspapers have talked much about their "rights and privileges," and have waged incessant struggles to maintain them. Today, the more enlightened segment of the press realizes a third—and even greater—element—responsibilities. The individual is no longer the "innocent bystander" in conflicts between the law and the press, but the person who makes the resolution of these conflicts imperative.

The people, through the Constitution, have been sweeping in the immunities they have granted to the press. But not even a free press is a sufficient price to pay for irresponsibility.

A book on law and the press should not be a "handy guide" as to what the press may, or may not do, legally. Rather, it should be an explanation of the joint responsibility of the law and the press in carrying forward democratic government.

Some liberties have endured because the press did fight to preserve their inviolability. The fight, of course, has not been carried on exclusively by the press, nor has it been directed solely at the courts. For the courts, in many phases of the struggle, have stood as bulwark for free expression. At other times, courts have circumscribed both the press and individuals, and the newspaper has been a powerful voice in the battle against legal oppression.

While the needs of society as a whole will be served best by a partnership of the law and the press, it should not be a "mutual admiration pact" in which one partner is reluctant to expose the faults of the other. Nor should it be for the press a "partnership of fear" in which it is afraid to take the lead in speaking out against legal abuse or legal circumvention of fundamental rights. Courts have never been infallible and less so today when society is so dynamic and social conditions change more quickly than the legal system either can, or wishes to, adjust itself.

With the mushrooming of the mass media of communications—newspapers, radio, magazines, books, movies, and now television—more conflicts seem just ahead. They will be waged over the same general paradox: the right of society to be informed fully versus the right of the individual to live in anonmity. Since society seems to be insisting more and more that the right of the group to be informed is superior to the right of the individual to be let alone, the press and the law are likely to find themselves at odds almost as many times in the future as they have been in the past.

These future conflicts need not be so prolonged nor so bitter as those in the past if the law and journalism will take a lesson from the branches of the federal government. The "check and balance" system, established with the most sincere of purposes and motives, finally had to yield to the inevitable. "Checks and balances" just do not permit efficient operation of a government as large as that of the United States. Now the three branches of government have come to regard themselves not so much as checks upon each other, but as partners in a greater over-all system of accommodation.

Some of the potential conflicts of the future could be avoided if the law and journalism had the vision to begin work today on the problems. The work should be undertaken in a spirit of partnership and not only of hostility or rivalry.

It takes no omniscience to predict that some of these conflicts and problems will arise in these areas:

1. **The archaic and much-patched framework of the law of libel.** Antique rules and procedures do not serve a society as dynamic as that of the American nation of today where the emphasis is upon free expression. Technology has contributed to the confusion by making the whole world the "beat" of even the smallest newspaper.

Certain suggested remedies, such as the right of reply, offer more idealistic satisfaction than practical solution to the problems of mass communications. What is needed is a complete rebuilding upon a 20th century foundation.

2. **Radio—and now television.** Here is a new medium with problems encountered by no other form of expression. No amount of patch-work upon already antiquated laws will solve the problems of broadcasting.

3. **Constructive contempt.** Courts are established for definite social purposes and not ordained and sanctified. Although the nation's highest court at the moment has swung toward the greatest latitude in permitting comment and criticism of the legal system, the principle needs a more secure basis than the will of judges.

4. **Privilege.** Bench and bar are too "legalistic" in their opposition to such confidence laws. Anticipated or possible abuse should not outweigh the actual record in those states which have such laws. The legal system, with its vast investigatory powers, should not be so insistent that it is denied access to information which a reporter, without similar resources or training, is able to uncover, many times, simply because he is more diligent. As indicated in the chapter on confidence laws, a study has shown no single instance where the fears of bench and bar have materialized. On the other hand, there is a record of newspapers uncovering "leads" that the law never could tap without the aid of the press.

5. **Press association defamation.** It seems foolish for the law to contend, in effect, that a newspaper has either the time or the facilities to check stories originating miles away. No one would deny to any individual the right of redress for a wrong, but recovery should be from the party primarily responsible.

6. **Photographs.** Pictorial journalism is so well-established that it requires a clear statement of its rights and privileges. It should not be forced to depend upon the day-to-day policies of particular courts.

7. **Reporting of crimes.** Somewhere there must be a balance between the right of the defendant and the necessity for society to be informed and perhaps protected. While courts have inveighed against "pre-trial" stories of newspapers, many have shown amazing reluctance to restrain prosecutors, attorneys, and law officers who are just as eager to get their record into print as the newspaper is to publish it.

8. **Administrative law.** For the press, the inconsistency of the Post Office Department and for radio, the confusing regulations of the Federal Communications Commission, must be resolved into more stable and uniform rules. A Commission should not arbitrarily waive aside the laws of a state. And post-office officials might do well to heed the suggestion of Justice Arnold that they enjoy relief by being "limited to the more prosaic function of seeing to it that 'neither snow nor rain nor heat nor gloom of night stays these couriers from the swift completion of their appointed rounds'." (2)

9. **Public records.** The confusion as to what constitutes a public record should be resolved by statute. Uniformity is not attained through whims of either courts or public officials.

10. **Privacy.** This "hybrid" doctrine has no real justification in law or logic. It's a "court-made" creation that is even denied recognition by many of those whom it was intended to serve.

11. **Public meetings.** Americans are showing an increasing fondness for meeting in person to thrash out public and semi-public issues. The old New England town meeting is not being revived because both the physical size of many present communities as well as their greater diversified interests militate against such rebirth.

Few communities are solidly aroused by any one issue. But when citizens come together, either as individuals or as groups, to debate matters affected with public interest, great leeway should be permitted in these discussions and also in publication of reports of them. Only three states have seen fit to clothe such discussions with privilege, both for the speakers and for the newspaper. More jurisdictions could profit from these examples.

Some restrictions, of course, are desirable. Statements made should be germane to the business at hand, and discussions should be moderate. Such public meetings should not become mere sounding boards for any one with a grudge against a fellow citizen.

There are no reported instances of this privilege being abused in the three states which have adopted it.

12. Group defamation. Here is an area that the courts are just beginning to explore. As in all uncharted fields, much experimentation probably will be continued, and the newspaper is likely to find, in the next few years, considerable confusion, uncertainty, and lack of uniformity among the several jurisdictions. All problems of group defamation are not identical with the normal situation in libel, and legislative action seems desirable rather than a period of anxious waiting until the courts agree upon a policy.

None of these problems will be solved by critics who go about with mental bombs, concerned not so much about finding the proper target as about the size of the explosion they can cause. Suggested remedies range all the way from self-appraisal boards set up by the press itself to compulsory standards originated by governmental agencies and backed by mandatory law. But neither seems adequate to meet the situation.

For both remedies bog down on definitions. They must employ such words as truth, falsity, right, wrong, significant, and other catch phrases repeated so many times in certain circles that they have brought convictions as strong as those of primitive man reciting his ritual to the gods. But all of them are value words, and value is a word that belies any common definition.

The problems wil not be solved satisfactorily either, if the complacency of the press permits remedies to come exclusively from those outside the industry. Newspapers, always eager to give away space to building up a new movie star, sports hero, or to exploiting a product under the guise of choosing a Miss Cherry Blossom, Miss Deep Freeze Unit, Miss Nylon, Miss Automatic Washer, and scores of others just to get a "cheesecake" picture, seem reluctant to devote any time or energy on their own problems.

Just taking one example at random, it has been noted that only a few states penalize the purveyor of false information. Here is a type of beneficial law that certainly would meet no objection from bench, bar, or press critics. Yet, in most states, the newspapers appear content to suffer embarrassment, and pay out damages, rather than take effective steps against hoaxers.

On self-appraisal, *Editor and Publisher* asks:

"Who is to be entrusted with that job? (of drawing up standards). The newspapermen in New York, Chicago, or San Francisco? Who is so omniscient that he, or they, can divine when the press is right or wrong?" (3)

On government appraisal, history long since has passed judgment. As Brucker says:

"Looking at past suppressions with the perspective of hindsight, one comes to the conviction that the more nearly inviolable free speech and free press are, the better for the common good. The risk of persecution, in denying them, is too great." (4)

Justice Learned Hand aptly put it another way:

"The newspaper serves one of the most vital of all general interests: the dissemination of news from as many different sources, and with as many different facets and colors as is possible. That interest is closely akin, if indeed it is not the same as, the interest protected by the First Amendment; it presupposes that right conclusions are more likely to be gathered out of a multitude of tongues, than through any kind of authoritative selection. To many this is, and always will be, folly; but we have staked upon it our all." (5)

Nor is the cause of proponents for change strengthened when one of the leading advocates returns from England with paeans for the British radio system and denunciations for American programs at the very time that press associations are carrying stories that tiny Luxemburg is pulling listeners away from English stations because Britons are dissatisfied. Who is then so omniscient that he can tell the public what it should have?

The newspaper, on the other hand, must not maintain it is "untouchable", or that in the general conduct of its business it has immunities granted to no other industry.

The situation is neither hopeless nor as discouraging as some critics fear. No one who has been in newspaper work during the past two decades can fail to note two distinct improvements—in the newspaper as a whole and in the type of men and women who staff them.

With all its imperfections, the newspaper of today is a vastly improved product over that of a quarter of a century ago. Social, economic, and political problems are reported today with all the emphasis and facility once reserved for crime. Old ideas about news have been supplanted by definitions fraught with social values.

Two bugaboos of critics—the "vanishing daily" and the economic aspects—have been largely disspelled in the minds of those who analyze for facts and not for substantiation for preconceived opinions. Five or six newspapers, struggling for financial favor in a community, may bring cheer to those who yearn to see ideas "competing in the market place," but the newspaperman knows from experience that such weak organs, susceptible to every temptation to maintain their existence, do not serve the city as well as one strong, secure organ which can afford to be independent of all the forces that may seek to use it for their own advantage.

No one yet has devised a way to make newspapers self-supporting from its readers alone. Speaking of the dire deductions drawn by some from the fact that newspapers are businesses, Edwin James, managing editor of the New York *Times*, has said:

"I consider it a very good thing that our newspapers are businesses and economically independent. Or what is the alternative? It is newspapers supported by some interest or party.

"I would rather see a newspaper standing on its own feet than leaning on the Republican Party, the Democratic Party, the Communist Party, the Chamber of Commerce, or the National Association of Manufacturers to meet his payroll." (6)

The hope for the future does not seem to lie in self-appraisal boards or in standards set by governmental or semi-public agencies. *It lies in the growing recognition by newspapermen themselves that the newspaper's role in the community must be that of informer, interpreter, voice, and leader to translate public wishes and opinions into enforceable policy.* It must be the community's "market place" for interplay of free expression and at the same time its guardian against encroachment by either the government or special interests.

The newspaper, realizing it is a powerful social instrument, must use its authority to further community understanding and progress. And one step toward that goal will be the recognition by the newspaper that the law is not its natural enemy but its partner, although partners, at times, are permitted to have disagreements.

Constitutions, statutes, court decisions, and administrative regulations are not the answer to the even better newspaper of tomorrow. For the newspaper, like any other social institution, can never be better than the men and women who produce it.

APPENDIX

All Footnotes May Be Found Herein

By Chapters

Footnotes Section

CHAPTER 2

"The Nature of Law"

1. Hertzler, J. O., *Social Institutions*, Lincoln, Neb.; University of Nebraska Press, 1947, p. 119.
2. Young, Kimball, *Sociology*, New York; The American Book Company, 1942, p. 72.
3. Barnes, Harry Elmer, *Social Institutions*, New York; Prentice-Hall, Inc., 1942, p. 355.
4. Frank R. Kennedy in *The Polls and Public Opinion*, Meier, Norman C. and Saunders, Harold W. (eds.) New York; Henry Holt and Company, 1949, p. 92.
5. *Ibid.*
6. Associated Press v. National Labor Relations Board, 301 U.S. 103, 130.
7. United States v. Associated Press, 52 F. Supp. 362.
8. Central Arizona Light and Power Company v. Akers, 46 P. 2d. 126.
9. Reported by the United Press, Dec. 27, 1949.
10. Pennekamp v. Florida, 328 U.S. 331.

CHAPTER 3

"Types of Laws Affecting the Press"

1. Barnes, Harry Elmer, *Social Institutions*, New York; Prentice-Hall, Inc., 1942, p. 354.
2. Galloway, George B., *Congress at the Cross Roads*, New York; Thomas Y. Cromwell Co., 1946, p. 4.
3. *Ibid*, p. 3.
4. Chicago *Herald American*, Nov. 26, 1949. For story of picture and comment see *Editor and Publisher*, Dec. 9, 1949, p. 44.
5. White, Paul W., *News On The Air*, New York; Harcourt, Brace and Co., 1947, pp. 179-80.
6. Beard, Charles A., *Economic Origins of Jeffersonian Democracy*, New York; The Macmillan Company, 1915, p. 37.
7. *Ibid.*
8. Article VI, Sec. 2.
9. Grosjean V., American Press Co., 297 U.S. 233, State ex rel. Pulitzer Publishing Co., 152 S.W. 2nd. 640, Giragi v. Moore, 301 U.S. 670, Arizona Publishing Co. v. O'Neil, 303 U.S. 543.
10. Many of these cases involved a religious sect known as Jehovah's Witnesses. See Lovell v. City of Griffin, 303 U.S. 444, Schneider v. State, 308 U.S. 147, Cantwell v. Connecticut, 310 U.S. 296, City of Manchester v. Leiby, 117 F. 2d. 661, Kennedy v. City of Moscow, 39 F. Supp. 36, Martin v. City of Struthers, 319 U.S. 141, Murdock v. Pennsylvania, 319 U.S. 105 and the two opinions in Jones v. Opelika, 316 U.S. 584 and 319 U.S. 103.
11. *Editor and Publisher*, Nov. 26, 1949, p. 12.
12. Near v. Minnesota ex rel. Olson, 283 U.S. 697.

13. United States v. Associated Press, 52 F. Supp. 362, affirmed 326 U.S. Reports, 1.
14. Pulitzer Publishing Co. v. Houston Printing Co. 11 F. 2d. 834.
15. *Esquire,* Inc. v. Walker 151 F. 2d. 49. See also Hannegan v. *Esquire,* 327 U.S. 146.

CHAPTER 4

"What Is Freedom of the Press?"

1. In talking of freedom of the press, it should be borne in mind that the First Amendment concerns itself also with freedom of speech, religion, and the right of assembly and petition.
2. Justice Holmes dissenting in Abrams v. United States 250 U.S. 616.
3. See for example, various issues, the London *Times,* Feb. 22-March 3, 1949.
4. *Editor and Publisher,* April 2, 1949.
5. Washington *Post,* Dec. 14, 1948.
6. London *Daily Mirror,* Nov. 20, 1949.
7. New York *Times,* Dec. 14, 1948.
8. Duniway, C. A., *The Development of Freedom of the Press in Massachusetts,* New York; Longmans, Green, 1906, pp. 64-65.
9. Bleyer, Willard G., *Main Currents in the History of American Journalism,* New York; Houghton Mifflin Co., 1927, pp. 66, 67.
10. Journals, Vol. 1, p. 57. The other four were: representative government, trial by jury, liberty of person, and easy tenure of land.
11. Bancroft, George, *History of the Formation of the Constitution,* New York; D. Appleton and Co., 1887, p. 716.
12. Bird, George L., and Merwin, Frederic E., *The Newspaper and Society,* New York; Prentice-Hall, 1942, p. 49.
13. Ford, P. L. (ed), *Writings of Thomas Jefferson,* Vol. 5, p. 47.
14. Elliott's (Jonathan) *Debates,* Philadelphia, 1896, Vol. 4, p. 47.
15. Grosjean v. American Press Co., 297 U.S. 233.
16. 1 *Annals of Congress, 1789-90,* p. 434.
17. Elliott's *Debates,* Vol. 4, p. 570.
18. Cooley, T. M., *Constitutional Limitations,* 8th ed., p. 901.
19. *Ibid,* p. 900, Note 3.
20. Schofield, Henry, *Freedom of the Press,* Publications of the American Sociological Society, Vol. 9, p. 67.
21. Grosjean v. American Press Co., 297 U.S. 233.
22. Bridges v. California, 314 U.S. 252.
23. Abrams v. United States, 250 U.S. 616.
24. *Ibid.*
25. *Editor and Publisher,* Sept. 28, 1940, p. 14.
26. *Ibid.*
27. Associated Press v. National Labor Relations Board, 301 U. S. 103.
28. Grosjean v. American Press Co., op. cit.
29. Bridges v. California, op. cit.
30. Schenck v. United States, 249 U.S. 47.
31. Reynolds v. United States, 98 U.S. 145.
32. Ford, P. L. (ed.), *Writings of Thomas Jefferson,* Vol. 8, p. 218.
33. Schenck v. United States, 249 U.S. p. 47.
34. *The Federalist,* Vol. 84, p. 23.

35. Thomas v. Collins, 323 U.S. 516.
36. Near v. Minnesota, 283 U.S. 697.
37. Grosjean v. American Press, op. cit.
38. Quoted in Mencken, H. L., *A New Dictionary of Quotations on Historical Principles*, New York; Alfred A. Knopf, Inc., 1942.
39. Report of the Commission on Freedom of the Press, *A Free and Responsible Press*, Chicago; University of Chicago Press, 1947 p. 5.
40. *Ibid*, p. 1.
41. Gerald, J. Edward, *The Press and the Constitution, 1931-1947*, Minneapolis; University of Minnesota Press, 1949, p. 9.

CHAPTER 5

"Problems of News and Newsgathering"

1. Bush, Chilton R., *Newspaper Reporting of Public Affairs*, New York; Appleton-Century, 1940, p. 1.
2. Clayton, Charles, *Newspaper Reporting Today*, New York; Odyssey Press, 1947, p. 22.
3. *Ibid*, p. 23.
4. MacDougall, Curtis D., *Interpretative Reporting* (revised), New York; The Macmillan Company, 1948, p. 85.
5. Schramm, Wilbur (ed.) *Mass Communications*, Urbana; The University of Illinois Press, 1949, p. 288.
6. A newspaper can prevent outright pirating of its news on the ground of unfair competition. See Associated Press v. International News Service 248 U.S. 215.
7. For these interpretative definitions, I have drawn upon Jones, Chester L., *Statute Law Making in the United States*, Boston; Boston Book Co., 1912. The wording and explanations, however, are not necessarily those of Jones.
8. Associated Press dispatch, Jan. 21, 1950.

CHAPTER 6

"Reporting the Federal Government"

1. Generally speaking, Congress possesses only those powers delegated to it by the Constitution. Under the Constitution, there are no common law offenses against the United States. Before the adoption of the Fourteenth Amendment, the Supreme Court consistently held that none of the first eight amendments applied to the states.
2. This historical summary of the news coverage of Congress is based on Steigleman, Walter, "Press Rights and Congress," *Newspaperman*, April, 1944.
3. *Washington Daily News*, June 30, 1935.
4. *Washington Daily News*, July 1, 1935.
5. "Press Rights and Congress," op. cit.
6. London *Daily Mirror*, Nov. 20, 1949.
7. Nugent v. Beale, Fed. Case No. 10375.
8. Rosten, Leo C., *The Washington Correspondents*, New York; Harcourt, Brace & Co., 1937, p. 82.
9. *Editor and Publisher*, Dec. 27, 1930, p. 6.
10. 76th Congress, House Document No. 30, p. 197.
11. New York *Times*, May 19, 1945.

12. New York *Times*, May 23, 1945.
13. *Ibid.*
14. *Editor and Publisher*, May 26, 1945, p. 13.
15. *Ibid.*
16. *Ibid.*
17. For these editorial protests see 91 *Congressional Record*, 2254 (appendix) May 28, 1945.
18. *The Washington Correspondents*, op. cit. p. 81.
19. *Editor and Publisher*, March 14, 1931.
20. Associated Press dispatch, Jan. 21, 1950.
21. *Congressional Directory*, 1949.
22. Hyman v. Press Publishing Co., 192 N.Y.S. 47.
23. New York *Times*, Jan. 11, 1931. Also see *Editor and Publisher*, Jan. 17, 1931.
24. *Editor and Publisher*, Jan. 10, 1931, p. 53.
25. For legal definitions of public records see Robinson v. Fishback, 93 N.E. 666, State ex. rel. Spencer v. Freedy, 223 N.W. 861.
26. 25 *Opinions of the Attorney General*, 326.
27. For the extent of the publicity clause see 43 Statutes 293 and for the repeal, 44 Statutes 51.
28. The Joint Chiefs of Staff of the United States have made this classification of information: Top Secret: paramount to security and disclosure of which would cause exceptionally grave damage; Secret: material which if disclosed could endanger national security, cause serious injury to the prestige of the nation, and be of great advantage to a foreign nation; Confidential: material, disclosure of which would be prejudicial to the interests or the prestige of the nation, cause unwarranted injury to an individual, or be of advantage to a foreign nation; Restricted: material which needs less strict protection than the other three types but still has an effect upon security.
29. Worcester (Mass.) *Gazette*, Aug. 7, 1948. For editorial comments on the affair see *Editor and Publisher*, Aug. 14, 1948.
30. Hartzell v. United States, 322 U.S. Reports, 680.
31. Des Moines *Tribune*, Feb. 4, 1950.
32. *Ibid.*
33. See series of articles on Hiss case written by Bob Considine and distributed Jan. 20-26, 1950, by International News Service.

CHAPTER 7

"Reporting State Governments"

1. Revised Statutes of Maine, Chap. 2, Sec. 35.
2. The reluctance of the courts to interfere with the legislative process is shown by an Indiana case in 1949. The legislature, following a long-standing custom, remained in session beyond the time permitted by the state constitution. The assembly kept turning back the clock for three calendar days. A taxpayer brought suit to void all laws passed by the legislature after the constitutional expiration of the session. The state Supreme Court, however, dismissed the suit, and the disputed laws went on the statute books.
3. *Editor and Publisher*, Feb. 19, 1949.
4. *Editor and Publisher*, June 11, 1950.
5. *Ibid.*
6. *Ibil.*
7. *Ed⁄tor and Publisher*, Feb. 18, 1950.

8. Most cases involving qualified privilege in reports of state agencies or state administrative bodies are so old as to be of doubtful value today. See: Spalding v. Vilas, 161 U.S. 483, Lewis v. Mercury Publishing Co., 165 Cal. 527. Statutes of California, Montana, Oklahoma, South Dakota, and Wisconsin extend qualified privilege to judicial and legislative acts and to *other official proceedings.* Presumably these *other official proceedings* refer to administrative acts, but that assumption has not been passed upon by the courts.

9. Mack, Miller Candle Co. v. The MacMillan Co., 195 N.E. 167.

10. See Reed, Thomas H., *Municipal Government in the United States.*

11. For example, see Accord v. Booth, 33 Utah 734.

12. Holway v. World Publishing Co., 44 P. (2d). 881. Also see: Montgomery v. New Era Co., 78 Atl. 85.

13. Trebby v. Publishing Co., 74 Minn. 84.

14. *Editor and Publisher,* Nov. 5, 1949.

15. *Editor and Publisher,* Feb. 25, 1950.

16. *Editor and Publisher,* March 19, 1949.

17. Laws of Texas, Art. 5431.

18. (Deering's) Civil Code of California, Sec. 47, Para. 5.

CHAPTER 8

"Public Records as News Sources"

1. Even Congress has engaged frequently in contests with the President over the demands of the lawmakers to inspect certain administrative records. In February, 1950, President Truman refused a demand by Congress that he turn over the "loyalty records" of State Department employees. Later, a compromise was worked out under which the president agreed to show the records to certain members of a Senate investigating committee. In an almost similar situation, Congress met President Roosevelt's refusal by directing that salaries of three men specifically named must not be paid from federal funds. The Supreme Court later annulled this provision in an appropriation on the ground Congress, in effect, had condemned the men without a judicial hearing. Congress could have abolished the three jobs but the conflict was resolved by their resignations.

2. Conner v. Standard Publishing Co., 67 N.E. 596; State ex. rel. Spencer v. Freedy, 223 Wis. 961.

3. Indiana *Publisher,* September, 1948.

4. *Ibid.*

5. Indiana *Publisher,* August, 1948.

6. Sec. 9, Art. 1 of the Indiana State Constitution reads: "No law shall be passed, restraining the free interchange of thought and opinion, or restricting the right to speak, write, or print, freely on any subject whatever."

7. *Editor and Publisher,* October 1, 1949.

8. Des Moines *Tribune,* September 26, 1949.

9. *Editor and Publisher,* October 8, 1949.

10. *Editor and Publisher,* May 29, 1949.

11. *Editor and Publisher,* February 19, 1949.

12. *Ibid.*

13. *Editor and Publisher,* February 12, 1949.

14. *Editor and Publisher,* May 29, 1949.

15. *Ibid.*

16. A 1938 Wisconsin decision (Kassowitz v. Sentinel Publishing Co. 226 Wisconsin 468) defines loathesome diseases as: leprosy, plague, or venereal disease.

17. This summary is based on a revision of Steigleman, Walter, "The Legal Problem of the Police Blotter," *Journalism Quarterly*, March, 1943.

18. Washington *Post* Co. v. Kennedy, 2 Fed. (2d) 207.

19. Thompson v. Boston Post Publishing Co., 189 N. E. 210.

20. Sherwood v. Evening News Association, 239 N. W. 305. But a Pennsylvania court ruled that in circumstances in which the public should be warned of possible danger from a man wanted by police there is privilege: Urban v. Pittsburgh *Times*, 1 Monongahela 135.

21. See Plummer v. Commercial Tribune Co., 208 Ky. 210.

22. This account of the legal status of a confession is summarized from Steigleman, Walter, "I Confess — But It May Be Libel," *Quill*, October-November, 1944.

23. Caller Times Publishing Co. v. Chandler, 130 S.W. (2d) 853.

24. *Eighteenth Report*, Judicial Council of Massachusetts, p. 44.

25. *Editor and Publisher*, July 23, 1949.

26. See *Editor and Publisher*, January 29, 1949, March 5, 1949, and also intervening issues.

27. *Editor and Publisher*, March 5, 1949.

28. *Editor and Publisher*, July 24, 31, August 7, November 6, November 27, 1948; June 11, 18, July 9, 1949; January 14, March 4, 1950.

29. *Editor and Publisher*, January 7, 1950.

30. For example, see *Editor and Publisher*, March 5, 1949, for such a dispute in Bridgeton, N. J. and *Editor and Publisher* for a similar dispute in Ashland, Wis. Laws of Wisconsin even designate as confidential traffic accident reports made to police.

CHAPTER 9

"Reporting Crime and Courts"

1. All states but Louisiana, where the primary influence is from the Napoleonic code, follow the English judicial system. The common procedure at a criminal trial, is for the defense, after the state has presented its case, to move for a directed verdict of acquittal. The defense contends the state has not proved the defendant guilty beyond a reasonable doubt. If the judge agrees, the defendant is discharged. If the court overrules the motion, the defense begins the presentation of its case. It is not up to the defendant to prove he is innocent but the burden is on the state to prove he is guilty.

2. For court interpretation of privilege in proceedings before a justice see: Augusta Chronicle Publishing Co. v. Arington, 157 S.E. 394.

3. Few justices are "learned in law," and most disputes between them and the press grow out of the justice's lack of understanding of his powers and limitations. Most disputes are resolved after the justice confers with the district attorney and discovers the limits of his authority. See *Editor and Publisher*, December 17, 1949, for a dispute of a paper with a Michigan justice. The justice opened up his records when the county attorney advised him they were public documents.

4. Several states do not make use of the grand jury. Instead, the district attorney files "information" with the court, and the case is listed for trial. In these jurisdictions, the paper may print the charges but may not claim privilege for any material not in the "information" filed with court.

5. See Watson v. *Herald Dispatch*, 222 Ill. App. 557.

6. Cf. Williams v. New York Herald Co., 150 N.Y.S. 838, and Cambell v. New York *Evening Post*, 245 N.Y. 320. The former was decided in 1914 and the latter in 1927.
7. (Kerr's) Political Code of California, (2d. ed.) Pt. I, Sec. 1032, permits inspection only by attorneys or interested parties or *by order of the court* in which the action is pending. Does this last clause mean, then, that the court may permit publication if it wishes?
8. *Editor and Publisher*, Sept. 24, 1949.
9. *Editor and Publisher*, June 18, 1949.

CHAPTER 10

"Limits of Criticism — Public Officials and Performances"

1. United States v. Associated Press, 52 F. Supp. 362.
2. Associated Press v. United States, 326 U.S. 1.
3. Pennekamp v. Florida, 328 U.S. 331.
4. *Editor and Publisher*, July 13, 1935. For the significance of this last paragraph see discussion below under "minority school."
5. *Ibid.*
6. Post Publishing Co. v. Hallam, 59 F. 530.
7. Nevada State Journal Publishing Co. v. Henderson, 294 F. 60.
8. Briarcliff Lodge Hotel v. Citizen-Sentinel Publishers, 260 N.Y. 106.
9. Pattangall v. Mooers, 113 Me. 412.
10. Jones v. Express Publishing Co., 87 Cal. App. 246.
11. Sniveley v. Record Publishing Co., 185 Cal. 565.
12. Arizona Publishing Co. v. Harris, 20 Ariz. 446.
13. Peck v. Coos Bay Times Publishing Co., 122 Ore. 408.
14. Moore v. Booth Publishing Co., 216 Mich. 653.
15. Marks v. Baker, 28 Minn. 162.
16. Lewis v. Carr, 178 N.C. 578.
17. Jackson v. Pittsburgh *Times*, 152 Pa. 406.
18. Lydiard v. Wingate, 131 Minn. 355.
19. *Editor and Publisher*, Feb. 18, 1950.
20. Cherry v. Des Moines *Leader*, 86 N.W. 323.
21. *Ibid.*
22. Outcault v. New York Herald Co., 102 N.Y.S. 534.
23. Hoeppner v. Dunkirk Printing Co., 254 N.Y. 95.
24. Stevens v. Moore, 185 Wis. 500.

CHAPTER 11

"Limits of Criticism — The Courts"

1. Patterson v. State of Colorado ex. rel. Attorney General, 205 U.S. 454.
2. Des Moines *Tribune*, March 14, 1950.
3. For discussion of this case, including the statements of the *News* and the action of the court, see *Editor and Publisher*, February 12 and 19, 1949.
4. *Ibid.*
5. See In re Shuler, 210 Calif. 377, for the case of a minister fined for contempt for making radio criticisms of a judge's rulings during a trial.

6. During the Iowa City murder trial already mentioned, a reporter was reprimanded in open court for printing a question and answer that was never asked or delivered. While a witness was being questioned, the reporter, from his prior knowledge, assumed the question would be asked and answered in a definite way, and he hurried out to call his paper. But the question was never put to the witness. The judge warned that future such occurrences would be dealt with severely. See Des Moines *Tribune*, March 23, 1950.

7. Bridges v. California, 314 U.S. 252.

8. Greeley, Horace, *The American Conflict*, Hartford; O. D. Case and Company, 1867, vol. 1, p. 106.

9. Jackson was speaking of the decision in Fletcher v. Peck. See Cotton, Joseph P., Jr., *Constitutional Decisions of John Marshall*, New York; G. P. Putnam's Sons, 1905, vol. 1, p. 228.

10. A Boston court in 1949 evoked for the first time a new law which permits the courtroom to be cleared at the trial of criminal proceedings involving a husband and wife. The judge acted at the start of a trial of a woman charged with adultery by her husband. See *Editor and Publisher*, August 27, 1949.

11. Reporters and photographers are not the only newspapermen likely to be cited in contempt. A managing editor, or city editor, who never leaves his office can be cited if he orders the reporter or the photographer to violate a court order.

12. Ex parte Sturm et al. 136 Atl. 312.

13. *Ibid.*

14. *Ibid.*

15. In re Sneed, 251 N.Y.S. 615.

16. *Editor and Publisher*, March 14, 1931.

17. *Editor and Publisher*, August 14, 1948.

18. *Editor and Publisher*, March 11, 1950.

19. *Ibid.*

CHAPTER 12

'Limits of Criticism — Constructive Contempt"

1. For a discussion of some of the types of constructive contempt and a partial historical account see: Nelles, Walter, and King, Carol Weiss, "Contempt by Publication in the United States," 28 *Columbia Law Review*, April, 1928. Also: Herman, R. E. (and others) "Recent Limitations on Free Speech and Free Press," 48 *Yale Law Journal*, November, 1938.

2. The early development of the principle of contempt is treated in Fox, Sir John Charles, *The History of Contempt of Court*, Oxford; The Clarendon Press, 1927.

3. Nelles and King, *op. cit.*

4. *Ibid.*

5. Gates and Seaton's, *Register of Debates*, 21st. Congress, 2d Session.

6. 28 United States Code, Sec. 385.

7. Patterson v. Colorado ex. rel. Attorney General, 205 U.S. 454.

8. *Ibid.*

9. Toledo Newspaper Co. v. United States, 247 U.S. 402. Justice Brandeis joined in the dissent.

10. *Ibid.*

11. *Ibid.*

12. Virtually the same decision came from the Supreme Court the next year, 1919, in Craig v. Hecht, 263 U.S. 255 with Justices Holmes and Brandeis again dissenting.

13. 314 U.S. 252.

14. *Ibid.*

15. *Ibid.*

16. *Ibid.*

17. *Ibid.*

18. *Ibid.*

19. *Ibid.*

20. Pennekamp v. State, 22 So. (2d) 875.

21. Pennekamp v. Florida, 328 U.S. 331. The paragraph quoted is from Justice Murphy concurring in the majority opinion.

22. *Ibid.*

23. *Ibid.*

24. Craig v. Harney, 67 Sup. Ct. 1249.

25. *Ibid.*

26. *Ibid.*

27. *Ibid.*

28. *Ibid.*

29. *Ibid.*

30. *Editor and Publisher,* January 14, 1950.

31. *Ibid.*

32. *Editor and Publisher,* April 23, 1949.

33. *Ibid.* The newspaper also had employed some "crime experts" to work on the case, including a lawyer known nationally as a writer of murder mysteries.

34. *Editor and Publisher,* November 27, 1948.

35. *Editor and Publisher,* August 14, 1948.

36. *Ibid.*

37. *Editor and Publisher,* November 27, 1948.

38. *Editor and Publisher,* May 7, 1949.

39. Ex parte McCormick, 88 S.W. (2d.) 104.

40. Some of this material is indicated in the reading section at the end of this chapter.

41. *Yale Law Journal,* March, 1950.

42. *Ibid.*

43. *Ibid.*

44. *Ibid.*

45. *Ibid.*

46. *Ibid.*

47. Cooke v. United States, 267 U.S. 517.

48. *Ibid.*

49. *Ibid.*

50. Patterson, Giles J., *Free Speech and a Free Press,* Boston; Little, Brown and Company, 1939, p. 152.

51. After this trial, press, radio and bar formed a joint committee to look into remedial action to curb such behavior in the future, but the recommendations have produced little concrete action.

CHAPTER 13

"The Right to Print the News"

1. Reeda v. Tribune Company, 218 Ill. App. 45.
2. See: Jenkins v. News Syndicate Co., 219 N.Y.S. 196.
3. The courts have ruled a number of times on the publication rights in letters. See for example: Baker v. Libbie, 97 N.E. 109; King v. King, 25 Wyo. 275.
4. *Editor and Publisher,* April 1, 1950, reported that the American Federation of Labor was using the letter method to get certain material published.
5. International News Service v. Associated Press, 248 U.S. 215.
6. International News Service v. Associated Press, 248 U.S. 215.
7. The court did have precedents for asserting a news gatherer had a quasi-property right in his news, but none of these cases had determined if that right was lost by publication. See: National Telegraph News Co. v. Western Union, 119 F 294.
8. Associated Press v. KVOS, Inc. 80 F. (2d.) 575.
9. For a popular account of this feud see: White, Paul W., *News on the Air,* New York; Harcourt, Brace and Co., 1947.
10. International News Service v. Associated Press, 248 U.S. 215.
11. Legally, the paper had no valid copyright because it failed to meet the requirements of the law, by having its application, fee, and two copies in the mails before releasing the edition on the streets. For a legal interpretation of this point see: New York Times Co. v. Sun Printing and Publishing Association, 204 F 586.
12. One of the important cases on copyright protection for foreign dispatches is: Chicago Record Herald Co. v. Tribune Association, 275 F. 797. See also: Tribune Co. v. Associated Press, 116 F. 126; New York Times Co. v. Star Co., 195 F. 110; and New York Times Co. v. Sun Printing and Publishing Association, 204 F. 586.

CHAPTER 14

"Protecting the Sources of News"

1. In fairness, it should be noted that some sections of the press agree with the bench and bar on this question. See: *Bulletin of the American Society of Newspaper Editors,* August, 1948.
2. For an historical account of the development of such laws in each state see: Steigleman, Walter, "Newspaper Confidence Laws," 20 *Journalism Quarterly,* September, 1943.
3. It was 31 years before a test case came before Maryland courts and the law was upheld.
4. Garnsey, John Henry, "The Demand for Sensational Journals," *Arena,* November, 1897.
5. Wigmore, John, *Evidence in Trials at Common Law,* Boston; Little, Brown & Co., 1940, Vol. 3, Sec. 2286, subdiv. 3.
6. For example, Louisiana includes certified public accountants. Oregon says stenographers may not be forced to testify about any communication made by their employers to them in the course of their regular work with him. Iowa includes confidential clerks and stenographers and also "counselors" although the Johnson County court ruled in 1950 that "counselors" did not include psychologists who are advisers to college students. Since Iowa also mentions attorneys, the word "counselors" is in doubt.

7. People ex. rel. Mooney v. Sheriff of New York County, 199 NE 415.
8. *Ibid.*
9. Burdick v. United States, 236 U.S. 79.
10. Associated Press dispatch, February 27, 1948.
11. United Press dispatch, February 28, 1948.
12. *Editor and Publisher,* May 29, 1948.
13. *Editor and Publisher,* November 26, 1949.
14. *Editor and Publisher,* February 18, 1950.
15. There are a number of decisions on the problem in Oklahoma, but see especially Bodine v. Times Journal Publishing Co., 110 P. 1096. The leading case in Utah is Williams v. Standard Examiner Publishing Co., 27 P. (2d.) I.
16. There have been cases in which judges in adjoining counties differed on the question. As far as can be checked, the New Hampshire Supreme Court has never ruled on the problem.
17. South Carolina attorney general unofficially believed there is a possibility newspapermen may be included but the courts there have not passed on the question.
18. The belief in Georgia is based on Code of Georgia, Sec. 105-704 which reads: ". . . a truthful report of information received from an arresting officer or police authorities, shall be deemed a privileged communication." Georgia in recent years, however, has modified some of its former liberal laws dealing with the press, and possible privilege has become more uncertain.
19. Joslyn v. People, 184 P. 375.
20. People ex. rel. Mooney v. Sheriff of New York County, 199 N.E. 415.
21. State v. Donovan et al., 30 A. (2d.) 421.
22. Revised Statutes of New Jersey, Sec. 2:97-11.
23. *Jersey Journal* (Jersey City), February 23, 1943.
24. The Chicago *Tribune* said the proposed law ". . . could do a good deal of harm in encouraging newspapers to publish rumor without investigation." See *Editor and Publisher,* May 21, 1949.
25. For views of some New York papers see: *Editor and Publisher,* February 19, 1949.
26. For the views of the New York Society of Editors see: *Editor and Publisher,* August 14, 1948. For arguments on both sides see reading list at end of chapter.
27. *Editor and Publisher,* January 15, 1949.
28. *Editor and Publisher,* February 19, 1949.
29. A Canadian paper collected $2,500 from a press agent who drummed up interest for his circus by announcing the owners were planning to set up a $10,000,000 motion picture industry in the newspaper's city. See Calgary *Herald* v. Barnes Corporation et al., 1 Western Weekly Reports, 428.
30. New York State Penal Code, Sec. 1348.
31. *Ibid.* Sec. 1349.
32. Utica *Daily Press,* March 30, 1945.
33. Ohio permits criminal action to be instituted not alone by the newspaper but also by any one ". . . injured in person, property, or reputation" by the false story. See Throckmorton's *Ohio Code Annotated,* (1940) Sec. 6319-7.
34. North Carolina General Statutes, Sec. 14-17. Michigan and Georgia permit a paper to recover any libel damages it must pay out in court from those who repeated the libelous material for publication.
35. Pennsylvania in 1949 increased the fine to $1,000 and the jail term to one year. North Carolina provides no specific penalty in its statute but the state's Supreme Court has ruled misdemeanors may be punished by jail terms up to two years.

36. *Editor and Publisher*, January 14, 1950.

37. MacKown v. Illinois Printing and Publishing Co., 6 N.E. (2d.) 526.

38. Curry v. Journal Publishing Co., 68 P. (2d.) 168.

39. Newark *Star-Ledger*, March 11, 12, 1950. On April 1, 1950, the Cedar Rapids (Iowa) *Gazette* printed as an April Fool stunt a story of the landing of another flying saucer, but its article was not so realistic as that of the New Jersey paper.

CHAPTER 15

"Photographs and the Law"

1. For a brief but good account of picture journalism in the United States see: Mich, Daniel D., "The Rise of Photo-Journalism in the United States," 24 *Journalism Quarterly*, September, 1947.

2. *Editor and Publisher*, February 18, 1950.

3. *Ibid.*

4. Worcester *Gazette*, August 24, 1948.

5. *Editor and Publisher*, October 9, 1948.

6. Indianapolis *Star*, April 4, 1949.

7. Altman v. New Haven Union Co., 254 F. 113.

8. Holmes v. Underwood & Underwood, 233 N.Y.S. 153. For criticism see: 15 *Cornell Law Quarterly*, 103.

9. Wandt v. Chicago *American*, 109 N.W. 70.

10. De Sando v. New York Herald Co., 88 N.Y. App. Div. 492.

11. Van Wiginton v. Pulitzer Publishing Co. 218 F. 795.

12. See Russell v. Brooklyn *Daily Eagle*, 153 N.Y.S. 450, and Alfred M. Best Co. v. Index Publishing Co., 9 N.E. (2d.) 439.

13. *Editor and Publisher*, March 26, 1949.

14. Associated Press dispatch, April 10, 1950.

15. Cooley, T. M., *A Treatise on the Law of Torts*, Chicago; Callaghan and Co. 1930, (3rd. ed.) p. 364.

16. Brandeis, Louis D and Warren, Samuel, "The Right of Privacy," 4 *Harvard Law Review*, December, 1890.

17. Slidis v. F-R Publishing Corp., 113 F. (2d.) 806.

18. *Ibid.*

19. *Time*, October 18, 1948.

20. Kerby v. Hal Roach Studios, 127 P. (2d.) 577.

21. *Editor and Publisher*, September 24, 1949.

22. Dawson, Mitchell, "Private Lives," *American Mercury*, October, 1948.

23. For some illustrative cases on the restrictions of personal photographs in advertisements see: Morrison v. Smith, 69 N.E. 725; Pavesich v. New England Life Insurance Co., 50 S.E. 68; Melvin v. Reid, 297 P. 91; Flake v. Greensboro News Publishing Co., 195 S.E. 55; Burton v. Crowell Publishing Co., 82 F. (2d.) 154 (permission granted to use the picture but an unusual camera angle distorted it); and Peck v. *Tribune*, 214 U.S. 185.

24. *Editor and Publisher*, October 2, 1948.

25. Metter v. Los Angeles *Examiner*, 95 P. (2d.) 491.

26. Dawson in *American Mercury*, op. cit.

CHAPTER 16

"The Origin and Nature of Libel Laws"

1. Othello, Act III, Scene 3.
2. Lee, Alfred McClung, *The Daily Newspaper in America*, New York; The MacMillan Co., 1937, p. 167.
3. Hollenbeck v. Hall, 72 N.W. 518.
4. Certain civil wrongs; for example, breaches of contract, can also be dealt with in equity as shown earlier.
5. For an actual case see: Sydney v. MacFadden Newspaper Corporation, 151 N.E. 209.
6. Brown v. New York *Evening Journal*, 255 N.Y.S. 403.
7. Towne v. Eiser, 245 U.S. 418.
8. The *American College Dictionary*, New York; Harper & Bros., 1948.
9. Republican Publishing Co. v. Mosman, 24 P. 1051.
10. Dusabek v. Martz, 249 P. 145.
11. Knapp v. Post Printing and Publishing Co., 114 P. (2d.) 981.
12. Tawney v. Simonson et al. 124 N.W. 229.
13. Morey v. Barnes, 212 Minn. 153.
14. Washington Post Co. v. Chaloner, 250 U.S. 290.
15. Robertson v. Bennett, 44 N.Y. Sup. Ct. 66.
16. Polakoff v. Hill, 261 N.Y. App. Div. 777.
17. Triggs v. Sun Printing and Publishing Association, 71 N.E. 739. Unusual devices in the lead to attract reader interest also may be libelous. See Dall v. Time, Inc., 17 N.E. (2d.) 138.
18. Grant v. New York Herald Co., 138 N.Y. App. Div. 727.
19. Ingalls v. Hastings & Sons, 304 Mass. 31.
20. Finkle v. Westchester Newspapers, Inc., 235 N.Y. App. Div. 817.
21. Garriga v. Richfield, 174 N.Y. Misc. 315.
22. Levy v. Gelber, 175 N.Y. Misc. 746.
23. Grant v. *Reader's Digest*, 151 F. (2d.) 733.
24. Spanel v. Pegler, 160 F. (2d.) 619. See also: Gallagher v. Chavalas, 199 P. (2d.) 408. The word "Red" was held to be libelous in Toomey v. Jones, 124 Okla. 167.
25. Associated Press dispatch, December 8, 1948.
26. *Ibid.*
27. Syndicated column, "Washington Merry-Go-Round," February 12, 1950.

CHAPTER 17

"Intent and Responsibility in Libel"

1. This list was made in a private memorandum to the writer.
2. See for example: Washington Post Publishing Co. v. Kennedy, 3 F. (2d.) 207; Switzer v. Anthony, 206 P. 391; Roth v. News Co., 217 N.C. 13.
3. *Editor and Publisher*, May 24, 1947.
4. As used here, press associations should be thought of as including feature syndicates and other organizations which supply non-local material to newspapers.
5. Roth v. News Co. 217 N.C. 13.
6. *Ibid.*

7. Wood v. Constitution Publishing Co., 194 S.E. 760.
8. Layne v. Tribune Company, 146 So. 234.
9. *Ibid.*
10. *Ibid.*
11. *Ibid.*
12. Morse v. Times-Republican Co., 100 N.W. 867. The court, however, recognized there are other defenses besides truth. These will be discussed later.
13. Coleman v. MacLennan, 98 P. 281.
14. Hatfield v. Gazette Printing Co., 175 P. 382.
15. Folwell v. Miller, 145 F. 495.
16. Merrill v. Post Publishing Co., 197 Mass. 185.
17. City of Chicago v. Tribune Co., 139 N.E. 86.
18. *Ibid.*
19. For a detailed study of these chain libel suits see: Davis, Norris G., "The Sweeney 'Chain Libel' Suits," 21 *Journalism Quarterly,* June, 1944.
20. Sweeney v. Philadelphia Record Co., 126 F. (2d.) 53; also Sweeney v. Steinman and Steinman, Inc., 126 F. (2d) 53; Sweeney v. Chronicle Publishing Co., 126 F. (2d.) 53.
21. See Sweeney v. Schnectady Union Publishing Co., 122 F. 2d. 288, and Sweeney v. United Feature Syndicate, 129 F. (2d.) 904.
22. Sweeney v. Caller-Times Publishing Co., 41 F. Supp. 163.
23. Benton v. Knoxville News-Sentinel Co., 174 Tennessee 658.
24. Bradt v. New Nonpareil Co., 79 N.W. 122. Also see: Sorenson v. Balaban, 42 N.Y.S. 654 and Wellman v. Sun Printing and Publishing Association, 23 N.Y.S. 577.
25. Hughes v. New England Newspaper Co., 312 Mass. 178. See also: Rose v. Daily Mirror, Inc., 284 N.Y. 335; Kimmerle v. New York Evening Journal Co., 262 N.Y. 99; Themo v. New England Newspaper Publishing Co., 306 Mass. 54.
26. See 170 F. (2d.) 941. The court later held this award to be excessive and reduced it.
7. Scott v. Times-Mirror Co., 181 Cal. 345.
28. Broughton v. McGrew, 39 F. 672.
29. Behrendt v. Times-Mirror Co., 96 Calif. App. 3.
30. See: O'Meara v. Haiden, 204 Calif. 354; Quinn v. Chicago, Milwaukee, and St. Paul Railway Co., 202 N.W. 275.

CHAPTER 18

"The Three Elements of Libel"

1. Tappan v. Wilson, 7 Ohio 191.
2. Rice v. Simmons, 2 Dela. 417.
3. Giles v. State, 6 Ga. 276.
4. For a summary of Hamilton's address in support of a new trial for Croswell see: Bird, George L., and Merwin, Frederic E., *The Newspaper and Society,* New York; Prentice-Hall, Inc. 1942, p. 49 ff.
5. Morse v. Times-Republican Co., 100 N.W. 867.
6. Schoenfeld v. Journal Co., 235 N.W. 442; Williams v. Journal Co., 247 N.W. 435.
7. Helmicks v. Stevlingson, 250 N.W. 402.
8. For further examples see: Woolf v. Scripps Publishing Co., 172 N.E. 389; and James v. Fort Worth Telegram Co., 117 S.W. 1028.

9. Express Publishing Co. v. Herrera, 234 S.W. 554.
10. Corrigan v. Bobbs-Merrill Co., 228 N.Y. 58.
11. Merrill v. Post Publishing Co., 197 Mass. 185.
12. Roth v. News Co., 217 N.C. 13
13. Behrendt v. Times-Mirror Co., 96 Calif. App. 3.
14. Post Publishing Co. v. Butler, 137 F. 723.
15. Palmer v. Bennett, 31 N.Y.S. 567.
16. Gross v. Cantor, 200 N.E. 592.
17. *Ibid.*
18. *Editor and Publisher,* October 25, 1947.
19. Levert v. Daily State Publishing Co., 49 So. 206.
20. Carter v. King, 94 S.E. 4.
21. DeHoyos v. Thornton, 259 N.Y. App. Div. 1.
22. *Ibid.*
23. Service Parking Corporation v. Washington Times Co., 92 F. (2d.) 505.
24. *Ibid.*
25. Norval v. Hearst, 102 Calif. App. 403.
26. *Ibid.* Also see *Times* v. Stivers, 252 Ky. 843.
27. Kassowitz v. Sentinel Publishing Co., 226 Wis. 468.
28. Helmicks v. Stevlingson, 250 N.W. 402.

CHAPTER 19

"How the Laws of Libel Operate"

1. Norfolk Post Corp. v. Wright, 125 S.E. 656. See also: Landon v. Watkins, 63 N.W. 615.
2. Hayes v. Press Company, 18 A. 331.
3. Shubert v. Variety, Inc., 219 N.Y.S. 233.
4. Adler v. Herald Co., 36 N.Y.S. (2d.) 905.
5. Lawyers' Co-Operative Publishing Co. v. West Publishing Co., 32 N.Y. App. Div. 585.
6. 170 N.Y. Misc. 217.
7. Cruikshank v. Gordon, 118 N.Y. 178.
8. Mount v. Welsh, 118 Ore. 568.
9. Bormann v. Star Company, 72 N.Y. App. Div. 633.
10. Marion v. Courier Publishing Co., 125 Ill. App. 349.
11. Martin v. The *Picayune,* 40 So. 376.
12. Potter v. New York Evening Journal Co.
13. Pentuff v. Park, 138 S.E. 616.
14. Ritchie v. Widdemer, 59 N.J. Law, 290.
15. Bigelow v. Brumley, 138 Ohio 574.
16. Williams v. Hicks Printing Co., 150 N.W. 183.
17. Ingalls v. Morrissey, 154 Wis. 632.
18. Weber v. Credit Office, 160 N.Y.S. 583.
19. Register Newspaper Co. v. Worten, 33 Ky. Law, 840.
20. Paris v. New York Times Co., 170 N.Y. Misc. 215.
21. *Editor and Publisher,* July 17, 1948.
22. *Ibid.*
23. Cafferty v. Southern Tire Publishing Co., 173 N.Y.S. 774.

24. Clark v. McBaine, 299 Mo. 77.
25. Paducah Newspapers, Inc. v. Bratcher, 274 Ky. 220.
26. D'Altomonte v. New York Herald Co., 139 N.Y.S. 200.
27. Zbyszko v. New York American Co., 239 N.Y.S. 411.
28. McDonald v. Sun Printing and Publishing Association, 45 N.Y. Misc. 441.
29. Vosbury v. *Utica Daily Press,* 172 N.Y.S. 609.
30. McKee v. Robert, 197 N.Y. App. Div. 842.
31. *Editor and Publisher,* June 11, 1949.
32. Kirkman v. Westchester Newspaper, Inc., 287 N.Y. 373.
33. Stone v. Textile Examiners and Shrinkers Employers' Association, 122 N.Y.S. 460.
34. Adirondack Record, Inc. v. Lawrence, 202 N.Y. App. Div. 251.
35. *Ibid.*
36. New York Society for Suppression of Vice v. MacFadden Publications, 260 N.Y. 167.
37. *Editor and Publisher,* February 19, 1949.
38. *Ibid.*
39. People v. Spielman, 149 N.E. 466.
40. *Ibid.*
41. Crane v. State, 166 P. 1110.
42. People v. Eastman, 101 N.Y.S. 1137.
43. Houston Chronicle Publishing Co. v. Martin, 5 S.W. (2d.) 170.
44. Bradt v. New Nonpareil Co., 79 N.W. 122.
45. Sorenson v. Balaban, 11 N.Y. App. Div. 164.
46. State v. Haffer, 162 P. 45.
47. Cohen v. New York Times Co., 138 N.Y.S. 206.
48. Lemmer v. Tribune Co., 148 P. 338.
49. Dall v. Times, Inc., 17 N.E. 2d. 138.

CHAPTER 20

"Defenses in Libel"

1. Justice Frankfurter in Bridges v. California, 314 U.S. 252.
2. See: 23 A. (2d.) 889; also: 191 S.F. 811.
3. Morse v. Press Publishing Co., 49 N.Y. App. Div. 375
4. Carpenter v. New York Evening Journal Co., 96 N.Y. App. Div. 376.
5. Cafferty v. Southern Tier Publishing Co., 173 N.Y.S. 774.
6. Times-Dispatch Publishing Co. v. Soll, 139 S.E. 505.
7. Constitution of the state of New Hampshire, Art. 22.
8. Hall, John M. "Preserving Liberty of the Press by the Defense of Privilege", 26 *California Law Review,* January, 1938, p. 227.
9. Mapel, William L., quoted in "Is Libel a Cloud Over Your Head?", a publication of the Employers Reinsurance Corporation, Kansas City, Mo.
10. Evans v. Star Company, 209 N.Y.S. 267. The courts later did reduce the judgment, but it still was costly.
11. *Editor and Publisher,* July 23, 1949.
12. Roth v. News Co., 217 N.C. 13. Also see Oray v. Times Co., 77 N.W. 204.
13. *Ibid.*
14. *Ibid.*
15. Park v. Detroit Free Press Co., 40 N.W. 731.

16. Hanson v. Krehbiel, 75 P. 1041.

17. Park v. Detroit Free Press Co. op cit.

18. 43 *Harvard Law Review.*

19. Comer v. Age Herald Publishing Co., 44 So. 673; Allen v. Pioneer Press Co., 40 Minn. 117; Neafie v. Hoboken Printing and Publishing Co., 68 A. 146; Osborn v. Leach, 47 S.E. 811; and Meyerle v. Pioneer Publishing Co., 178 N.W. 792.

20. Post Publishing Co. v. Butler, 137 F. 723.

21. *Editor and Publisher,* June 11, 1949.

22. *Editor and Publisher,* August 6, 1949.

23. *Editor and Publisher,* April 22, 1950.

24. Morris, Clarence, "Inadvertent Newspaper Libel and Retraction," 32 *Illinois Law Review,* May, 1937.   Morris, however, opposes limiting recovery to actual damages on the ground that many times a plaintiff cannot prove actual money losses, yet he may have suffered sharply.

25. Mississippi has a "right of reply" law which applies only to political campaign stories. See: Mississippi Code, 1943, Sec. 3175.

    Louisiana legislature in June, 1950 defeated a bill to establish the right of reply.

26. (Hillyer) Nevada Compiled Laws, 1929, Sec. 10506.

27. *Ibid.*

28. Chafee, Zechariah, Jr., *Government and Mass Communications,* Chicago: University of Chicago Press, 1947, Vol. 1, p. 184.

29. *Ibid.,* p. 178ff.

30. Finnish Temperance Society v. Riavaaja Publishing Co., 219 Mass. 28.

31. *Editor and Publisher,* October 29, 1949.

32. *Ibid.*

33. *Indiana Publisher,* November, 1949.

34. Siebert, Fred S., "Communications and Government," in *Mass Communications,* Urbana; University of Illinois Press, 1940, p. 141.

35. *Ibid.*

CHAPTER 21

"Restrictions on Use of Names"

1. State v. Hinkle, 229 P. 317.

2. Hannegan v. *Esquire,* 327 U.S. 146; and *Esquire* v. Walker, 151 F. (2d.) 49.

3. Report of the American Public Welfare Association, May 20, 1950. The Association also reports that six additional states are about to adopt the same rule.

4. For a good legal discussion of this case see: Thayer, Frank, "Law on Naming Victim of Assault Reviewed," *Editor and Publisher,* December 31, 1948.

5. *Ibid.*

6. *Editor and Publisher,* January 7, 1950.

7. *Editor and Publisher,* August 14, 1948.

8. *Ibid.*

9. *Editor and Publisher,* February 4, 1950.

10. *Editor and Publisher,* February 4, 1950.

11. *The Indiana Publisher,* August, 1948.

12. *Ibid.*

CHAPTER 22

"Post Office Regulations"

1. United States v. Loring, 91 F. 881.
2. Hannegan v. *Esquire*, 327 U.S. 146; and *Esquire* v. Walker, 151 F. 2d. 49.
3. 4 Statutes 238: Sec. 6.
4. 15 Statutes 196: Sec. 13.
5. United States Code Annotated, Title 18, Sec. 336.
6. Postal Laws and Regulations, Sec. 601.
7. St. Louis *Star-Times*, September 12, 1947.
8. Brooklyn *Daily Eagle* v. Voorhies, 181 F. 579. Since this decision was handed down, the "in whole or in part" clause was added to the law.
9. *Editor and Publisher*, January 17, 1948.
10. *Ibid.*
11. *Editor and Publisher*, October 22, 1949.
12. *Editor and Publisher*, May 12, 1949.
13. *Editor and Publisher*, January 17, 1948.
14. Private letter to the writer.

CHAPTER 23

"Advertising — Rights and Restrictions"

1. Shuck v. Carroll *Daily Herald*, 247 N.W. 813.
2. Private letter from some of the principals.
3. Wooster v. Mahaska County, 98 N.W. 103.
4. McLaurin v. Hamer, 164 S.E. 2.
5. Nebraska Seed Company v. Harsh, 152 N.W. 310.
6. *Editor and Publisher*, November 12, 1949.
7. *Ibid.*
8. Peck v. Tribune, 214 U.S. 185.
9. Morrison v. Smith, 69 N.E. 725.
10. Central Arizona Light and Power Company v. Akers, 46 P. (2d.) 126. The trial court verdict, however, was reversed on the ground that the word "racket" was not libelous per se as the lower court had ruled.
11. United States Compiled Statutes, Sec. 7314.
12. Lewis Publishing Company v. Morgan, 229 U.S. 288.

CHAPTER 24

"Radio — Rights and Restrictions"

1. National Broadcasting Company v. United States, 319 U.S. 190.
2. Federal Communications Commission v. Sanders Radio Station, 309 U.S. 470.
3. National Broadcasting Company v. United States, 319 U.S. 190.
4. Sec. 326
5. United States Code Annotated, Title 18, pgh. 1464.
6. Press association dispatches from Washington, May 1, 1950.
7. Press association dispatches from Washington, June 2, 1949.
8. Federal Communications Commission Reports, 333.

9. Press association dispatches from Washington, April 14, 1950. Also see *Broadcasting*, May 1, 1950.

10. *Ibid.*

11. *Broadcasting*, May 1, 1950.

12. *Ibid.*

13. *Ibid.*

14. This fear was expressed by Harry Boyd in his syndicated newspaper column, "This is America," May 5, 1950.

15. Communications Act of 1934, as amended, Sec. 315.

16. For an account of this "war," see White, Paul, *News On the Air*, New York; Harcourt, Brace and Co., 1947, Chap. 3 and 4.

17. Walters v. Sentinel Company, 169 N.W. 564.

18. *Ibid.*

19. Sorenson v. Wood, 243 N.W. 82.

20. *Ibid.* It is interesting to note that in the same year, 1932, an Australian court was deciding that radio defamation was slander. Meldrum v. Australian Broadcasting Company.

21. *Ibid.*

22. See: Coffey v. Midland Broadcasting Co., 6 F. 889; Plakoff v. Hill, 261 N.Y. App. Div. 777; Hryhorijiv v. Winchell, 180 N.Y. Misc. 574; Miles v. Wasmer, 172 Wash. 466.

23. Weglein v. Golder, 177 A. 47.

24. Irwin v. Ashburst, 158 Ore. 61.

25. Locke v. Gibbons, 299 N.Y.S. 188.

26. Summit Hotel Co. v. National Broadcasting Co., 8 A. (2d.) 302.

27. Thayer, Frank, *Legal Control of the Press*, Chicago; The Foundation Press 1944, p. 224.

28. Louisiana Code of Criminal Law and Procedure, 1943, 740-47. Defamation is defined as "the malicious publication or *expression in any manner*, etc."

29. 243 N.W. 82.

30. *Ibid.*

31. Coffey v. Midland Broadcasting Company, 8 F. Supp. 889.

32. *Ibid.*

33. Miles v. Louis Wasmer, Inc. 20 P. (2d.) 847.

34. Summit Hotel Company v. National Broadcasting Company, 8 A. (2d.) 303.

35. Josephson v. Knickerbocker Broadcasting Company, 38 N.Y.S. (2d.) 985.

36. *Editor and Publisher*, July 16, 1949.

37. *Editor and Publisher*, September 18, 1948.

38. Communications Act, op. cit. Sec. 315.

39. Volvia v. Station WCBD, 39 N.E. (2d.) 685; also Josephson v. Knickerbocker Broadcasting Co., op. cit.

40. *Broadcasting*, February 2, 1948. Also see *Broadcasting*, February 16 and 23, 1948. The ruling came as part of the license renewal proceedings of Station WHLS, Port Huron, Michigan.

41. *Broadcasting*, February 23, 1948.

42. Communications Act, op. cit.

43. Volvia v. Station WCBD, op. cit.

44. Press association report, January 16, 1947, of a letter from the Commission to the Texas Quality Network.

45. *Broadcasting*, May 1, 1950. Also see same, March 20, 1950.

46. Indiana Statutes, 2-518; North Carolina General Statutes, Sec. 99-2-B.

47. Metropolitan Life Insurance Co. v. Knickerbocker Broadcasting Co., 15 N.Y.S. (2d.) 193.
48. Irwin v. Ashurst, 74 P. (2d.) 1127.
49. Haggard v. First National Bank, 8 N.W. (2d.) 5.
50. Summit Hotel Company v. National Broadcasting Company, op. cit.
51. Ex parte Shuler, 292 P. 481.
52. Elmhurst v. Shoreham Hotel Co., 153 F. (2d.) 467.
53. Mau v. Rio Grande Oil Co., 28 F. Supp. 845.
54. Binns v. Vitagraph Company, 103 N.E. 1108.
55. See editorial in *Editor and Publisher*, July 16, 1949.

CHAPTER 25

"Conclusion"

1. Siebert, Fred, "The Law and Journalism," 32 *Virginia Law Review*, June, 1946.
2. *Esquire* v. Walker, 151 F. (2d.) 49.
3. *Editor and Publisher*, March 25, 1950.
4. Brucker, Herbert, *Freedom of Information*, New York; The Macmillan Company, 1949.
5. United States v. Associated Press, 52 F. Supp. 362.
6. *Editor and Publisher*, February 19, 1949.

INDEX

Post Office regulations, 342ff; What is barred from mails 342ff; Lottery laws, 343ff; History of lottery laws, 344; Recent case in St. Louis, 345ff; Official interpretation, 346ff.
Power, Legal, Definition of, 56.
President, U. S., Reporting of, 74ff.
Press, Freedom of, Chap. IV, 31ff; Difference between American and English concept, 38-41; Historical concepts, 36ff; Is it an absolute right, 42ff; Threats to, 43ff; American concept and foreign press, 46ff; Commission on, 47ff; Problems of change of concept of, 48.
Principal defenses, in libel, 308.
Privacy, Invaded by Radio, 381-382.
Privacy, Right of, 225ff; In news, 225ff; In Pictures, 228ff.
Privilege in confessions, 111ff.
Privilege of Congressmen, 69.
Privilege in county government stories, 91ff.
Privilege, Legal, Definition of, 56.
Privilege of legislators, 86.
Privilege in reports of legislative action, 86ff.
Privilege in municipal government stories, 90ff.
Privilege of newspapers, 56ff; List of privileges, 60-61.
Privilege, Qualified (see Qualified Privilege).
Privilege in reporting, Radio, 382.
Problems, Legal, of advertising, 353.
Problems of Constructive contempt, 167ff.
Problems, Legal, in photographs, 211.
Products, Criticism of, 148.
Professional people, Libel of, 289ff.
Providence (R.I.) Evening Bulletin, 103, 198.
Providence (R.I.) Journal, 103, 198.
Public institutions, Criticism of, 148ff.
Public life, Criticism of persons in, 141ff.
Public meetings, Reporting of: Definition of public meeting, 93ff; Right to report, 92ff.
Public officials, Criticism of, 133ff (see Criticism, Public Officials).
Publication, in libel, 275ff.
Publick Occurrences, 36.

Qualified privilege, as a defense in libel, 313.

Racing Form, 309.
Radio: Chap. XXIV, 361ff; Differs from newspapers, 361-362; Constitutional freedom of, 362ff; Negative censorship of, 363-364; Right to express views, 364ff; Defamation in, 368; Libel or Slander, 368ff; Responsibility in libel, 373ff; Political speeches, 377ff; Defenses in libel, 378ff; Retraction laws, 378; Who may be sued, 379ff; Where suit may be maintained, 379-380; Contempt of court, 380; Invasion of privacy, 381-382; Privilege in reporting, 382; False information, 382; Facsimile, 382; Television, 383.
Records, Court, Use of, 132.
Records, Minor judiciary, Use of, 119ff.
Records, Public, Chap. VIII, 95ff; Definition of, 96; As news sources, 95; Privilege in, 95.
—State Records: Governor's office, 97; Attorney general, 97; State police, 97; Fire marshal, 98; Treasurer, 98; Auditor, 98; Banking commissioner, 98; Motor vehicle commissioner, 98; others, 99ff; Disputes over state records, 99ff.
—County Records: Types of, 101ff; Right to see, 101ff; Enforcing right to see, 102ff.
—Municipal Records: General, 103; Police records, 106ff; Police Blotter, 106ff (see Police Blotter).
—Hospital Records: General, 104; Right to see, 104ff; Privilege in using, 106.

Reed, Justice Stanley, 176.
Refusal, Right of, in advertising, 353ff.
Regulations, Post Office (see Post Office Regulations).
Reporting Government: Chaps. VI, VII, and VIII.
—County Government: Right to report, 91ff; Privilege in stories, 91ff.
—Federal Government: Reporting Congress, 65ff; Right to report Congress, 66; House, 66ff; Senate, 69ff; History of reporting Congress, 66ff; Congress compared to House of Commons, 68; Disciplining of press by Congress, 68ff; Privilege in Congress stories, 69; Congressional committees, 70, 73; Disputes between Congress and press, 70ff; Disputes concerning disclosure of news sources to Congress, 71ff; Off-the-record news, 71.
—Federal Government: Reporting the President, 74ff; Cabinet Members, 75ff; Attorney General, 75; Administrative agencies, 76ff; War Department, 76; Independent agencies, 76ff; Right to attend administrative hearings, 77ff; Security information,